THE PETITE BOURGEOISIE IN
EUROPE 1780–1914

THE PETITE BOURGEOISIE IN EUROPE 1780–1914

Enterprise, Family and Independence

Geoffrey Crossick and Heinz-Gerhard Haupt

London and New York

First published 1995
by C.H. Beck'sche Verlagsbuchhandling
This edition in English first published 1995
by Routledge
11 New Fetter Lane, London EC4P 4EE

Simultaneously published in the USA and Canada
by Routledge
29 West 35th Street, New York, NY 10001

Typeset in Garamond by
Ponting–Green Publishing Services, Chesham, Bucks
Printed and bound in Great Britain by
TJ Press (Padstow) Ltd, Padstow, Cornwall

British Library Cataloguing in Publication Data
A catalogue record for this book is available from the
British Library

Library of Congress Cataloguing in Publication Data
A catalogue record for this book is available from the
Library of Congress

ISBN 0–415–11882–4

To Rita, Matthew and Joshua
and Heidi, Anna, Sarah, Lotta and Andréas

CONTENTS

CONTENTS

PREFACE

This book is an analysis, based on our own researches and those of other historians, of the history of the petite bourgeoisie of shopkeepers and master artisans in Europe during the long nineteenth century. Our separate interest in the subject was given shape and developed in the context of the Research Group on the Petite Bourgeoisie in Nineteenth- and Twentieth-Century Europe which organised a succession of round tables between 1979 and 1990. The round tables were important for all those who participated in them regularly, stimulating the research of others but also providing an essential stimulus for our own ideas. They were also enjoyable and friendly occasions which encouraged our belief in the personal as well as the intellectual benefits of co-operative projects. We are immensely grateful to our fellow organisers of those round tables, Philippe Vigier of the University of Paris X, Nanterre, who sadly died while this book was in the process of publication, and Ginette Kurgan-van Hentenryk of the Free University of Brussels. We are also grateful to all participants in the round tables, from which we learned a great deal about the petite bourgeoisie, and where we also made many good friends. In particular we would like to thank those who became regular members of the round tables, and whose support and conversation over the years have so strongly influenced our own ideas, in particular David Blackbourn, Josef Ehmer, Serge Jaumain, Friedrich Lenger, and Philip Nord.

This book is a combination of personal research and our reading of the work of other historians. While writing this book we have continued our own separate primary researches on the history of the petite bourgeoisie, and in the book we have drawn extensively on that research, as well as on our reading of a large primary printed literature from the period. The references make that clear, but they make even clearer our debt to the work of other historians, some of whom have worked on the petite bourgeoisie but the great majority of whom have been interested only incidentally in the history of small enterprises and their owners. It is for that reason that we have been able to carry out one of our main objectives in this study, which is not so much to write a self-enclosed history of a social group, but rather to place a neglected group within the social history of modern Europe.

The book was written jointly, and readers attempting to work out who wrote which chapters will be disappointed, for there was no such division of labour. We did not write separate chapters, but worked on each other's drafts, passing the drafts backwards and forwards for further discussion and development. It is a form of joint authorship which takes longer, and there were moments when each of us wondered whether the book would ever see the light of day, not least as a succession of changes of university temporarily distracted one or the other of us from his work on the book. Only the reader can judge whether the extra effort of this form of writing was worth it, but we found it very rewarding, in the sharing and developing of ideas, and above all on the personal level. Our comparative approach extended to the very writing of the book itself, as we became increasingly aware of the different expectations of the writing of history in our two countries which each of us brought to the book. It may have taken longer, but we have enjoyed it.

Our main academic debts have been recorded above, but we are specially grateful to Lars Edgren and Friedrich Lenger who each read a chapter of the book in draft form and offered valuable comments. We would like to express our gratitude to the universities and colleagues with whom we worked while writing the book, and who supported and stimulated us in ways of which they are probably not even aware. For Geoffrey Crossick: the University of Essex, for Heinz-Gerhard Haupt: the European University Institute in Florence and the Martin Luther University of Halle-Wittenberg, and for both of us: the University Lumière Lyon 2 and its Centre Pierre Léon, then directed by Yves Lequin, where each of us worked, though at different times. Our most important thanks are acknowledged in the book's dedication.

Geoffrey Crossick and Heinz-Gerhard Haupt
Colchester and Halle

LIST OF ABBREVIATIONS

AN	*Archives nationales* (France).
Commission Internationale	Commission Internationale d'Histoire des Mouvements Sociaux et des Structures Sociales, *Petite entreprise et croissance industrielle dans le monde aux XIX*^e *et XX*^e *siècles*, 2 vols; 1981.
Crossick and Haupt	G. Crossick and H.-G. Haupt (eds) *Shopkeepers and Master Artisans in Nineteenth-Century Europe*, 1984.
PP	*Parliamentary Papers* (Great Britain).
Round Table	Round tables in the series on the Petite Bourgeoisie in Nineteenth- and Twentieth-Century Europe.
1851 London Census Sample	Sample of London enumeration districts in 1851 Census. For fuller details see Chapter 5, footnote 3.

1

INTRODUCTION

The master artisans and shopkeepers of nineteenth- and twentieth-century Europe have not always been looked upon kindly by their contemporaries. They have often found themselves identified with unfavourable character-istics, such as meanness, narrowness of spirit, xenophobia, an anxiety for respectability, and an excessive concern for order and propriety. Unflattering portraits of petits bourgeois have been presented by some of the period's major writers, from Honoré de Balzac to Emile Zola, H.G. Wells and Bertolt Brecht. These images were not entirely divorced from historical reality, for such images rarely are, but in their very distortion they are doubly interesting to the historian. In the first place, they allow the historian of the petite bourgeoisie to explore the political and social motives behind these severe pictures. To what extent can we see in them the fear of established bourgeois that they might be confused with those trying to imitate them, so that the differences were exaggerated and caricatured as a defence mechanism? A good number of these critics came from petit-bourgeois origins, ridiculing the class they believed that they had left as they closed the door behind them. Alternatively, such images might be seen as part of an attempt by a section of the bourgeoisie to impose upon workers, along with the middling groups of small business owners and clerks, cultural and social standards which they could rarely hope to achieve. This literary condescension has received too little attention for those questions to be answered, but the similarity of the images across Europe is indeed striking. They could even be found amongst the Social Catholics who tried to defend the petite bourgeoisie from the end of the nineteenth century. The very individualism which the petite bour-geoisie was supposed to correct appeared even to its defenders to be more deeply rooted amongst them than amongst any other social class. 'Its qualities of order and frugality are not always the most attractive', a meeting of Lyon Social Catholics was told in 1909, 'and its egoism and narrowness of spirit are faults which are far too common'.[1]

Texts denigrating the petite bourgeoisie have a second interest for the historian, for they could provoke reactions amongst shopkeepers and master artisans themselves, of the kind which Jacques Rancière has shown amongst

1

workers in mid-nineteenth-century France, who reacted against their negative image in contemporary discourse with a vigorous defence of their own honour.[2] The concern of better-established masters and more stable shop-keepers to stress the differences that separated them from the more fragile margins of small enterprise is evidence of an analogous strategy. In debates on the electoral system to be established for the Retailers' Chamber in Bremen, for example, shopkeepers as well as bourgeois deputies agreed that fishmongers certainly had no place in such a Chamber.[3]

The leading schools of European thought have generally offered a no more flattering picture of the petite bourgeoisie which could be used as the basis for analysis. Karl Marx's reflections on French history presented an insis-tently negative image of the petite bourgeoisie though, of the two classic texts, *Class Struggles in France* contains a much finer perception of the ambiguities of petit-bourgeois politics than the more acerbic denunciations in *The Eighteenth Brumaire of Louis Bonaparte*.[4] Marx's belief that the situation in 1848 had been ripe for revolution made him judge severely and in moralistic terms the decisions of the *démo-socs*, whom he identified essentially with the petite bourgeoisie. This negative image became integrated in his analysis of the logic of capitalism, which would progressively eliminate middling social groups. Marx's successors drew the conclusion that only social classes inserted within the process of capitalist evolution could properly understand their social position and their political interests, which meant that the petite bourgeoisie was condemned perpetually to deceive itself and to attach its political flag to the cause of one or other of the main classes. Marx may have rejected, in his *Critique of the Gotha Programme*, the proposition of the German Social Democrats that all classes other than the proletariat were inherently reactionary, but a polarised image of the class structure nonetheless continued in the SPD which, in its Erfurt Programme of 1891, could find little of significance in a small business sector that was simply waiting to disappear.[5] This catastrophic vision may have come into question at the end of the century,[6] but few Marxists sought to advance beyond the negative picture of the petite bourgeoisie that had dominated Marx's own analysis.

Liberal writers in many countries believed during the first two-thirds of the nineteenth century that small masters and shopkeepers could be inte-grated within a larger middle class that would oppose both aristocracy and populace. In German liberalism's most representative text, the *Rotteck-Welckersches Staatslexikon* of 1838, liberals found in the artisanat,

> the source of a secure, independent and contented condition; for their families the possibility of a good education and a positive future; and finally for the state the solid base of an independent desire for legal freedom, combined with an instinctive hostility to violent transforma-tion, and even to risky and precocious attempts at change.[7]

In the last third of the century, however, artisans and shopkeepers in various European countries distanced themselves from liberal values and turned towards social and economic protectionism. The advance of industrial and urban concentration thus shattered the unity of property owners. Some German, and indeed French, liberals saw in this evidence that petits bourgeois had dangerous anti-liberal leanings which would push them into the camp of the friends not of progress but of order. The following century saw this readily adapted into an explanation for fascism.

However, as far as conservative social thought was concerned, the petite bourgeoisie stood alongside aristocrats and peasants as the positive foundations of social stability, and it is through conservative idealisations of small enterprise that its most favourable characterisation emerged. Its disappearance, or even its substantial weakening, would remove the middle of society, and with it, the rampart against class division. A terminology of the middle came to be used for this group – *classes moyennes* and *Mittelstand* – which signified the social role that conservative thought attached to it. As early as the middle of the century Wilhelm Heinrich Riehl had claimed that 'amongst the citizens of a town the artisan is the conservative *par excellence*. But he will not remain a conservative if he is pauperised or allowed to degenerate.'[8] It became a powerful refrain amongst conservatives, especially Catholic conservatives, from the late nineteenth century. Hector Lambrechts, the Belgian lawyer and civil servant who from the 1890s was an indefatigable presence formulating policy on behalf of the petite bourgeoisie, stressed that 'the *classes moyennes* . . . are dying, and their disappearance will prove fatal to the social order, for their existence is a condition of both progress and peace'.[9] Here was a recurrent Aristotelian vision which identified an influential middle as the basis for social equilibrium.

Each of these different perspectives drew upon real aspects of the situation of petits bourgeois within European societies. Each started from the threat hanging over the world of small enterprise, though proceeding to draw very different conclusions from that threat. They remain relevant to the analyses which follow, for they were part of the framework within which petits bourgeois came to define their place in society, but they lack the analytical force to guide a historical study. For that it is necessary to turn to the theory of social class which has been such a powerful influence on the analysis of industrial society. However, class identification of the petite bourgeoisie is by no means straightforward. Composed of master artisans and shopkeepers who generally owned their own tools of work or of production, but who at the same time contributed their own personal labour power, the petite bourgeoisie cannot be readily incorporated within an approach to class which centres on the social relations of production. In that Marxist perspective its specific character derives precisely from the fact that it straddles the class of those who own the means of production and those who are separated from them, those who extract surplus-value and those who produce it. The approach of Max Weber seems more helpful, stressing that the non-monopolistic position of small producers and small retailers in the market place constituted the essence of their social position. Unlike wage-earners, they enter the market to sell a product rather than to sell their labour power. On the other hand, their lack of monopolistic control means that they find themselves pitted in an unequal struggle with large-scale enterprise. It is Weber's emphasis on the market rather than production that is particularly valuable, for it directs attention to the economic ambiguities in the position of small enterprise, as well as to the significance of the market in defining both the situation and the demands of artisans and shopkeepers in nineteenth-century Europe. Weber's conception of social class stressed the role of such social ties as marriage, occupational inheritance and social proximity in unifying diverse social categories. Although no social class is wholly united or homogeneous, the examination of proximity and distance amongst different occupations makes the question of class coherence a central one. This is particularly relevant to the petite bourgeoisie, whose diversity of circumstances might tempt the historian rapidly to conclude that little could unify shopkeepers and master artisans.[10]

The petite bourgeoisie has rarely engaged the interest of those concerned with the theory of social class in twentieth-century Europe. The major exception has been the experience of German fascism, which stimulated a sociological reconsideration of the place and character of the petite bourgeoisie. Nazism was rapidly diagnosed as a movement based on the owners of small enterprise and salaried employees, shaping itself around their fears and ambitions. The concept of *Ungleichzeitigkeit* had already become prominent in discussions of the petite bourgeoisie towards the end of the Weimar Republic, indicating a disjuncture or time-lag at the root of petit-bourgeois disquiet, confronting modernity from the perspective of a past from which they found it hard to adjust. Authors as different as Theodor Geiger and Ernst Bloch laid emphasis on the way in which the world of the workshop and the shop, while participating and living in the twentieth century, remained attached to a pre-industrial and guild-based set of values through which they interpreted society and their own problems. That disjuncture supposedly produced irrational solutions to the problems of the present, solutions ultimately expressed in petit-bourgeois support for fascism.[11]

Sociological writings about the petite bourgeoisie thus draw heavily on the social and ideological atmosphere of the time in which they were produced. They were in this respect no different from work on any other social class, but the relative paucity of attention to the world of small business has made that relationship a more acute one. Sociologists have more recently given only intermittent attention to the petite bourgeoisie, and it is interesting that it has come especially into focus for those whose goals were primarily concerned with resolving theoretical problems of class analysis, such as Nicos Poulantzas or Erik Olin Wright.[12] Sociological attention to the petite bourgeoisie has rarely assumed a serious historical dimension, beyond the rather formulaic attachment of the small enterprise petite bourgeoisie to an older (and hence historically situated) mode of production, which for the French sociologist Christian Baudelot and his colleagues had to be distinguished from managers and white-collar employees in private and state employment.[13]

Most sociological attention has understandably been directed at the latter groups, those who have been variously termed the 'new middle class' or the 'new petite bourgeoisie', the range of educated and salaried occupations whose emergence is certainly the most striking difference between the nineteenth-century social structure and that which has developed during the twentieth century, and most rapidly since the 1960s. The debates concerning the enlarging of the social middle were not unknown during the period covered by this book, for the broadening of the concept of the *classes moyennes* or petite bourgeoisie to incorporate such groups as white-collar employees, managers, schoolteachers, and civil servants was an attractive option for writers anxious to identify the middle as a force to be won for the existing order, but having little confidence in the viability or even the advisability of saving small enterprise. Even if their main period of growth came later, the new occupations were expanding in the period before 1914 as more advanced economies, scientific management, and bureaucratised states provided the basis for their growth. It is therefore not surprising that sociologists have addressed themselves more to the new than to the old petite bourgeoisie. Erik Olin Wright's efforts to define the ambiguities of an increasingly complex class structure through focusing on the middle represents one of the most intellectually ambitious engagements, but his interest amongst the middling groups is not focused on the independent petite bourgeoisie. By placing the ambiguities of class position at the centre of his analysis Wright has touched on what are central historical concerns of this book, but his focus is resolutely that of the later twentieth century, and in its concern for the new salaried occupations he echoes the interests of other sociologists.[14]

The notable exception to this generalisation, both in their focus and in their sensitive historical perspective, is the work of Frank Bechhofer, Brian Elliott and their colleagues, whose work combined general discussions of the significance of the petite bourgeoisie in contemporary Britain with empirical studies of small shopkeepers. At an early stage of their project they noted 'the stubborn, almost incomprehensible persistence of the stratum in all industrial capitalist societies (and some socialist ones too)'.[15] Its persistence during the present century has derived above all from its flexibility and from its positive relationship to capitalism for, they argue, 'the secret of its survival is that it adjusts to its habitat – to capitalism in all its phases'.[16] For Bechhofer and Elliott its varied politics and its social values embodied an essential defence for capitalist societies, expressing not only 'sentiments supportive of capitalism and the institutions of liberal democracy',[17] but also distinctive moral values bound up with such ideas as individualism, the family, hard work, thrift and personal aspiration. The petite bourgeoisie may have become more economically marginal in the course of the twentieth century, but its social and ideological role in sustaining and reproducing the values of a capitalist society remains fundamental.[18] In their distinctive approach linking empirical analysis to sociological theory, Bechhofer and Elliott have firmly resisted the temptation to place the petite bourgeoisie within a larger social grouping, insisting that it was different not only from workers and capitalists, but also from the so-called 'new middle class'.

Neither diverse sociological approaches nor the historical record suggest that it would be fruitful to begin an analysis of the petite bourgeoisie in classic terms of class analysis, to follow some process of class formation through the period under study here. The petite bourgeoisie, we argue, has a place in the social formation which makes it very much a part of industrial capitalist society, and as such it emerges alongside the processes of industrialisation and urbanisation that were central to the construction of class societies in Europe. Nevertheless, it would be inappropriate to seek it in terms of fundamental economic relations, relative homogeneity of economic situation or social relations, a class culture, and organisation in political parties. The danger of freezing social experiences, and losing sight of the ambivalent and dynamic nature of those experiences over time, is one that applies to the historical analysis of any class, but it is an especial danger with a social group which was particularly and necessarily ambiguous in relation to classic ideas of class.

How far do the master artisans and shopkeepers who are the subject of this book constitute a single social group, even a single social class? Enough has been said already to indicate the difficulties in giving a rapid affirmative answer to those questions. If by social class we imply a group which can be distinguished from others by its specific productive relations, close social and institutional contacts, distinctive social characteristics, demographic continuities and sense of class identity, then it must be concluded that the economic heterogeneity, ambiguity of productive relations, social instability and lack of political unity of master artisans and small shopkeepers combine to complicate the notion of the petite bourgeoisie as a social class. Not only were artisans primarily concerned with production whereas shopkeepers earned their living from the distribution of goods and services, but the relation of each to the development of industrial capitalism differed during the period under study here. The artisanat was caught up earlier and more intensively in the process of capitalist industrialisation, with sectors producing for consumer markets finding by the 1830s and 1840s that merchants were reconstructing relations in their industry in a way that exposed them to increasingly vigorous competition and the challenge to artisanal methods of production. During these years individual shopkeepers suffered the pressures common to all small enterprises, but retailing as a whole expanded with industrial and urban change, and the small independent shopkeeper was at the heart of the expansion. It was not until the late nineteenth century that independent shopkeepers were faced with the entry of large-scale capital into retailing. It is therefore hardly surprising that when European petits bourgeois began to organise extensively towards the end of the nineteenth century it was shopkeepers who were at the heart of the movements, everywhere except in Germany where the timing of industrialisation, the strength of corporate expectations and the attention of political elites combined to give artisans a significant role.

A profound social heterogeneity within the world of small enterprise complicates matters further. At one extreme stood the well-established traders and master craftsmen of a town with several employees, and where businesses often passed to the next generation. At the other were the owners of tiny and marginal shops or workshops, who had only opened them because personal or economic crisis denied them other ways of earning a living. Between the two lay the mass of small enterprises, a myriad of individual positions shaped by the experiences of their trade, their town, their level of capital, their family circumstances, their skill, and the economic conjuncture in which they had opened their business. Social classes always include a great variety of personal circumstances and levels of relative well-being, but the problem was compounded for petits bourgeois by the very high rate of social instability which characterised them. If a degree of demographic stability is a requirement for a social class, indicating that a high proportion of the class remained in it through their lives and passed on that class position to their children, then the petite bourgeoisie fails to meet the criterion to the extent that other social classes did. Such instability will not have helped the development of a sense of common experience, which will also have been limited by the distinctive position of the petite bourgeoisie within the overall structure of class relations. Whereas the working class and the bourgeoisie might be seen to take definition from their relation to each other, master artisans and small shopkeepers, by reason of their relations to the means of production and the multi- dimensional character of their social relations, were orientated towards both bourgeois and proletarian positions and values.

Structural ambiguities thus inhibited the development of class coherence amongst petits bourgeois, but so too did the introspection that often characterised these owners of small enterprises, turned in as they were on the family and the business, and in competition with their fellow petits bourgeois. It is this introspection as much as any lack of structural coherence which explains why politics was so significant for the development of petit-bourgeois identity during this period, and why times of economic as well as political crisis were especially important for establishing a petit-bourgeois presence. As Arno Mayer suggested, in one of the first articles to attempt to put the petite bourgeoisie back on the agenda of historical enquiry, 'however amorphous the petite bourgeoisie may be in times of normalcy, in times of severe crisis it develops considerable internal coherence'.[19] Here is a social group which hints at a class character only at times of crisis, when its very existence seemed under threat.

The boundaries that divided the petite bourgeoisie from the working class on one side and from the more substantial bourgeoisie on the other cannot be marked precisely. The observation is hardly new, for Etienne Martin Saint-Léon, a Le Playist sociologist writing in France in 1910, had noted the difficulty.

> There is a contested zone between two neighbouring classes, which does not depend clearly on one class or the other, but which in certain respects shares the characteristics of both. Is that a reason to deny that the *classe moyenne* exists? Not at all.[20]

Rather than seeing this fluidity and ambiguity in purely negative terms, we would argue that the way in which the petite bourgeoisie shaded into other classes, the instabilities and ambiguities, were not so much a hindrance to defining them but a part of the definition. In our view, the obstacles to petit-bourgeois coherence can be too easily overstated, and it is important to consider those forces which might have given the social group a degree of identity and cohesion within the social structure. The sustained answer to the question lies in the rest of this book, which will explore these issues in greater historical detail.

The boundary between master artisans and shopkeepers was indistinct and frequently crossed. Not only did many craftsmen retail their own produce – many tailors and shoemakers fall into this category – but some of the most common of those normally thought of as retailers were themselves craft producers, such as bakers, *charcutiers* and butchers. In any case, the extent to which individuals' concern for independence led them to move between artisanal and retail enterprise suggests that structural distinctions might not be the whole question. Of twenty-eight grocers in the small German town of Gifhorn in 1900, for example, eleven had previously been artisans. A full third of Lyon master bakers who left the profession between 1850 and 1876 went into a retail trade, generally as grocers, café-owners or wine-sellers.[21] Such evidence points towards common concerns and ambitions which transcended sectoral distinctions and the instability of enterprise. In any case, we shall see that the differences between artisanal and retail enterprise and their relations to industrialisation have been too sharply drawn in the past.

The same might be said of the role of social instability as an obstacle to petit-bourgeois identity. The question of whether a group marked by a considerably fluctuating membership can be seen as a coherent social entity is a significant challenge to the historian of the petite bourgeoisie, though it should be observed that mobility – whether geographical or social – has been too little considered in the historical analysis of class relations and class formation. Nevertheless, much of the instability, both within and between generations, involved movement inside the world of small enterprise, and even more so inside the larger lower middle-class world that embraced white-collar employees. Career instability amongst artisans often took them into retailing, as we have noted, but there is also clear evidence of vigorous inter-generational movement between craft enterprise and shopkeeping, as in Bremen between 1890 and the First World War.[22] It became increasingly common for shopkeepers and master artisans to seek white-collar careers for their children, in order to keep them within an occupational group of equivalent status, indicating the significance for the owners of small enterprise of a middling status that was bound up with perceptions of independence.

The distinctiveness of the petite bourgeoisie, which remains ambiguous in terms of productive and class relations, becomes clearer when the structural characteristics of petit-bourgeois enterprise are considered, along with the social and cultural patterns that accompanied them. The unique feature of the petite bourgeoisie lay in the fact that its livelihood was derived from the use of both its own capital and its own labour. Its income was derived from small-scale property which it worked itself, often with the assistance of family labour, and any labour that may have been hired was on a limited scale.[23] Here was a particular form of enterprise, and a particular form of running the enterprise, which placed the family at the centre of economic activity, even where some wage labour was employed. What Balzac, describing the popular neighbourhoods of early nineteenth-century Paris, called 'the bizarre union of household and production'[24] was in no way bizarre, but one of the most fundamental characteristics of nineteenth-century small enterprise. This particular form of enterprise structured petit-bourgeois consciousness in relation to the society within which they lived, and gave them a distinctive culture and patterns of behaviour. Independence was a challenging ideal, repeatedly under threat yet tenacious in its ability to inspire ambition, and it was accompanied by a passionate concern for small property, one whose definition was often too broad for the comfort of larger bourgeois. Independ-ence and property were frequently defended more against the ravages of the rich and powerful than against the threat from the propertyless. In most cases, the petit-bourgeois way of life was an introspective and family-centred one that concentrated on their immediate world of family and neighbourhood. From this came their characteristic suspicion of the outside world and the unknown which turned them against both the bureaucratic state and the forces of banking and high finance. These and other social and cultural characteristics came from the way in which their structural position interacted with what was increasingly felt to be a threatening society. If they do not in themselves define a class, they point towards a package of features which mark the petite bourgeoisie out as a distinctive part of the social formation. Furthermore, they do at times – above all in crises such as that of the 1890s where economic pressure and political anxieties coincided – seem to act as a class. These years saw increasing organised action by craftsmen and shopkeepers in continental Europe. The traditional Marxist view of the petite bourgeoisie as an irresolute social formation, swinging backwards and forwards in response to outside manipulation and in the service of whatever forces required it, stands in need of considerable revision.[25] The political position of the petite bourgeoisie may have been awkward, but in its pattern of development and its political trajectory we shall see further evidence of petit-bourgeois identity.

Even though our analysis neither begins nor concludes with the argument that shopkeepers and master artisans constituted a social class, the petite bourgeoisie was a group whose experiences were shaped by the fact that it lived within a class society. They grew within class societies whose internal structure and power relations followed the structuring principles of wealth, qualifications and achievement. These principles constituted a challenge to the world of master artisans and shopkeepers who for much of the nineteenth century – in many ways for all of it – had other cultural horizons. As far as personal relations were concerned, notions of the moral economy and quality of product, of the personal rather than an anonymous market, and of the right to a trade, played an important role in the world of small enterprise that in many countries kept it at a hesitant distance from the dominant values of the class society in which petits bourgeois lived. The chapters that follow will trace those tensions, and it is from those chapters, rather than this brief and necessarily elliptical discussion, that the meaning of the petite bourgeoisie in European societies will emerge.

The societies at the heart of this analysis are Britain, Germany, France and Belgium, though examples drawn from other countries such as Italy, Sweden, Austria and the Netherlands will appear without any pretension to systematic coverage. It is a geographical balance derived from both the areas of specialised knowledge of the two authors and the state of research in the field. The petite bourgeoisie was long neglected by historians more concerned with the heroic classes whose initiatives and whose conflicts have shaped the modern European world. Initial research was primarily derived from attempts to explain fascism,[26] but by the 1970s studies were beginning to emerge which focused attention on the petite bourgeoisie rather than on fascism, even though they remained largely within the same problematic and still focused primarily on Germany.[27] The middle of the 1970s saw attempts to enlarge the field of study from its narrowly political perspective,[28] and a major impetus was provided by the decision of the Commission Internationale d'Histoire des Mouvements Sociaux et des Structures Sociales to make small enterprise in its social, economic and political dimensions the focus of its research initiative in the late 1970s, culminating in the publication of a set of often useful but rather uneven national reports in 1981.[29] It was from that initiative that contacts were made which culminated in the Research Group on the Petite Bourgeoisie in Nineteenth- and Twentieth-Century Europe, which organised six round tables over the following ten years.[30] These meetings drew together a group of hitherto often isolated researchers working on the world of small enterprise, and played an important part in developing the broader questions for the analysis of the petite bourgeoisie, whether by focusing on economic, social and cultural questions, or by removing the political study of the group from the stranglehold of an approach concerned only to trace the prehistory of fascism and anti-modernism.[31] The history of the petite bourgeoisie ceased to be simply read off from its political behaviour, while its political behaviour ceased to be simply interpreted through its presumed culmination in interwar extremism. The last fifteen years have seen a growth of historical research and publication on the petite bourgeoisie which has transformed our understanding of the subject, including research theses which remain small in number but very significant in providing dense material and analyses of specific occupations and towns.[32]

The four countries to which most attention is given in the chapters which follow were of course the main industrialising economies of nineteenth-century Europe, but the variations between them provide a valuable basis for the comparative analysis of the petite bourgeoisie. Their experience of guilds and corporations differed, from the precocious withering of guild controls in Britain, through straight abolition in France and Belgium in the aftermath of the French Revolution, to hesitant and never complete abolition in Germany during the nineteenth century. Two other major variables concerned with the experience of small artisanal and retail enterprise also provide a good basis for comparison – industrialisation and urbanisation. It was not simply the speed of change which differed, though the early processes of both in Britain distinguished that country from France, where industrial expansion and especially urban development were more gradual and in many ways less traumatic processes, or from Germany whose industrialisation was not only later but based more heavily on capital goods industries, and whose urbanisation in the second half of the century produced a particularly rapid growth of large-scale towns. The contrasts were greatest in terms of political systems and processes, even in the second half of the nineteenth century when there was a degree of convergence between European political systems. France moved towards universal manhood suffrage and an often turbulent republicanism, while in Britain the electorate was increased more hesitantly and a more stable parliamentary system saw the alternating of Conservative and Liberal governments. A mass electorate appeared in Belgium in 1893, though one whose weighted voting system gave the petite bourgeoisie a distinct if temporary advantage from which they benefited in terms of policy attention, but the mid-century Liberal government had by then given way to the rule of a socially conservative Catholic Party that was particularly concerned to develop its petit-bourgeois base. Conservative governments and imperial authority were in firm control in Germany, where universal manhood suffrage at the level of the Reich contrasted with limited tax- or property-based franchises in the towns and regions.

The implications of these differences will be a central strand of the chapters which follow. The four countries offer distinct paths of transition to freedom of trade, to industrial economies and urban societies, and to democratic political cultures. These comparisons operate on at least three levels. In the first place, the analysis is enriched not simply by the contribution of each national historiography, but also by the confrontation between different national historiographies. Second, examples drawn from different countries permit us to accumulate material that allows a more general analysis to be developed. Without being able, or indeed wanting, to compare country by country or town by town within each chapter, we draw upon material from a wider variety of situations than exist within a single country, in order to advance broader explanations or interpretations. Finally, several chapters permit us to establish distinct patterns of national development. In this last respect selective use of the comparative approach will enrich our understanding of the petite bourgeoisie, but analysis of the petite bourgeoisie also advances our understanding of comparative history. The reflection on sources for the study of the petite bourgeoisie makes it clear just how the use of statistical data in quantitative comparative social history often assumes an accuracy in the data collected, which belies the fact that such varied sources as the *patente* business licence tax or census tables are deeply implicated in the ideological and political concerns of each country.[33] Reflection on the comparative study of the petite bourgeoisie also leads one to question the unit of analysis that has dominated comparative history – the nation state. Comparative social history which works within the unit of the nation state will of necessity privilege those variables which are contained within its boundaries: state policy, legal systems and political organisation rather than the geographically more ambiguous economies and societies.[34] Family life, neighbourhood experience, workplace relations, associational culture and a dozen other social variables are better explored at the level of the town or even neighbourhood, and better compared between types of town or neighbourhood or industry, than they are within units set by national boundaries. If the chapters that follow raise comparisons between countries, comparisons between trades, and comparisons between types of town, then this is because the significance of adjusting the unit of comparison has emerged from our study of the petite bourgeoisie.

Language is a problem for comparative history, for the translation of terms from one language to another can strip them of their original meaning, but it is also a source of rich material for reflection. The term *artisan*, central to the concerns of this book, derives from the corporate expectations within which it made sense, though it was rarely used in the seventeenth- or eighteenth-century trades of either Britain or France. During the nineteenth century, Britain's leaner conceptualisation of the social structure came to read in the term artisan a skilled wage-earner, while the expectation of the German *Handwerker* was that it included, and sometimes was even exclusively

12

composed of, masters in the craft trades.[35] Even more striking is the language to describe the occupational groups with which this book is concerned, as terms such as *Mittelstand* in German or *classes moyennes* in French came to be narrowed from their earlier nineteenth-century breadth to a much more precise focus on the owners of small independent enterprises, before debate began again at the end of the century on their enlargement to the new salaried employees. The very conception of the middle and the average in these ideas is vital to an understanding of contemporary designations of the group, but so too is the difference between the use of *classe* in the French and Belgium term but *Stand* (estate) in the German. As we weave between the uses of these terms in self-ascription and outside description, we can understand that the terminology was itself an active participant in the processes which this book explores. The fact that social discussion in English found it difficult to establish a consistent term for the owners of small enterprises will be seen as particularly significant when we come to examine the political voice of the British petite bourgeoisie.

The long nineteenth century was a period in which small enterprise, and with it its petit-bourgeois owners, failed to disappear in the way expected by those who have seen it as ill-suited to the needs of an industrial society in which large-scale capital, large bureaucratic institutions, and the antagonism of labour and capital came to prevail. It was indeed a period which proved difficult for small enterprise, though the difference between sectors and trades makes such generalisations crumble almost as soon as they have been made. We shall certainly encounter the real challenges to the success and viability of small workshop enterprise, especially the early pressures on those in the consumer goods trades such as clothing and furniture, where merchants were rapidly reorganising the industry and depressing the independence of work-shop owners, the skill of their now sub-divided trades, and the prices they received. Yet we shall also see the more extensive and varied ways in which industrialisation, and above all urbanisation, served as stimuli to the opening of small enterprises. The retail trades expanded rapidly with urban develop-ment, and for most of the century almost exclusively through the proliferation of the independent family shop. Only in the closing decades of our period did large-scale retail enterprises begin to pose a threat, and even then the threat was exaggerated by shopkeepers' organisations reluctant to accept that it was the competition between individual shopkeepers themselves which was the most significant challenge they faced.

By the end of the century only a handful of industrial sectors – amongst them cotton, textiles, iron- and steel-making and chemicals – had come to be anathema to small enterprise, and no sectors of the retail trade. Yet these were not untroubled times for small enterprise, and it is one aim of this book to explore the pressures upon the owners of small enterprise which grew in spite of the survival of their role in so many economic sectors. Survival was generally predicated upon changes that brought added pressures. Throughout industrial Europe, workshop owners and, to a lesser extent, retailers found their much-vaunted independence undermined by increasingly organised economic relations which tied them to the needs and commercial techniques of larger capital. The ever-more insistent assertion of petit-bourgeois independence in the late nineteenth century represented the adaptation of a once proud and radical ideal to a world in which they felt less and less at ease. Independence now became an increasingly conservative cry of anger at a world where change seemed only a threat. As organised labour and the working class pulled apart from the owners of small enterprise, as urban space became more segregated, as the organised state seemed to join organised capital in undermining the local social relations on which petit-bourgeois conflict rested, so the petite bourgeoisie became increasingly uncomfortable.

The response to this discomfort was not uniform, for nowhere is comparative analysis more effective than in identifying the different political responses to pressure, but it saw petits bourgeois strengthening the commitment to privacy, family and introspection which had always been present in the world of small enterprise. It also saw the increasing mobilisation of petits bourgeois in trade organisations and political movements which carried their complaints into a larger public sphere, one in which others were prepared to respond and make promises as they sought to construct an electoral base. The interaction between political parties and groups, outside observers and intellectuals and the movements of the petite bourgeoisie itself is a recurrent theme of the book, above all in the chapter devoted to politics.

The chapters which follow recognise the great diversity of small enterprise: diversity of sector and trade, diversity of wealth and income, diversity of stability, and diversity between country and town. All combine to make generalisation awkward. Yet without carefully drawn generalisation, historical analysis becomes impossible. The diversity is in many ways our starting point, as we explore the different relations to guilds and corporations and to their abolition, which we argue were such a determining element in petit-bourgeois experience through the nineteenth century. It continues with the chapters on economic change and on mobility and movement, which stress both the common experiences of much small enterprise and the way in which those experiences made common identity difficult. If common traits and identity are to be found amongst at least sections of the owners of small enterprise, then they must be sought through exploring the distinctive meanings of the family and the town within the world of the petite bourgeoisie, and their distinctive patterns of culture and sociability. It is not that their structural position precluded identity, but it made it difficult and fragile, and any attempt to understand the petite bourgeoisie must reach into the areas covered by other chapters. The clearest expression of petit-bourgeois identity came through its politics, and it is also the least trustworthy expression, because of the inevitable concern as to the representative nature of those organisations which claimed to speak for shopkeepers and master artisans as a whole. The study of petit-bourgeois politics in the book's longest chapter explores the way the place of petits bourgeois in the radical world of the *menu peuple* progressively fragmented along with the popular politics that it had sustained. The late nineteenth century saw the beginnings of a turn to the right by at least the political heart of the petite bourgeoisie, and arguably by the majority of the owners of small enterprise, but it was a change which varied between countries and which, even in its clearest expression, carried with it continuing themes from the petite bourgeoisie's more radical past. If the petite bourgeoisie played a significant role in fascist mobilisation in the interwar period, and, as the Conclusion argues, this is by no means self-evident at the European level, then it did not do so as the inevitable final stage of a journey that had begun in the middle of the nineteenth century.[36]

2

THE TRANSITION FROM CORPORATIONS

For the French historian Jacques Revel, the essential characteristic of *ancien régime* society was the corporate order rather than the feudal tie.[1] He was describing less the material importance of corporations than the power of corporate communities, as representations of economic and social relations, to shape the ways in which people perceived the social order in which they lived. The *avocat général* Séguier, in his famous speech attacking Turgot's controversial plans to abolish trade guilds in 1776, made the point powerfully when he told the King:

> All your subjects, Sire, are divided amongst as many different bodies as there are states in the kingdom. The clergy, the nobility, the sovereign courts, the law courts, the officials of these courts, the universities, the academies, the finance companies, the trading companies, represent throughout the State existing bodies which one might see as links in a great chain, the first of which is in the hands of Your Majesty, as chief and sovereign administrator of all that constitutes the body of the nation.[2]

Historical research may have revealed the gap between such representations and the realities of corporate life, but it remains the case that the transition from corporate structures to freedom of occupation was fundamentally important to the future of artisanal – and to a lesser extent retail – small enterprise throughout Europe. This transition shaped not only the chronology of the transformation of small-scale enterprise, but also the organisations that petits bourgeois formed, the demands that they made, and certain aspects of their mentality throughout the nineteenth century.

IDEALS AND CHALLENGES

Where corporations held sway in mid-eighteenth-century Europe – and that means everywhere but Great Britain where their influence had long been waning – their defining function was the organisation of craft production and trade. Yet their multi-faceted character meant that they were always more

16

than simply economic institutions.[3] Their basic principle was to secure a monopoly of production and distribution which would guarantee a livelihood to those practising a trade within a corporation. In its ideal form, the cohesion of the order was maintained by strict rules on those to be admitted as masters, their mode of access, family origins and sober lifestyle. It was, not surprisingly, easier for the sons of master artisans themselves to reach the status of masters. For others, there was the classic *cursus honorum*, which began with formal apprenticeship, passed through the status of *compagnon* or journeyman in the course of which a number of years were spent travelling and practising the trade, and ended when the journeyman finally set up as a master on his own account, having satisfied the jurors of the corporation that his technical standards were satisfactory by producing a piece of work, literally a masterpiece. The corporate body of masters was unified by the symbolic rituals through which it identified itself as a harmonious community, one that protected its members and looked after their families in times of need. At the same time, the corporations were part of the hierarchical order of their town, and setting up as a master was frequently (particularly in Germany) linked to obtaining rights of residence and to marry as well as political status. Membership of a corporation was closely bound up with the political and juridical identity of urban citizens – in German and Swedish towns guild membership and citizen status went together, while guildsmen in early-modern Britain were freemen of their towns. Throughout Europe, corporate communities took their place in electoral colleges and public processions, as well as in the policing of urban economic life. Even if the reality did not generally match up to this ideal picture, corporations were indeed multi-faceted institutions regulating economic activity, disciplining the labour force, maintaining the standards and traditions of the craft, providing a career pattern marked by elaborate rites of passage, and contributing to the orderly functioning of the urban community. These roles converged on the master as citizen, as head of household, and as independent craftsman.[4]

This was a very masculine vision of order, rooted ideologically in the vision of the *pater familias* imposing his authority in workplace and family alike, and materially in the secondary role ascribed to women in corporate institutions. When a master died, the corporation would ensure the well-being of the family where necessary, allowing significant rights to the widow who could continue operation of her husband's business and confer master's status on a journeyman whom she married. These were rights of dependence, however, and women secured few rights of independence through the guild system, whatever their economic role. Eighteenth-century Paris saw female trades such as linen-makers, hairdressers, and seamstresses, which had formal statutes and apprenticeships, and whose organisations functioned in many ways like male corporations, but these lacked the public role or legal standing that went with the male institutions.[5] Outside those few cases, women had few formal roles in guilds. The admission to the guild of female owners of enterprises in certain eighteenth-century Breton building crafts was permitted primarily in order to keep the business under guild control, but they received none of the public and political rights of male masters.[6]

The juridical ideals of the corporation or guild[7] rarely matched the reality. There were many sources of divergence: the inequality of power and resources within corporations; the economic changes that saw increasing activity carried on outside corporate control as well as subordinating guild masters to merchant capital; and the way geographical dispersal within the town weakened the strength of relationships amongst masters, making a broader solidarity amongst artisans in general transcend purely corporate divisions.[8] Indeed, the introspection and cohesion of guild life have been too readily extrapolated from the image guilds presented of themselves and to which their enemies responded. Corporate identity was no automatic expression of the economic cohesion of a trade, but was constructed to play a political or social role within a town and to manage the economic interests of those involved. Guilds and corporations thus existed as economic and political institutions, and as public images or representations of those institutions. We should not be surprised if the two did not coincide.

Corporations were under threat in eighteenth-century western Europe, long before political revolutions and economic liberalism combined formally to destroy them. The threat came from three distinct directions. First, from the state which in many countries enlarged its public functions to replace those of increasingly ineffective corporations, asserting its monopoly of jurisdiction and policing while at the same time pursuing economic policies aimed at increasing production. Yet the state often restrained its hand in the eighteenth century, seeing the advantages of an institution which offered stability and social protection whatever its effects on economic progress. That explains the ambivalence of French governments, which alternated between reform and support in the century that followed Colbert's rationalisation of the system in 1673. Where corporations survived best was where their capacity to assure order was most appreciated. As a Berlin municipal councillor expressed it as late as 1843, 'each master is a policeman. In raising the prestige and the honour of masters we would at the same time enhance a body of great value for the maintenance of discipline and order.'[9] The second factor corroding the corporate world was the divergences which emerged between the wealthy and the humble within each trade. Guilds were essentially restrictive and exclusive bodies aimed at controlling competition within a given market, and in this sense they 'embodied the individual's search for security within apparently limited and inelastic markets'.[10] Yet as markets expanded, guilds were unable to prevent the growth of substantial inequalities amongst their members. Indeed, even if protective controls could prove a barrier to some capitalist enterprises, many a wealthy merchant or manufacturer used the guild as an instrument to advance his business. It would therefore be wrong to see corporations as synonymous with economic stagnation. Finally there was the assertive and independent voice of journeymen who, faced with decreasing prospects of mobility to master's status and the pressures of economic subordination, broke the constraints of corporate ideology and regulations and clashed openly with their employers.

Against the image of the corporation as cohesive must thus be set a reality of inequality and conflict,[11] and against the image of inertia and stability must be set the reality that corporations constituted a resource, which could assist action at many levels. The radical revolt and its outcome in the small Dutch town of Deventer, for example, show the corporations providing a basis for radical mobilisation that placed the town's masters at the heart of the revolution against both Orange rule in the Dutch Republic and that of the *rentier* oligarchy in municipal affairs. The democratic revolt of 1782–83 in Deventer was led by lawyers and other professionals, but the bulk of the participants were guild masters mobilised through their guilds: 68 per cent of those who signed all three of the crucial petitions were guild members, mostly signing together as guildsmen with their officers at the head of the page. Here was the capacity of the corporate community, more homogeneous in this small town than it would have been in large metropolitan centres, to provide a base for organisation and protest, to use its sense of independence to back a radical and democratic movement. The movement that had made the revolution in Deventer then split. The professional elite that had led the movement proposed an abolition of economic controls and restrictions that was unacceptable to the localist and corporate interests of its artisanal rank and file, who now turned to support the Orange restoration. Yet as Te Brake observes in his analysis of this revolt, 'The Orangist version of the future had precious little to do with the Prince of Orange; rather, its cutting edge was the established artisans' and shopkeepers' defence of economic interests defined in old-regime corporatist terms.' Democratic radicalism and economic protectionism were no more contradictions amongst the masters of Deventer than they were to be in the urban revolutions of 1848 in Germany, but it was the very strength of the guild resources which had mobilised them in the democratic movement which subsequently led to a corporatist and superficially loyalist reaction.[12]

The German territories present the clearest example of persistent guild structures, with corporations in German towns able to defend their monopolies with the support of regional and state authorities. The rights of citizenship were more intricately tied up with practising membership of guilds in Germany than they were in other parts of Europe. In the free imperial cities of Aachen and Cologne citizenship was conferred on men who were Catholic, self-supporting, and members of the town guilds, providing one reason why many German guilds contained wealthy merchants and even nobles.[13] Citizenship was but one aspect of the way in which state administrations saw in corporations the means to guarantee social stability and to secure the position of the sovereign ruler. Yet guilds were not universal in Germany, being most secure at the end of the century in the free cities and small towns in the north and south-west, least so in the agrarian towns of eastern Prussia. Their importance varied with the strength of the artisanal population. In Munich in 1792 they comprised 9 per cent of the whole urban population, 11 per cent in Berlin in 1801. They thus constituted a central element of the broader middling strata which made up some one-third of the male-occupied population of towns.[14] Nevertheless, these corporations were far from having a monopoly of industrial and commercial activities. At the turn of the century about one-half of German artisans lived in the countryside and outside corporate regulation,[15] but certain occupations escaped it even in urban areas. The tailors' guild in Hamburg, which boasted a mere 120 members in 1789 while 2000 worked outside its control,[16] was an extreme case, but much depended on the extent to which the individual state was willing to protect a particular guild. One must not in any case exaggerate the power of German state administrations in the eighteenth century, particularly outside Brandenburg Prussia, where the *Allgemeine Landrecht* of 1794 recognised guilds as privileged corporations, but placed them under the ultimate control of the state. Guilds found it difficult to secure government protection when the interests of the state appeared to lie in expanding production. In the dispute concerning Berlin calico printers in 1783, for example, the state came down firmly on the side of entrepreneurial auton-omy.[17] In contrast, the small and introverted towns of central and southern Germany, for which Mack Walker coined the term 'home towns',[18] saw the guilds play a central role in urban government, securing the political independence and internal stability which allowed them to defend their interests.

Although the slower pace of economic development and the general state endorsement of guilds ensured that the world of artisanal production was retained more securely within its corporate framework in eighteenth-century Germany than in Britain or France, strains were already becoming clear. The practice of masters housing and feeding their journeymen was no longer uniformly followed. The corporate rules preventing marriage before acces-sion to master's status were being flouted in those towns where journeymen were losing confidence in their ability to set up on their own relatively early in life. Married journeymen living outside their master's household comprised 5 per cent of all journeymen in late-eighteenth-century Nuremberg, but were as many as 30 per cent in the small north German town of Hildesheim.[19] Furthermore, the established pattern of internal recruitment of master artisans from the same occupational and geographic milieu was breaking down not only in large cities such as Berlin but also in the little town of Nürtinger.[20] Tensions emerged between masters and journeymen, though these were less extensive than in either Britain or France, and less corrosive of the corporate identity. The brotherhoods, which supported journeymen as they spent their years travelling, provided temporary housing for them, and placed new arrivals in jobs assumed a larger role, akin to the *compagnonnages* in France, in defending journeymen in disagreement with individual masters and municipal authorities. As tensions between masters and journeymen became more frequent, the brotherhoods began to assume a role in strikes.[21] A study by Kocka of 259 strikes by journeymen in six German cities, mainly between 1780 and 1805, reveals some of the dimensions of these conflicts. The vast majority saw journeymen pitted against the masters or their guild – in only 16 per cent of strikes did masters and journeymen join together to defend their common trade interests, and, as journeymen took joint action across different trades in a town, so the masters were less likely to support them. These tensions were at the same time largely contained within the structures and discourse of the corporate world. Journeymen generally left work in response to grievances over the denial of their traditional rights, their sense of honour, and the moral standards of the trade. Nearly one-third of these disputes concerned questions of corporate custom and honour without any evident connection with economic questions, such as strikes over a master having touched a dead animal. It was not only that narrowly economic issues appear not to have been the dominant concern (23 per cent concerned wages and related issues), but that even wage and related demands were presented and justified in largely non-economic and defensive traditional terms.[22] The theme is a common one across Britain, France, and Germany, with journeymen action in the world of the later eighteenth-century workshop shaping their protests in terms of artisans' traditional rights and the defence of the community of the trade against misguided masters. The continuing vigour of corporations and the support of German states gave a particular force to such defences in Germany.

A particular feature of the German case was that the corporation remained a structure recognised by the state as being essential to the urban economy and to the organisation of a town's citizens. Nowhere was this more true than in the home towns, those small towns of up to 15,000 inhabitants which in 1800 contained about a quarter of the whole German population, and where the guildsmen's role in town government, their ability to protect themselves against often weak wider state apparatuses, and the absence of severe economic pressures from outside combined to create a stable and introspective world for the guild masters who dominated it. Their most precise defence derived from all of these – their ability to control the access of outsiders to economic, residential and burgher status within their town. In the words of Mack Walker, 'the German home towns in the peaceful years from Westphalia to Austerlitz created an unusual mechanism to repel intrusion, and that mechanism became the basis of its political and social life'.[23] The German home towns were of course not typical of German urban life, merely one segment of it, but they represent the *locus classicus* of the closed guild world, hierarchical and stable, defending its local autarchic economy against immigrants and the intrusive state alike, and it was an image to which later generations of petits bourgeois returned for the source of their utopian dreams. We must take care, however, not to mistake the classic formulation for the typical.

If guild controls simply faded into disuse in Britain, as we shall shortly see, and if they were suppressed in a few days in France, they were weakened in Germany and abolished by the actions of a multitude of states over three-quarters of a century. Between the first suppression of guilds in the Rhineland in the 1790s and the last in Mecklenburg in 1869 lay a period of progressive but uneven abolition, as states struggled with the apparently competing demands of economic development, social and political stability, the ambitions of bureaucratic apparatuses, and political pressures from inside and outside their own territories. The earliest pressure came from outside, with the areas of the Rhineland and Westphalia, occupied and influenced by the French, never restoring the guilds which were at that time removed. In Prussia, the trade tax edict of 1810 and the law on the policing of trades in the following year established freedom of occupation, in the sense that it was now possible to practise a trade without being admitted to a guild. Bureaucratic hurdles remained, however, for no German state passed straight from corporate structures to the untrammelled freedoms proposed by British political economists. In Prussia, the payment of a trade tax and the need to be a citizen of good standing ensured that the policing of trades passed from guilds to the state, indicating that the image of a rapid throwing open of artisanal trades in Prussia while they remained closed in many other parts of Germany was in many ways illusory. Furthermore, the links between the practice of an artisanal trade and the rights of urban residence allowed many municipalities to control the number of masters. Prussian guilds remained influential as quasi-public associations (*Innungen*) which extended specific features of corporations into the era of trade freedom, such as representing trade interests, supervising the education of apprentices, and undertaking a variety of benevolent activities. The Prussian government in 1845 increased their influence by restricting the training of apprentices in forty-three artisanal trades to masters who were members of *Innungen*. Guilds did not disappear in Prussia or more widely in Germany, they were simply stripped of many of their legally enforceable functions, and their continued existence as bodies straddling the public and private spheres left the corporate option firmly in place for successive generations of German artisans seeking an alternative to the decline that they feared.

The period between 1815 and the final turn towards freedom of occupation in various German states in the late 1850s was one characterised by tension between, on the one hand, guilds seeking traditional self-regulation and, on the other, bureaucratic states which successively took over many of those regulatory functions for themselves. In areas where guilds seem to have remained entrenched, they were often being reformed and partially deprived of their real significance. The reforms of the 1830s in Hamburg put guilds under the political control of the Senate, which proceeded to forbid alliances with corporations outside Hamburg as well as all attempts to control imports into the city.[24] Monopoly was limited and trade was encouraged, but the corporate framework itself was left in place. Württemberg chose a different route, freeing thirteen sectors while maintaining the legal position of masters in forty-four others. These surviving corporations saw their functions limited, with restrictions on the number of apprentices lifted, the admission of masters who had not received a traditional training, and the abolition of their right to limit the size of workshops.[25] State authorities in such areas were torn between their desire to maintain corporations as barriers to proletarian-isation and as forces for stability on the one hand, and their concern to eliminate what they saw to be a brake on economic development on the other. In Saxony the government allowed a chaos of conflicting economic regu-lations to accumulate rather than establish undisputed freedom of trade before they felt convinced that social upheaval would not ensue. They waited until 1861.[26] Some state administrations were torn internally by the question, as in the Grand Duchy of Baden in mid-century, where local and cantonal administrations supported existing guilds while the higher levels of the bureaucracy wanted restructuring and even abolition.[27] Nevertheless, after a flurry of reaction in much of Germany after the 1848 revolutions, the late 1850s saw the imperatives of economic change and the influence of liberal economic ideas make freedom of occupation the rule. The final states, such as Hamburg, Hanover, Bremen, Württemberg and Bavaria held out until the 1860s. In 1869 the Reichstag of the North German Confederation abolished all corporate laws, and the new German Empire followed suit in 1871.[28]

The structures of the artisanat under official freedom of trade in Prussia, and those elsewhere where reformed corporations remained significantly in place, probably came much closer to each other in reality than any juridical polarisation would lead one to expect. Nowhere could corporations preserve their old autonomy and exclusivity, and in the face of state authorities and their production-oriented economic policies, they were forced to fall back on self-regulation, professional training, and mutual trade support and soci-ability. The survival of state-supported corporate frameworks or at least quasi-corporate institutions nevertheless remains important, as was the extent of bureaucratic intervention in trade life.

The contrast with the British experience was striking. George Unwin, whose studies at the start of this century remain amongst the few detailed examinations of the corporate experience in post-medieval Britain, observed that the transition from guild rule, which elsewhere in Europe was generally linked to political conflict and revolution, was in England the result of far more gradual processes. However, 'the victory of one type of economic organisation over another was none the less effectual because it was achieved in silence'.[29] The decline of guild authority was an uneven process, but by the beginning of the eighteenth century the role of guilds cannot be compared with that of equivalent institutions elsewhere. The early unification of the national state and of national legal structures partially explains that difference, as does the absence of struggles over sovereignty between different levels of urban, regional and state or imperial authority which elsewhere in Europe sustained competing structures of law and privilege. By the early seventeenth century guilds can be seen to have begun a period of declining authority, though new guilds continued to be formed and in some towns at least their economic vitality may have been maintained.[30] The guilds and companies ceased to represent the interests of master artisans precisely as they came to be dominated by larger-scale merchant and then manufacturing capital. In particular, the London livery companies (the capital's name for its corporate bodies) came to be ruled by their oligarchic Courts of Assistants, as artisanal interests became subordinated to those of larger capital.[31] As the municipal authorities lost interest in guilds as a method of policing local industry, few other than the legitimately installed small masters were left to defend their regulatory and corporate powers. The seventeenth century saw guilds failing even in their most essential function – ensuring that the practice of a trade was restricted to those who had served a legal apprenticeship and who had secured the freedom of their guild or company.

At the heart of a European comparison lies not just the precocity and gradualness of the decline of guild controls in Britain, but the fact that the defence of the artisan came to depend more on statute law than on guild law. The apprenticeship clauses of the 1563 Statute of Artificers and Apprentices required a seven-year indentured apprenticeship for those exercising a craft, and until repeal in 1814 these clauses provided the essential basis for all legal attempts to defend apprenticeship, restrict access to the craft and maintain its standards – the essential goals carried out by corporations elsewhere in Europe. Apprenticeship now rested on the ability of journeymen to insist upon its enforcement (for example by refusing to work with 'dishonourable' labour), or to bring successful legal actions. Industrial conflict prevailed because the courts became reluctant to enforce apprenticeship until, after a sustained journeymen's campaign to reassert the clauses' authority in the early years of the nineteenth century, they were repealed by a Parliament fearful of workers' combinations and beginning its conversion to liberal economic ideas.[32] The way in which statute and common law in Britain became more important than guild law confirms this weakening of guilds: London liveried companies even realised that they lacked the capacity to enforce their own rules on recalcitrant journeymen, and turned to the public courts to prosecute them for conspiracy. Increasing intervention by magistrates, and laws such as those to prevent journeymen leaving work unfinished, mark an advance of the state which signified the decline of guild authority.[33]

Guilds did not disappear from eighteenth-century Britain, but they became less and less relevant to artisanal production and its regulation. Nowhere was this more apparent and more paradoxical than in London, where the decline of the liveried companies' authority over the trades whose name they carried stood in stark contrast to their pride and pretensions, as they assumed their modern status as wealthy, propertied, educational and charitable institutions. The trades had escaped their control, whether through the expansion of production into the suburbs, the influx of masters and journeymen who never accepted the authority of the company, the complexities of sub-contracting and sub-division of labour which older trade regulations could not handle, or the fact that the companies were in the hands of men of influence who had little interest in the detailed enforcement of artisanal regulations.[34] Companies did periodically seek to enforce their still extant regulations, but successes were limited and short-lived.[35] The authority of the London Weavers' Company, for example, was increasingly flouted from the early years of the eighteenth century, with most of those summoned to apply for the freedom of the company simply ignoring the call. Many qualified weavers failed to take up their freedom, and the Company could do little to prevent the excessive number of looms, to limit the numbers of apprentices, or after 1736 even to practise the traditional right to search the trade for illegal or sub-standard goods.[36]

Divisions within the world of production and trade thus opened up in eighteenth-century Britain, with growing inequality between ordinary masters and the elites of the trade, as well as between journeymen and their masters. It is hard to judge whether the extent of conflict differed from that in contemporary France, but in Britain it increasingly took place outside the framework and the discourse of guilds. Conflict between masters and journeymen was reflected in increasing strike action and the emergence of workers' associations. A London petition from masters in various trades made their fear of organised journeymen clear. 'The exclusive Right of Exercising Handicraft and Retail Trades within this City and Liberties is a great and Valuable Franchise,' they wrote, but one which was being degraded because of its exclusivity.

> The greatest part of the Free Journeymen presuming on this their exclusive Right are becoming Idle and Debauched, Negligent in their Callings, Exorbitant in their Demands, and Disrespectful to their Superiors, often entering into unlawful Combinations and busying themselves more to prevent others from Working than to procure or deserve employment for themselves.[37]

Under the combined pressures of increasing division of labour and sub-contracting, reduced opportunities to reach the status of master, and pressure from masters to cut costs by employing unapprenticed workers, journeymen were in many trades coming regularly into conflict with their employers. The hatters and tailors formed continuing organisations, while others rested on the informal association around a trade's public house, 'house of call', to sustain industrial action when needed. Certain trades such as hatters, tailors, woollen workers, silk-weavers, coopers and printers were renowned for such conflict, but by the later decades of the century they were a feature of industrial life in many trades and most larger towns.[38] Although the enforcement of apprenticeship was a cause of strikes, wages and hours of work dominated strike demands quite explicitly in Britain, at a time when parallel workplace tensions in France and Germany were generally still articulated within the discourse of honour and custom.

The defence of the trade, in terms of the enforcement of customary ideals of work practice and apprenticeship, was thus increasingly left to the journeymen. In their eyes, this right to work at the trade had been earned when they had completed their apprenticeship, and constituted a form of property which could not be legitimately removed. The defence of the custom of the trade, an idea fundamental to eighteenth-century British artisans, is reminiscent of aspects of artisanal discourse elsewhere in Europe. The customs sustained their rights, and the two were reinforced by initiation ceremonies, rites of passage, workshop rules, conviviality, and symbolic rituals that included saints' days, such as the shoemakers' celebration of St Crispin.[39] In the face of ambivalent masters and hostile merchants and manufacturers, journeymen came to assert regulatory and quasi-corporate rights over their trade. As early as 1725, a journeymen woolcombers' club in the town of Alton in Hampshire was said to have presumed

> to act as a Body corporate, by electing two Supervisors and a Book keeper, using a common seal, and making By Laws or Orders, by which they pretend to determine who hath a Right to the Woolcombers Trade, how many Apprentices each Master should keep at one time, and who is qualified to take them.[40]

At the end of the century the caulkers in the Thames Dockyards, seeking to prevent the employment of non-indentured men, tried to incorporate their trade as a company.[41] The language of guilds was, however, less common than that of 'the trade', which asserted that the journeymen and masters shared common interests in the defence of the traditions and rights of their craft, and that the natural harmonious state of the trade had been undermined by the misguided abandonment of those ideals by many masters. The trade had to continue to organise itself to defend the artisan's property in his skill, to limit competition, and to maintain the standards of the craft. In the journeymen's vision of the trade we surely find the corporate idiom without corporations. It was a cause which in Britain was increasingly identified with the journeymen. It came to be so in France too during the first half of the nineteenth century.

France during the *ancien régime* might seem to have approached the German model, for Colbert's reorganisation of French corporations in 1673 sought to impose the corporate form on all economic activity, with the aim of both unifying the kingdom and finding additional fiscal revenues. Corporations had never been ubiquitous in France and they did not become so in the years after Colbert's measure. In Provence, their layered diversity reveals both the absence of corporate regularity and the presence of corporate ideals. Late *ancien-régime* Provence boasted privileged corporations established by letters patent from the Crown only in specific trades that were either rich, such as drapers or haberdashers, or sensitive, such as goldsmiths and apothecaries, and then only in the most important towns of the region – Marseille, Toulon and Aix. Far more widespread were second-rank guilds in lesser trades, whose statutes were simply ratified by the *Parlement* in Aix. Many trades lacked any formal corporations at all, especially in smaller urban centres, but even here Agulhon finds an associationist tendency which expressed itself in brotherhoods or chapels identified with a particular trade and serving what were effectively informal corporate functions.[42] The corporate presence was thus less systematic than the ideal might suggest in eighteenth-century France, but the corporate impulse remained important.

The French state was more ambivalent about corporations than its German counterparts, supporting a source of both stability and income, but at the same time anxious to stimulate production in sectors where guilds were deemed to be restrictive. The Controller General Turgot's abolition of guilds in February 1776, in pursuit of the Physiocratic version of liberal economic ideas, was to remain in force for no more than a few months, but it was the most extreme of a series of measures throughout the eighteenth century by which the absolutist state sought to loosen guild restrictions on production – such as the 1736 ordinance seeking to limit guilds to large towns or those in the 1740s and 1750s which lifted specific restrictions in textile production. In reality, however, the Bourbon state saw itself as dependent on the corporate order for stability and finance, and the horrified attacks of guild masters and the agitation of political opponents combined to ensure Turgot's resignation and the restoration of corporations by August of the same year. Events during those six months tell us much about the distance between French corporations and their ideal. Most masters were indeed appalled – though the Parisian glazier Jacques-Louis Ménétra was not alone in welcoming the end of an institution which stifled his business and irritated him with its affectations to exclusiveness, and its intrusive *jurandes*.[43] The mass of masters who sought to regain their corporations defended them not in terms of the warmth of workshop relations between masters and journeymen that was to so attract those who romanticised the institution in the later nineteenth century, but by stressing the idleness and indiscipline of apprentices and journeymen who would never work seriously if the only incentive was offered by the market place. Journeymen's joyful celebrations of Turgot's reform confirmed not only the masters' worst fears, but also the judgement of historians who have pointed to the decline of workplace relationships within eighteenth-century French crafts.[44] The shock administered by Turgot, the modified corporations which returned in the summer of 1776 under more oligarchic control, and the inevitable fiscal charges placed upon those re-entering the system, combined to weaken the hold of corporations in their fifteen remaining years of life. Industrial conflict appears to have become more acute during those final years of the corporate trades.[45]

The corporation's idealised image of itself in France was thus under challenge from various directions. First, there were the increasing ambiguities of master independence, above all in those trades such as textiles, clothing and furniture where merchant organisation opened up wider markets. Specialisation and sub-contracting were undermining the notion of an independent master even within the corporate system that was intended to protect him.[46] In these growing industries, the specialisation of workshops on a single process within a complex division of labour undermined the corporate ideal of distinct workshops each under the control of an independent master. Parisian corporations were less able to keep control of artisanal production as the century went on, with the growing problem of *faux ouvriers*, masters and journeymen operating outside the guilds, whether simply illegally or in privileged places such as the faubourg Saint-Antoine. Far from inhabiting some eighteenth-century version of the black economy, these producers were tied into the same systems of sub-contracting and wholesaling as the legitimate masters. They also produced nearly one third of the bread consumed in the capital every day.[47]

Inequalities and tensions amongst the masters themselves constituted a second element undermining the corporations' self-image of internal cohesion and harmony. Differences of wealth, age, and economic dependence turned most guilds into hierarchic organisations dominated by their more prosperous and powerful members. Larger employers – who might indeed be men of substance but in many guilds need have no more than half a dozen journeymen – would become *anciens* and *jurés* and build their social world around the meetings and conviviality of the guild. The tendency to oligarchy increased in the reformed corporations after August 1776, with even more guilds now excluding the mass of ordinary masters from personal involvement in assemblies. Ordinary members of the card and paper-makers' corporation in Paris, protesting in 1775 at new rules increasing the permitted number of apprentices in a workshop, complained that the *anciens* and *jurés* 'who between them control the greatest part of the manufacture, [are] anxious always to maintain their despotism in the corporation'.[48] Occasional opposition movements demanded greater guild openness and democracy, protested against the webs of family and business connections which dominated the guilds in larger towns at least. Kaplan has found such movements amongst many Paris trades – clockmakers, wigmakers, roofers, grocers, caterers, and bakers amongst them.[49] This trend to oligarchic control of guilds in France provides one explanation for the ease with which most master artisans shed their attachment to the institution during the Revolution, in comparison with countries such as Germany and Sweden where guild participation by smaller masters continued for much longer, and with it their defence of the institution.

The revisionism of recent research depends largely on evidence for Paris, but there were parallel developments elsewhere, with business and merchant elites frequently using the guild to advance their interests. One should not assume too readily that merchants and manufacturers were struggling to escape from corporate constraints, for guilds could provide an excellent mechanism by which merchants could keep control of production quality, markets, credit, and the disciplining of workers and sub-contractors. In Lille merchants used the textile corporations they dominated to exercise controls over quality and limit competition from outsiders. The *marchands–fabricants* of Lyon used guild regulations to control the silk-weavers who supplied them, for example by preventing weavers from working for more than one guild merchant at a time, while a similar pattern in Orléans kept hosiery masters subordinate to the merchant–manufacturers who dominated the guild.[50]

Finally, if the world of guild masters did not match the harmonious image, nor did that of their relations with their journeymen. In many trades journeymen no longer had a reasonable expectation that they would one day set up for themselves, and where access was easy, as among the textile trades of Bayeux, the overstocked industry was hardly worthy of the effort.[51] Masterships were becoming expensive for those who were not sons of masters, and with an increasing ratio of journeymen to master many workers, instead of waiting for their own independence, sought to advance their interests as workers, albeit workers in a world they still perceived through a corporate lens.[52] Tensions were more marked in larger workshops, where foremen acted as intermediaries between masters and men, and strikes in Paris were more common in trades such as printers, hatters, silk-workers and building workers where larger workshops prevailed.[53] Journeymen strikes and protests across a remarkably wide range of trades in Lyon and Nantes, linked to growing levels of journeymen association, shows that the problems were not limited to the capital.[54] A wide range of grievances surfaced in these disputes: payment, working conditions, numbers of apprentices, the employ-ment of unapprenticed workers (*alloués*), work practices and, above all, control over the labour market as journeymen insisted that they should control the placement of workers arriving on the *tour de France*. Attempts by masters to impose the *livret* employment document represented an attempt to win back the freedom to choose their own labour force.[55] While town-wide disputes rested on a general decline in the quality of relations between masters and their journeymen, this was particularly the case with respect to conflicts within a single workshop, and often produced protests embedded in trade traditions and charivari. The massacre of cats carried out in the 1730s by the apprentices and journeymen of a Parisian printing shop in rue Saint-Séverin represents the best-known example of such action, where simmering anger at their distant master who neither worked nor ate with the men exploded in the mock trials and ritualised massacre of the cats around the house and shop, including the favourite *grise* of the mistress of the house.[56]

Journeymen's associations proliferated in the eighteenth-century French artisanal world, whether the increasingly important *compagnonnages* which eased the passage of those making the *tour de France*, or the religious *confraternités* or brotherhoods in Paris whose chapels and religious rituals provided the associational foundations of the struggle against master violations of the rules of the trade.[57] The *compagnonnages* and *confraternités* provided sociability, welfare support, the placement of workers, religious ritual and the maintenance of trade traditions, and they were the natural basis for organising disputes. The *compagnonnages* were hierarchical institutions in many ways modelled on the corporations that mistrusted them, with their own concern for ritual, history and myth. They provided a distinctive basis for labour solidarity, expressive of the moralised world of the eighteenth-century trades.

The ideal corporation, with its harmonious and structured relations, existed only as a golden age to be evoked by those who found the present wanting, whether guild masters or their journeymen and apprentices. By the end of 1791 the formal existence of corporations in France had itself become a memory, as the threat raised by Turgot was brought to fruition by the Revolution. 'From the 1st of April next, every citizen will be free to exercise whichever occupation or trade he chooses, so long as he has obtained and paid for the appropriate trade licence [*patente*].'[58] With these words the *loi d'Allarde* abolished corporations in March 1791, and three months later the *loi Le Chapelier* forbade the formation of workers or masters associations. The reaction of masters to these important changes seems to have been surprisingly muted. Those guilds which had produced their lists of grievances (*cahiers de doléances*) in the winter of 1788–89 concentrated on a very narrow defence of guilds, as if taking their continuation for granted, espousing few general principles, and primarily concerned that abuses be stamped out.[59] The upholsterers of Orléans could see nothing but chaos ensuing. 'Every worker would want to set up on his own account. Today's masters would see their shops abandoned.'[60] This did not prevent masters denouncing the exclusive privileges of others, and by 1791 commitment to the progress of the Revolution, combined with a sense that little could be done to save their corporations, led masters to acquiesce in the *loi d'Allarde*. Lille's merchants and artisans accepted the end of corporations but, according to Hirsch's recent study, they were less willing to see the destruction of all regulation of trades. If corporations found few to defend them in commercial and artisanal circles, the same could be said for freedom of trade. The onset of war and the speeding up of revolutionary change on the one hand, and the commitment of public authorities to apply the laws on the other, combined to speed the transition from the old order to economic freedom.[61] There was an additional incentive to acquiescence: the municipal revolutions had offered masters, particularly those who had been prominent in their corporations, the chance of a new political and administrative role, and the gain in political prestige made the loss of corporate status less threatening.

The Napoleonic years saw some discussion of the advantages of guilds by social conservatives nostalgic for the stability they remembered from the *ancien régime*, by a small number of Napoleonic administrators attracted by the role of guilds in policing economic activity, and by certain small retailers and artisans seeking shelter from competition.[62] Several hundred Parisian wine merchants petitioned in 1806 for the return of their guild, to be protected by hefty registration fees, inspection of goods for sale, and a limit of one shop per master.[63] Demands interpreted as seeking the return of guilds were generally a more limited search for legal restrictions on competition rather than attempts to reconstruct a corporate world which by now had few defenders, as in the case of the retailers and artisans who demanded legal protection from itinerant *colporteurs*.[64] The butchers' and bakers' trades, whose importance in the feeding of towns allowed them guild-like organisations and municipal regulation, consistently opposed these restrictions, and greeted as a liberation the abolition under the Second Empire of controls on prices and on access to their trades.[65] The few petitions in favour of corporations received by the Chamber of Deputies in the auspicious years of ultra-Royalist domination immediately after the Restoration were ignored by deputies.[66] Even the Villèle government, the most reactionary of the Restoration monarchy, declared in 1824 that all attempts to restrict the number of enterprises were 'contrary to the freedom of industry and ... to the competition which is so beneficial to consumers'.[67] The corporation as a structure for industrial organisation was dead in France, with neither small enterprise nor state authorities willing to contemplate its return.

A comparison of Britain, Germany and France presents us with different models of transition from corporate institutions, involving distinct chronologies as well as distinct relationships between corporatism and the state. The experience of other countries can be located within this framework, as with Belgium where the economic strains of the eighteenth century had significantly undermined the effectiveness of corporations even more strongly than in France, and where the country's Habsburg rulers saw corporate privilege as a block to reform of the political order as well as to industrial and commercial development. They also saw guild reform as a necessary aspect of improving public morality, anxious about the banquets, drinking, and lengthy festivals which characterised corporate life and which seemed as much of a threat to the good order of society as they were to economic activity. The state made a series of unpopular efforts to reform corporations in 1738, 1761 and 1784, few of which seriously inhibited their activities, and they were finally abolished in the 1795 proclamation which attached the country to France.[68] The pattern in Austria itself, on the other hand, resembles that in Germany, with the late formal abolition (in 1859) of guilds which had for some time been experiencing strain, the continuation of the corporate idiom in quasi-public associations, and the strengthening of these bodies in the changed political situation of the later nineteenth century.[69]

THE CORPORATE IDEA IN A CHANGING WORLD

This comparative picture highlights fundamental aspects of the social history of each country: the heavy weight of the *ancien régime* and the importance of state bureaucracy in German society; the way in which the Revolution did indeed constitute a rupture in the longer-term development of mentalities in France; the freedom of trade in Britain which, alongside the distinctly less bureaucratic and interventionist pattern of the eighteenth-century state, meant that alliances and conflicts were defined by economic more than by juridical or political characteristics. The different modes of transition from this corporate order helped shape the physiognomy of the petite bourgeoisie of nineteenth-century Europe. The idea of the trade as a self-regulating moral body was a continuing influence on both small employers and their work-force, offering a lens through which to view their experiences, and a set of memories and images with which to fashion solutions to their problems. The eighteenth century's corporate discourse provided the context within which the social and economic relations of small enterprise were defined and negotiated, and one in which the comparative perspective was important. In Germany most master artisans clung to the corporate ideal longer than their journeymen who after 1848 sought other solutions to their problems. In Britain, on the other hand, the early nineteenth-century labour movement developed in part around the journeyman's defence of those traditional craft rights and the moral universe of the trade which were being rejected by the majority of their masters. The issue is thus not simply the transition from corporations, but the more subtle transition from corporate expectations and the corporate idiom.

The survival of corporate organisation in nineteenth-century Germany encouraged master artisans' nostalgia for the security of guilds, as well as influencing the models of organisation which they adopted. The guild in some form seemed a solution to the problems they faced. When King Frederick William IV passed through Cologne in 1841, 600 of the city's master artisans took advantage of his brief stop to present him with a picture of their misery and to demand the return of closed, compulsory corporations with formal masters' examinations.[70] Such pressure for the restoration or strengthening of guilds was not a simple appeal for state protection, but an expression of the need for collective and autonomous defence of the kind guilds were thought to have once provided, a defence bound up in the introspective and stable urban communities where guilds had been so important.

The position of German master artisans in the revolutions of 1848 makes sense from that perspective, looking simultaneously to corporate institutions and more democratic government. The restoration of guilds, limitations on factory production, the banning of non-artisans from selling artisanal products all shaped master artisan demands, from the artisans' pre-congress in Hamburg through to the Frankfurt Artisans' Congress which met from the end of July. The master artisans who gathered in Frankfurt, and who sought unsuccessfully to press their case on the liberals of the Frankfurt Parliament, launched an onslaught on trade freedom. In demanding that limits be set to factory production and that artisanal work be restricted to masters, they set themselves against both manufacturers and retailers. The renewed guilds were to limit excessive numbers of apprentices, to prevent craft production outside the guild structure, and maintain the journeymen's Wanderjahre, although decisions concerning temporary limitations on numbers of masters were to be left to local officials. Guilds would constitute the base of a structure that looks corporatist in a twentieth-century sense, with guild representatives on industrial councils and chambers that would legislate on artisanal matters. At the same time the Congress called for progressive income and property taxes, free state education, and financial support for journeymen as they travelled.[71]

The corporatist demands were echoed at the local level. Many of Cologne's trades set up Innungen to press their case: masons, painters, locksmiths, cabinet-makers and others. In Düsseldorf demands for guild restoration came not from trades which most closely resembled the traditional guild ideal, such as butchers and bakers, but the tailors, shoemakers, and cabinet-makers who were in structural crisis.[72] The availability of corporate solutions was important, but the commitment of master artisans to democratic and progressive social demands through 1848 emphasises the danger in simply attaching guild ideals to reactionary politics. In a town such as Düsseldorf, where freedom of trade and enterprise had long existed, the artisans who supported the resolutions of the Frankfurt Artisans' Congress were the same as those who actively supported the local democratic movement.[73]

After its affirmation in 1848, the defence of corporations passed into the background, taking second place to attempts at co-operative and other self-help organisations, amongst them the now essentially voluntaristic Innungen. The early years of the new German Empire, however, saw the return to guild demands by the re-emerging artisanal movement. The small German Association of Independent Artisans and Manufacturers in the early 1870s and the General Union of German Artisans from 1882 were only the most prominent of a succession of associations that turned again to corporate regulation and organisation as the solution to artisanal problems.[74] The 1890s saw a new vigour to corporatist demands, notably amongst Catholic masters involved with the developing politics of the Catholic Centre Party, seeking compulsory guilds, the exclusive rights of masters to open a workshop and train apprentices, and asserting the right of the master to live by his specialist trade, to be protected from unfair competition, and to be assured of a fair clientèle. The particular German transition from corporations is essential for an understanding of the ideas and organisational forms upon which German master artisans drew.

They were encouraged by state support for the masters' *Innungen*, to which increasing rights and privileges were attached. The government re-organised them in 1881, though still as voluntary organisations that were now set within a framework defined by the bureaucratic state, and they began to proliferate in numbers and members. The law in the long term reinvigorated the corporatist ideal, while in the short term it provided the basis for local employers' associations. In the 1889 tinsmiths' strike in Nuremberg it was the newly-formed Tinsmiths' Guild which negotiated with the workers' union.[75] The 1897 Handicrafts' Law went further, permitting the imposition of *Innungen* on a trade when two-thirds of masters in that trade in the town voted for it, and giving guilds stronger control over the training of apprentices and participation in new handicraft chambers. Contemporaries claimed at the end of the nineteenth century that at least one-quarter of all masters were members of an *Innung*, a high level of organisation in comparison with other social groups, especially when one bears in mind the heterogeneity of the artisanal milieu.[76] The master artisans' guild organisations may not have regained a monopoly of production or the right to regulate prices, but the control over the education, qualifications and advancement of apprentices was not negligible, nor was the formal position now accorded to such organisations. As the successors of older corporations, albeit renewed and reduced successors, the *Innungen* drew upon a long tradition of self-regulation and organisation amongst German artisans, as well as a long tradition of state concern in Germany to handle with care an institution which policed the interior life of trades. The notion of the master persisted in Germany, with a significance long stripped from it in Britain and France, reinforced by the legal status of artisans in Germany – *Handwerk* and *Industrie* continued to be bound into separate associations and chambers. The corporate past, continuing juridical distinctions, and state concern for the regulation of sources of potential disorder, combined to shape a master artisanal identity of considerable force. Corporate institutions provided a continuity over time which sustained this identity. In contrast to the situation in England, here was a master's world and identity of which even those small master artisans whose social and economic situation differed little from that of workers nonetheless felt themselves a part.

The anti-guild rhetoric of the early German labour movement is more readily comprehensible in a context where masters defended the corporate ideal through the period of industrialisation.[77] In the early labour movement in France, on the other hand, the corporate idea played a considerable role.

The *compagnonnages* did not disappear with the guilds, and during the Restoration organised some 200,000 journeymen.[78] Their form and their aims carried the imprint of their eighteenth-century past, continuing the integrating rituals and traditions of *compagnonnages*, seeking to maintain the quality of artisanal labour, and where necessary to lead combined action against masters. The *tour de France* continued for journeymen, and provided the *compagnonnages* with the basis of a control over the labour market which they used to put pressure on recalcitrant masters. With reception houses and a *mère* to receive travelling journeymen in larger towns, and the ritual commitment to each of the separate orders of *compagnonnages* which could descend into violent confrontations between their members, here was a unity of work and daily life on the *tour* reminiscent of the patterns of the guild age. The joiner Agricol Perdiguier, whose writings perhaps made him France's most celebrated nineteenth-century journeyman, underlined this unity, describing 'an entire world, a distinct world, with its own customs, habits, forms of dress, ceremonies and celebrations which one would not find anywhere else'.[79] There were limits to their influence, remaining weak in Paris as they had always been, and primarily organising journeymen only in the early stages of their careers, but they constituted significant bearers into post-Revolutionary France of corporatist labour ideas that were to decline only during the July Monarchy.

The early French labour movement bears witness to the continuing significance of corporate ideas – the importance of associationism and co-operation, the anti-capitalist impulse rooted in the defence of the trade and artisanal rights, the notion of the trade as property, the commitment to self-organisation rather than to a state-led social transformation, and in the broadest terms the power of moral conceptions of production and a moral critique of productive relations.[80] The result was a commitment to co-operative production and workshop organisation which was to be a formative influence on French socialism.[81] The American William Sewell has presented the case for the very specific forms of these continuities[82] and, although doubt has been cast on his stress on the continuities of journeymen's organisations, and although it is clearly the case that in not all artisanal trades did workers take the classic eighteenth-century craft as the starting point for their response,[83] the continuing power of the corporate tradition remains necessary to an understanding of the French working-class movement through to 1848.

As artisanal dependence on larger capital grew during the first half of the nineteenth century, so the absence of formal status distinctions between masters and journeymen of the kind which continued on the other side of the Rhine permitted joint action against *monopolisateurs* – a term used to describe merchants, sub-contracting merchant manufacturers and bankers. The involvement of master artisans in popular political movements through the first half of the nineteenth century will be explored in a later chapter, but comparison with the German experience suggests the significance of the different transition from corporations in explaining that politics. French labour and socialist movements could continue to appeal for support from small shopkeepers and small masters. The potential for such alliances dissolved only in the closing twenty years of the century, when the distinctive organisation of master artisans and, above all, shopkeepers created a distinctively petit-bourgeois mobilisation.

French petits bourgeois formed their own organisations much later than had those in Germany, a reminder of the disorganising consequences of the demise of corporations. A French commentator, seeking to explain in 1904 why German master artisans had such a more effective level of co-operative organisations, observed that 'the corporatist traditions have remained so much more firm in that country than in ours'.[84] The abolition of corporations was one of the bases of a continuing and widespread ideological distrust of organisations in French public life during the nineteenth century, a belief rooted in the republican ideal that no intermediary bodies should interpose themselves between the individual and the state. Employers' organisations were certainly not absent in France from the early nineteenth century, and they received far more indulgent treatment from the state than did those of workers, but they were much less substantial than parallel organisations in Germany. The *chambres syndicales* (employers' unions) whose numbers grew from the mid-1880s united large and small enterprises within a trade, so that it was a sector of industry which was united rather than its master-artisan component. With the abolition of corporations, and the growing influence of commercial and industrial capital, the French artisanat was progressively losing its identity over the course of the nineteenth century. In the absence of common modes of regulating careers and managing enterprises, the milieu disintegrated not so much as a social aggregate but as a moral community. The term *artisanat* gave way to the broader and less explicit *métier* (trade), and the term *maître* largely went out of use. It had disappeared from the electoral lists in Lyon, for example, before 1914.[85] The decline and crisis of apprenticeship emphasised this loss of identity, constituting less the initiation into artisanal identity it once had been, and more a form of cheap and easily exploited labour.[86] In the world of French artisanal and commercial small enterprise, the transition from corporation to occupation had left only minor traces of the corporate past.

Nevertheless, such traces can be discerned in the shopkeepers' movement that developed from the 1880s and to which we shall return in more detail. The calls of the *Ligue syndicale* for restrictions on the number of shops, the assertion of the right of the retailer to live by his trade, the ideal of specialisation and the need for the state to defend the specialist trader by prohibitive taxation of department stores which accumulated trades, were ideas that only made sense within a corporatist idiom.[87] The shopkeepers' campaign was primarily based on the *patente* business tax to penalise large capitalist traders, the same *patente* which had been established by the

Constituent Assembly in 1791 to provide a system based on individual specialisms as a means to license and tax business enterprise, and that link of corporate trades to the new *patente* was one route by which corporatist ideals were carried into the late nineteenth-century movement.[88] Only a small section of the French petit-bourgeois movement dreamed of true corporations,[89] as the idea passed to the right and was actively promoted by Social Catholics seeking a new source of stability in a divided society.[90]

The formal corporate past was simply too distant in Britain to have any influence on social relations or social status. British shopkeepers and small masters in the second half of the nineteenth century identified themselves not with residual notions of the corporation but with the individualised business world, signalling a transition long achieved, and one which coloured their political and organisational presence in contrast with other European countries. Self-help was to be the solution to their problems, without the corporatist or state-directed demands that surfaced in France and, above all, Germany. Yet the idea of 'the trade', a quasi-corporatist idea according to which masters and journeymen should together defend the customs and practices of the industry against the attacks of outsiders and of misguided masters, continued to be a powerful force in the early nineteenth century. As Behagg has shown for Birmingham, that ideal came to be identified with the journeyman alone.[91] Journeymen cutlers in Sheffield intriguingly recalled the past role in regulating the trade of the now essentially ceremonial Company of Cutlers, urging all 'corporate trades' to form combinations of masters and men to drive out false practices, fix prices and enforce apprenticeship.[92] The concept of the trade rarely carried those formal corporatist meanings, however, and was in any case of little attraction to the masters. The absence of a corporate structure in the recent past denied small producers even the myths of an idealised guild age to inform their responses to change. In the comparative perspective that distinction was to prove significant.

3

SMALL ENTERPRISE
Survival or decline?

The *Communist Manifesto* offered a straightforward response to the title of this chapter.

> Modern industry has converted the little workshop of the patriarchal master into the great factory of the industrial capitalist . . . . The lower strata of the middle class – the small tradespeople, shopkeepers, and retired tradesmen generally, the handicraftsmen and peasants – all these sink gradually into the proletariat, partly because their diminutive capital does not suffice for the scale on which modern industry is carried on, and is swamped in the competition with the large capitalists, partly because their specialised skill is rendered worthless by new methods of production.[1]

Marx and Engels were concerned with broad tendencies, but their followers turned them into dogma, as in the Erfurt Programme of the German SPD in 1891, while even outside socialist circles the predictions seemed to confirm the gloomy future for small enterprise. Small production in particular seemed to many bourgeois economists to be blocked by industrial and financial concentration. The historical school of economics in Germany was, by the end of the nineteenth century, describing a catastrophic future for both artisans and small retailers.[2]

There were other economists, however, insisting that the survival of small enterprise was not only a social necessity, but also an economic possibility. As the 'social question' loomed in importance during the second half of the nineteenth century, and as the organised working class began to haunt contemporary opinion, the survival of small enterprise seemed to offer the prospect of social equilibrium. The French political economists Adolphe Blanqui and Michel Chevalier returned from the 1851 Great Exhibition in London convinced that the range and quality of France's craft industries were the only basis for future success in free-trade world markets. Their belief that only through the flourishing of small enterprise could France avoid class conflict was probably as persuasive as economic argument. According to Blanqui:

It has been shown that the total value created in small industry exceeds that in large, and that small industries require less capital, employ more labour, create more intelligence and general well-being with fewer social complications than those manufacturing processes where machinery dominates and where an extreme division of labour prevails.[3]

A quarter of a century later Gustav Schmoller, author of a major study of German small enterprise, concluded that 'the lower classes must come increasingly to accept in their everyday family and working life the values of the *Mittelstand*, the solid tradesmen'.[4] Many economists now argued that the needs of large-scale enterprise itself and the growth of the mass consumer market could together enable workshops and small shops to avoid any inevitable decline. By the late nineteenth century, it was no longer unrealistic to envisage the co-existence of large and small capital.

It would be agreeable if contemporary statistics could tell us whether this optimism was well founded, but the weaknesses of these statistics are intimidating. They prove an unwieldy tool with which to analyse the petite bourgeoisie. The fiscal, census and registration data produced by each state varied not only between countries but also over time. If historians cannot escape these sources, neither can they rely uncritically upon them. The French and Belgian *patente* provides a good example of the difficulties. The registers of this professional and business tax have been used by historians to calculate the number of enterprises of different sizes and to compare these across time as well as place. Yet the *patente* was an instrument of policy and a focus for political agitation, with the result that groups of artisanal and retail enterprises were progressively extracted from its tentacles: those who worked alone, or who worked in a family workshop with no salaried labour. Exemptions removed some 20,000 blacksmiths from the French *patente* registers in the twelve years after 1850 and a similar number of shoemakers.[5] All workshops, whatever their size, were inspected by the Brussels municipal authorities under health at work regulations, unlike those liable to the *patente*, and the difference between the totals for each in 1892 indicates the limits of the tax registers: locksmiths and stovemakers were well represented in the *patente*, with 91 per cent of those workshops known to the authorities for inspection also registered for the *patente*, but not so joiners (46 per cent) or cabinet-makers (27 per cent).[6] A section of influential opinion wanted to protect small enterprise against excessive taxation, but the vagaries of contemporary social theory or contemporary fiscal politics cannot be allowed to define our social group for us.

Population censuses need to be handled with similar caution. The apparent rigour of printed census tables can be seductive, with their serried ranks of statistics presenting occupations and status as if the classification emanated from the material itself. In reality ideological concerns, often bound up with the relationship between raw materials and the morbidity or character of

39

those who worked with them, shaped the presentation of occupational statistics in many countries.[7] Nineteenth-century social statisticians were moved by concerns distant from those of late twentieth-century historians, and they were not even moved by the same concerns at the same time in different European countries. In the aftermath of the 1830 Revolution, the French census began to distinguish between wage-workers, independent artisans and employers; while during the following decade Dieterici's reform of the Prussian census introduced similar distinctions. Yet German statistics, long after the abolition of corporations, continued to differentiate between *Fabrik* and *Handwerk*, industrial and artisanal work.[8] The persistence of this terminology shows how long a pre-industrial vision of economic facts could shape analysis. By the late nineteenth century the French census was repeatedly reshaping its categories in this area: in 1891 distinguishing employers, employees, and workers, while introducing a new classification ten years later which separated employers with non-family labour and their workers on the one hand, from *travailleurs isolés* – independents working on their own – on the other. The British census attached little importance to such questions. The 1851 report announced that 'it was thought desirable to distinguish masters from men' and asked individuals to write the word 'master' after their occupation where relevant,[9] but the information had been unevenly recorded and there was no further attempt to distinguish between workers and masters before the end of the century. The vitality of small enterprise was not sufficiently important in Britain to shape the gathering of census statistics.

If the resulting statistics were unclear, so too was the social world of independence, dependence and mastership which they tried to capture. Even those European censuses which sought to enumerate small enterprise struggled to cope with the plethora of small and family workshops, often organised by merchant capitalists. The workers' report in an 1867 French Commission used the ambiguous expression *ouvrier–patron* for those who owned their working equipment and moved frequently between employment and independence.[10] The 1872 census recognised them when it devised the category of *chefs–ouvriers attachés aux arts et métiers* (worker–masters in artisanal trades).[11]

Statistical sources were a representation rather than a reflection of reality, and the evolution of statistical categories followed both changing economic realities and the perceptions of contemporaries. The ambiguity of the boundaries drawn was itself an eloquent representation, reflecting the way so much small enterprise straddled the world of labour and the world of employers. What was to be done with the French *travailleurs isolés*, those independents working on their own who constituted as much as 23 per cent of the occupied population in 1896?[12] If they are enumerated as masters the world of employers is inflated, because the bulk of such people were only formally independent; if they are excluded, then intermediary categories between populace and employers will have been insufficiently identified. This is not a problem which better statistics will somehow solve, but an issue central to both the identification and the analysis of the petite bourgeoisie.

INDUSTRIALISATION AND ARTISANAL ENTERPRISE

In spite of the limitations of national statistical data for small enterprise, can any broad trends be identified? Not for Britain, of course, where such statistics were not collected, and only with great caution even for France and Germany where they were. The French data indicate that during the second half of the nineteenth century industrial and commercial enterprise more than maintained its position. Those paying the *patente* increased from 1.3 million in 1845 to 1.8 million in 1896, a growth of 37 per cent during a period when the population as a whole grew by only 8 per cent.[13] This includes all professions and trades, but small enterprise accounted for most of the expansion, even though small family enterprises present in 1845 had been exempted from the *patente* by the later date. In the food, wood and clothing trades small enterprise remained prominent throughout the century, though it lost ground in the building and the leather trades and virtually disappeared in spinning and weaving, glass, steel and chemicals. Caron concluded from his investigation of French industry before 1914 that 'small and even very small industrial enterprises still played a very important part in the French industrial structure'.[14]

In Germany, on the other hand, the later nineteenth century saw a serious contraction in the numbers of small artisanal enterprises. The proportion of artisanal and industrial workers employed in enterprises with five employees or fewer fell from 60 per cent in 1882 to 31 per cent in 1907. During the same period the number of small enterprises employing labour declined from 2,173,083 to 1,867,829, while those where no outside labour was employed fell from 1,430,140 to 994,570. The period of major industrial development in Germany was indeed marked by the retreat of small-scale production.[15]

These distinct French and German patterns reflect different models of industrialisation. The once pessimistic image of French industrialisation has more recently been revised to emphasise that growth rates were not as deficient as once thought, and that France's mode of industrialisation was well adapted to the country's configuration of human and natural resources. Bouvier argued that, once one stops testing it against some idealised model, French industrialisation appears well adapted to a peasant population without a great surplus for consumer expenditure, to urban and export markets for higher-quality goods, and to a national market that was slow to unify. According to this perspective small and medium enterprises, far from being a brake on industrial development, were the medium through which France's industrialisation took place, assuring the major part of economic growth through to the 1930s.[16]

German industrialisation was characterised by rapid economic growth from the middle of the nineteenth century; large-scale enterprise in the first industrialisation based on capital goods rather than consumer goods; and a major role for large-scale finance. If France represented labour-intensive change, Germany has long been seen as capital-intensive, with the attendant challenges to small enterprise. The extremes have been drawn too starkly, for artisanal industry continued in many German regions in the late nineteenth century. Even in Bochum, the diversification which followed initial heavy industrial development created widespread opportunities for small producers, whose numbers grew substantially.[17]

The German pattern was nevertheless exceptional, with France joining Belgium and Britain within the mainstream of nineteenth-century industrialisation. Individual industries in Britain and Belgium became large-scale to a greater extent than in France, but those sectors were very limited. Belgium, the first economy on the European continent to industrialise, remained in the 1850s essentially a country of small industry and artisanal production, with large enterprise confined to the textile towns of Flanders and the industrial basins of Hainaut and Liège. The second half of the century saw substantial concentration in mining, metallurgy, glass and textiles, but urban as well as economic growth produced a parallel flourishing of small enterprise in most sectors. As late as 1896 36 per cent of all industrial workers were employed in the 95 per cent of industrial enterprises with four employees or fewer.[18]

Large-scale production appeared in only a handful of industries during Britain's industrialisation, mostly in certain textiles and the more slowly developing producer goods industries. In most industries production grew through the proliferation of small enterprises and other forms of dispersed production, rather than by heavy inputs of capital and powered machinery. The great expansion in the use of steam engines came, after all, in the last quarter of the nineteenth century.[19] Industrialisation did not leave small producers in Britain untouched, but operated in most industries through their expansion rather than their contraction. This is clear whether we look at major industrial centres – such as the light metal region around Birmingham or the cutlery trades of Sheffield – or at the consumer goods industries that supplied Britain's commercial and urban revolutions: clothing, leather, boots and shoes, food and drink, printing, hosiery, lace, together with the building industry where small units dominated much longer than they did even in France.

National models and explosive transformation, two long-cherished elements in the analysis of industrialisation, have in any case come under scrutiny in recent years. The national accounting approach has reduced the rate of growth of the British economy during industrialisation, while other economic historians, still insisting that the emergence of industrial societies produced fundamental transformations, nevertheless doubt whether rapid economic discontinuities capture the realities of European industrialisation.[20] The historian of small enterprise can only agree: explosiveness and scale are not the essential features of European industrial change. Until the later nineteenth century concentrated production made economic sense in no more than a handful of sectors. As a result, most industries expanded output through a variety of forms of small-scale production, and small-scale producers proliferated in European industrialisation. At one extreme stood domestic outwork, shown by Lancashire cotton weavers in the short term, and Swiss watchmakers over a longer period, which was in no way incompatible with the capitalist organisation of production.[21] Increasing specialisation in high-quality craft production stood at the other. Transformation of the economic relations of production was certainly subordinating small producers within networks controlled by large capital, but these small units of production were nevertheless expanding throughout industrial Europe.

All typologies simplify, but three distinct ways in which industrialisation stimulated petit-bourgeois producers can be identified. In the first, a small producer sector grew without substantial change in either technology or size of enterprise. The nature of markets need not change – one thinks of bakers or farriers serving local customers – but in most cases they did, as national and international competition transformed the relations of production without altering the technology. The metal industries of Birmingham, Sheffield, Solingen or Paris provide the classic example, where the production of hardware, cutlery, locks and the like expanded through intense sub-division of trades under the organising influence of merchants and factors.[22] If artificial power provided a competitive advantage, as with the Sheffield cutlery trades by the 1860s, small firms might rent space and access to the distributed power of a steam engine in a larger building. There were twenty-six power-sharing engineering establishments in the 10th, 11th and 12th *arrondissements* of Paris in 1872, renting power to 1,473 tenants who between them employed over 9,000 workers.[23] Tenement blocks, with workshops around a central source of steam or pneumatic power, were often planned, but the occasional success, such as in faubourg Saint-Antoine in the 1870s, cannot hide the fact that they were often born more in philanthropic or commercial optimism rather than any realistic hope of success.[24] German artisans nevertheless urged municipal authorities to establish bases for water, gas, or pneumatic power.[25] Artificial power remained the exception. The expansion of small enterprises was in most trades characterised by market integration, the sub-division of processes, and no more than low-level mechanisation.

This first category of small enterprise expansion rested on the integration of the producer into a capitalist structure characterised by merchants and factors on the one hand and sub-contracting on the other. The tailoring trades of Paris, London and Düsseldorf in the 1830s and 1840s provide the most striking example, as they faced the competition of ready-made clothing produced for the new wholesale merchants. Many masters retreated into sub-contracting and turned their workshops into what would later be known as sweatshops, while others became domestic pieceworkers. Independence became an illusion for all but a minority of bespoke tailors and viable sub-contractors.[26] By the 1860s, department stores and merchants in Paris were making independent tailors no more than outposts of larger capital, and the same process in Berlin saw producers of ready-made clothing employ through the *Zwischenmeister* (sweating master) a mass of domestic workers.[27] Tailoring was an extreme case, but most petit-bourgeois producers operated in sectors being transformed by merchant capital. A lockmaker in the English Black Country might continue to work as his father had done, with a small workshop employing two or three journeymen and an apprentice, but the merchant who bought his product dealt with distant markets, drove down prices to compete, advanced credit to ensure that the producer was under pressure to sell his product regularly even at low prices, and thus bound the small firm into new structures of dependency.[28] By the late nineteenth century this factoring system produced the sweated workshops denounced by so many observers, but sweating was only the extreme version of a system which left most small enterprise viable but dependent.

The burden of fluctuations and competition was thrown on to the workshop master, in a system particularly suited to sectors where sudden changes in demand were caused by unstable markets or changes in fashion.[29] In the silk trades, vagaries of taste and the long preparation needed to set up short production runs maintained a system of external merchant control rather than concentrated production amongst the *canuts* of Lyon or the ribbon-weavers of Saint-Etienne. The nineteenth-century French sociologist Frédéric Le Play devised the term *fabriques collectives* (collective manufactures) for systems where a mass of small workshops specialised in manufacturing distinct parts of a product under the control of a merchant–manufacturer. If many producers were little more than outworkers, others were not. The classic case for Le Play was the cutlery and sword-making industry of Solingen in the Rhineland. He described one sword assembler who

> works in a workshop which he has rented on his own account; he supplies the tools and the additional materials needed for doing the work; he hired his assistants and is in general in no way different from a master artisan, except that he neither owns the raw materials on which he works nor disposes of a clientèle to whom he sells.[30]

The gun quarters of Birmingham and Saint-Etienne provide more prosperous examples of the proliferation of workshops through the division of labour. The master gunmaker gathered in his warehouse the parts made in independent workshops – items such as locks, barrels, sights and triggers – before putting them out to further specialised workshops for assembling.[31] The artificial flower trade of Paris was similarly organised – the 'rosemaker' would construct his flower from the products of ten separate independent workshops.[32] This proliferation of workshops based on a detailed division of labour was not new: the watchmaking trades in the Clerkenwell district of London, and the coachmaking and hatting trades of Paris, provide eighteenth-century examples.[33] The nineteenth century placed the system at the heart of expanding production in many industries.

These systems of production, proliferating networks of formally independent workshops, were firmly integrated within the processes of capitalist industrialisation. The economic logic which lay behind small-scale production was precisely the force determining the vulnerability of individual petit-bourgeois producers.[34] Here was the most common relationship between industrialisation and small producers. The masters' viability often depended upon their willingness to respond to market pressures by extracting more rapid production from the workforce, by hiring less skilled labour, and by breaching the traditional expectations of the trade, from whose sense of community they increasingly detached themselves. It is hardly surprising that this world of pressured, market-oriented small production created the journeymen metal-workers, tailors, silk-weavers and the rest who were so central to early working-class movements.

The second type of relationship between small enterprise and industrialisation was in industries where technological change actually favoured the growth of small firms. The most significant of such innovations was the sewing machine in tailoring and shoemaking, though one can also point to early powered machines in the English hosiery trades, where access to power could be hired and second-hand machinery easily acquired.[35] The sewing machine enabled small shoemaking firms to act as a transition between earlier domestic outwork production and the larger-scale factory production towards the end of the nineteenth century. The English shoe trade had been controlled in the early part of the century, especially in Northamptonshire, by substantial wholesalers organising rural and urban outworkers, though craftsmen all over the country continued to meet much local demand. From the 1860s the sewing machine was a stimulus to the formation of small firms which combined workshop production with some putting out. This efflorescence of small firms was only temporary, for larger manufacturers responded to the competitive difficulties from the 1880s with increased mechanisation and factory rationalisation, as well as by opening their own retail chains.[36] Increased workshop specialisation often accompanied such technical innovations. In Paris, new cutting equipment in the leather trades and the power saw in cabinet-making encouraged a more advanced division of labour.[37] Into this category one should perhaps also place those artisans tied not into production but into the repair and installation of industrial products – electricians, car mechanics, bicycle repairers, plumbers and so on – a group which grew substantially from the 1890s.[38]

More flexible sources of power could also stimulate workshop production, at first the gas engine but then the electric motor. Small-scale industrial towns such as Saint-Etienne, Remscheid and Solingen were pioneers in the use of electricity from the 1890s, while in the Netherlands the electric motor allowed small firms to flourish after 1900 in industries such as bakery, printing, cabinet-making and metalwork. Clapham felt that by then 'electricity was a diffusive force in industry' in Britain, encouraging small workshops in lighter trades.[39] Werner Siemens had as early as 1886 declared that 'the technique will serve to remove the obstacles standing in the way of a return to competitive manual work, offering a cheap source of power as the basis for production in small workshops and workers' apartments'. The Belgian government pressed the electric motor on small enterprise at the Liège Exhibition of 1905. One Dutch Catholic trade paper subsequently predicted that as 'steam power has driven the people into the factories, the electric current will drive them out again into their own workshops'.[40] Contemporary observers, however, magnified the impact of developments that offered to strengthen petit-bourgeois enterprise, and verdicts on France and Germany suggest that hopes far outstripped reality.[41] In any case, as the Social Catholic Etienne Martin Saint-Léon observed in 1905, the fact that it was primarily used by workshops that were sub-contracted to large enterprises meant that it served to increase dependence.[42]

Under the third and final type of relationship between small production and industrialisation, small firms survived in the interstices of a system based on large-scale production, interlocking rather than competing with it. The anarchist writer Peter Kropotkin, who admittedly sought evidence of thriving small-scale independence at every turn, felt that in Britain in 1912 'each new factory calls into existence a number of small workshops'.[43] Highly-capitalised large businesses chose to sub-contract to small firms in times of high demand or for auxiliary services. Thus the handful of factories in the clothing industry of Leeds in 1881 had become fifty-four a decade later, but there was a simultaneous boom in client workshops to whom the large firms sub-contracted production.[44] Cyclical and seasonal high demand was thus met more cheaply than by the expansion of high fixed-cost production. Lévy-Leboyer has described such small enterprise in France as a safety valve for large firms.[45] Small firms – as in the edge-tool or chain-making trades in the English Black Country – could be left with inferior or lighter parts of the range of products, allowing factories to concentrate on heavier goods or on export markets for which quality control was important.[46] Or they could produce one part of a product, as in mid-century Cologne where the expanding Eau de Cologne industry spawned some sixty sub-contracting joinery workshops producing wooden cases to hold the bottles.[47]

The central feature of small-scale production in nineteenth-century Europe was that its survival and expansion were accompanied by increasingly severe constraints and pressures. The process affected not only established industrial areas, but essentially administrative and commercial towns as well, as recent studies of Edinburgh and Toulouse have made clear.[48] Not only were the defences of corporations being removed, but during the second half of the nineteenth century the constraints of capitalist competition transformed the conditions of work, the nature of specialisation, and the economic prospects of almost all artisanal trades. Furthermore, artisans producing for local consumption were now losing the protection of distance. Changes in transport, marketing and financial structures removed the boundaries of the world within which they sheltered, and exposed them to regional, national and often international competition. The very forces that increased opportunity for many artisans increased the vulnerability of them all. With the protection of localism now lost, one can understand why later political movements of the petite bourgeoisie were to retreat into the ideals of an economic autarky.

URBANISATION AND RETAILING

Urbanisation was the second structural transformation that shaped the opportunities and problems facing artisans and shopkeepers and its impact was as ambiguous as that of industrialisation. The growth of urban societies meant a decline in self-sufficiency, an increase in monetarised wage labour, improved distribution systems, and the demand for services, all of which shaped an urban culture that offered new opportunities to small enterprise. The significance of the urban-service sector can be seen even in primarily industrial towns such as Bradford, where in mid-century a full 82 per cent of the city's private businesses operated in the provision of urban services, and a mere 12 per cent in the worsted industry on which Bradford's growth rested.[49] Yet urbanisation brought challenges as well as opportunities, for it was accompanied by the concentration of capital and the undermining of distance which threatened the independence of small enterprise.

Retail enterprise played a dynamic role in the restructuring of the urban fabric, as competition for central sites by larger retailers raised land and property prices, and stimulated central redevelopment. Yet the urban reconstruction symbolised by Haussmann's rebuilding of central Paris seemed to threaten the position of small enterprise in the heart of old towns, by destroying the small-scale neighbourhoods in which it had flourished while providing the sites for the new department stores. Did urban growth create opportunities on the suburban periphery while destroying the very world of the inner-city *quartiers* in which small enterprise had flourished? The answer must be yes, but the challenge should not be exaggerated by taking contemporary denunciation, whether from petit-bourgeois protest or romanticisers of an urban past, at face value. Jeanne Gaillard showed how Haussmannisation in Second Empire Paris could operate as a force that created as much as it destroyed opportunities, a revisionism confirmed in Florence Bourillon's examination of the rebuilding of the Arts et Métier *quartier* as new boulevards were driven through its heart. Its reconstruction after 1855 far from eradicated the small retailers and workshops in the metal and *articles*

47

de Paris trades. The manufacture of *articles de Paris* came to prevail, increasingly organised by merchants and wholesalers, while more specialist shops sprang up to serve the better-class residents of the new streets. Behind the new boulevards an artisanal and shopkeeper world formed anew: formed in the image of the new Paris, for sure, but certainly not destroyed.[50]

Urbanisation's most powerful impact on small enterprise was in retailing. Retail trade expanded through the proliferation of independent family-based shops. The Toulouse branch of the Bank of France could have spoken for many a town of the period: 'Toulouse is nothing more than an immense bazaar whose shopkeepers, helped by the speed and convenience of communications ... meet all the needs of their customers with a service of rapidly growing and direct supplies.'[51] Shopkeepers became the dominant element in urban small enterprise. In 1830, retailers and café-owners had made up 53 per cent of Toulouse's small businesses, with artisans comprising the other 47 per cent. By 1872 those proportions were 63 per cent and 37 per cent.[52] Brussels shopkeepers represented 49 per cent of all businesses at the start of the period but 63 per cent at the end.[53] While the total number of master artisans declined in Germany between 1882 and 1907, the number of commercial enterprises doubled.[54] While artisans were reshaped by industrial and urban growth, retailers were multiplied by it. Nor did shopkeepers face competition from large capital to the extent experienced by workshop trades for, although various forms of large-scale retailing did emerge in the decades before the First World War, the greatest competition faced by independent shopkeepers came from amongst themselves.

At the end of the eighteenth century fixed shop retailing was at its most advanced in Britain. Stockport, a Cheshire town of some 11,000 population, could by the 1790s boast sixty-nine provision dealers and bakers, twenty-seven grocers, seven butchers, four wine and spirit dealers, and sixteen mercers and drapers, amongst a range of other retail traders.[55] The fifty years that followed saw a rapid expansion of retailing in Britain equivalent to that elsewhere in industrialising Europe. In Britain, shop numbers grew faster than population in the first half of the century. In one group of northern towns there was one shop for every 161 inhabitants in 1801, but one for every fifty-six inhabitants fifty years later, a proportion which then stabilised through to 1881.[56] German retailing understandably grew more slowly than that in Britain, but a fall in the population per shop seems to have begun in the 1840s, and speeded up in the 1860s.[57] Shop provision was growing faster than population, as shown in studies of Cologne between 1850 and 1875, Brussels between 1847 and 1892, Milan between 1880 and the turn of the century, and Lyon's butchers between 1866 and 1906.[58] In Germany as a whole between 1882 and 1907 population grew by 40 per cent, but retail shops increased by 68 per cent, with growth concentrated above all in large towns.[59] Opportunities fuelled the inherent tendency of retailing to expand too fast, and this tendency was exacerbated on the supply side by industrial change, above all the merchandise emerging from the consumer goods industries that were now being mobilised by large capital. Nevertheless, much of the apparent over-supply occurred amongst the smaller shops: for example, the small bakers, butchers, food shops and cafés of Milan's explosive growth.[60] Here was where competition was at its worst.

The location of traders within the city often depended on the importance of the shop, as property prices made central areas the preserve of more prosperous enterprises, except in poorer inner-city neighbourhoods where petty shopkeeping continued. On the periphery, suburban middle-class districts provided opportunities for those with enterprise and ambition, while the new populous *faubourgs* of cities like Paris, Berlin and Milan drew humbler shops whose ambitions frequently outstripped their resources. Urban retailing was thus a heterogeneous world. There may have been far fewer grocery shops in the old inner *arrondissements* of Paris from the 1860s, but those which remained increased dramatically in average size. Yet the city's populous outskirts saw the rapid growth of enterprises that were all too often underfunded and thus ephemeral, as small food dealers followed the people from the central areas.[61] The same was true beyond the *octroi* walls in late nineteenth-century Milan, with food traders, tobacco dealers and bars attracted by working-class customers and lower taxation.[62] The impoverished and often (but by no means always) short-lived shops were especially common in the grocery, fruit, and general shopkeeping sectors, whereas drapers, ironmongers, wine and spirit dealers and bakers, all needing capital, tended to be the more substantial enterprises. This retailing hierarchy did not just exist in large cities. The butchers and bakers of a small provincial town such as Bourg-en-Bresse were relatively wealthy in the first half of the century when entry was restricted by the state, and the cost of acquiring a business rose fast. The other trades – the ironmongers and grocers and haberdashers and so on – were marked by a great variety of wealth even within each trade.[63] As with artisanal small enterprise, expansion and differentiation were closely linked.

Large-scale retailing was never as great a threat to the independent shopkeeper as late nineteenth-century retailer organisations suggested. Its growth lay in the expansion of effective consumer demand with rising real incomes, the emergence of a white-collar lower middle class, and the way urban concentration and advertising permitted standardised goods and a certain democratisation of fashion. Large-scale retailing took the form of department stores, consumer co-operatives, and multiple chains. If the first loomed large in the eyes of many retailers, it was not because their market share necessarily justified the fears but because their luxurious style, large capital investment, and city centre sites seemed to symbolise a future without small shops. Aristide Boucicaut's Bon Marché in Paris in the 1860s is seen as the first genuine department store,[64] and the city's new boulevards provided the perfect setting for their spread. English towns may have lacked the grandeur of French boulevards, but department stores rapidly located them-selves where broad new streets appeared: the Kensington improvement scheme in London after 1867 drew Pontings, John Barker, & Derry and Toms, and Birmingham's new Corporation Street proved similarly attractive. The Kurfurstendamm in Berlin saw the opening of the Kaufhaus des Westens.

As delivery vans and mail order extended the stores' range, even distant shopkeepers came to feel threatened. Galeries Lafayettes had a regular motor delivery service running between Paris and Trouville by the early years of this century, while la Capitole in Toulouse delivered by motor vehicle within a 50-kilometre radius goods ordered from its catalogue.[65] Developments were slower in Germany, but by the 1890s department stores were appearing all over the country. There were 121 in Prussia by 1912.[66] In all countries customers were drawn from the comfortable bourgeoisie and the fashion-conscious new middle class of professional and office workers – a clientèle exemplified by the Civil Service co-operatives in London, or the Warenhaus für deutsche Beamte that attracted the particular ire of shopkeepers. They drew their clientèle with fixed and competitive prices, immense publicity in the proliferating newspapers and journals, regular specialist sales, the promise to exchange mistaken purchases, mail order, and free delivery.[67] Zola's promise that the sleepy Au Vieil Elbeuf would succumb to the grand Au Bonheur des Dames seemed real,[68] yet the former's proximity ought to have helped. Trade was stimulated in the vicinity of the bright new stores. Shopkeepers near La Samaritaine in Paris, needing the animated atmosphere it created, petitioned for it to stay open on Sundays.[69]

An even more potent threat in the eyes of small retailers was the consumer co-operatives which began growing from the 1860s in industrial Europe, and which expanded rapidly from the 1880s. They symbolised the power of organised labour as effectively as department stores did that of organised capital. They were best organised in Britain, and by the 1890s threatened to dominate the working-class market in many industrial towns, with stores moving to occupy central shopping streets and diversifying from the previous staples of bread, groceries and shoes. Membership rose from 100,000 to three million between 1863 and 1913, turnover from £2.5m to £88m.[70] The same years saw explosive growth in Belgian co-operatives, as well as in Germany where a mere 173,000 members of 198 societies in 1888 had grown to nearly two million members and 1451 societies on the eve of the War.[71] Their main strength everywhere did not lie in the most populous cities. Co-operatives may have been a more symbolic than real threat for most retailers, particularly in Germany where they could legally sell only to members, and everywhere that they sold only for cash, but food shops selling to better-paid workers had to fight for market share in the smaller industrial towns where co-operatives did best. In England that meant Rochdale and Bury, for example, rather than Manchester.[72]

The multiple chains were the third challenge, above all the national companies whose goods were characterised by the two great consumer innovations of the late nineteenth century: mass production and the international trade in food. In Britain they appeared first in the food trades, but by the 1880s they were spreading rapidly throughout retailing, involving a far more diverse range of trades than elsewhere in Europe. It has been estimated that the twenty-nine multiple firms in 1875 with 978 branches had grown by the First World War to 433 firms with 22,755 branches – half of them concentrated in food, clothing and footwear.[73] Their low prices, product specialisation, uniform shop appearance and vigorous advertising guaranteed success in skilled working-class and lower middle-class suburban markets where quality and new products needed the added incentive of competitive pricing.[74] If multiples were most widespread in Britain, they became a serious presence in France (grocery, shoes and restaurants), and to a lesser extent Germany (tobacco, cafés, shoes and food). The grocery and provision chains were the largest: look at the 500 branches of Les Docks Rémois or Les Comptoirs français in France on the eve of the War, the 900 of Maypole and 500 of Liptons in Britain, the 1,400 branches of Kaisers Kaffee Geschäft in Germany, and the 744 shops of Delhaize Frères in Belgium.[75]

By the 1890s shopkeepers throughout industrial Europe were feeling the pressure of these new retail forms. The old challenge of itinerant traders, who had attracted the anger of small shopkeepers since the early nineteenth century, seems to have been weakening, though their control remained a major demand of both Belgian and German retailers.[76] The real threat, however, now appeared to be large-scale retailing. In the earlier part of the century, while artisanal masters and journeymen were resisting the capitalist reorganisation of production, the distribution network was growing through the proliferation of individual enterprises. The trading sector had therefore known a long period of growth by the time that it was itself threatened by large-scale business. The intense threat to each sector came at different times, which was important for petit-bourgeois experience, and for the fact that shopkeepers played a more active role in the late nineteenth-century organisation of the petite bourgeoisie. Yet how real was the threat posed by these new forms of retailing? It seemed real enough to most shopkeepers, faced with the glass, light and extravagant architecture of a Galeries Lafayettes, or the blatant publicity-seeking of a Karstedt, a Thomas Lipton or a Felix Potin – but their challenge to market share is harder to judge. The estimate for Britain in 1900 that co-operatives accounted for 6 per cent of the consumer market, department stores between 1 and 2 per cent, and multiples 4 per cent, is based on insubstantial data. German calculations suggest 1.1 per cent for co-operatives (1905) and 2.3 per cent for department stores (1913).[77] The national picture is in any case not the issue. Co-operatives in England probably posed their greatest threat to retailers in older industrial towns of the north whose peak growth lay in the past and which were now somewhat stagnating. In an expanding town such as Leicester, on the other hand, individual traders would have been less damaged by a rate of co-operative expansion that did not exceed population growth.[78] The real result of new forms of retailing was to restructure the consumer market, so that small enterprise was frequently left with the least desirable customers, those who paid least regularly and needed the credit that only independent tradesmen afforded. As a tradesman in the Kent town of Dartford complained, the multiples drew working-class customers when they had cash, but when money was in short supply they returned to traders like himself for credit.[79] The independent retailers' onslaught on the new forms of retailing in any case evaded the key issue, which was the ease of entry into many sectors of retailing, and the resulting level of competition amongst independent traders themselves.

ECONOMIC CRISES

The economic fortunes of small enterprise were shaped by short-term fluctuations as well as long-term structural trends, and there is a danger that the former will be viewed merely as the inevitable moment when small enterprise, poorly equipped to cope with shrinking markets and financial pressures, finally succumbed. The reality, as we have seen, is that much of the small-business artisanal and retail world was viable, and while individual small enterprises were certainly more vulnerable in crisis, small enterprise as a whole need not have been threatened. However, crises were experienced by petits bourgeois because of the credit and debt that made small business so vulnerable. Depression reduced orders at a time when credit from larger manufacturers, wholesalers and merchants was harder to obtain. It is hardly surprising that small producers supported movements for currency reform, as in Birmingham during the 1830s; or political movements which attacked the illegitimate manipulations of speculative capital; or denunciations of the bankers and financiers whose tight monetary policies undermined those needing petty credit. These were not just comforting explanations of their own vulnerability, but analyses which seemed to address the realities of their daily struggle to survive.

Economic crisis is never simply economic. The Parisian crisis of the later 1830s may well have been economically more severe than that which occurred a decade later, but the sense of political and social uncertainty made the latter more devastating and deepened its economic consequences. The onset was a classic *ancien régime* crisis, as successive harvest failures from 1846 produced rising food prices and a consequent narrowing of demand for manufactured goods. The food trades of Paris suffered the most – above all the drink sellers and small grocers – but larger retail and artisanal enterprises were drawn in by the summer of 1848, as the collapse of smaller firms which were indebted to them pulled down the larger ones in an uncertainty exacerbated by political flux.[80] In contrast to the 1828–32 crisis, when medium and even larger firms in Paris suffered more than the small ones, that in the late 1840s saw the reverse, and therefore some concentration of business size.[81] In the city's central quarters, a full 27 per cent of the 2,357 *patentables* in existence at some time between 1847 and 1851 disappeared during those four years. Nevertheless, the period was also one of growth – only in 1848 itself did the curve of new business creations actually turn downwards – but the growth was accompanied by concentration. The firms which disappeared came disproportionately from smaller businesses, while the new enterprises concentrated at the upper levels of the *patente*.[82] The crisis did not restructure the Parisian economy, but it gave an impetus towards concentration.

While crises might advance a structural process of concentration, they also served to increase the dependence of small business on large capital. Furthermore, at times of crisis, small employers had the greatest need to increase their control of the work process while unemployment weakened journeymen's ability to resist changes in work practice.[83] Each economic crisis put renewed pressure on individual small masters, whose survival depended on the willingness of merchants to maintain credit and orders, and those who seemed the most 'business-like' and creditworthy were inevitably more favourably regarded. In this way, the crisis of the late 1840s assisted the viability of small enterprise within industrial capitalism, by compelling adaptation to its demands.

The Great Depression of the last quarter of the nineteenth century occurred when the impetus towards industrial concentration was greater, and the consequences for small producers were more serious. In this depression of falling prices, enterprises with narrow margins were unable to take advantage of low interest rates to improve their long-term competitive position, at a time when larger businesses, both industrial and retail, were innovating to cut costs and to restore profit levels. Enterprises in Europe's metropolitan centres also faced rising rents, the one exception to the downward pressure on prices. By the 1860s in Paris and the following decade in London, small enterprises in central areas saw rents and local taxes rising at the very time when they most needed to keep down their costs of production.[84]

In Germany, the late nineteenth-century depression saw small units of production and distribution under severe pressure. The shoemaking and building trades of the large towns led the surge towards bankruptcy, followed by bakers. Bankruptcies in Baden, for example, were disproportionately numerous amongst artisans with a modest capital of between 1000 and 10,000 thaler. The very small are as ever lost to view, those who closed their doors without legal procedures, but a broader picture of the disappearance of businesses there between 1875 and 1882 reveals the losses to have been most severe amongst glaziers, turners, shoemakers, saddlers and joiners, all of whom lost between one-sixth and one-quarter of their numbers. The impact on small industry is inescapable.[85]

While the Great Depression certainly weakened the position of small industrial enterprise throughout industrial Europe, the impact of depression was very variable. The Great Depression particularly affected areas where small-scale industry was strong, such as the metalworking districts of Britain. In Birmingham and the Black Country, larger firms sought to reduce costs by using more powered machinery, with a resulting increase in the average size of firm, though the most rapid concentration took place in the years after the crisis itself. Yet the crisis also lay behind the simultaneous increase in the number of marginal garret masters, as unemployed journeymen set up producing goods such as buttons or brassware.[86] The Viennese picture similarly emphasises the variability of the effects of depression, showing that the crisis at the end of the century may have been a severe check for small producers as a whole, but that its impact was very uneven. Amongst Vienna's bakers, bookbinders and the building trades, the expansion of earlier years was not undermined by the depression; other trades, operating in international rather than metropolitan markets, saw their rate of growth slow down – tailors, goldsmiths, umbrella-makers; hatters, coopers and brass-workers, on the other hand, now saw their earlier expansion reversed, under the pressure of factory competition; while elsewhere in Austria one can find declining trades, such as ironwork and nail-making, whose problems simply intensified in these years.[87]

There is, indeed, considerable evidence that small enterprise was fostered by crisis, as can be seen if we return to the crisis of the 1840s. In Germany, the agrarian crisis of 1845–47 was weakening when an industrial crisis took off that was to last for a good part of 1848. This conjuncture produced a crisis in credit and finance. Yet in this context, Prussian artisans saw an increase in the number of masters alongside a fall in the number of journeymen employed, especially in the wood and metal trades. There was a parallel growth in the number of retailers between 1846 and 1849. Far from being a sign of well-being, this growth of small enterprise was a symptom of the crisis, as shops and workshops offered a means of survival to those who had little hope of work.[88] Apparently contradictory figures for Cologne confirm this interpretation. The number of artisans advertising in directories in the 1830s and 1840s rose during bad years and declined during good. Many were journeymen setting up on their own, and generally returning to wage employment as times improved, while others would have been established sub-contractors, advertising to obtain orders from a wider public when their contracts from larger firms had dried up.[89] It was a pattern repeated later in the century. The average number of employees in each enterprise that employed labour in Baden and Württemberg during the 1880s increased at the very time that the number of independent proprietors without hired labour also grew.[90] Here was the other dimension of economic crisis for small enterprise, for the disappearance of small firms was numerically compensated by the proliferation of tiny workshops and shops, as displaced journeymen and other workers sought some source of income in crisis. The use of minimal savings or a few tools to provide a shelter from the storm, rather than as an expression of ambition, is a theme to which we shall return in the next chapter. It explains the rapid multiplication of small cutlery masters in Sheffield during depression. As Mayhew noted of London cabinet-makers, 'whenever there's a decrease of wages, there's always an increase of small masters'.[91] Capital and equipment requirements meant that not all unemployed journeymen could respond in this fashion: unemployed tailors and bricklayers were therefore far more likely to start up on their own account when unemployed than were smiths and bakers, who were more likely to go on tramp.

The conjunctural and structural dimensions of crisis thus need to be distinguished when considering their effects on small enterprise. For industries in which small enterprise was faced by large-scale markets and the potential for concentration and mechanisation, economic crises could constitute major moments of sectoral restructuring, severely weakening the relative position of small firms. The consequences of crisis in the 1840s depended upon the extent to which merchant capital had in the preceding years reshaped small-scale production and marginalised a large proportion of small producers in sectors deeply dependent on levels of consumer demand. Amongst tailors, shoemakers, cabinet-makers and small metal goods firms, short-term economic difficulties thus became major structural crises. A far greater proportion of industries were to find themselves in that situation during the late nineteenth-century depression. The Great Depression did not eliminate the small-scale producer, but it provided the opportunity for a shift of balance towards the larger scale in many industries, amongst them metal goods and hardware, cutlery and tools, light engineering, and shoemaking. Yet even the crisis of the 1880s contained within it innovative trends for the opening up of new sectors such as electricity, plumbing, automobiles, and bicycles which offered substantial and growing opportunities for small enterprise.

RURAL SMALL ENTERPRISE

European agriculture was particularly severely hit by the late nineteenth-century depression, especially sectors producing arable crops for the market. The result was to intensify the migration from the countryside which had long fed the world of urban small enterprise, for in many European cities retailers in particular were drawn disproportionately from rural migrants. This transfer of people and capital provides one thread in the chapters which follow. So too does a transmission of culture, for in many countries migration from rural farming and business enterprise served to nourish urban ideologies of small proprietorship.

This relationship between the countryside and the urban petite bourgeoisie should not, however, lead us to forget the artisans and shopkeepers within rural areas. Their importance varied between countries, not least because of the different proportions of the population living in the countryside. England was the most urbanised country in Europe throughout the period: 45 per cent of the population lived in towns of more than 5000 inhabitants in 1850, and 75 per cent in 1910. Some like Belgium advanced in similar fashion (34 per cent and 57 per cent); German urban growth came relatively late (19 per cent and 49 per cent); while French urbanisation was particularly slow (19 per cent and 38 per cent).[92] The rural sections of the French petite bourgeoisie would inevitably be more important than those in Britain, and one-third of all those paying the *patente* in France at the end of the nineteenth century lived in rural communities of fewer than 2000 inhabitants. At the same time in Germany, there were 26.4 master artisans to every 1,000 inhabitants in rural districts – virtually the same as the proportion in towns.[93]

The character of this petite bourgeoisie varied with patterns of landholding and cultivation, for viable peasant farming generated the commercialised villages and *bourgs* which were dotted amongst the small farming communities, and whose artisans and shopkeepers served expanding rural markets. Agrarian reform in the provinces of Brandenbourg after 1807 increased the purchasing power of the peasantry and favoured the growth of an internal market. The result was a noticeable increase in the numbers of rural artisans.[94] Peasant agriculture also encouraged pluriactivity, the construction of a family income from a combination of farming with artisanal or retail activities. 'Artisans in rural society were closely tied to the soil', wrote Annie Moulin of nineteenth-century France.[95] Inequalities within the French countryside did not prevent land being more accessible to rural families with some limited resources than it was in the greater part of Britain, or in those areas of Prussia dominated by large Junker estates, where the link between the occupation of land and artisanal activity was much weaker in the early nineteenth century, and where artisans devoted themselves full-time to their trade and, millers and bakers apart, derived a poor living from it.[96] The blacksmith–farmer in Maire (Sarthe) whose family budgets were examined by Le Play in the early 1850s was, however, a far more familiar figure in the French landscape. He had progressed from journeyman to owning a workshop of his own where he employed his former apprentice, now himself a journeyman. The small amount of capital he had accumulated was invested in the house and land where he lived. He ran the blacksmith's shop, while his wife spun hemp to augment their income, and they together tended the garden and fields.[97]

In areas of peasant agriculture pluriactivity was both more common and more necessary. It is not so much the multiple occupations that had long accompanied industrial activity in the French countryside with which we are concerned, such as the domestic textile and metal workshops in the Department of the Loire which sustained small-scale cultivation well into the present century,[98] but a world where agricultural activities supported artisans with independent enterprises and shops. In the canton of Janville (Eure-et-Loire), a high proportion of artisans and traders also had peasant holdings, and this was particularly true of millers, masons, innkeepers, *cabaretiers* and grocers, for all of whom farming was a complementary but secondary activity. Nearly all artisanal houses had agricultural buildings and tools, and labour often included hired workers as well as members of the family.[99] The work of a mason or shoemaker could be integrated into the agricultural calendar in these arable districts, while that of a *cabaretier* fitted into the shared family labour of the farming day. Pluriactivity was equally common in peasant districts of Germany. In Adelsheim (Baden) in the mid-1880s, two-thirds of artisans were at the same time peasant farmers, and this was true of half the artisans in Schleswig-Holstein in 1907.[100]

The relationship between artisanal prosperity and a rural social structure dominated by small-scale farming was seen by Gustav Schmoller, who found a late nineteenth-century reality that endorsed his own social vision.

> Small industry is most widespread where small landownership and small scale farming prevail, in areas where large villages rather than farms with substantial numbers of labourers are dominant, or where there are many small and medium-sized towns rather than large cities surrounded by a depopulated countryside.[101]

The English experience seems to confirm the importance of Schmoller's variables. On the one hand, the larger-scale landowning and farming structure that characterised most of England increased purchasing power in the countryside, for larger farmers sustained agricultural artisans and services, while a rural population dependent on money wages constituted a local consumer market, however humble in scale. On the other hand, larger-scale farming and wage-labour systems provided less scope for an independence resting on pluriactivity. It existed nonetheless.[102] A middling group of independents had once been prominent in the English countryside combining income from trade, a smallholding, and perhaps a little carting, and they had long sustained the cultural vitality and political radicalism of village life. The shoemaker in the north Yorkshire village of Aysgarth traded extensively over a 20-mile radius in the 1860s, but he combined with it some farming, and still took a good deal of his payment in kind.[103] The long-drawn-out process of enclosure had seriously weakened this group by mid-century, however, whittling away the easy access to land which had been essential to its income.[104] Yet it survived in many places, such as Corsley in Wiltshire where a large proportion of the artisans held small farms in the early twentieth century, and over one-third of the farmers had another occupation, generally in a craft or trade.[105] In the 1880s and 1890s, when rural smallholdings became a politically fashionable solution to the problem of the agricultural labourer, it is not surprising that they were generally taken not by labourers but by village tradesmen and artisans.[106]

Artisans and shopkeepers, with or without land, played a major role in the rural economy throughout Europe. There were those who served agriculture – the ubiquitous blacksmith, who might double as farrier and general metalworker, and the wheelwright, who would act as general carpenter and often undertaker. Others provided for the general village population, above all the tailors and shoemakers whose decline was clear by the later years of the century. The distribution of artisans and traders varied with size of settlement, as well as with its function. A study of Picardy in northern France during the nineteenth century shows artisans supporting local agriculture and consumption to have been far more numerous than shopkeepers. Even the smallest of villages will have had its joiner, smith and miller in the 1830s. By the end of the century, the presence of grocers, butchers and bakers, as well as clothing and textile retailers, provides a measure of the greater complexity of the village economy and the decline of self-sufficiency.[107] Isolated areas had the weakest implantation of artisans and shopkeepers: in Loir-et-Cher, small enterprise was strongest in those districts where road, river and then rail transport produced denser population and marketing structures.[108] Transport, which was in the long run to undermine rural small enterprise, served for much of the nineteenth century to stimulate its growth. Transport enabled artisans and shopkeepers to smooth the workings of the rural economy in small-scale farming systems such as existed in much of France, and from their ranks came the middlemen who linked small agriculturalists to wider markets. In the wine-growing village of Condrieu in the northern Rhône, coopers acted as intermediaries linking *vignerons* to merchants.[109]

Village shopkeepers spread more rapidly in England than in France, which matched the former only in economically advanced regions such as the Nord in France. Medium-sized villages in north Yorkshire boasted a grocer, butcher, draper and publican by mid-century, at a time when village artisans were already under strain.[110] Many a traditional English village craft was in decline by 1850 – amongst them thatching, straw-plaiting, and the making of hurdles, baskets and lace. The decline of the water mill and windmill, and the growth of larger-scale carriage and cart-making enterprises, narrowed the wheelwright's functions, but crafts that served the expanding horse population continued to thrive: blacksmiths, saddlers, and harnessmakers. Urban competition forced an increasing proportion of artisans who served agriculture to concentrate on repair work, but even though the adaptable smith might turn to maintaining farm machinery, farmers were wary of them. As one contemporary observer of the rural scene noted, 'owners of costly reapers and steam ploughs, and threshing machines, will not trust them to the coarse hands of a country blacksmith', and called in the manufacturer's representative.[111]

The agricultural depression from the later 1870s thus provided a point of transition for rural tradesmen in Britain, their ties to the village weakened as much by urban competition as by the decline of agricultural prices. The fall in farm incomes was a further blow, as buildings and equipment were neglected by economising farmers.[112] Many a wheelwright, harnessmaker or smith found it hard to compete with urban production, but the decline of tailors and shoemakers was even more abrupt, unable to compete in price or fashion with ready-made goods available in towns.[113] The impact was felt hardest in the large market villages such as Ashwell in Bedfordshire, whose shops and crafts had once served the smaller settlements in a 10-mile radius. It was the sons of Ashwell's tradesmen who left, a rising generation driven out in larger proportions than were the labourers.[114] The depression meant rising real incomes for labourers, but while one or two village traders might benefit – perhaps the grocer–cum–draper and the butcher – competition from nearby towns aided by improved transport services weakened irrevocably the range of village shops. Villagers would do the bulk of their week's shopping in market towns each Saturday, while town butchers, grocers and drapers sent their vans into the countryside.[115]

The variations in forms of agriculture and degrees of market integration mean that it is harder to generalise about the impact of depression on artisans and traders in the French and German countrysides. The proportion of rural artisans in the population of the Württemberg village of Kiebingen fell from 36 per cent in 1882 to 17 per cent in 1910, with those such as shoemakers and weavers producing for local needs suffering the most. The wealthier trades who formed part of the local elite, and those who continued to serve the daily needs of the village both held their own. Building artisans were in demand, but suffered increasing instability of hire.[116] In France, areas as varied as the Beaujolais, Calvados and the Beauce saw artisanal activities narrow; but decline is less clear in economically advanced regions of growing population, where a substantial non-peasant population could benefit from falling food prices, and where the decline of self-sufficiency provided opportunities for new enterprises.[117] The prosperous countryside of Pas-de-Calais now boasted not only its bakers, but its butchers and *pâtissiers* as well.[118] A small commune in Eure-et-Loire shows the diversity of experience, even within a single community. The numbers of tailors, shoemakers, and millers all declined in the closing decades of the nineteenth century, as did those of innkeepers whose market amongst travellers declined with the railway. However, many trades were stable – the smiths, saddlers, joiners, and most shopkeepers. Behind this pattern lay a trend apparent in most parts of Europe: these rural petits bourgeois were ageing, as the young left.[119] Migration removed young artisans and shopkeepers, or the sons of village petit-bourgeois families, in greater proportions than any other group. Petit-bourgeois families not only had the resources for their young to move and establish in the town, but their greater expectations made harsh times more difficult to accept.

By the turn of the century a degree of stabilisation was setting in, as those enterprises which survived found a reasonable local market for the supply of food or services. Yet artisans and retailers, whether or not supported by agricultural income, had substantially decreased as a part of the village community. The English novelist Thomas Hardy noted that his Dorset villages 'used to contain, in addition to the agricultural inhabitants, an interesting and better-informed class, ranking directly above these – the blacksmith, the carpenter, the shoemaker, the small higgler, the shopkeeper [who] formed the backbone of village life'.[120] He felt that by the 1880s they were in decline. Even if everything was in decline for Hardy by the 1880s, their retreat impoverished village communities.

THE VAGARIES OF INDEPENDENCE

How well did the much vaunted independence of the petite bourgeoisie survive these processes of economic change? Independence, in its more secure forms, had shaped not only occupational pride but also a radical social vision in which independence was central to their political ideals. The social vision of the *sans-culottes* in the French Revolution or of Painite radicals in Britain rested on the proud and assertive independence of small producers. By the time of the late nineteenth-century depression this had changed, and independence came to be asserted more stridently, within a defensive and increasingly conservative discourse. Dependence may have grown, but the ideal of independence survived as a homogenising value, to which all sections of the petite bourgeoisie could subscribe in the face of the advances of large-scale capital and the bureaucratic state.

Independence was undermined above all by the forces of credit and contract.[121] We have seen the structures of dependence that tied artisanal enterprises to the merchants for whom they produced. Behagg has argued that small firms in the Birmingham trades were dependent on large capital as early as the 1840s.[122] If dependence is based on the absence of direct access to the consumer and the market, then it was general amongst all but the most local of artisans in industrial Europe by the last third of the century.[123] Even where the ties between producer and merchant were loose, credit relationships generally constrained any real independence. Small-scale London brushmaking firms needed a large and varied stock of raw materials, but without the resources to purchase directly they came to depend on merchants who supplied on credit. By the 1880s most firms were totally dependent on the orders they received from City wholesalers, however much their own minor retailing operations provided a facade of independence.[124] By the late nineteenth century few artisanal sectors escaped the intervention of a third party between producer and consumer, or escaped the links of financial dependence, which is why the Belgian economist Victor Brants decried most small producers as 'vassals of their suppliers of raw materials'.[125] The Cologne artisans who developed their businesses with mortgage loans from their suppliers were financing their upward mobility at the price of increased subordination.[126] Independence for most artisans became more an ambition than a reality. As one small producer in Birmingham wrote in 1858, 'the large manufacturer, or possibly the factor, who gives him orders knows who he is, how he is circumstanced, and taking the natural trade advantages of his securities, grinds him down to the lowest point consistent with his having any'.[127]

The structures of dependence that surrounded shopkeepers were weaker, partly because large capital entered at least a generation later, and partly because the pressures they experienced resulted primarily from intensive competition amongst themselves. Credit nonetheless narrowed the realities of their fragile independence. One attentive German observer commented at the very end of the nineteenth century, 'if one looks closely at the mushroom-like growth of grocers in a newly constructed neighbourhood, one finds that each one rests on credit'.[128] Denmark was hardly at the forefront of capitalist change in nineteenth-century Europe, and the small market town of Thisted was hardly at the forefront of the Danish economy, but when a small master baker set up in the late 1870s, with credit provided by the master bricklayer who altered the shop, he knew that he had to balance the debt against earnings. He did not succeed, and at his bankruptcy in 1880 the importance of wholesaler credit was clear: only one-fifth of his outstanding debts were local (mostly to that same bricklayer), while the other four-fifths were owed to big wholesalers in the large towns of East Jutland for supplies of flour, sugar, chocolate, and sweets.[129]

Shopkeepers experienced three types of dependency on larger capital. Wholesaler credit was the most common, for few retailers could purchase for cash. Bakers were increasingly tied to the millers whose capital on setting up and supply of flour on credit were essential to many businesses.[130] It is hardly surprising that those seeking to reinvigorate the independence of small enterprise at the start of the twentieth century attached such importance to the establishment of co-operative credit associations.[131] Purchasing co-operatives, which might have enabled shopkeepers to retrieve power lost to wholesalers, were even rarer. A French parliamentary inquiry in 1913 learned that a mere 12 per cent of retailers used them, while the great majority bought from just one wholesaler. They were no more common in Germany, even though they were regularly demanded by shopkeeper organisations towards the end of the century.[132] The use of purchasing co-operatives was even rarer in Britain. The commercial travellers sent out by wholesalers needed the business, they needed the dependency of the shopkeepers in debt to them, but they also needed a steady flow of repayment. One Salford grocer escaped bankruptcy at the eleventh hour when a commercial traveller, who had insisted on payment or no supplies during the bad days of 1911, collapsed on the floor in an epileptic fit. He allowed the credit to stand – supported from his own pocket – in return for his employer being told nothing of his disability.[133] Few retailers were as fortunate – London grocery wholesalers would carry out thorough enquiries into the prospects of a small shop and the reputation of its owners before granting them credit, while simultaneously soliciting the more desirable custom of larger retailers.[134]

Formal loans from wholesalers and suppliers constituted a second form of dependency, tempting many to enter with insufficient capital. These ties could become more formal when debts led to the wholesaler taking control. In late nineteenth-century London,

> If a small draper is failing he almost always applies to his chief creditor among wholesale firms for assistance; the firm sends a man to look into his affairs; if they are in such a condition that he can be pulled out of the mire, they put a man in to help him through, and practically control the business.[135]

Large retail concerns came to act as wholesalers with regard to smaller ones, providing a means of control and sometimes acquisition. Josiah Chater, a successful Cambridge retail draper, regularly supplied cloth in small quantities to a small shop in the nearby town of Royston. When the latter got into financial difficulties in 1855, 'he wanted us to do something for him', Chater recorded in his diary. 'So I went over and took stock, made out a balance sheet for him, and we agreed that the business should be ours and he should be our servant.'[136] Such cases shade into the third category of dependency, where small shops were sponsored by wholesalers and city centre retailers: many a large grocer in Manchester with a wholesale trade would set up a married couple as small grocers in a suburban district.[137] European retailing developed many such schemes, including those where manufacturers set up retailers dependent on them for starting capital, circulating capital, and goods. This was common among clock manufacturers, millers, perfume manufacturers, producers of hairdressing supplies, and above all the drink trade. A majority of Parisian wine-sellers were attached to distillers, while two-thirds of Amsterdam's drink sellers owed their launch to money from large brewers. In France, Félix Potin supplied the provision shops that bore his name with pre-packaged and branded goods, but each shop was an independent enterprise, in a precocious example of franchising. Similar examples included the Niederlage wine concession in Germany, and the Delhaize food stores in Belgium.[138]

Independence was undermined all by these trends. Moreover, dependency enabled larger capital to shape small business in its own image, the mechanism by which the need to appear creditworthy diffused a model of correct behaviour for small businesses. Bankruptcy was one such mechanism, for although businesses fail, it needs others to take legal action for an individual to be made bankrupt. The decision to do so was not necessarily related to the size of debts. Why otherwise did the creditors in the small western French town of Niort unite in 1872 to liquidate one enterprise (run by someone barely known in the town's business circles), while allowing another to repay his immensely larger debts over twenty years? The latter came from a family of long-established butchers, one of the town's best-known business families. 'Whether or not a shopkeeper was supported by his fellow businessmen, that was the question.'[139] It came down to creditworthiness, and bankruptcy was one means by which the business community regulated itself, ensuring that certain standards of business and personal behaviour were observed so that a creditworthy appearance could be maintained.

There were other ways in which large business could use credit dependency to restructure small enterprise in its own image. Charles Walters was a small screw manufacturer in Birmingham in the 1830s. Behagg's examination of the letters Walters sent to his brother shows how Walters felt himself in the grip of the factor who advanced him credit and marketed his product. A small producer such as Walters had to retain total credibility in the eyes of his factor, in this case Nettleford, who would call in unannounced, inspect the books, look over the workshop. Walters was pleased when Nettlefold 'expressed himself in a gratifying way at the regularity of the people and the aspect of things'. He had to be judged to be running the firm in a business-like fashion if he was to obtain the support that guaranteed his slender profits.[140] In these and other ways, dependency was one element transmitting the values of larger business to the world of the more ambitious small enterprises. For small enterprise in nineteenth-century European economies, the issue was not so much survival or decline, but transformation. Dependency and credit were essential forces within that process of change.

4

A WORLD IN MOVEMENT

The world of the petite bourgeoisie was a world in movement. Firm points of personal and structural stability meant that movement did not imply chaos, but movement is more relevant to a consideration of the petite bourgeoisie than for any other social group. There is a paradox here. Contemporary defenders of the petite bourgeoisie valued the opportunity for mobility which it offered to the working class. As Frantz Funck-Brentano told the *Congrès International de la Petite Bourgeoisie* in 1899, the disappearance of the petite bourgeoisie would mean,

> growing discontent amongst the working classes .... The *classe moyenne* was the wide and open road by which the thrifty, skilful and assiduous working man could reach the ranks of employer. Even those who never get there can keep alive the hope of so doing, whether for them or for their children. And everyone knows that men live by hope more than by reality.[1]

As Belgian Catholics were told, 'it would be a great evil if the intermediary groups disappeared entirely .... the image of the social ladder must be preserved.'[2] Yet at the same time these petits bourgeois were lauded for their stability, and often by the same people, for they represented the permanence of the family enterprise. The stability of the hard-working shopkeeper or artisan provided not only reassuring continuity but also a guarantee that hard endeavour and the careful husbanding of resources were rewarded.

Mobility and stability at the same time? The paradox derives from the ideologies of those Le Playists, Social Catholics and *Kathedersozialisten* who sought an alternative to class society without sacrificing private enterprise, but it also identifies a social group whose very existence appears threatened by its personal instability. In comparison with other classes, a greater proportion of the petite bourgeoisie had been born into a different class; a greater proportion spent only a period of their lives as independent craftsmen or shopkeepers; and a greater proportion saw their children enter other classes. The world of small enterprise was thus a world in movement. A world of geographical movement, first, for a small shop or bar frequently provided rural migrants with their point of entry into the urban economy. Most of this movement, however, was only metaphorically so: the business instability caused by both economic conjuncture and the way small enterprise operated; the resulting insecurities that qualified the much-vaunted independence of the petite bourgeoisie; the way in which the continuity between generations affected professional solidarity and the creation of patrimonies; and the larger issues of inter-generational mobility. In considering these questions we are forced to reflect upon the way social mobility analysis often works with models of society that are constructed around hierarchies of occupations. The petite bourgeoisie constitutes the most complex of worlds on which to impose a social mobility grid, yet it was in the very nature of nineteenth-century society that the bulk of social mobility involved movement into and out of this middle ground.

SMALL ENTERPRISE: OPENING AND SURVIVING

Following a single occupation throughout one's life was by no means the nineteenth-century norm, and nowhere was this more true than in small enterprise. Evidence of instability, bankruptcy, and sales of businesses point to the same conclusion, even in trades with a reputation for permanence. Of the 197 butchers' shops in Lyon in 1844, only twenty-one were in the hands of the same family as twenty-five years earlier.[3] Bankruptcy statistics are a common measure of instability. They exclude the very marginal enterprises that no-one pursued through the legal procedures of bankruptcy, but which simply put up the shutters and abandoned the struggle to survive. They also excluded those businesses able to come to an arrangement with their creditors and close down in public silence. The Fourchambault Shopkeepers' Association noted in 1913, 'for the small shopkeeper it is a matter of pride to avoid that shame, and by dint of hard work and self-denial he manages to do so, but he simply sells the stock, shuts the shop and leaves'.[4] In the words of the Social Catholic Hector Lambrechts in 1901, they were 'merely silent shipwrecks in which all is lost except honour'.[5] The bankruptcy evidence is nonetheless striking. Over a quarter of all French bankruptcies between 1903 and 1905 were accounted for by just two occupations – bakers and grocers, for the food trades were vulnerable everywhere.[6] As the chairman of the London grocers' association told Charles Booth, 'the grocer's trade is in the proud position of supplying more work for the bankruptcy officials than any other'.[7] The late nineteenth-century French economist, Charles Colson, claimed that one in twelve French shopkeepers and wholesalers went bankrupt during their career, even more if we consider only retail traders [8] It is striking how marginal were most of these failed businesses. Of those who went bankrupt in the town of Niort in western France between 1817 and 1874, 59 per cent had never appeared in the town's directories, and only 11 per cent had lasted for more than a decade.[9] Bankruptcy among shoemaking firms in the English town of Northampton between 1885 and 1912 reveals a similar fragility – 60 per cent had existed for less than five years, 38 per cent for less than two.[10]

Sales of businesses tell a more ambiguous tale. In 1912 10 per cent of all Paris businesses were sold: as more than half the sales were under 5000 francs, and a quarter for under 1000 francs, many were very small enterprises with tiny initial investment.[11] Not all were the result of owners abandoning their trade, for traders shifted round the city as their fortunes changed. One grocer's assistant used his wife's dowry to open a shop in Belleville, only to sell it at a loss within three years. His next little shop did better, and within four years he was able to move up again, this time to a larger place in avenue Saint-Ouen.[12] Artisans moved as well, seeking greater proximity to suppliers or merchants or a better workshop, though most moves were within a small district.[13] However, most movement involved the closure of businesses, and the French experience was repeated elsewhere. In Bremen at the beginning of the twentieth century, a third of all retail businesses did not survive for as long as six years.[14] In Braunschweig, the same was true of 50 per cent of greengrocers, 40 per cent of grocers, and 30 per cent of drapers.[15] High rates of turnover and marked differentiation between trades are confirmed by a study of Edinburgh retailers in the second half of the nineteenth century, showing that one-third disappeared over a five-year period. Differences between trades reflected initial capitalisation and therefore ease of entry, with spirit dealers and victual dealers losing 61 per cent and 51 per cent of their enterprises respectively between 1890 and 1895. At the other extreme were the wine merchants (17 per cent) and ironmongers (27 per cent). As with retailers, one-third of the city's artisans disappeared over the five years, with building trades and bakers the least stable.[16] Lest such high levels of turnover were thought to be the preserve of larger urban economies, consider Malmö in Sweden where only one-half of all masters in 1820 were still active in the trade ten years later.[17] These are no more than bare statistics whose full social meanings vary, including the death or ill-health of the owner without a successor, the movement to a better situation, and bankruptcy or failure. Most instability rested on failure rather than success, and underlines the social fluidity of the petit-bourgeois milieu. Entry into most sectors of small enterprise was too easy, especially now that corporate controls had disappeared or weakened. The result was undercapitalisation and accumulated debts.

By no means all small enterprise shared these characteristics of marginality and fragility. Indeed, in mid-century Naples a fixed small enterprise was a sign of stability and social promotion in a retail economy still dominated by itinerant traders.[18] The fragility of much small enterprise, however, can divert attention from better-established sections of small enterprise. A Belgian inquiry in 1905 discovered that 49 per cent of grocers in Ghent had been established for less than five years, but also that a stable core of 13 per cent had been there for more than twenty years.[19] This unstable fringe must be emphasised, however, for small business statistics are skewed by tiny firms more likely to be short-lived. It would be specious to fit divisions at precise points between the widow who turned her front room into a confectioner's shop at one extreme, and the city centre draper with a dozen shop assistants at the other, but the range existed, and statistics record each as a distinct enterprise. The lines blur most at the lower end. In Germany the majority of artisans in 1848 worked alone or with only family labour, a pattern which persisted – in 1907 about one-half of all *patrons* in the small enterprise sector were working alone.[20] These included the fringe which we encountered in the last chapter, where independent craftsmen merge with sub-contracting piece-workers. They also included those known in Britain as penny capitalists, but it existed everywhere where workers sought to survive financially by adding some tiny independent source of income to wage labour, or even by relying on that independent activity alone. In Britain, it was most commonly found in older labour-intensive branches of manufacturing such as clothing, watch and clock repairing, shoe repairing and so on; in the jobbing sector of the building industry, where the craftsman worked on the customer's premises and could obtain materials on credit; or in petty retailing – parlour shops, the rush of small beerhouses after the 1830 Beer Act, or of course that itinerant trading to which the poor, unemployed or old could turn, and which was seen as the enemy of fixed retailers.[21]

The most marginal shops were described to a British parliamentary inquiry in 1892 as

> small shops in back streets, or perhaps in a parlour window, or small cellar, (that) sell almost everything, a little hosiery, chips, and bath bricks, and all that kind of thing, and sweets; a little bit of everything that they think that they can dispose of.[22]

Sunday trading inquiries inevitably explored the most marginal of retail enterprises, forced of necessity to remain open at any time that a customer might chance to pass. Of the 669 shops open in Bradford one Sunday in 1904, 257 were described by the Chief Constable as 'merely houses used as shops'.[23] They did not need many customers to make their efforts worthwhile. In turn-of-the-century Cologne a general shop in a working-class area could maintain itself on the custom of no more than fifty families. This petty retailing was a search for neither status nor real independence, but merely for some kind of income. A Cologne tax official referred to them as 'proletarians of commerce'.[24]

They included the small enterprises born out of economic and personal conjunctures. It was not their shops that made their owners poor, but their poverty that made them shopkeepers, as small enterprises were brought into existence by the need for a subsidiary family income. The Chamber of Commerce of Allais (Gard) told a French inquiry in 1913 that small shops were most frequently opened by workers with savings, often leaving the grocer's or haberdasher's shop to be run by their wives while they stayed in wage employment.[25] Others were founded to provide earnings while unemployed, an income in widowhood or illness, or when blacklisted by employers for political or trade union activity. A full 60 per cent of London's women shopkeepers in 1851 were widows. The concentration of these widows in the most marginal of trades (such as victuallers, tobacconists, confectioners, and simply 'shopkeepers') suggests that they opened the shop to provide earnings after their husband's death.[26] The same was true in Bremen around 1890, when 48 per cent of all enterprises headed by women were in the hands of widows.[27] When strength or health declined, an independent enterprise might be the only alternative to poverty. The café-owners of the Berry region in central France had the very high average age of 48, turning to the trade when physically incapable of continuing with manual labour, or on the death of a spouse.[28] There were also the working-class militants who opened shops and bars, especially coal-miners in close communities. John Catchpole, founder of the Derbyshire Miners' Association, gave up the mines in his early forties, exhausted by insecurity and threat of the sack, and opened a small bookshop.[29] Mine safety delegates in French coal mines, elected by the men but paid by the employers for half the month, often opened a bar to make up the rest of their income: ordinary work at the mine for the rest of the month could have made them vulnerable to employer pressure.[30] There were as many conjunctural reasons for opening a small enterprise as there were conjunctural problems. This was not the heart of the petite bourgeoisie, but it comprised a substantial proportion of the small enterprises that passed into and out of existence in the nineteenth-century European city.

Ease of entry was a root cause of the instability of small enterprise, but it did not affect all sectors equally, nor all countries. However incomplete the corporate controls in early nineteenth-century Germany, they provided an institutional constraint absent elsewhere in Europe. Artisans everywhere needed some background in the craft in a way rarely true in smaller retail trades. A London greengrocer told Charles Booth that no provision existed for training entrants to the trade. 'There is no reason why there should be, as there is nothing to learn.'[31] As a result, whereas the lower sections of artisanal trades renewed themselves from workers in the trade itself, marginal retailers tended to come from outside. Ease of entry differed, however, even amongst the workshop trades. The labour-intensive trades of later nineteenth-century Edinburgh – such as masons, joiners, or shoemakers – were easier to join than were even small-scale engineers or printers, whose modest initial capital requirements remained too great for aspirants with skill but few financial resources. The substantially higher rates of business turnover in the labour-intensive category confirm the greater ease of entry.[32] Amongst retailers, far more capital was needed to set up as a draper, ironmonger, wine-merchant or chemist, than as a greengrocer, tobacconist or general shopkeeper. The latter were therefore far more likely to attract proprietors whose lack of skill or resources put them out of business in the first year or so.[33] The father of the English writer V.S. Pritchett began as a shop assistant in north London, but in a burst of optimism and ambition he opened a small newsagents and stationers in the Suffolk town of Ipswich. He knew neither the town nor the trade, and had no capital, but he launched himself in the enthusiastic conviction that he had a superb 'opening'. The enterprise rapidly failed, not least because of the absence of capital with which to acquire adequate stock.[34]

The sources of finance for better-established enterprises were similar throughout industrial Europe, mixing personal savings, family loans, marriage dowries and wholesaler credit, with the sale or mortgage of rural property playing a role in regions and countries with peasant agriculture. Dependence on credit from suppliers to finance a new business was a measure of vulnerability. In the small-scale grocery trade of Paris formal loans played a greater role in the initial finance for former grocers' assistants, indicating a greater ability to persuade lenders of their prospects than former workers, whose savings usually had to play a larger role.[35] Marriage was a moment to start new enterprises, partly because many rested on the work of a married couple, but also because the dowry was a crucial supplement to other sources of capital. Dowries in the Lyon bakery trade often matched the purchase price of the business, with the father-in-law additionally acting as guarantor for the lease.[36]

There were thus a variety of financial routes into small enterprise, and most new businesses used more than one of them. It was, however, too easy to enter many trades with little in the way of finance or skill. 'France is the richest nation in the world and the banker of other countries,' observed George Mauss, President of the Federation of French Retailers, '. . . yet it is terrible to see how small and medium retailing and small and medium industry weakens, collapses, lives from one day to the next, all because of a lack of adequate financial support'.[37] Many a small workshop, bar or shop could be opened in mid-century Paris with a mere 1000 francs, but even this represented the annual income of a skilled worker. Those without savings, dowry or property could only establish themselves by going into debt with their suppliers. 'Wholesalers not only supply small shopkeepers with their goods, they are also their source of advice and even assistance through short-term credit.'[38] The result was vulnerability to the failure of customers to pay their debts, or long-term ill-health. These were the enterprises whose owners were tersely described by the Paris bankruptcy courts in their dossiers as 'more a worker than a shopkeeper'.[39] Charles Booth commented that London's small family shops of the 1890s 'enjoy, or suffer, a varying fortune. Many a small inheritance, and many a sum of savings slowly accumulated in some other occupation, is dispersed and lost by the rash entering into a "little business".'[40] Frank Bullen would have agreed. Increasingly bored by his life as a clerk on two guineas a week in London during the 1880s, he began trading on the side as well as doing picture-framing for his colleagues. His wife inherited a small sum – less than £200 – and persuaded him that they should set up in business. They took a double-fronted shop in East Dulwich and sold picture-framing services, art supplies, needlework and fancy goods. They ran up heavy debts in fitting up the shop, and took their stock on wholesaler credit. With so much tied up in the shop, and so many debts around their neck, the enterprise had to be kept afloat at all costs. Even when the business was going through a good phase they never earned enough to shift the burden of debt, and life became a continuing and embittering struggle.[41]

THE FLOW FROM THE COUNTRYSIDE

The relative ease of entry explains why rural migrants were often prominent in urban small enterprise. Joseph Bernard, explaining the crisis in French shopkeeping of the early years of this century, noted 'during the past twenty years a mass emigration from the countryside into small retailing in the towns'.[42] This was not in fact new, for nearly two-thirds of Parisian petits bourgeois in the early nineteenth century had been of rural origin, while the subsequent expansion of the city's grocery trade rested on migrants bringing rural savings from the Paris basin. Food trades, with their generally low requirements of capital and skill were particularly easy to enter, and rural migrants from Loire Moyenne who set up in Parisian small enterprise in the mid-nineteenth century were disproportionately to be found in food shops and cafés. Not only Paris, for the same was true of smaller towns such as Caen, or a provincial capital like Lyon where 86 per cent of bakers between 1836 and 1852 were of rural origin, a figure which still stood at 78 per cent between 1878 and 1914.[43] Not all migrants from the countryside came from agricultural backgrounds, though the combination of peasant savings and family ambitions meant this was often the case. Amongst the shopkeepers or artisans in Paris between 1830 and 1870 who had migrated from Loire Moyenne, 31 per cent were from peasant backgrounds, 31 per cent retail and 25 per cent artisanal. Their trades in Paris might be closely connected to these origins – as with the sons of *vignerons* and coopers who became wine merchants – but such links were unusual, for the skills learned in village crafts were difficult to transfer to the specialised urban labour market.[44]

The London pattern was different. In 1851 the proportion of shopkeepers born outside the capital was virtually identical to the proportion of migrants in the adult population as a whole (45 per cent and 46 per cent respectively). A comparison of London-born and migrant trades reveals no clear pattern: beershop keepers (66 per cent migrants) might confirm the French picture of a flow into trades relatively easy of access, but the same could not be said of drapers (71 per cent); London-born strength amongst the urban trades of oil and colourman (32 per cent migrants) and outfitters (21 per cent) might have been expected, but not amongst the ubiquitous general dealers (31 per cent).[45] The contrast with France derives partly from different agrarian structures. British urban small enterprise with rural origins was most notable in regions with small agrarian proprietorship: the small-scale hill-farming districts of Cumberland, whose yeoman capital enabled migrants to set up as shop-keepers and trading artisans in the coastal industrial towns during the middle of the nineteenth century, or the emigrants from peasant farming districts of south-west Wales who opened shops in the mining communities of south Wales towards the end of the century, drawing their supplies from relatives and friends back home.[46] Such links were rare in Britain which, though not as dominated by large-scale farming as traditionally portrayed, was far less characterised by peasant agriculture and peasant aspirations than many other parts of Europe. Thomas Lipton, who later founded a national retail grocery chain, was increasingly frustrated by the way his parents ran their Glasgow provision shop. They had fled from their smallholding in Ireland after the Famine, and opened a small shop in Glasgow that drew much of its hams, butter and eggs from an Irish farmer. A stay in the USA taught Lipton business methods different from those of his parents, whose shop provided for them the security that the family smallholding had once done.[47] This link between peasant mentality and urban enterprise was unusual in Britain, but more common in France. Parisian small businessmen of Auvergnat origins brought with them a culture of frugality, economy, hard work, and a reluctance to display what wealth they made.[48]

Independent enterprise was the means by which a peasant or rural craft family could step into the urban world without renouncing their commitment to independence. Accumulated savings or a mortgage on inherited land would allow a child to move to the town, drawn more by the status of urban culture than by any real expectation of increased income. Such ambitions required no break with the rural past. The owners of small artisanal and retail enterprises in Paris tended to marry wives from the same region, while Parisian grocers generally obtained loans from their home district.[49] For the Auvergnats who set up in the metal or wine trades, or in a café or small hotel, the wife's dowry and land expectations guaranteed the urban loans that were crucial to the business. Those who prospered in Paris often bought land or a house in their home community, one that they rarely visited but which provided both security for urban credit and an affirmation that they would return home, if only on retirement. They rarely did so.[50] These Auvergnats built unusually dense networks within Paris and between the capital and the provinces, but they highlight the complex relationships in many countries between rural origins and urban small enterprise. We know far less about Germany, where contemporaries were less struck by the rural inflow and historians therefore less stimulated to explore it. The survival of corporations and municipal rights acted as a break on rural inflow into artisanal and retail trades. In Esslingen, a genuine Württemberg 'home town', 77 per cent of the masters in 1803 had been born in the town, while the rest were married there, and the proportion of locally-born actually rose a little over the next twenty years. The constraints then lifted as corporations lost their vigour and municipal rights their exclusivity, but only after 1845 did this proportion fall to 50 per cent.[51] Here is a specific feature of German towns about which more needs to be known.

A HIERARCHY OF ENTERPRISES

The characteristics which made small enterprise so attractive to many rural migrants were the same features that made much small enterprise structurally weak, and amongst strategies for survival was a pluriactivity similar to that already found in the countryside. It might involve the combining of different trades, perhaps adding a bar to a shop or workshop. When families combined wage employment with a small enterprise, we enter the ambiguous but important margins of the petite bourgeoisie, and often go beyond them as with penny capitalists. One thinks of the tiny shops kept by the wives of workers to supplement the wage income. Over half the 298 beershop keepers in mid-nineteenth-century Merthyr were employed at the local ironworks.[52] In late nineteenth-century east London, according to Booth, most small shops 'were kept by the wives of men otherwise employed'.[53] If the picture from the 1851 census continued, they were most likely to be the wives of skilled workers in the less well-paid crafts, such as tanners, carpenters, tailors and hatters.[54] The man would often be formally credited with both occupations, whatever the reality. In Bremen in 1907, 31 per cent of all shops were supplementary to some waged employment, above all in sectors such as dairies and greengrocers that required little capital.[55] For some it was a means of augmenting a working-class income; for others an outlet that might result in real independence and the abandonment of wage labour; while many others lead us beyond the pluriactivity that permitted a shop to maintain itself, and into the use of petty enterprise within working-class subsistence strategies. In such cases we leave the ideals of the independent artisan or the comfortably-established shopkeeper, and enter the world where the conditions of many owners of small enterprises mixed with those of wage-earning workers.

Businesses with family labour alone were not necessarily marginal, as was well understood by those larger traders pressing for state regulation of shop opening hours in Britain. The representative of the Manchester and Salford Grocers' Association told a parliamentary enquiry in 1895 that he wanted the very small shopkeeper excluded, because he was of no commercial significance yet his numbers would vote down any closing propositions submitted to a local shopkeeper ballot. Yet he did not include all family shops in this category, for many an enterprise run by husband, wife and children was a successful and stable competitor.[56] One must of course be careful not to take the discourse of shopkeepers' representatives, anxious to present to the outside world an image of a respectable and responsible trade, for an accurate description. Only then can we understand the opposition of the Saint-Etienne Chamber of Commerce to the enlargement of its electorate, or the concern of the President of Bremen's principal shopkeeper organisation to ensure that Jewish shops and those without employees were not members.[57] Unstable and marginal small enterprises nonetheless existed, and inflated both the statistics of turnover and the atmosphere of instability, but they were only one part of a petit-bourgeois world that contained layers of stability and relative prosperity. Witnesses before British parliamentary inquiries into shop opening hours during the last fifteen years of the century illuminate the way in which these layers of small enterprise were perceived.[58] There were the tiny shops that were an adjunct to wage employment; the small shops dependent on family labour alone and deemed to be too marginal to concern established traders in the drapery trade, but which were central to competition in grocery and food retailing; there was the contrast between established town centre traders and those on the suburban periphery, often family enterprises which would stay open all hours and whose owners would vote down any local early-closing proposals; there was the very large number of organised traders with between two and five assistants; and finally, striding across the pages of these inquiries, came the wealthy figures, such as the drapers with upwards of twenty assistants, who claimed to speak for all shopkeepers. The conflicting images we receive of the world of small enterprise make questions of range and hierarchy fundamental, with statistics dominated by the marginal operator and organisations run by the better-established. The range can be grasped not only through the longevity which we have already considered, but through wealth, trade hierarchies and gender.

The wealth left at death by shopkeepers and artisans reveals the range of small enterprises. The absolute levels of wealth are less important than the evenness of the pyramid of distribution revealed. The poorest of Edinburgh retailers who died between 1889 and 1892 left under £100, and constituted 9 per cent of all retailer deaths; a further 29 per cent left between £100 and £300; 31 per cent left between £300 and £1000; and the most prosperous 32 per cent left over £1000. The spread of craft-retailers (e.g. bakers and shoemakers) and craft businessmen (e.g. masons, engravers and printers) was similar.[59] In the same way, pyramids for French cities were similarly much more gently rounded than other occupational groups, where uneven distributions were more common. Of shopkeepers and master artisans dying in Paris in 1847, 7 per cent left under 1000 francs (in contrast with 85 per cent of workers); 26 per cent left between 1000 and 5000 francs; 37 per cent between 5000 and 20,000 francs; and 31 per cent over 20,000 francs. The equivalent figures for 1911 show a relative decline in the smaller fortunes and a swelling of the larger ones, but an overall distribution that remains strikingly broad.[60] German examples show a similar pattern. Wealth at marriage of Esslingen's master artisans after 1845 ranged from 28 per cent at under 200 florins through

28 per cent between 200 and 499 florins and 28 per cent between 500 and 999 florins, to 22 per cent at the top with over 1000 florins.[61] The world of small enterprise covered a wide range of prosperity.

These hierarchies within small enterprise as a whole necessarily hide the different experiences within each trade. Insurance policies in nineteenth-century Leicester show the specialist retailers, such as drapers, ironmongers and chemists, at the top of the hierarchy; butchers and bakers were mostly fairly comfortable; general shopkeepers were at the bottom; and grocers were widely spread across the range, indicating the sheer breadth of that occupational title.[62] The small French town of Bourg-en-Bresse in the first half of the century produced its own hierarchies, with the butchers and bakers, legally protected from competition and with a range of legal obligations to fulfil such as the baker's substantial deposit of grain in the municipal reserves, showing a relatively uniform position towards the top of the retailer hierarchy, alongside hairdressers and wigmakers, whereas bar keepers and drinks sellers covered a great variety of conditions. The town's artisans ranged from the more prosperous metal and leather trades, through the middling-wealth of wood-working and building artisans, and the relative poverty of weavers and tailors.[63] In the German canton of Münster in 1907, at the head of the table of incomes in small enterprise stood masters in building (carpenters, masons, plumbers) and food (butchers and bakers), in comparison with the saddlers, shoemakers, turners, coopers and hairdressers who stood at the bottom.[64]

These case studies suggest the range of conditions in the world of small enterprise, and it was a diversity on which a division by gender can be fitted. Women proprietors were rare in nineteenth-century artisanal trades, though the distinctively female artisanal trades of millinery and dressmaking were often degraded in reputation simply because they were run by women, but were often successful small enterprises. The picture is clearer among shop-keepers, with women firmly entrenched at the foot of the hierarchy of trades. In mid-nineteenth-century London, the overwhelmingly male retail trades were also the more prosperous ones – oil and colourmen, drapers, pawn-brokers, chemists and druggists, cheesemongers and wine merchants. The very heavily female trades, on the other hand, were generally the poorest – 'shopkeepers', chandlers and fancy goods dealers – though the predominantly female florists were an exception to this general rule.[65] The picture for Bremen at the start of the twentieth century was somewhat less bleak for, although women were strongly represented in such undercapitalised and fragile trades as grocery, haberdashery and greengrocery, their substantial presence in such specialist trades as stationers and such generalised women's trades as dress shops suggests that they had a place amongst the town's more successful retailers.[66]

The more stable sections of small enterprise were necessary for the development of distinctively petit-bourgeois cultural patterns and organisations. These rested, first of all, on the core of stable petits bourgeois who developed the culture and values of the social group and, second, on aspirations to patrimony. The transmission of a patrimony to the next generation was an ambition which could be achieved by only a minority of those who opened small enterprises in the nineteenth-century European city, but the ambition is proclaimed in the shop or workshop signs announcing 'and son', in the headed notepaper that was becoming common by the turn of the century, in the assertion of family in the photographs taken in front of shops at the same time. The existence of a stable core that kept alive the ambition for patrimony provided a basis for the hopes, strategies and cultures of a larger group.[67] The patrimony was most real for city-centre traders: virtually all the Parisian grocery shops that had been passed down generations were the more valuable city centre enterprises.[68] This continuity, indicating the survival of the family but also of the corporation, was particularly strong amongst butchers. Evidence from northern Belgium at the end of the *ancien régime* and from Limoges and Lyon in the nineteenth century shows elite groups of butchers creating hereditary family enterprises through strict marriage strategies, continuity between generations, family cohesion and, at least in the Limoges case, militant Catholicism. Yet a sample of 187 bakers across France in the closing decades of the nineteenth century finds a mere eleven sons involved in the same trade at the time of their marriage. Even if one makes allowances for the early career stage of these sons, it is a lack of continuity that contrasts strongly with the image of butchers.[69]

The practice of patrimony produced amongst butchers a social cohesion that approaches the social if not the institutional expression of the corporation, as also revealed in Henning's portrait of inter-generational continuities and prosperity amongst an aristocracy of Westphalian artisans.[70] These were exceptionally cohesive trading and artisanal elites, but a more general process produced a stable and successful stratum of petits bourgeois in most towns. Jacquemet demonstrated such an elite drawing away from the mass of small businessmen in the Parisian popular suburb of Belleville during the second half of the nineteenth century, and even Bremen at the end of the century, whose rapid turnover of small shops has been noted, saw drapers, ironmongers and similar trades laying the foundations for local commercial dynasties. In a sea of uncertain existences, here were forces for stability, families whose enterprise often survived beyond the first generation, and whose significance at the local level was far greater than their relatively limited wealth might suggest. The larger group of small enterprises stood below the elite to which they were closely linked – the more substantial businesses with a number of employees and a real sense of continuity. Together they constituted the bedrock of most petit-bourgeois organisations. Thus very few of the eighty members of the Manchester and District Grocery Trade Defence Association in 1886 employed no outside labour, though they claimed to speak for the smaller firms as well, while the hundred varied traders in the

Vauxhall and Wandsworth Road Tradesmen's Club from the inner suburbs of south-west London included no general shops and no small family enterprises, and represented a membership of stable and established businesses, each with a handful of assistants.[71] In Bremen, the *Verein Bremer Ladeninhaber* was similar, with a committee dominated by those employing a number of assistants, and a membership in the food and textile trades whose enterprises were much longer established than the average.[72]

The ideal of the corporation as a cohesive and hierarchical unit often survived in the ideology of small enterprise long beyond the abolition of formal corporate institutions, and it was an ideal which contrasted bleakly with the diversity and instability identified in this chapter. The corporatist vision retained its power – for only in Britain did masters decisively distance themselves from it – yet the model that was admired was one which even under the *ancien régime* had differed from the reality: a certain equality of wealth, an equal distribution of journeymen, heredity of occupation, marriage within the same milieu, and a prevailing sense of continuity. Nowhere were questions of corporate and class images more relevant and more ambiguous than in Germany, where the weight of corporations might lead one to expect a certain homogeneity of milieu in small enterprise. The Rhineland towns of Cologne and Düsseldorf had been freed from corporatism by the Napoleonic invasion, whereas Esslingen in the south retained its corporations until the 1860s. The degree of heterogeneity that one finds in these towns with such varied corporate experiences suggests real limits to explanations that are based on the survival of some corporate *ancien régime* alone. The declarations of income at marriage made by Esslingen master artisans in 1845 shows 15 per cent with incomes that were similar to the working class, 50 per cent in the range of middling incomes, and 35 per cent amongst the wealthier sections of the town's population. The artisanal world in Düsseldorf was more unevenly balanced than that in Esslingen, and the degree of hardship greater: the municipal tax registers reveal that three-quarters of masters had incomes barely of subsistence level, something true of only half of shopkeepers. Esslingen's diversity within a corporate setting was confirmed by the unequal distribution of journeymen and apprentices, for in 1860 approaching half of the town's master artisans worked without apprentices or were subcontracting pieceworkers.[73] On the other hand, patterns of occupational heredity were closer to the ideals of the corporation in Esslingen and in the Rhineland alike. Two types of heredity need to be distinguished: that in which master artisans continued in the same trade as their fathers, and the continuity of broader master artisan status though not necessarily in the same trade. Direct continuity was more marked in corporatist Esslingen than in free-trade Cologne. In Esslingen, 45 per cent of master artisans were in the same trade as their fathers, though there was a marked distinction between the earlier part of the period when the rate of continuity was two-thirds, and the years between 1846 and 1870 when the rate dropped to only one-third. Occupational heredity was stronger among those locally born, as one might expect, and stronger amongst those with middling incomes than amongst those who were relatively prosperous or relatively poor, which appears surprising.[74] The experience of Cologne's free-trade economy suggests that the answer might lie in the stagnation of the artisanal sector which encouraged a continuity from father to son as 'the artisanal world protected itself'. Artisanal trades were growing more slowly than other parts of the town's economy, which made it difficult for the sons of workers or peasants to enter the crafts. The artisanal milieu of Cologne defended itself less by continuity within the same trade – the 19 per cent of master artisans marrying in 1855 whose fathers had the same trade had increased only slightly to a figure of 24 per cent twenty years later – than within the artisanal milieu as a whole – in 1855 49 per cent of master artisans were the sons of master artisans, whether in the same or a different trade, but by 1875 the proportion had risen to 66 per cent. In Düsseldorf, 60 per cent of the sons of master artisans remained in artisanal occupations, two-thirds of those as independents.[75] Personal contacts between masters in different trades and collective controls over training were the mechanisms by which heredity grew. Crisis and difficulty can thus enclose people within the narrow world in which they grew up, a milieu that was narrowed further by the reluctance of others to enter in difficult times. Furthermore, a lack of capital resources meant that these artisans were not well equipped to move themselves or their sons into better situations. The picture is thus a complex one, with patterns of recruitment and continuity in these German towns by no means following a simple link to guild institutions, or some simple equation of prosperity and inheritance of status. Even in Cologne and Düsseldorf, with their early abolition of corporations, the artisanat retained traces of a cohesion which might be traced to a corporate past, but which also related to the opportunities within each urban economy. These German towns show the ways in which economic situation, corporate structures, and the petit-bourgeois milieu might interact, but they also lead us to ask about the meanings of social mobility, and about the complex relationship between that social mobility and the European petite bourgeoisie.

SOCIAL MOBILITY: AN IDEA UNDER CHALLENGE

If the petite bourgeoisie was important to social mobility, it is by no means clear that the reverse was true. Writers proclaimed the opportunities small enterprise provided for aspiring workers, but the middling groups to which access is relatively easy are the least stable element in any social system. Yet how helpful is the concept of social mobility for an understanding of the petite bourgeoisie itself? Interest in social mobility is often driven by ideological preoccupations, from exploring the heredity of eugenic civic worth for Francis Galton and the eugenics movement from the late nineteenth century to the empirical research of the 1950s and 1960s investigating the openness of liberal society.[76] The concept should not be assumed to describe some self-evident social phenomenon, and we need to ask what is meant by historical social mobility. Historians sometimes refer to social or occupational change within an individual's lifetime (career mobility), at other times to the extent to which an individual's social position differs from that into which they were born (inter-generational mobility). These approaches share a common difficulty, in that analysis generally works through the names of occupations announced to public officials. Occupational titles are taken to describe more than a daily working activity, but to represent a social as well as an occupational position and, furthermore, each occupational designation is taken to refer to something reasonably homogeneous. Groups of occupations are ranked in a linear hierarchy, and movement up or down that hierarchy constitutes social mobility. The concept of social mobility is a metaphor that seeks to grasp individual movement within linear images of a society. It also tends to focus on individual mobility, even though working-class and petit-bourgeois occupational mixing means that the occupational composition of a family might be more important.[77]

The petite bourgeoisie raises particularly difficult questions for classic perceptions of social mobility. The transition from wage-earner to small master or shopkeeper was not necessarily experienced as upward mobility, for although it offered freedom from the constraints of wage labour, there was no automatic change of social identity such as the hierarchical grouping of occupational titles would lead one to expect. Those London small masters of the 1860s and 1870s who kept their trade union membership were acknowledging not simply the insecurities of their new position but their continuing identification with their craft milieu.[78] In any case, movement in and out of small enterprise characterised many urban trades. In 1874 a Paris engraver observed of his craft,

> when you ask an engraver: are you an employer, are you a worker? He replies: wait until tomorrow, perhaps I'll be able to give you an answer, because today I don't know what I am. The biggest employers in our trade employ at best four workers for a few days, after which they become workers again themselves the day after.[79]

As the engraver was making the case for a mixed *chambre syndicale* for engravers, he tried to minimise the gap between workers and employers, but the fluidity within many small-scale trades was well captured. Hasty assumptions should be avoided about the long-term meanings of descriptions of occupational status. The pattern has been noted all over Europe, especially in domestic trades such as the Berlin tailors in the 1870s, or Hanover trades on the eve of the First World War.[80] The Registrar-General for Scotland told the 1890 Committee on the Census that 'people who are employers one day and employed the next' were common 'in all small trades'.[81]

The power of popular sociability, craft culture, personal values, or family position shaped the way occupational change was experienced. In any case, such change depended more on the opportunities available than on aspirations to climb an agreed status ladder. Unskilled industrial workers who changed occupation went into semi-skilled and, less commonly, skilled work: factory employment provided the possibility of advance within the working class. Miners, on the other hand, operated in an industry that offered little significant advancement within the trade, and aspirations for change in a town such as Bochum therefore concentrated on becoming small tradesmen – not simply because miners could accumulate savings, but because their ambitions were shaped by the opportunities available.[82] Self-employment would not necessarily have seemed a superior option, however, given the importance of security in working-class life. The social complexity of petit-bourgeois positions, and the lack of homogeneity within petit-bourgeois occupational titles, create problems for classic notions of historical social mobility. Movement through an occupational hierarchy must be relinquished as an organising idea, and replaced perhaps by seeking to establish the empirical connections between occupations, as revealed by actual patterns of inter-marriage and occupational succession. The complex realities of the social landscape might then be grasped.[83]

The sources used by historians present an additional problem. Analyses of nineteenth-century social mobility generally use marriage registers which recorded the occupations of the groom and his father. The source privileges relationships between men, for studies of marriage as a source of social mobility tend to compare the occupation of the groom (or his father) not with that of the bride but of her father.[84] It tells us nothing of the occupational trajectories of the unmarried, and finds it hard to deal with the children of widows. Even more serious, perhaps, is the age-specificity of the data, which records the son's occupation at the age of marriage (on average about 26 in mid-nineteenth-century western Europe), an early moment in his career. Finally, the occupations of father and son are compared at different moments in their careers, even though segments of the social structure subject to instability of occupational position are those where the timing and life cycle stage of observations are most significant.[85] Children of peasants, artisans and shopkeepers would commonly enter wage employment before joining the family enterprise.[86] In any case, people set up on their own at an age older than that at which occupation was normally settled. In mid-nineteenth-century London, only one-eighth of male shopkeepers were unmarried, compared with nearly one-third of the adult male occupied population as a whole. Marriage registers thus understate the flow into shopkeeping.[87] The same can be found amongst the owners of artisanal enterprises, for whom a period of salaried employment was a necessary part of craft training. As a result it took longer to become a petit bourgeois than a wage-earner or a white-collar employee. Small business men in mid-nineteenth-century Marseille were on average markedly older than those in working-class, service or white-collar positions, [88] as were London shop-keepers. In 1851, 33 per cent of London's adult male occupied population were aged between 20 and 29, but only 17 per cent of male shopkeepers were. The difference was even more acute amongst women, where 54 per cent of occupied women were in their twenties in comparison with a mere 10 per cent of shopkeepers, the result of the particularities of the female labour market and the fact that women shopkeepers tended to be substantially older than male ones.[89]

The accuracy of the occupational title raises a further problem about sources, for the range of fortunes and social position was often considerable. In Braunschweig it was impossible to distinguish wholesale merchants from retailers in the marriage registers because they were both inscribed as *Kaufleute*, whereas in Bremen, where the confrontation between merchants and retail traders forced its way into everyday language, the distinction is expressed in the sources.[90] It is often impossible to distinguish between employer, self-employed and employee in census and registration sources. Finally, there is pluriactivity, nowhere more important than in small-scale enterprise, and difficult to identify from such sources, as are the variations in occupational title used by the same individual over time. In 1872 Louis Dantoine, a tradesman in the small French town of Givors, was listed as an *épicier ambulant* (itinerant grocer), but the title then changed to *marchand fruitier* (fruiterer, 1876), *épicier* (grocer, 1881), *négociant* (merchant, 1886), and *marchand de fromages* (cheese seller, 1891).[91] How often had he actually changed occupation over these years, or was he simply offering different titles to local officials?

In any case, it must not be assumed that there was widespread ambition for upward social movement in a social group, so that low levels of upward social mobility represent thwarted ambition. This is especially true for petits bourgeois, whose attachment to patrimony and continuity might have restrained ambition. Security and movement were in tension, and each constituted a form of ambition. When the future of the young Henri Béraud became a matter for family discussion in their Lyons bakery, *La Gerbe d'Or*, mother and father had different views. Henri's father wanted him educated for a better future, perhaps in the liberal professions. His mother disagreed. 'Why should one have to go to the trouble of chasing after people and business, when one is the only son of an honourable and respected shop-keeper, the vice-president of his corporation?' As Henri Béraud later commented, 'Was I not the heir of *La Gerbe d'Or*, its business, money, customers and flour? Wasn't that worth all the offices, all the studies, all the piles of paper in the world?'[92]

THE MOVEMENT BETWEEN GENERATIONS

The owners of small urban businesses came from a popular world of petits bourgeois, peasants and skilled workers. The shopkeepers and master artisans in the 4th *arrondissement* of Paris in 1846, were the sons of petits bourgeois (54 per cent), peasants (17 per cent), and workers and servants (20 per cent).[93] This diversity of backgrounds emerged as traditional routes into small enterprise declined, those from apprentice to journeyman to master artisan, or from shop assistant to shopkeeper. The older routes declined with the corporate structures that had once sustained them, and as an increase in the employed labour force reduced the proportion of employees who could set up on their own account. Although 60 per cent of grocers in late nineteenth-century Paris had started as a shop assistant, only a minority of the 6000 grocers' assistants in the city in 1890 could hope to become independent shopkeepers.[94] The same trend could be seen amongst London drapers, whose assistants' prospects of starting on their own were reduced by the increasing scale of enterprise.[95] The cost of entry was a key element. In the Austrian city of Graz upward mobility occurred only in trades serving local demand and requiring modest capital. Whereas 46 per cent of employed cabinet-makers in 1857 had acquired their own workshop twelve years later, and 38 per cent of those in the clothing trades, only 10 per cent of the town's skilled engineering and metal workers had done so, and none of its printers.[96]

Increasing popular recruitment responded to the opportunities created by urban economic expansion for those with skill, resources or merely ambition. The new retailers in a fairly stagnant eastern German city like Leipzig, in contrast, came from peasant and petits-bourgeois families, with those few of working-class origin mostly drawn from domestic service or the military in which the accumulation of savings was common.[97] The Edinburgh petite bourgeoisie, on the other hand, shows social origins broadening in a more expansive economic context. Although these included professions, large bourgeois and unskilled workers, the town's small enterprise came above all from the sons of the petite bourgeoisie itself and those of the skilled working class, which together accounted for some two-thirds of petits bourgeois in 1890.[98]

The origins of a social group usually emphasise continuity far more than would the occupational destinations of its children. Half of a cohort of late nineteenth-century Lyonnais shopkeepers, for example, were the sons of shopkeepers, but only 16 per cent of the sons of shopkeepers were themselves shopkeepers.[99] It was never easy for the European petite bourgeoisie to maintain petit-bourgeois status for its own children, whether by passing on the enterprise or by providing the resources to secure equivalent status. Even without the problem of resources and stability of enterprise, there were demographic difficulties. In mid-century Paris, the average male *boutiquier* would have married when he was 28 years old, which left some twenty-five years before his death at the age of 53.[100] This did not leave much time in which to raise and then set up the eldest son or daughter, let alone the younger ones who were everywhere less likely to have remained within small enterprise. If the petite bourgeoisie was characterised by openness, it was one that turned to the classes below rather than to those above. The occupations of the sons of retailers in a group of English towns and industrial and agricultural villages in 1871 reveals striking diversity, though these comparisons were drawn from different stages of the life cycle. Of 108 sons of retailers, 33 per cent were in retail trade, mostly the same trade as their fathers; 30 per cent held skilled working-class occupations; 25 per cent were white-collar employees; and 12 per cent were in mine or factory employment.[101] A more substantial study of Leicester shopkeepers for 1879–81 reveals comparable figures: 9 per cent of sons marrying were in the professions or non-retail business, 41 per cent in retailing, 9 per cent in white-collar occupations, 33 per cent in skilled crafts (a figure which will have included a number of small masters), and 8 per cent in other working-class jobs.[102] Shopkeepers were more likely to have sons in non-working-class occupations than were artisans. This could indicate the relative weakness of artisanal over retail small enterprise, but is more likely to be due to the closeness of master artisans to the working-class milieu, their attachment to craft work, and the tendency of the owners of craft businesses to begin as journeymen. The predominance of craft workers amongst the sons of Toulouse's petits bourgeois was due to precisely that social proximity in a town with a diverse economy.[103]

A meticulous study of the antecedents and the children of artisanal and retail *petits patrons* in the 4th *arrondissement* of Paris between 1835 and 1845 provides some clues as to the family (as opposed to the structural) influences at work in determining the likelihood of an eldest son himself becoming a business owner. The key variables were size of family and early death of the father. Once a small enterprise family had four children, the chances of the eldest son himself becoming a *patron* were substantially reduced, and the already limited prospects of upward mobility virtually eliminated. The death of the father within fifteen years of marriage greatly increased the likelihood of the eldest son ending up in an unskilled manual occupation.[104] The maintaining of petit-bourgeois status was a fragile affair, subject to personal as well as structural forces. The petite bourgeoisie was in that respect no different from any other part of nineteenth-century society, but the power to shape one's children's occupational choice was not equally distributed. However many sons of petits bourgeois took up skilled working-class occupations, however much social openness and proximity is stressed, it remained true throughout Europe that being born into a small business family greatly improved one's occupational opportunities. A broad survey of English marriages between 1839 and 1914 concluded that sons from petit-bourgeois backgrounds were some fourteen times more likely themselves to occupy petit-bourgeois positions at the time of their marriage than were the sons of working-class fathers; nine times more likely than even the sons of skilled craft workers.[105] The growth of the white-collar option only strengthened that inequality of opportunity.

Little has been said of the petite bourgeoisie's role as a stepping stone to substantially higher status, which would have surprised those contemporaries who lauded it in those terms. The reality was different, for the already restricted opportunities offered for small entrepreneurs or their children to advance to substantial bourgeois positions progressively diminished as the nineteenth century went on. The chances of master artisans becoming merchants or industrialists were virtually non-existent in Düsseldorf and Esslingen well before the 1870s.[106] A longer-term process of upward mobility has been traced amongst third-generation descendants of the wealthier of Westphalian artisans, however, with a full third occupying positions as university-trained civil servants and army officers as well as manufacturers.[107] Mobility through official and professional education was clearly possible – at the beginning of the twentieth century the traditional petite bourgeoisie provided 19 per cent of university professors in Germany as a whole, while in Württemberg it supplied 32 per cent of Catholic priests, though only 14 per cent of Protestant clergy.[108] Education rather than business was the mode of major occupational change, and for a small minority in Germany it provided a precocious form of upward mobility.

Progress for French artisans and shopkeepers was no easier, as more substantial bourgeois milieux became closed to them. Such mobility as existed was not to the industrial or land-owning bourgeoisie, which had been reduced to the narrowest of bridges according to studies of Paris, Bordeaux and Rouen,[109] but into large-scale retailing, which came to provide better prospects than did manufacturing. In the context of burgeoning suburbanisation, new styles of marketing, and rising real incomes, many of the huge multiple grocery chains in turn-of-the-century Britain, as with department stores in France, had started from fairly humble petit-bourgeois origins.[110] There were alternative paths of progress, as amongst the Rouennais petits bourgeois who occupied the posts of notary abandoned in the countryside,[111] but for the bulk of the petite bourgeoisie social movement took place within the lower middle class rather than outside of it. Sinking below the skilled working class was immensely more likely than the very limited prospects of upward movement. In the German town of Minden 4 per cent of children of the petite bourgeoisie reached substantial bourgeois positions in the period between 1860 and 1918, in comparison with the 40 per cent who were to be found in working-class occupations.[112] Most movement took place within a world of artisanal and retail petits bourgeois on the one hand, and upper sections of the working class, white-collar workers and lower civil servants on the other.

In the later nineteenth century structural change, depression and an atmosphere of crisis presented particular problems for the core of more stable petit-bourgeois families and those who shared their ambitions. Continuing petit-bourgeois status for children was not only more difficult to achieve, it was also less attractive. New opportunities were, however, appearing in the world of offices and clerical occupations, in expanding state bureaucracies, and in new minor professions such as elementary schoolteaching. The way petits-bourgeois parents sought such posts for their children points to the emergence of a larger *classe moyenne* in these years, with social mobility for small enterprise families increasingly horizontal. This trend disturbed many friends of small enterprise, weakening the petite bourgeoisie while enlarging a group less able to act as social intermediary.[113] Yet it proceeded apace. The dual strategy of Malthusianism and secondary education amongst the French petite bourgeoisie during the twentieth century saw family size fall while resources were concentrated on educating the children for white-collar occupations.[114] This strategy of reconversion, as it has been christened, [115] had its roots in the latter half of the nineteenth century. The Director of the École Turgot in Paris reported in 1875 that his school recruited largely from workshop masters and the like. 'The principal goal of the great majority of both children and parents is office employment.'[116] It was a tendency that grew with the problems of small enterprise, and not only in France. In Wilhelmine Germany, Walter Hofmann's father came to feel that his engraving business no longer fulfilled the hopes he had once invested in it.

> The father, once so ardently bent on handing over his 'fine little business' to his son, would see occupational salvation for his children and grandchildren in an official's post – not because it was 'the best', but because it was the 'most secure.'[117]

The obvious next step for Norman Hancock, on leaving school in 1911, was apprenticeship in the drapery trade before entering his father's business, but the other alternatives he considered were becoming a chemist, commercial traveller or journalist.[118]

Parental ambitions had by the end of the century come to focus on a petit-bourgeois world that was laterally extended, and education was the key to this extension. The petite bourgeoisie was the group least attended to in nineteenth-century educational development, sandwiched as it was between the established secondary schools for bourgeois families, on the one hand, and the growing religious and state provision of elementary schools for the working class, on the other. The gap was recognised in both public inquiries and private philanthropic ventures in Britain during the middle decades of the century.[119] Nevertheless, petits bourgeois rapidly made use of the expanding educational opportunities that appeared everywhere from the 1860s. In the German towns of Minden and Duisburg about a quarter of all master artisans and shopkeepers provided their children with a secondary education by the end of the century, a number which had grown substantially from earlier years,[120] while in a fast-growing industrial town like Bochum, the *Gymnasium* and *Oberrealschule* were dominated by the children of small urban business owners and white-collar employees who used the schools for stability rather than progress.[121] The German petite bourgeoisie, in using secondary education to maintain family status, turned to the practically-oriented *Realsschule* more than the classical *Gymnasium*. The traditional petite bourgeoisie in Germany, according to Peter Lundgren, used education more as a means of resisting decline than as an instrument for upward mobility, and in more normal conditions parents favoured their children entering the family enterprise, even if they might then be regarded as over-educated for such careers.[122]

The parallel with France and Britain is striking. *Ecoles primaires supérieures* from the 1860s, and Higher Grade Schools from the 1880s, offered a more advanced level of education that was extensively used by the traditional petite bourgeoisie. This had been the intention of many who had campaigned for such schools. Félix Pécaut wanted them in the small towns of France to educate the elite of small rural proprietors and retailers who had influence over the rural lower class.[123] The *écoles primaires supérieures* came to prevail over the competing Catholic schools by the 1880s, offering a more practical education that channelled children into expanding careers as engineers, accountants, managers, white-collar employees and schoolteachers.[124] Surveys of pupil and parent expectations reveal that nearly half the sons of shopkeepers in secondary schools hoped to follow their fathers' occupation, while the goal for the others was this kind of horizontal mobility. The programmes chosen illustrate the limited horizons. While larger bourgeois and professions chose the classical programme which gave access to the *grandes écoles* and other elite institutions, the shopkeepers, peasants and artisans opted for the special and more modern programme.[125]

The outcome was clear in Britain as elsewhere. Whereas in the years 1859–61 only 3 per cent of all Leicester bridegrooms from shopkeeper families were in white-collar employment, that had risen to 17 per cent in 1899–1901.[126] This new white-collar world was itself stratified. The better-paid positions that were linked to career ladders – such as those in banking and insurance – tended to be occupied by sons from more substantial small-business families with incomes of upwards of £300 a year.[127] Most opportunities were at the lower end of the white-collar occupational world, and for these petit-bourgeois enthusiasm for educating their children coincided with increasing competition from working-class children emerging from improved public schooling systems.[128] State service was a particularly appealing option in countries like France and Germany where it carried traditional prestige, as well as in Britain where its security was attractive, but those who entered via secondary or higher primary education found themselves trapped at the lower end where most expansion took place: clerical work, postal systems and elementary schoolteaching. It is ironic that the petite bourgeoisie which railed against the growth of the bureaucratic state now sought posts within it to resolve family anxieties. Georges Duplat, a Belgian lawyer and defender of the *classe moyenne*, commented on this 'strange fascination for the civil service'.[129] The rapid growth of teachers in the decades before the War likewise drew heavily on petit-bourgeois children – not least in Britain, where they made extensive use of the direct route through the pupil–teacher system (a form of school-based apprenticeship).[130] Primary schoolteaching and veterinary medicine recruited many petit-bourgeois children in the French countryside during the Second Empire, for these professions, unlike others, could be followed without moving to larger towns, [131] but entry into such newer professions was everywhere easier than into those where social groups already in control had to be displaced. A relatively lower status for such professions was the unavoidable consequence.

The patterns of movement examined in this chapter are essential to an understanding of the social layers of the petite bourgeoisie, their ambitions and anxieties, and above all questions of petit-bourgeois identity. No social group is ever homogeneous, least of all classes,[132] but whether a group characterised by a considerably fluctuating membership can be seen as a coherent social entity remains problematic. The notion of a demographic core is relevant here, a relatively stable component within a greater flux, because we have identified continuities and stabilities that were the basis of petit-bourgeois social, professional and political organisations. John Goldthorpe has taken the notion of a core identity one step further, suggesting that the fact that people enter, leave and then re-enter the twentieth-century petite bourgeoisie through their working lives indicates a milieu that might have been economically precarious but which remained highly desirable, for some people at least. His conclusion, that the 'snapshot' approach presented in inter-generational mobility tables suggests a lower association between petit-bourgeois position and specific individuals and families than actually prevails, proposes widening the notion of a class core to include those not currently in a petit-bourgeois position but who regard their (or presumably their children's) absence as merely temporary.[133] According to this perspective, our consideration of mobility, aspirations and stability might not preclude a petit-bourgeois identity, so much as indicate the mechanisms which gave it a very specific character. If we are to go beyond that characterisation, however, we have to explore the social relations of the nineteenth-century petite bour-geoisie: their relations in the town, the nature of petit-bourgeois cultural and associational identity, and the emergence of a petit-bourgeois political consciousness. Given the contradictory structural position of petits bourgeois within emerging industrial capitalist societies, it is in these fields that the questions surrounding petit-bourgeois identity can best be answered.

5

THE FAMILY
Images and necessities

Small shopkeeping ... does not destroy family feeling. The whole family takes part in it: all its members have their role and make themselves useful . . . . The wife keeps the books, the husband sells, and the children deliver to customers' homes. No division of labour is more natural and moralising, no co-operative society is so harmonious, and nowhere is so little energy wasted, or the organisation so elementary and flexible. Above all, no association is more democratic, for the family, fully fashioned as it is by the hand of nature, is thus the most basic of institutions.[1]

These comments by a Belgian Social Catholic towards the end of the nineteenth century were an idealisation, but they remind us of the importance of the family to an understanding of the petite bourgeoisie. The concept of the family enterprise was not primarily about inheritance, but about a business world in which family was intimately involved. In the course of the nineteenth century social ideology came to attribute the earning of income to individuals, and essentially to men. This was a poor reflection of the reality for most families in society, but the growth of proletarian labour outside the home on the one hand, and bourgeois ideals of feminine domesticity on the other, combined to make it appear a powerful prism through which to observe the world. However, the vision made even less sense for the petite bourgeoisie than for other social groups: in the world of small enterprise family and business were bound inextricably together.

'In this business you have to be a couple, and firmly attached', insisted a Parisian café-owner, born in the Aubrac and, like a good many of his fellow Auvergnats who had migrated to the capital, combining the café with a tobacconist and coal-dealing business.[2] The owners of small enterprises were indeed more likely to be married than other sections of the occupied population. In mid-nineteenth century London a mere 12 per cent of male shopkeepers were unmarried (in comparison with 31 per cent of adult men as a whole), while in 1881 male shopkeepers over the age of 50 had by far the lowest rate of bachelorhood of any occupational category.[3] German master artisans in 1880 were far more likely to be married than other men of the same age.[4] Marriage was intimately bound up with independence, originally the passage from journeyman to master's status in the traditional world of the guild-based crafts, but marriage and setting up went together long after the guild structures had lost their influence, and strongly characterised shop-keepers for whom guild experience was less significant. German and Austrian evidence, however, cautions against oversimplifying the relationship between corporate traditions and the frequency of marriage. On the one hand, marriage was becoming increasingly common during the second half of the eighteenth century amongst journeymen artisans.[5] On the other hand, the guilds themselves and local government acted to restrain marriage, linking the right to open an enterprise to the availability of resources as well as to the honourable family origin of the bride-to-be.[6] The traditional link between mastership, municipal rights, and the establishment of a family continued, and was reinforced by economic necessity. Running a workshop or a shop was generally a family affair.

For many, this binding together of family and enterprise evokes the continuing power of a pre-industrial pattern within the world of small business. The Austrian historian Josef Ehmer, however, has questioned that equation between artisanat, family production, and the importance of the family unit.[7] A study of household structure, work patterns and continuity between generations amongst Austrian artisans, led him to conclude that the fundamental artisanal institution under the *ancien régime* was not the family but the guild. Guild rather than family determined the transfer of the business between generations, while the labour needs of the enterprise were met by apprentices, journeymen and servants rather than by the master's wife or sons. These sons served their apprenticeship in other households, and travelled elsewhere as journeymen, and if they themselves became masters then it was by inheriting influence and resources rather than craft and workshop. This priority of guild over family changed during the nineteenth century, for the more prosperous trades, with a greater tendency for sons to stay in the workshop, and to inherit what might now genuinely be seen as the family enterprise. According to Ehmer, these trends towards family labour and family inheritance in the better trades reveal not the continuity of a pre-industrial tradition, but the adoption of a bourgeois family model in the face of the declining influence of the corporation, the reduction in apprentices and journeymen living in the household, and the subsequent spread amongst more prosperous master artisans of an individualistic and family-based conception of property. The family-based artisanal enterprise, in central Europe at least, represented innovation rather than tradition.

While the Swedish artisanat passed through a similar process,[8] it remains difficult to assess the European extent of this transition from guild household to family household. Parisian artisans and traders were by the eighteenth century using the contacts of neighbourhood and trade to place sons and often daughters in apprenticeships, suggesting that guild influence was already weakening in the face of wider social networks.[9] In any case, although Ehmer raises important questions about the character of the 'traditional' artisanal family, the distinctions should not be overstated. Guild and family were closely connected in eighteenth-century Europe. The guild would oversee the education of apprentices and journeymen, celebrate the *rites de passage* of the master's family, protect widows and generally tie together corporation, household and family. This may not be the traditional conception of family labour and family inheritance, but even in the guild period the household, containing both family and employees, was deeply involved with the production process. The practice of sending sons into other small enterprise households rather than retaining them in the family enterprise, although partially a central European characteristic, was widespread through much of Europe before the middle of the nineteenth century.[10] It was part of a larger process of journeymen migration which was concerned on the one hand to relieve pressures on the local labour market (especially where stable married journeymen were the norm), and on the other, to maintain a high level of skill, especially in the luxury trades.[11] For artisanal sons, leaving the family enterprise meant that the values and status of an artisanal position could be assured independent of any particular inheritance, while tightening the connections between different artisanal households. It was a systematic practice amongst the tailors of Turin during the first half of the eighteenth century, and the simultaneous presence of apprentices and journeymen in households from which sons were departing precludes absence of work as an explanation. The aim was rather 'to ease the tensions bound up in the inheritance of the workshop, while securing more solid alliances for both the son and the family'.[12] Nevertheless, as guilds disappeared or narrowed in function, and as the world of craft production became more unequal, so the family indeed became increasingly important, in terms of both family labour and the aspiration to inheritance. The downward diffusion of a bourgeois family model is not the principal explanation: structural changes, the gradual decline of living-in labour and the narrowing of households, and the changing role of the couple, all combined to alter the small enterprise family. In any case, the aspiration to inheritance meant different things for those in prospering trades compared with those whose trade was in decline. In the former, it would be a sign of social success to continue in one's father's trade, as with the metal workers in a study of Esslingen. For the textile workers in the same town by the middle of the nineteenth century, however, family continuity was accepted with resignation, in a declining trade which could not provide the resources to turn to other occupations.[13] Inheritance had ambiguous meanings, coloured by a wider framework of expectations. In contrast to the central European case examined by Ehmer, the family firm in western Europe often experienced the decline of corporations as the basis for diversification in family occupations. For the master artisans and retailers of the southern French town of Montauban, the abolition of corporations and the new inheritance laws that went with the Revolutionary and Napoleonic periods combined to effect a significant shift in inheritance practice. The patrimonial property of the *ancien régime*, where a small business was bound up with the rights of mastership and public status, gave way to family inheritance that was narrowed to more formal possessions. The family enterprise came in this context to be seen as a way to generate resources for children as a whole rather than a resource which was itself to be preserved and transmitted to a single heir. It was a setting in which wives became more important in the business, as the core relationship of the enterprise became the married couple, rather than father and son.[14]

BUSINESS SPACE, FAMILY SPACE

The bourgeois family model was in any case less relevant to the small-enterprise household which was, in contrast to that of bourgeois, professionals, civil servants and white-collar employees alike, characterised by close links between the spheres of production and reproduction, between business space and private space. This overlapping of space was not simply the tumbling together of domestic and work life in cramped and struggling families. At its most extreme in the pressurised space of the small corner shop or in the crowded workrooms of the *canuts* in Lyon, it was a characteristic of most small enterprise. The case of the locksmith Friedrich Hemminger in Esslingen shows the cost in terms of family accommodation. The large furnace he installed meant reducing to a mere 56 square metres the space available for kitchen, living room and bedrooms.[15] The mingling of family and home seemed as inescapable culturally as it was economically, and the alternatives were difficult to imagine: Lyonnais silk-weavers continued to set up family workshops even in bleak and depressed times because the stability of marriage seemed to be built around them.[16] The unattractive alternatives would fracture a comfortable world, as with the baker in a small Kent town in England at the start of the twentieth century who could not hide his contempt for a fellow tradesman who had left the accommodation above his shop for a gloomy and demanding house. 'Spent his savings to buy this,' the baker complained. 'Got to keep a servant to run it. Next thing you know he'll be trying to sell it.' The baker was unwilling to contemplate such a move. 'He was snug and happy there and saw no point in spending money to be made uncomfortable.'[17]

If the wealthy European business and professional bourgeoisie separated workplace from home in the course of the nineteenth century, most precociously in Britain where districts such as Birmingham's Edgbaston and Glasgow's Kelvinside stood testimony to the simultaneous desire for distance and domesticity, it was a process that touched the petite bourgeoisie but little.[18] This was necessarily due to a lack of resources. When the French sociologist Paul de Rousiers visited a successful small Birmingham tool-maker in the 1890s, he found a comfortable lifestyle but workshop and home still linked.

> He was, in fact, at home, for the workshop, the other buildings surrounding the court, the shop which bounded one side of the porch, the neat well-cared-for dwelling, the little bit of garden with its walls covered by creepers, were all his own property.[19]

This combination of workshop and home is well established in nineteenth-century industry: in the metal trades of the English Midlands, the workshop was usually in the dwelling itself or an outhouse attached to it, while the tinsmiths of Lyon, irrespective of income, would have their workshop and shop looking out on to a court with the living accommodation at the side or above the work premises. The court structure, in which household space and productive space converge, recurs across much of Europe.[20] In the small and still rural town of Esslingen during the first decades of the nineteenth century, the general rule for artisanal housing was a two-storey building, the first devoted to the workshop and perhaps stables, the second to living space for one or more families.[21] Its presence amongst better-established firms is important, because it was in the marginal trades that the identification of household and work was normally commented upon: for example, garret masters in the cabinet-making and tailoring workshops of mid-century London, or the matchmakers of Niort in western France who worked and lived in a single room.[22] Between the two extremes, and typical of those sectors of small enterprise organised by merchant capital, were the two-roomed apartments in the large tenement blocks on the slopes of Croix-Rousse to which the Lyon silk industry moved in the course of the early nineteenth century from its humbler location in the old town, and where the masters organised their complex domestic and working space. In the one large room would stand four looms, worked by the *chef d'atelier*, his wife, a journeyman and an apprentice; and alongside them a large table and a stove for cooking. At night the beds were pulled out from under the table, and the looms moved aside to convert the room into a bedroom for the children and the employees, while the couple slept in the smaller room.[23]

The mixing of domestic and private space was even more common in retailing, where the family almost invariably lived above or at the side of the shop.[24] Lock-up shops appeared slowly, even in England where sub-urbanisation was most strong. In a large city like Birmingham even the more prosperous retailers in the main central shopping area continued to live alongside or above the business in the middle of the century. As late as 1911, when one in seven shops in the London district of Camberwell were lock-up premises, the bulk of these were branches of multiple chains.[25] Long opening hours and close attention to customers meant that most shopkeepers had to be almost continuously available – a requirement that both created and divided the movements for the early closing of shops in the later decades of the century. The Greig family built up a successful dairy business in the Holborn district of central London, and the accumulation of savings and the lure of a suburban lifestyle took them out to a four-storey house with a large garden which they bought in Hornsey. The Holborn shop was open for long hours, and the move was only possible because Hannah's two brothers continued to live above the shop, looked after by one or other of their sisters. The family gathered together in Hornsey only on Sundays.[26]

In most shops, there was a continual movement between residential space and business space, especially for the women and children. One daughter of a small Lancashire shopkeeper remembered that 'I never knew anyone burn so many meals, every day you went in our kitchen we had a pan soaking that was burnt, every day. Because every day she was in the shop and forgot the meal.'[27] This inter-weaving of space could be reinforced by the inter-weaving of activities, above all in public houses, cafés and many food shops where items for sale would often be prepared in the family kitchen. The world of the shop, even more than that of most urban workshops, was one where family and business were hard to separate physically. The typical housing for small shopkeepers in Niort consisted of two rooms, the first opening on to the street and acting as the shop, the other a back living room which led into a courtyard and the stairs to the bedrooms, a pattern repeated in the north-German city of Bremen.[28] Larger shops may have enjoyed more space, but the consequences of proximity were the same. One substantial English draper was remembered by his son as always mentally in the shop, even at meal times. 'Even when he sat down he was still, as it were, attached by some invisible thread to the activities of the shop.'[29]

This fusion of separate spaces was but one aspect of the reluctance to conceptualise separately the spheres of business and of private life. The two worlds fused mentally in the accounting procedures of many small enterprises. Household and business expenditure had once been jointly reckoned in the larger bourgeois world, but the early nineteenth century saw the growth of distinct accounting methods. These made least headway with the owners of small enterprise, amongst whom it was hard to establish even elementary book-keeping. Frank Farmer and his wife, with the help of their young daughter, ran a double-fronted drapery, millinery and hosiery shop in east London. When accountants reported on the business in 1888 to assess the amount of compensation when the shop was demolished in a road-widening scheme, they found the account book confusing. 'We are informed that the amount entered as Takings is the money left in the till at the end of each day after various payments for housekeeping and other payments have been made.'[30] The practice, commonly found in all but the better-established of enterprises, rested on a genuine mixing of household and business in the minds of petits bourgeois, above all retailers. Only one in four respondents to the Landry Inquiry in France just before the First World War said that retailers used regular accounting procedures, while only seventy of the 647 respondents said that the precise accounting requirements of the Commercial Code were followed. We must take care with such findings, for wholesalers and social reformers alike were keen to criticise shopkeepers' accounting practices, agreeing that their problems were caused not by competition, but by the absence of professional training and skill. The reply of the President of the *Tribunal de Commerce* of Alais (Gard) is fairly typical. 'The organisation of accounts,' he observed 'is nearly always inadequate. As a result, the shopkeeper does not know the exact situation he is in, nor the state of his business.'[31]

The explanation lies in the way that the business was conceived as a source of direct consumption rather than a distinct enterprise that would yield a calculable profit. Charles Booth's investigator looked at a small general shop in a working-class district of London.

> An attempt was made, at my request, to separate the two accounts by keeping two purses, and letting the house pay for all its supplies, but it failed; and what the house used was never considered part of the takings of the shop.[32]

The practice reflects a reality which better accounting procedures might have concealed: with living-in employees in some trades, family labour, and the employment of servants to release family members to work in the enterprise, it was unrealistic to distinguish between household expenditure and business expenditure.

'YOU HAVE TO BE A COUPLE'

Family commitment to the shop or workshop was built upon the couple, as the Auvergnat café-owner recognised. Women were not only partners, of course, and we have seen the extent of retail enterprises headed by women, as in Bremen where in 1904 they held 30 per cent of all the town's shops.[33] Many more were recorded under the husband's name while in reality the responsibility of the wife. They were increasingly the less stable businesses, and do not challenge the nineteenth-century trend towards the marginalisation of women in small enterprise. Their presence was more secure a century earlier when a town like Colchester boasted substantial millinery and clothing shops run by single women in the most prestigious shopping streets. These were usually enterprises taken on at specific points of the life cycle when their owners stood outside a family economic unit, as young unmarried women or as widows, but they were nonetheless viable and often successful businesses, unlike many of those owned by widows a century later.[34] Women's ownership of good independent shops declined during the first half of the nineteenth century, with the marginalisation of women traders, and fewer women's artisanal businesses in trades such as tailors, saddlers, whitesmiths, and butchers. By the middle of the century these had narrowed to the needle trades, and women's independent enterprise in general was limited to the more marginal levels of retailing, though florists remained a continuing exception. In Bremen, women were important in the fruit and vegetable trade and haberdashery, as well as in women's clothing shops: dresses, hats, ribbons and so on.[35] There was thus both marginalisation and specialisation. As businesses needed credit links to larger traders and suppliers, and as ideas of femininity and separate spheres became entrenched in western Europe, so women's enterprises found it harder to command the necessary resources with which to grow.

Women nevertheless remained essential to family businesses, as the officials who devised the British population censuses knew well. In 1851 they required that the wives of specified tradesmen – primarily innkeepers, publicans, shoemakers, butchers and 'shopkeepers' – be recorded as innkeeper's wife, butcher's wife, and so on, even when no occupation had been declared on the form. The list was thought at the time to be far too limited.[36] The role of wives in family enterprises varied from production in certain household-based crafts, through responsibility for sales and records in many artisanal trades,[37] to an equal place in many retail shops. In addition, they often managed large households of living-in employees and family workers for a major part of the nineteenth century.

The silk-weavers of Lyons have already alerted us to those branches of textile production where husband, wife and employees shared an intensive involvement in both productive and domestic aspects of the household. The wife organised and serviced the household while also spending a good deal of time working the loom.[38] Wives were also widely involved in production in shoemaking and tailoring. In general, however, the gender division of labour was clearer in artisanal than in retail enterprises. By the early nineteenth century women were excluded from formal apprenticeships outside what were seen as women's trades, and therefore tended to concentrate on subsidiary tasks or on the business rather than the production side of the enterprise. In the artisanal trades of *ancien régime* Paris, the wife was already taking responsibility for the shop, cash desk, business records, and the payment of employees.[39] In sub-contracting trades under the *Verlag* system, the wife would often carry the goods produced to the merchant and negotiate with him over issues such as price, quality, and colour. The result, as in the ribbon-weaving workshops of Saint-Etienne, was an equality based on a specialisation of functions.[40] The workshop unit in most trades was a group of skilled men – master, apprentices, journeymen, possibly sons – and even in the tailoring workshops of early nineteenth-century Paris the wife would become fully involved in production only in peak periods, while taking responsibility at other times for sewing hems and buttons, handling cash, and managing the productive household.[41]

The retail sector rarely produced the well-established gender division of labour which characterised much artisanal production. It certainly existed in more prosperous shops, as with the south London cheesemonger and grocer whose wife worked on the cash desk.[42] It also existed in trades where artisanal and retail activities were combined. In the butchery trade, with the husband needing to be away at markets and abattoirs for long periods, the wife not only served and took cash, but often cut the meat, especially in shops without employees.[43] Bakery provides the most striking example, with the husband baking with his apprentice or journeymen, and the wife running the retail side. Their responsibilities were as distinct as the times of their working day, in a division of labour which in France has survived until the present.[44] The *boulangère* was in this setting vital to the success of the enterprise, which is why French bakers, although themselves often of peasant origin, frequently married women from retail or artisanal backgrounds. It also explains why they remarried so quickly after widowhood.[45] René Barjavel remembered his mother's marriage to a baker in turn-of-the-century Nyons.

> Marie was ... gay, hardworking, and skilful, knew the value of every piece of work, and how hard it is to make an ear of corn or a penny grow. In spite of her young years she learned rapidly how to organise the working of this small family and business unit. She kept the house, the shop, and the books of customers who only paid at the end of the month, and she cooked, cut and sewed dresses, and in every free moment she read.[46]

The majority of shops, however, saw no such clear division of labour. 'Grocery was an occupation for couples,' explained Faure in his study of Paris.[47] The same could be said of most trades, reinforcing the overlapping of space with an integration of roles. 'With an iron will and the involvement of my wife,' explained a German small greengrocer at the start of the twentieth century, 'I have been able to sustain my shop and to make it grow.'[48] Here are additional reasons why marriage was important for setting up. The motives were complex. One was the need for the financial support provided by dowry and family connections. The use of the wife's dowry to finance the purchase or enlargement of a shop was common throughout Europe. In Naples, Teresa Rippo made over 2,000 lire of her dowry to her future husband so that he might purchase furnishings for his grocery shop, 'so that it could develop and grow'.[49] There were further motives, including the classic guild tradition in which an independent household was formed only when master's or burgher's status had been achieved, a practice which survived not only in Germany but also in Sweden, where the great majority of Malmö masters married within one year of their formal status being obtained.[50] The co-incidence of business independence and household independence continued, in a perception of the life-cycle that transcended the guild world in which it had originated. There was, above all, the need to establish a couple as an effective working relationship for running an enterprise. This was not new.

It helps explain why artisans and traders were so over-represented amongst those who used the divorce procedures established by the French Revolution: these were couples who had married in the early years of the Revolution, enticed by radical ideology into what has been called 'the adventure of marrying for love', an adventure entered into without economic calculation.[51] The disasters of their relationships may have been no greater than those of others, but the demands of such marriages, as working and financial partnerships, meant that, if they were ill-founded and if Revolutionary legislation provided a solution, they rapidly fell apart.

The marriage partnership remained crucial to the success of retail enterprise. Paul de Rousiers described in the 1890s the son of a Birmingham toolmaker, himself in the fruit trade, who was marrying the daughter of a clockmaker in the town. She was

> accustomed to mind her father's shop and help him in keeping his books, and quite ready to do the same for her husband. The young man told me with some satisfaction of the commercial aptitudes of his intended wife, on which he founds . . . his hopes of the future.[52]

Many a Parisian artisan or shopkeeper had done the same fifty years before – of heavily provincial origins themselves, they chose wives from the capital's business world. 'Brought up in trade and better educated than her husband, she brought with her both her labour and her skill, and kept a watchful eye on the running of the business.'[53]

The image of family and enterprise bound together, which we encounter in the postcard photographs which retailers had taken of themselves in front of their shops in turn-of-the-century Europe, was thus more than an image for the outside world. The photographs were as much family as business photos, for alongside the male shopkeeper stood wife and children. The couple might be framed by the shop doorway, their children in front of them, and their employees standing at a distance along the shop front. In other pictures, the male butcher, wine merchant or grocer would stand dominating the centre of the photo, asserting the authority of husband, father and employer in enterprises conceived as families, whatever the reality experienced by employees and apprentices. The image of male authority was more firmly asserted in artisanal businesses, where masculinity was bound up with craft work, and women's involvement more readily subordinated. The shops were much more equal, and the photographs – often but by no means always – tell us that.[54] There was nothing new about the patriarchal character of much small enterprise, especially amongst artisans where its heritage has been traced in Germany to the early-modern years, and the indissoluble link between home and work. 'The dominant role of the father, the readily understood order of the house, and the interdependence of the various household members' constituted the most striking characteristics of this family.[55] The family enterprise had long been an unequal one. The involvement of wives helps explain why petit-bourgeois widows more frequently inherited the firm than did their contemporaries among the larger bourgeoisie. Their experience meant that they were in a position to run it themselves. In Bremen at the end of the nineteenth century, amongst those shops run by women which had existed for more than twenty-five years, more than half were being run by widows.[56] The widow might often be directing affairs until the son was in a position to take over.[57] In Britain, where trusts and other legal devices were used by wealthy bourgeois to provide for widows without giving them effective control over either the capital or the business, it was more normal in small business for the widow to inherit outright, and often to continue the enterprise.[58] Yet male authority need not vanish with the husband's death. Thomas Carr was a fairly prosperous draper with a shop and house in south London's Old Kent Road. The fact that his will left the buildings, the business and all the property to his wife, Ellen, who was his sole executrix, followed the petit-bourgeois norm, but he proceeded to use most of the will (drawn up in 1858 some eighteen years before his death) to give her detailed instructions as to what she might do with the property: to maintain and insure the houses; to accept a good offer for the business should it be forthcoming; to invest the proceeds in government stock; how much she should spend on another house to live in should the issue arise; while all the time insisting that she would of course be free to make her own decisions.[59]

The role of wives in the family enterprise created its own difficulties for socially aspirant petits bourgeois. J. D. Milne observed in 1857, in relation to the British census's acknowledgement of the wife's active business role, that this was 'a supposition inconsistent . . . with the present arrangements of the middle classes, where a wife takes no part whatever in the business affairs of her husband'.[60] As Davidoff and Hall have noted, 'the contributions to the enterprise through women's labour were contradicted by her role in displaying rank through the appearance of a non-working lifestyle'.[61] The ideology of domesticity grew powerfully in early nineteenth-century Britain, insisting that the wife should be detached from the corrupting world of business and placed in the moral private sphere of home and family, and it found its parallels elsewhere in Europe.[62] The separation of business and home which became central to bourgeois culture was rarely feasible in small-enterprise families. This would have mattered little to those with limited aspirations. Yet the ideology was widely diffused: through literature, education, and religion, and through the fact that many a daughter of a farmer or tradesman spent a period as a domestic servant in more substantial households before her marriage. The conflict between the ideal of the wife at home and the realities described in this chapter could produce tensions for aspirant petit-bourgeois families. The wife might genuinely withdraw, as in the successful gentleman's outfitters in the Oxfordshire market town of Woodstock around 1900, where the fact that the house and the shop adjoined had little effect on the link of family to business: there was no connecting door, and the father ran the shop with shop assistants and without family labour.[63] The ideal was more commonly expressed as an aspiration, as in those postcard photographs where the wife and children were placed firmly in the domestic space – looking out of windows above the shop, standing in the doorway to the residential area, dressed in smart clothing and without aprons or other signs of work. It was not only in Britain that women's work in the business clashed with a vision of the world in which it was excluded. This is graphically portrayed in the autobiography of A. Muscetta, who was both a shopkeeper and manager of the station buffet at Avellino. He recounted how, on seeing his wife working in the buffet, he took refuge in the toilets to weep at such humiliation. 'I wanted to increase my work a hundred times over to avoid having to witness such a sight again.' An Italian novel of the end of the century echoed that anxiety over the wife's labour.

> Luisella, for sure, did not look down on the life of a shopkeeper. But she would have liked to have been the lady of the house and not of the shop, a housewife and not a seller of sweets, a mother to her family and not a seller in a shop.[64]

This tension between the ideal of separate spheres and the reality of the wife's labour helps explain the stress on respectable behaviour and lifestyle that was such a stifling feature of petit-bourgeois families by the close of the century.

Members of the family and domestic servants were not only cheap, they could be called upon at peak moments of the day or week, and their flexibility reduced the need for more than the minimum employed labour force. Family labour could also be coerced by pressures far beyond those to which wage labour was susceptible. This intensity of family labour reached its most extreme form when artisanal trades responded to crisis by turning in on the family. The Lyon silk-weaving industry was classically built around a household unit that included apprentices and hired journeymen, but this was challenged by the crisis of the 1850s and 1860s, when competition from factories and rural production led to intense pressure to reduce costs. The result was a retreat into family labour: 35 per cent of households of *chefs d'atelier* contained only family members in 1847, but by 1866 the figure was 63 per cent. The exclusively family workshop was here a defensive response to crisis, one reminiscent of peasant family strategies. It produced a high degree of self-exploitation in the struggle to defend the craft, the family, and some faith in 'independence'.[65] German artisans used far more family labour during the late nineteenth-century depression, especially those in the food-producing, textile and clothing trades.[66] It was a common response to crisis.

The intensification of family labour in crisis is an extreme manifestation of the involvement of family workers in small enterprise, as the memories of those brought up in petit-bourgeois households testify. The historian A.L.

Rowse remembers his childhood in a Devon village grocer's shop at the end of the nineteenth century.

> Saturday I came to detest most of all, for as I grew bigger I had my 'work' to do: there was chopping sticks to light the fire with through the week, weighing up quarter-pecks and half-pecks of flour in the stores and bringing them over to the shop, measuring out lamp-oil at intervals all day for people, sometimes – deepest humiliation of all – going round the village selling oranges, at the end of the day making up books and bills. That was my 'work'.[67]

Children were less involved in artisanal production than in retailing, outside the more marginal enterprises and outwork. A good artisanal workshop required more formal preparation and often more sustained labour. Yet the presence of children – certainly of sons, for the workshop was generally a more masculine world than the retail shop – was long established, notwithstanding Ehmer's central European pattern. According to his son's memoirs, Jacques Ménétra was anxious to keep both his son and son-in-law within the family's glaziery workshop in mid-eighteenth-century Paris. The guild was important but Parisian artisanal trades were already precarious and good business sense lay behind the family's increasingly tense relationships.[68] The role of children continued, out of necessity in the poorer trades and out of choice in the more successful ones. The accountants estimating profits at the time of shop demolition in London included in their calculations the notional wages of assistants who would have been employed had family labour not been used,[69] indicating the non-payment of the latter, but in good artisanal workshops sons would probably be paid. The son of a Birmingham toolmaker received thirty shillings per week in the 1890s, a third of which he handed over to his mother as a contribution to housekeeping expenses.[70] Family labour and its informality were inevitably stronger in retailing – in Germany in 1907 54 per cent of those working in commerce were members of the owner's family, a figure which would have been even larger had wholesale enterprises been excluded.[71] Even small local chains could rely on family labour. Daniel Noel, a tinsmith in the London working-class district of Hoxton, had three shops selling tin goods and utensils in 1886, all managed by members of his family with no employees other than errand boys.[72]

FAMILY SIZE AND HOUSEHOLD STRUCTURE

Care is needed, when considering the demographic contours of these families, to ensure that definitive conclusions are not drawn from what are no more than scattered indicators. Nevertheless, there appears to have been a precocious decline in completed family size amongst shopkeepers and master artisans. In eighteenth-century France, there had certainly been very high fecundity amongst the urban artisanat, shopkeepers and middling merchants, though high mortality rates reduced completed family size, and the age spread and departures from the household meant that the actual size of the co-residential group was rarely as large as that suggested by birth rates.[73] The case of the Lyonnais butchers is the most remarkable, with half of them having children at annual intervals throughout the wife's fertile years. Twelve to sixteen births per family were the typical pattern. Yet the wife's labour was central to the enterprise, and therein lies at least part of the explanation. Garden argues that the extensive use by artisans and shopkeepers of wet-nurses helps to explain their high birth rate, reducing the maternal breast-feeding which limited fertility.[74] A downward trend began in France even in the eighteenth century. In Rouen completed master artisan families fell from six and a half in the early decades of the century to under five by the end.[75] Even the Lyonnais butchers were by then extending birth intervals in the later years of marriage.[76]

The fertility decline amongst the European petite bourgeoisie by the end of the nineteenth century was part of a wider demographic transition which affected all social groups. Declining fertility, which can be seen in France by the early nineteenth century, did not appear significantly in most western European countries until the closing decades of the century. Extensive research on the geography and timing of this decline has not been matched by analysis of its social and occupational composition, though occupational change and ambiguity of title mean that it is not easy to account for these variables in demographic analysis. In any case, historical demographers exploring the transition from natural fertility have been more concerned with examining data at the ecological than at the individual level.[77] Occupation was probably not the most significant variable in European fertility decline, for cultural–linguistic–religious patterns seem more effective as a way of identifying trends, but it is one about which we need to know more.[78]

The evidence nevertheless suggests that the petite bourgeoisie was reducing family size in advance of most other social groups.[79] Retailers were the second most Malthusian social group in France during the second half of the century, after the liberal professions, white-collar workers and civil servants.[80] Local studies confirm this pattern: in the small industrial town of Saint-Chamond, an early downward movement in fertility in the later ages of marriage amongst the retail and commercial middle class was converted by the marriages of the 1860s into a strikingly low total marital fertility rate.[81] The German petite bourgeoisie was similarly reducing family size. In the southern town of Esslingen, the petit-bourgeois trend was in advance of the decline of fertility in the population as a whole: a clear difference appears in the demographic behaviour of master artisans and peasants between the middle of the eighteenth and the middle of the nineteenth centuries. The average age of the woman at the time of her last birth fell in artisanal families from 36 years 8 months to 34 years 7 months, while it stayed higher and fell little amongst peasant farmers (39.0, 38.4). The average number of children fell from 6.6 to

6.1 amongst artisans, but stayed at 7.8 amongst peasants,[82] though that might indicate a rural–urban as well as an occupational divide. Spree has found that the retail and craft petite bourgeoisie throughout Germany was by the later nineteenth century reducing its family size faster than most other social groups.[83]

The limited evidence available for Britain suggests a similar trend. While most occupations in England and Wales experienced a decline in fertility from the 1860s,[84] the 1911 Census of Fertility, which must be used with considerable caution, suggests a particularly acute fall in fertility amongst a broadly-defined lower middle class from the 1880s, second only to that of the professional and upper business class.[85] A study of Sheffield has emphasised that the town's fertility decline began amongst the small business, teacher and white-collar lower middle class. The most dramatic change was experienced by shopkeepers whose control of fertility in the later years of the reproductive period had by the 1870s developed into spacing out births from the early years of the marriage as well.[86]

Not only does petit-bourgeois family size appear to have been falling, but the petite bourgeoisie occupied an advanced position within the demographic transition. In contrast to the protoindustrial family model, with which one might have anticipated similarities, neither the age of setting up an independent household, nor the need for extensive child labour, would have encouraged high birth rates. On the contrary, the situation of the nineteenth-century petite bourgeoisie encouraged smaller families. In the first place, there was the need to avoid losing the wife's labour for extended periods. Owners of small enterprise might dispatch babies to relatives, or they might use a wet-nurse (and the Lyon butchers have indicated one aberrant consequence of this practice), but pregnancies, childbirth and the rearing of young children at times of high infant mortality would all remove the woman from the family enterprise. There were also broader social imperatives at work, above all those already encountered when discussing mobility: the need to guarantee resources for the next generation, to assure children's future through property or education, and to secure good marriages. The more prosperous non-guild trades of mid-nineteenth-century Vienna, such as innkeepers and builders, thus combined a high continuity in male succession with low fertility in a strategy devised to protect family resources and opportunities.[87]

The petit-bourgeois family was often part of a larger household. The single-person households headed by an unmarried or widowed person were essentially a feature of poorer small enterprises, of retailing rather than artisanal trades, and above all of shops headed by women. In mid-nineteenth-century London 93 per cent of male shopkeepers were in two-parent families, but only 19 per cent of female ones. The majority of the latter were widows. Non-parent or one-parent households certainly existed, but these were far less common in small enterprise than in most other non-elite groups. London shopkeepers had far fewer households in 1851 where no family connections were present (9 per cent) than did the population of the city as a whole (15 per cent)

The household of Andrew Rogers, a master baker in the St Pancras district of north London, is closer to our image of the complex small enterprise household. He was thirty years old at the time of the 1851 census. His household contained his wife but no children; a foreman baker and three journeymen bakers, all unmarried and called 'servants' because the census did not distinguish between household and business employees; one female servant; a shopwoman, who perhaps worked in the shop but might simply have been a lodger; Andrew Rogers's sister-in-law, described as a 'visitor'; and an 18-year-old cousin with the occupation of governess. Here was a household of ten people, which combined the family, business employees, a domestic servant, and wider kin.

Was this the classic small enterprise household or an exaggerated version of an older household structure already in decline? It was probably a little of both. Shopkeeper and master artisan households tended to be both larger and more complex than those of either the bourgeoisie or the working class, characteristically including employees in the enterprise, one or two domestic servants whose role was more ambiguous than their title suggests and perhaps members of the wider family. Amongst the Glasgow middle class in mid-century, the households that contained only nuclear family members (apart from any domestic servants) were far more common among merchants, manufacturers and clerks than among the owners of small retail or artisanal enterprises.[88] A look at Andrew Rogers's fellow London shopkeepers in 1851 provides a more detailed picture of these complex households. The average size of shopkeeper-headed households, with 5.27 members, was substantially larger than the 4.30 for all London households. Who were these additional household members? They were partly a larger number of non-conjugal kin (0.34 per household compared to 0.23), and slightly more visitors and lodgers, but the main difference was the presence of both business and domestic employees (0.91 compared to 0.38). The shopkeeper households were thus distinctive: 55 per cent of London households were made up of related people only, but only 37 per cent of shopkeeper households were. The complexity of these households derived from two related characteristics – the labour needs of a trade and its general level of prosperity. The simple households which were identical with the family group were found amongst the poorer trades, such as fishmongers (67 per cent family only), greengrocers (60 per cent), and general dealers (77 per cent). Mixed households, on the other hand, were over-represented amongst more prosperous trades such as drapers (18 per cent family only), wine merchants (17 per cent), licensed victuallers (32 per cent) and chemists and druggists (30 per cent).

Petit-bourgeois households, with their diverse labour needs and a tendency towards resident employees were larger and more diverse than those of either workers or substantial bourgeois, but the second half of the nineteenth century saw a reduction begin, a shedding of some of the non-family members, and the emergence of the more introspective and narrowly-based petit-bourgeois family of twentieth-century Europe. The transition in Germany from households that included non-family members to a more restricted household, with journeymen living out and fewer resident servants, was well established by the late nineteenth century.[89] The Swedish town of Orebro indicates the same trend, with mean household size amongst shop-keepers falling from 5.7 in 1850 to 4.4 in 1890, and even more sharply amongst craft masters from 7.4 to 5.4. The reduction was almost entirely due to a radical decline in the number of both business and domestic employees living in the household.[90]

This pattern was repeated all over Europe, as the classic small enterprise household was slowly transformed. The presence of apprentices and journey-men in the master's household was a characteristic of artisanal production throughout eighteenth-century Europe, though it weakened with the decline of guilds. In its classic form journeymen would wait until they were masters before marrying and forming households of their own. The master headed a patriarchal household which subsumed within it a range of both household and business servants who were in theory subordinate in the same way as were wife and children. Civic, legal, economic and social status were bound together, and only when able to set up in his own enterprise could the journeyman make the transition to adult independence. The structure was strongest where the corporate system sustained it – Sweden and much of Germany until the middle of the nineteenth century – but its persistence in France, Belgium and even Britain, and its extension into the purely retail trades, indicate the benefits of such a household even where guilds did not dictate it. The presence of apprentices, journeymen and shop assistants within the household bound together even more closely the experience of the family and the life of the enterprise.

The second half of the nineteenth century saw an uneven decline. In the German town of Oldenburg it was shoemakers, tailors and masons who housed their journeymen, rather than the butchers and bakers whom one might have predicted. Resident apprentices were most common amongst carpenters, shoemakers, tailors and smiths.[91] In much of Germany, living-in apprentices remained the norm until the end of the century, even though the proportion of resident journeymen was falling.[92] The practice went into decline in Orebro once guilds had been abolished and Swedish indus-trialisation got under way: 64 per cent of retail and 78 per cent of craft households had employees resident in 1850, but only 24 per cent and 31 per cent in 1890.[93] Journeymen in late nineteenth-century Vienna generally lived apart from their masters, but even when they lived in it was as cash-paying *Bettgeher* rather than as members of a family community.[94] Britain dispensed with living-in far earlier – it was close to extinction in Edinburgh by mid-century: in 1851 only 9 per cent of retail households, 10 per cent of craft-retailers (e.g. shoemakers and tailors), and 2 per cent of purely craft households contained resident apprentices or journeymen.[95]

There was no single explanation for the progressive departure of journeymen from their masters' households. A growing journeymen consciousness made workers unwilling to accept this particular form of subordination; the declining chances of becoming a master meant that journeymen were less willing to delay marriage; and some masters wanted the status attached to a family-centred household. In certain settings residence nonetheless remained strong, and actually grew in branches of the expanding retail sector. Only one in every seven employees of Lyon butchers were living away from the shop in 1866 – and that proportion actually fell over the next forty years.[96] With its long hours and women employees, retailing sustained living-in longer than did the mass of artisanal trades. Charles Booth was told that it remained dominant, though in decline, in the London grocery trade around 1890.[97] Although nearly a third of Bremen apprentices lived with their employer in 1912, the practice was only really strong in the grocery trade, with its long hours and low wages, and incentives for employers to have staff available at all hours. Indeed, a German survey in 1892 revealed a close correlation between the length of opening hours and the housing of apprentices.[98] Insofar as housing the workforce was continued, it had largely abandoned the ideal of family-based training for future independence, and survived best in labour-intensive retail sectors with long opening hours.

Domestic servants were the other main addition to petit-bourgeois households. In Britain, 'service' designated employment in an agricultural or artisanal household enterprise, and only gradually came to describe purely domestic responsibilities. The census thus used the term 'servant' for those who worked in either sphere, and in mid-nineteenth-century Britain their disproportionate presence in the households of farmers and small petit-bourgeois employers suggests precisely that ambiguity of function.[99] Even specifically domestic servants were often involved in the enterprise, above all if it was a shop. They also released other family members to work in the business. The more prosperous bourgeois who employed domestic servants to support an attractive lifestyle while releasing the wife from domestic work, might be emulated by more successful petits bourgeois, but considerations of money and space limited what was possible. Thus, while 442 master artisan households in Oldenburg in 1870 contained only 162 female domestic servants, there were 373 employed in 235 merchant households.[100]

The employment of domestic servants was not primarily a question of status. Servants could meet life-cycle gaps in the household structure, and could release other family members for remunerative work. The servants one finds in working-class households were not a sign of status aspirations, but a means for wives to be released to earn outside the home.[101] This role was even more important in petit-bourgeois households. Consider the Lyon butcher with a small but thriving enterprise in the bourgeois 6th *arron-*

dissement, whose wife served in the shop and was helped by a servant who did the cooking, the housework and delivering to customers in return for fifty francs per month plus board and lodging.[102] As one English shopkeeper's son recalled, 'mother used to be in the desk, take the money, do the books. There was always a certain amount of housework she had to do but we used to keep two girls.'[103] Or the London patten-maker and dry fish seller in 1847 whose wife worked in the business, and who always had a servant to look after the children.[104] The importance of the wife's involvement in small enterprise made domestic servants necessary at that stage in the life cycle when young children had to be cared for and were too young to contribute their own labour. It is not surprising that domestic servants were more common in retail than in artisanal households, nor that one historian described retailers as 'the most typical servant employer' in mid-nineteenth century Britain.[105] In Glasgow in 1861, 43 per cent of retail households had at least one servant, but only 28 per cent of those in artisanal trades did. The status attached to having a servant was not normally the main consideration. If it had been, then Glasgow's prosperous booksellers with their larger and more highly valued property would have had more servants than the bakers. In fact, the reverse was true, with the latter having an average of 1.0 servants per household compared with the former's 0.5. Bakers, with the wife's responsibilities for the shop and for living-in journeymen, could not have easily functioned without a servant.[106]

The petit-bourgeois household did not lose its non-family residents entirely, but by the end of the nineteenth century it was narrowing down towards its family core. The one group which we have not considered, however, are those we associate with more complex family structures – the presence of kin outside the conjugal group itself. The stem family – with parents and married child in the same household – was exceptionally rare in the artisanal or retail petite bourgeoisie. They comprised fewer than one per cent of all shopkeeper households in mid-nineteenth-century London, and they were no more common elsewhere. The relatively low rate of inheritance of petits-bourgeois enterprises provided no rationale for this complex family form, while the relatively older age-structure of the owners of small enter-prises made it demographically less likely. In any case, the stem family was rare in modern European urban society – if family extensions occurred, they were far more likely to do so laterally rather than between generations.[107]

Wider kin, on the other hand, were more common in nineteenth-century urban households, and in Britain these nieces, siblings, grandchildren and the like were particularly present in the households of the self-employed, small employers and farmers.[108] The reasons included the need for additional labour at specific points of the family life cycle, the taking-in of orphaned relatives, and support for kin migrating to the town. Labour needs seem to have been a strong motive. Of the London shopkeeping trades which in 1851 had disproportionately large numbers of servants, none also had above-average numbers of resident non-conjugal kin. They were most common when shopkeepers were young or old, least when they were in their forties and likely to have older children at home, and married shopkeepers were far less likely to have kin present in the household than those who were single or widowed. In the French town of Givors complex family households were concentrated in specific trades – butchers, bakers, *cafétiers*, grocers – all of which had intensive labour demands.[109] Shopkeepers were more likely to offer a home to such relatives than were master artisans – twice as likely in Glasgow in 1861.[110] The complex, as opposed to the conjugal, family may have been more common amongst petit-bourgeois households than amongst the population as a whole, but it remained the exception. However, census sources exaggerate the dominance of the nuclear-family household by freezing the population on a given day: a much larger proportion of households were complex at some point in their life cycle, as Segalen found amongst peasant households which showed over a forty-year period a fluctuating balance of children, kin, servants and employees, but which maintained a fairly constant number of potential workers over that time.[111] Urban small business was less likely to provide such continuities, of course, but although most petits bourgeois were living in nuclear-family units at any one time, the complex experience remained a real option.[112] In the Dutch industrial town of Tilburg during the second half of the nineteenth century, for example, extended family households were more common amongst the petite bourgeoisie than other social groups, especially so when one considers the number of households established in a longitudinal study as ever being extended.[113] The petit-bourgeois household was a dynamic unit, balancing family, labour and resources. The presence of non-conjugal kin constituted one element within that balance.

The extended family was more generally relevant to economic survival. There were extreme cases, such as the clan-like networks that dominated the butchers' trade of Limoges and whose control was maintained through a policy of tight inter-marriage. Nightly meetings of patriarchs would set the next day's prices.[114] The general importance of kin was more pervasive, whether through partnerships or helping with the starting capital. The wider family played an important role throughout the eighteenth-century business world, with finance, guaranteeing loans, providing business liaisons, and so on, but this slowly receded for the larger bourgeoisie through the century that followed, as more impersonal legal and institutional devices came to serve those needs. The owners of small businesses, on the other hand, remained tied to familial connections for far longer, both for setting up businesses and when things were going badly. A south Wales draper from a peasant family background, with business failing and the spectre of bankruptcy looming in the early 1860s, obtained loans from his father, brother and other kin which enabled him to survive.[115] The help in times of difficulty could go further. The wider reputation of a family was important in securing credit, and a case from the Niort *Tribunal de Commerce* in 1872 shows how influential that could be in a crisis. At a time when lesser bankrupts saw their enterprise liquidated by creditors, the fact that one heavily indebted tradesman came from a family of butchers widely respected in the town secured his long-term creditworthiness. As observed in a previous chapter, he was allowed twenty years to repay his debts.[116] Kin could also ease migrant integration into larger urban centres. Raison-Jourde's excellent study of the Auvergnats in Paris rests on the careful reconstruction of ties of kin, place and enterprise, ties between Paris and the Auvergne, and ties within the capital itself. Networks of kin were essential for setting up, and also for larger purchasing operations. The Parisian businesses of Auvergnats continued to rely on family contacts, showing little interest in the new legal structures that were becoming available.[117]

HARMONY AND INTROSPECTION?

Family, kin and close personal relationships were thus essential to both shop and workshop. As a sense of petit-bourgeois detachment from the popular milieu around them grew towards the end of the century, so too did the intensity of this familial world. The concentration of resources on fewer children, the assertions of a respectability that distanced them from a working class that was more organised and more culturally distinctive, and the anxious insistence on what was special about the world of small enterprise combined to accentuate a lifestyle which had always been centred on the family. Was this one of the distinguishing marks of the nineteenth-century petite bourgeoisie, with the family taking into its embrace outsiders such as journeymen, shop assistants and servants? Perhaps, though we should remember that employees and domestic servants frequently changed employer and that the familial embrace looked warmer from outside than it was in reality.

The evidence for this introspective late nineteenth-century family world comes mostly from Britain, which is probably coincidental, and primarily from retailers, which is not. The demands of a shop on the family were more dominating, more irregular, and more overwhelming than most in artisanal production. Those brought up in petit-bourgeois households recalled the intensity of their introspective world. It was associated in their memory with atmosphere and even smells, for the odour of the shop suffused the small world of children who grew up in it, a world that seemed to be enclosed within those walls rather than opening up on to street and neighbourhood. Norman Hancock was born into a medium-sized west of England drapers, and recalled

> the characteristic smells of the interior of the shop. There was the hot muffled dampish smell of blankets and flannels, the rank farmyard smell of corduroys, and . . . the smell of dyes from the cretonnes and chintzes 'dressed out' round the windows and entrance lobbies.[118]

René Barjavel remembered 'the sweet warm smell of the husks of bran' in the

Nyons bakery shop of his childhood.[119] This classic view of the small business family retreating into a comforting inward-looking home to escape from the disturbing world outside must be treated with caution, because introspection is exaggerated when remembered through the limited vision of the child. Other chapters in this book reveal enough about the wider social relationships, the place in the neighbourhood, and the associational life of petits bourgeois to qualify the intensity of that introspection – but it was a characteristic which increased in the more anxious atmosphere of the later nineteenth century.

The burgeoning importance of photographs emphasises the significance of family in this world, for petits bourgeois seem to have been particularly prominent as photography was popularised from the 1880s.[120] Photographs were gathered in family albums, as well as being used for postcards to be sent to friends, relatives and customers. Surviving postcards proclaim the variety of ties between family and enterprise. The man and wife, the children, the employees, often the pet as well: no-one looking at those photographs could ignore the fact that amongst their various meanings was a powerful statement about family. Photographs were also framed and displayed, as in the Hancock drapery shop where photos of the shop and the family hung in an office upstairs, and where the parlour displayed in silver and stained oak frames photographs of more distant kin.[121]

Family was therefore more than space and work. It was also a force in petit-bourgeois lives that was constructed through images and memory. Cultural introspection was the response not only to fears of the rough world outside, but also to the economic and social imperatives of a demanding small enterprise. These demands did not guarantee a warm family life, as is starkly revealed in the café run by a hard-working Auvergnat couple in Paris.

> After seventeen or eighteen hours of work each day, they would retire
> to their bedroom on the sixth floor. They may have spent all day in the
> cafe, but it would be wrong to speak of a life together. One went to bed
> at one o'clock in the morning, the other got up at half past four.[122]

An extreme case, but it reminds us that the intensity was not that of a comfortable bourgeois family. The home could nevertheless provide a protective domesticity. Helen Corke was born into a shopkeeping family in the 1880s, and had reached the age of eight before being allowed into a neighbour's house.[123] The Vincent family kept a shop and lodging house in a poor docks area of Cardiff, where strict discipline and morality at home were the rule, as the parents sought to isolate their private life from the district around them.[124] This tendency was exacerbated by the later nineteenth-century pressures on small enterprise and on its owners. Blackbourn has argued that the emphasis on respectability, modest revenues and family labour which characterised the German petit-bourgeois family in those years explains the severity, the moral rigidity and the authoritarian patriarchy which was one of the group's most striking characteristics.[125]

The distinctive family atmosphere was thus not some cultural eccentricity, but was rooted in the complex relationship between family, household and enterprise which this chapter has explored. Seen from the outside by those who idealised a threatened world of small enterprise, the family became one of the distinguishing features of the petite bourgeoisie. 'One must not forget', wrote Henri Vouters, a late nineteenth-century Belgian commentator, 'just how important small enterprise is to the maintenance of, and respect for, the family. It is there above all that children can best work with their parents. It prevents the home being disrupted.'[126] Family and labour were seen as bound together in a world of honest effort and close personal relations, where paternal authority in the family was reflected in the patriarchal nature of the business. 'In this way the disciple of St Crispin has the joy of being at home, in the centre of his affections, near his wife and his children,' claimed a report on the Louvain shoemakers in 1904.

> He takes his meals when he chooses. Does he need some relaxation? Engravings hang on the wall, while a song-bird adds a note of gaiety to the severity of the workshop. The shoemaker himself can sing while he works, can glance out at the busy street, can speak to his family. That is why work at home will always be more human than collective labour in a factory .... Having his children in sight he can watch over them, advise them, set them the example of his working life. He can teach them the practice of his trade.[127]

This coincidence of family, morality and work attracted writers and politicians repelled by a proletarian social order which appeared atomised and bereft of either morality or cohesion. As Hector Lambrechts, leading figure in the Social Catholic movement for the defence of small enterprise, told the readers of an Antwerp newspaper in 1901:

> Happier than the workers exiled to the factory who return exhausted fit only to collapse on their bed, these middle-class folk work at home, amongst their family. To their kids they are more than just a nocturnal shadow, and family life is a reality. Will it last?[128]

It offered an ideal for society as a whole – structured, moral, intimate, and hierarchic. 'Enter the shop of a small draper, grocer, butcher, *charcutier*, or hairdresser', wrote Etienne Martin Saint-Léon.

> The *patron* occupies himself with the practical side of the business, helped by his son or his daughter; his wife is on the cash-till. Family life thus coincides with business life. As for the young assistant or shopgirl, they work under the master's eye.[129]

The involvement of employees in the idealised family of small enterprise was now regularly used as an argument for its defence. 'The employee is the real colleague of the *patrons*,' explained G. Levy in 1911. 'He knows the price goods were purchased for, he is treated as one of the family, lives with the *patron* and eats at his table, shares his sorrows and his happiness.'[130]

This ideology of defence was strikingly absent from Britain, where the image of the petite bourgeoisie as an alternative vision of social organisation was rarely used by either social observers or petit-bourgeois movements. The shopkeepers' campaign against co-operative stores in St Helens in 1902, for example, appears to have made no connections at all between the independent trader and the character of the family work and social unit – an absence unthinkable in parallel movements elsewhere in Europe, where defending family production was a powerful tradition, often drawing on the social vision of Frédéric Le Play, whose attachment to independent rural production derived from its linking together of land, workshop and family.[131]

This idealisation was encouraged by petit-bourgeois organisations in Germany, France and Belgium. In the ideology of the German master artisan, the independent workshop not only represented the achievement of years of training and effort, but was an extension of the family home which constituted the centre of his moral and social values. The journeymen and apprentices were as much the responsibility of the master and his wife as were their own children.[132] Petit-bourgeois defence movements built on these images of the family. Patriarchal authority was particularly emphasised in Germany, transposed on to the remoralised state through the ideal of the stern but loving father, while the family as the basis of republican harmony was stressed in France. The virtues of the family working environment were a recurrent image in petit-bourgeois campaigns. The *Ligue syndicale*, founded in France in 1888, saw itself as defender of little communities bound together by hierarchy and sentiment. Department stores threatened all of this: the shop assistant, who had once lived *en famille* with his employer, was no more than a number in the new department store.[133] In this discourse, the department store's threat to family came from many directions. The relations between employer and employee became anonymous. Furthermore, using fashionable pro-natalist arguments, a Lyonnais shopkeeper newspaper denounced 'the encouragement to celibacy, because in department stores the assistants are housed separately, children are an obstacle, motherhood is impossible'.[134] One even finds the denunciation of the stores for their destructive effects on the bourgeois family, their bright electric lights seducing once moral housewives into the excitement of shopping, spending and artificial luxury. The impact of electricity need not be all bad, however, for electric power could halt the decline of small-scale production, and with it boost the small enterprise family. Electricity would enable society to halt 'the process of industrial concentration with its inevitable consequences: the promiscuity of the factory, the domination of married women by the machine, desertion of home, abandonment of children, corruption of young girls, revolutionary contamination'.[135]

This idealisation of the family reappears wherever we turn in the defence of the petite bourgeoisie in later nineteenth-century continental Europe. The general characteristics explored in this chapter help explain why the ideologists of the petite bourgeoisie were able to seize upon the family as one of its defining features, however great the distance between their idealisations and the experiences of petit-bourgeois families themselves. The centrality of the family was a fact of the petit-bourgeois world, even if it was not necessarily the fact dreamed of by its defenders. Occupational and geographical differences dictated variations in the relationships between household, family and enterprise. It remained true, nonetheless, that the petit-bourgeois family embraced a wide range of functions and dimensions. That is why the role of the family was more important for the petite bourgeoisie than for any other social group.

6

THE PETITE BOURGEOISIE AND THE TOWN

'The town, the city provides the inevitable setting for small-scale industry and retailing; it is their base, and at the same time their limits, while within it they constitute an important and vital element.'[1] Georges Duplat, a Catholic lawyer in early twentieth-century Belgium, may have been pleading petit-bourgeois communal rights that seemed under threat, but he also affirmed a historic intertwining of urban economies and small enterprise, of urban social orders and the owners of those small enterprises. In a historical perspective, artisanal production and shopkeeping have been fundamentally urban activities. Small-scale property was, of course, always important in the European countryside, whose peasant populations were the core of a rural petite bourgeoisie, and whose artisans serviced their agricultural communities. Nevertheless, the intersection of economic and juridical structures in Europe since the Middle Ages concentrated artisans and retailers disproportionately in towns.

Towns had often been defined by the exclusive rights to hold markets granted to them by royal and imperial authorities, and they came to be constituted around the juridical framework which gave the right to exercise a trade or profession to a town's guilds and corporations. As we saw in Chapter Two, corporate bodies were not only a mode of trade defence, but also the basis for representation in urban affairs. Its corporations were a town's most basic institutions, bridging the private world of economic interests and the public sphere of urban government and ritual. If the juridical boundaries were more strict than the economic reality, they themselves underpinned a certain conception of the urban. The masters and *jurandes* of urban corporations provided the town's freemen and burghers. In seventeenth- and eighteenth-century Germany, for example, only those who were citizens of a town had the right to sell in a market, to brew beer or to open a workshop.[2] Manufacturing might be excluded from the countryside by law, as in Prussia before the early nineteenth-century reforms or Sweden before the 1850s, whose restrictions sought to concentrate within towns the conflicts which surrounded industry and trade, and to protect the countryside and its subordinate peasantry from such tensions. Even where rural production was

112

permitted, precise distinctions would protect the exclusive rights of urban guilds, as with the laws which forbade country shoemakers round Bologna from selling in the town itself, while permitting their urban counterparts to sell higher-quality shoes in the countryside. As Bologna's shoemakers insisted throughout the eighteenth century, crafts were an urban activity and had to be defended as such.[3] Towns and small enterprise were thus historically bound together, even if frontier artisanal districts such as Paris's faubourg Saint-Antoine show that the boundary between town and country was more clear in law than on the ground. In the words of Fernand Braudel, 'the town accumulates and amasses shops, markets, houses and artisans',[4] and his judgement was as true for the modern as for the early-modern era. By the middle of the nineteenth century, in spite of the continuation of rural industry and industrial villages, production and commerce were concentrated ever more firmly in the towns of industrialising Europe.

Urban society cannot be understood without the petite bourgeoisie, nor the petite bourgeoisie without the setting of the town. If we seek the elements that gave shape to an identity amongst these small employers and business owners, then we need to explore these urban characteristics and urban connections. The economic role was of primary importance, as small enterprise grew not just under the stimulus of industrialisation but also in response to the demand for urban consumption and services. The shifting centre of gravity of small enterprise which we observed in Chapter Three, from artisanal producers to the providers of retailing and other services, was a result of urbanisation itself. Yet this was an inward-looking urbanisation, for the economic life of small enterprise remained bound within the perspectives of the town itself, however much merchants tied them into wider economic relations. As Duplat observed of small enterprise, 'trade and industry attach the citizen to his city'.[5] The process was accompanied by an introspection which served not only to increase their dependence on intermediaries, but also to generate a politics of closure and of autarky.

The relationship between the petite bourgeoisie and the town was more than economic activity alone, and it is upon these wider spheres which this chapter will focus. Shopkeepers and master artisans were central to neighbourhood life, helping define both neighbourhood sociability and the urban space within which it took shape. Their ownership of small-scale property gave them a major role in the provision of working-class housing. Finally, their economic and property interests combined with their localist perspective to give petits bourgeois a place in the contest for municipal authority. Family, property and enterprise together bound shopkeepers and master artisans to local worlds which they invested with a distinctive importance, reinforcing a parochialism to which we shall return in Chapter Nine. As Friedrich Engels, a perceptive observer of mid-nineteenth-century German society, commented, 'the petit bourgeois represents local interests, the bourgeois universal ones'.[6]

Economic, social and ideological forces thus bound the owners of small enterprise to their towns. The nature of those ties meant that notwithstanding the fact that the expansion of small enterprise rested on the growth of large towns, it was in the small and medium-sized towns that petits bourgeois felt most at home. In such towns they had been protected by localism of markets, they enjoyed more stable daily relations which made control as well as mutual support possible, and they faced only limited competition for domination of municipal affairs. The 'home towns' of southern Germany portrayed by Mack Walker are the best-known example of these introverted small communities, whose institutional and economic life long resisted pressures from outside, but most of the older small towns in Europe shared some of these characteristics, especially those with a vigorous guild tradition. Deventer in the Dutch Republic was one such town, with a population of 8,000 in the 1780s, and an economic world that was mostly based on local markets. Deventer's public life was built around its artisanal, trading and merchant guilds, their civic and social prominence symbolised by the town's ancient and beautiful *Gildehuis*.[7] Guilds may have reinforced the comforts of small-town life for small enterprise, but they were not essential, as many a small market centre in nineteenth-century France or England testified. Montrichard in central France, with a population of some 3,000 in mid-century, was described by its historian as 'a democracy of small proprietors, shopkeepers and artisans'. Even the larger regional capital of Blois, with 18,000 inhabitants and a wealthy bourgeois elite, offered a comfortable if more abrasive setting for the traders and artisans who constituted one-third of its occupied population, serving both local peasants and resident bourgeoisie.[8]

Vigorous urban growth provided threats as well as opportunities for small enterprise. Indeed, as a town became more heavily populated, so the proportion of petits bourgeois declined. In Belleville, to the east of Paris, 58 per cent of the occupied population was in retailing in 1836, a mere 23 per cent by 1851 after its initial period of growth. Small industrial towns, such as Saint-Chamond near Saint-Etienne or Rheine in Westphalia, saw the proportion of artisanal enterprises decline as they underwent modest mid-century growth.[9] For small towns, the advent of larger markets, modern transportation, and intensified migration all disrupted the secure habitats of small town artisans and shopkeepers even when urban growth itself was limited. Even without such pressures, the relative decline of small towns diminished the world where established small enterprise and its owners had once been most at home.

THE PETITE BOURGEOISIE AND THE NEIGHBOURHOOD

With the declining importance of the small town, not all was lost for petits bourgeois. Their relationship to local space reconstituted itself in the neighbourhoods and *quartiers* of large towns, and their role within these neighbourhoods has been too little observed by urban and social historians. None of this was new, for in early-modern Europe the life of urban communities took shape around the ties of work, housing and sociability, which for most people intersected within local neighbourhoods. In a fine study of eighteenth-century Paris, Garrioch has revealed the *quartier* as the centre of most Parisians' world.[10] It was a mental as well as a spatial universe, animated by the *quartier*'s role in providing protection, support in hardship, intervention in family affairs, and sociability in the street, shop or *fontaine* where the women obtained water and did the laundry. These neighbourhoods should not be idealised, for the interventions could be violent and the support as readily withdrawn as granted, but it was a world of familiar daily relationships. Garrioch shows the importance of reputation, correct behaviour and honour, and the ways in which the informal daily sociability of the *quartier* determined the assignment of status in local communities. These were not closed worlds – immigrants to the town or to the neighbourhood would arrive while others would leave – but newcomers were incorporated through the social relations of the *quartier*.[11] Master artisans and shopkeepers were at the heart of the local community in eighteenth-century Paris, with certain shops particularly important – the baker, wine-seller, *traiteur*, grocer, *perruquier* (primarily a barber in popular districts), and of course the café, where business and employment as well as leisure were frequently organised.

The importance of the neighbourhood continued in the growing towns of nineteenth-century Europe, as did the owners of small enterprise within it, though it is not easy to establish whether the greater attention to the question of the *quartier* in France is the result of its greater significance there, or the greater attention of a historiography concerned to identify intermediary structures between society and individual.[12] There was no one type of neighbourhood. The popular residential neighbourhood was the most common, where many found their employment within the district but even more outside it, and in which traders and artisans within the community serviced local consumption. There were also, however, the more classic artisanal neighbourhoods dominated by a single craft, of which historians have long been aware, the artisanal districts: the silk-weaving districts of Krefeld, or Spitalfields in London or, most famous of all, la Croix-Rousse in Lyons, rising above the city to a plateau upon which there stood a *quartier* of fierce independence; the cutlery districts in Sheffield or Thiers, with their closely linked specialised workshops; the faubourg Saint-Antoine in Paris, whose cabinet-makers practised an intense and ultimately self-destructive division of labour. These were productive neighbourhoods producing for national and international rather than local consumption.

As the nineteenth century progressed, artisans and shopkeepers steadily abandoned the traditional specialised locations to which street names alone still stand witness today. The activities of small enterprise were increasingly dispersed within the town. Dispersed, but certainly not undifferentiated, as can be seen from the distribution of small enterprises in Göttingen around 1830. In the centre of town, shopkeepers lived alongside innkeepers and pharmacists in a bourgeois district where few workers were to be found. Outside the centre, though still within the walls, gathered artisans in the food, textile, leather, wood and metal trades, together with more general retailing in a popular area where wage-earners and small business owners mixed. In the houses beyond the walls petits bourgeois were lost in an increasingly proletarian world of tailors and weavers.[13] This pattern of uneven dispersal through the town came to characterise small enterprise. Later nineteenth-century Milan saw more shops in lower-class areas, for those living in prosperous residential districts tended to use city centre shops. The better-class areas nonetheless boasted more clothing, furniture and stationery retailers than popular districts. Hairdressers and cobblers were to be found everywhere in the city, but as one moved further from the centre so one found increasing concentrations of shops dealing in basic goods (food, tobacco, fuel, bars), and these were especially numerous in the populous areas beyond the walls where most workers lived and where the tariff on goods entering the city was not paid.[14]

The scatter of small enterprise across the nineteenth-century city thus followed the urban social map, but was not exclusively tied to it. Whatever the shape of a neighbourhood, whatever the turnover of population or fluctuations in economic activity, whatever the balance between production and residence, there was a strong and continuing presence of artisans and small shopkeepers who lived and worked in the same building and within the same neighbourhood. They constituted the least segregated of any occupational groups,[15] present in virtually all urban districts – working-class central neighbourhoods or *faubourgs* on the edge of town, central shopping areas, prosperous suburbs. By the turn of the century it could be observed of south London that 'in all the boroughs, poor as well as rich, lining all the main roads and many of the side streets is the class of tradesmen who ministers to the needs of the vast populations which are hidden behind'.[16]

The shops and workshops that played such an important role in the popular neighbourhood were only a section of small enterprises. They were not so much the highly unstable elements highlighted in Chapter Four, though the business could remain important to the *quartier* even where ownership changed, nor were they the more prosperous city-centre enterprises or those in middle-class districts. The key group was the owners of relatively stable small enterprises located within popular neighbourhoods. Their place was ambiguous, part of the community yet rendered distant by the way they earned their income, by their often commercial relationship with those amongst whom they lived, and perhaps also by their aspirations. As the larger middle class moved out to districts of their own, the owners of local small enterprises were often left behind to serve as the neighbourhood's elite.

In the working-class districts of British industrial towns at the end of the nineteenth century, shopkeepers frequently organised seasonal rituals and informal neighbourhood charity. As one man who grew up in Salford recalled, shopkeepers were 'the only upper class that I knew'. They were both part of the community yet apart from it. Another resident of a poor district in Salford remembered that for the neighbourhood's young women clothes fashion was set by the daughters of the shopkeepers and publicans.[17] Indeed, in the recollections of workers whose childhood was spent in inter-war Wiesbaden, the local shopkeepers and master artisans appeared as part of another class, almost as the mediators of bourgeois culture.[18] The distance was not always so great. The disproportionate number of local traders and artisans amongst the witnesses at working-class weddings indicates their place both within and slightly above the community. In the French metal-working town of Saint-Chamond shopkeepers were frequently witnesses at the marriages of workers in the town's ironworking *quartier*. Jean-Claude Côté, for example, was a metalworker at the local Petin ironworks, who took as his three witnesses a grocer, a master stovemaker and a master tailor. Witnesses from outside the family were disproportionately drawn from the owners of local small enterprise, indicating either daily familiarity or a sense of who were the respectable members of the local community, or probably both.[19] The Vincent family, with their shop and lodging house in Cardiff at the end of the nineteenth century, coped with the poverty around them by turning in on the home, but their father's role in the community remained, for 'when anyone died they'd come for him to head the funeral'.[20]

The role of the owners of small enterprise within a popular neighbourhood was intensified by the fact that they were always there, living and working in the same *quartier*. In late nineteenth-century Hamburg, seven out of every ten owners of small enterprises worked within the neighbourhood within which they lived – mostly working at home or adjacent to the home, sometimes elsewhere in the neighbourhood.[21] Their daily involvement in the activities and relationships of the *quartier* was most powerful in the first half of the nineteenth century, when the urban neighbourhood's mixture of workers, small independents, domestic outworkers, artisans and shopkeepers mirrored a society still small-scale and complex, in which the neighbourhood was popular rather than proletarian. The democratic radicalism and social egalitarianism of popular radicals, the attacks on parasites and the idle rich, the assertion of the rights of the *menu peuple* (ordinary people) against the large and powerful, are not so much a reflection of some failure of working-class movements to adapt to proletarian values, but rather the accurate expression of the communities that were genuinely popular and which comprised far more than the working class alone. For a good part of the nineteenth century, what historians have called working-class culture and working-class politics should more appropriately be called popular. In neighbourhoods such as these – and outside a handful of heavy industrial and coal mining communities they remained the norm to the end of the century – social and political life bound workers and petits bourgeois together, often even in new districts. Jalla's study of the Turin metalworking suburb of Borgo San Paolo, which grew explosively from the 1890s, led him to conclude that the key to understanding social relations was 'the solidarity between workers in a single town, and between them and the *petit peuple* of artisans, shopkeepers and white collar employees'. The attachment that he found in Borgo San Paolo was as much territorial as it was social, often fragmenting to the level of streets and local neighbourhoods.[22]

Small enterprises often constituted places of popular sociability, where people met and talked. It was a familiar role for the village shop or workshop – especially the latter, it would seem, with the shoemaker's shop or the smithy a place for gossip, sociability, and, in the rural culture of Scotland in which performance played such a major part, story telling and singing.[23] Neighbourhood shops similarly served as places of informal sociability in towns. Robert Roberts described his mother's general shop in Salford. 'Here, back and forth across the counters, slid the comedy, tragedy, hopes, fears and fancies of a whole community: here was market place and village well combined.'[24] As we have already seen, gossip was not merely a way to make the shop agreeable to customers and the working day agreeable to the shopkeeper, but the means by which those who sold on credit could keep in touch with the prospects of those who might be in debt to them. The success of a business could depend on the accuracy of such information.

Conversation was essential to the success of a shop in other ways. A grocer and bar keeper in a poor district of Cologne in the 1840s argued, with a self-consciousness that is instructive, that

> in order to acquire and retain a clientèle, one must be able to chat with the customers . . . . In the evening one discusses politics over a glass of beer, or simply shows off; if the small shopkeeper cannot exercise this magnetic attraction over his neighbours, then that is the end of his shop.[25]

Hence the seats that were a common feature of French bakers' shops. As the century progressed, ordinary seats gave way to benches and even sofas, as people met and talked on their frequent visits to buy bread. It was not always welcome – Henri Béraud's mother complained of the endless chatting in the shop which kept her from other tasks – but it was necessary.[26] The clocks in these Lyons bakers' shops, increasingly impressive clocks to show the success and standing of the enterprise, also distinguished the shop as a public space serving public functions. The ambiguities of public and private that bedevilled the petit-bourgeois family, and which drove many to insist on private respectability, were compounded by the way in which their enterprise was marked out as public space. Shopkeepers might establish with precision where customers could come – who talked in the body of the shop, and who in the intermediate space between the shop and the domestic rooms. The division was meticulously observed according to the memories of a Brighton newsagent's daughter, with the back parlour serving as a frontier zone that symbolised those ambiguities of public and private, involvement and distance, in the social relations of shopkeeping.[27]

Sociability was easier in trades where the shop was warm and the smell agreeable. The baker's shop would always seem more welcoming than that of the butcher. The frequency of visits also affected the social role of the shop, enhancing the place of those which sold items of daily consumption, such as the baker, grocer, general shop, and tobacconist. Cafés and public houses held a special place, for sociability was their *raison d'être*. Sociability around retailing was primarily feminine, but one should not see that around cafés as intrinsically masculine. Public houses and cafés had their own daily social cycle, with the clientèle varying with time of day, following the rhythm of neighbourhood daily life. Some establishments were segregated by occupation or gender, but many were genuinely mixed and integrative, not least where their role was played out as community spectacle. The distinction in this respect between the French café with its terrace on the street and the English public house with its closed door and opaque windows reminds us of the very different roles even of enterprises constructed for sociability.[28] Artisanal workshops could play a similar role to that of shops, especially the shoemaker, blacksmith or wheelwright whose customers often waited for work to be carried out. The shoemaker's workshop throughout Europe was a meeting place where men, women and children would gather and talk. Their numbers would be fewer than in a tavern, but with a social atmosphere animated by the often radical and literate shoemaker. Alice Foley remembered the long waits as a young girl in Bolton in the 1890s, sitting on a bench in the shop awaiting her turn and then for the work to be done, during regular visits to the clogger's shop to have new irons fitted to her clogs.[29] The owner of a pottery in the French Midi insisted that he had not been active in the political opposition to Louis Napoleon's *coup d'état*, explaining to the police in 1852 that 'people used to come to warm themselves by my furnace, and they would discuss politics'.[30]

The sociability of the neighbourhood was thus essential for many small enterprises, while small enterprises themselves were essential for the sociability of the neighbourhood. The functions were hard to distinguish, as Burguière discovered in his study of a twentieth-century Breton commune. 'During the day, the shops provided a sort of office for impromptu purchases, chats, moments of relaxation' and 'for the client, the purchase is often the means of paying for his relaxation or little chat'.[31] Shops were always about more than selling. It was not just department stores which accumulated a myriad of other functions, though they were extravagantly conspicuous as places of visibility, as tearooms for fashionable ladies, as propagators of fashion and as shapers of consumer culture.[32] The neighbourhood shop was as varied in its functions, most of them casual and informal, but some more specific. With bookmaking in Britain permitted only on racecourses, illegal betting often took place in shops (as in the coal shops of west London) or public houses.[33] Only the most prosperous of clubs or *cercles* could afford their own premises, so not only workers' but also bourgeois societies would hire the semi-public and semi-private space of a room in a café or public house to hold their weekly or monthly meetings. The proprietor often encouraged their establishment, for they were a source of regular custom.[34] Retail premises could also thus provide the setting for middle-class sociability, even if the principal focus here is on the working-class neighbourhood. Although domestic servants would shop for everyday items, the premises of the draper, jeweller, or *parfumier* would be equipped as a place of calm and conversation for the bourgeois client, while bookshops and stationers might host middle-class reading and discussion groups.[35]

With the exception of the public house or café, shops provided a social space primarily used by women. The sociability of the shop played a central role within the culture of working-class women, linking domestic space to public space,[36] and providing a place for relaxation in a daily routine where leisure was generally taken in the midst of work, in contrast to the increasingly clear division within the masculine working day. The neighbourhood, like all social space, was gendered. Burdy has shown how in the working-class *quartier* of Le Soleil in Saint-Etienne, women's daily lives focused on household, shop, market and street, while that of the men revolved around workplace, café and *jardin ouvrier* (allotment). Women depended more upon the neighbourhood for their daily routines and, as Ross has shown for Bethnal Green in East London, they used its networks and sociability to sustain the household and secure its survival.[37]

Apart from the café, only workshops, which were a less significant part of neighbourhood sociability, and the barber's shop might play a similar role for men. One writer recalled the enthusiastic discussion of horse racing throughout the day in the Aberdeen barber's shop in which he had worked as a young man. In the village barbers of twentieth-century Burgundy, the men gathered on a Sunday morning. 'They would chat and tell hunting stories, crowded round the iron stove.' The *salons de coiffure* in late nineteenth-century Lyon might serve as a social centre for migrants to the town. Such was the salon in the Old Town whose owner came from Annonay, where the Annonay press was always available and where old and new migrants could meet.[38]

The petite bourgeoisie may have been a world in movement, but it contained more stable elements which were fundamental to the identity of a neighbourhood and to the representation of social spaces within a town. Rates of residential and geographic mobility were high amongst urban workers in nineteenth-century Europe, perhaps reaching their peak by the 1880s in Britain's more advanced urban society but in other countries continuing at a high rate up to the First World War. In this context, the grocers, bakers, shoemakers and publicans of a neighbourhood provided the stable poles for its sociability, identity, memory and for the incorporation of newcomers. Shops were the most common local landmarks given in evidence in court cases in late eighteenth-century Paris,[39] they marked out the detailed urban space in which people lived their lives and provided its skeleton through the following century, as oral testimony and memoirs confirm. Alice Foley's memories of her Bolton childhood and its routines revolved around the premises of its tradesmen: shops, clogger's workshop, coalyard. Her references to town-centre shops are quite different, establishments which she walked round on an occasional Saturday evening, providing entertainment rather than the spatial and social framework of her daily life.[40]

Against the instability that characterised much small enterprise, stood the residential and neighbourhood persistence of those who remained. In mid-nineteenth-century Düsseldorf, master artisans and tradesmen, if they survived in business in the town, were far more likely to stay in the same district than were workers.[41] A study of the *quartier de la Gare* in Paris at the very end of the century shows that one half of all shopkeepers and master artisans left the *quartier* during the decade after 1896, the same proportion as workers. Those who remained in the neighbourhood, however, were far more likely to remain in the same premises. Shops and workshops could thus provide stability and memory in neighbourhoods where population often turned over at a striking rate. 'Owning a shop,' concluded Jean-Luc Pinol for Lyon, 'fixed individuals and reduced their mobility.' This was particularly true of those such as *charcutiers* with greater investment in premises or equipment. Bakers might move twice in their career if they stayed in business, butchers and *charcutiers* not even that.[42] It is hardly surprising that the more stable of these petit-bourgeois tradesmen were central to the social world of the *quartier*, providing its network of meeting places, its milieux of sociability and performance, its construction of identities and associations.

Myths of the neighbourhood can be seductive, and we must be careful not to create an idealised vision of *quartiers* in the past. There was conflict and even violence between workers and shopkeepers, between workers and masters, and the relationship remained an ambiguous one, as we shall see in Chapter Eight. The neighbourhood is too easily pictured through a haze of nostalgia, whether one imagined by late twentieth-century campaigners against urban renewal, by visionaries for urban villages, or by late nineteenth-century political movements such as the French *Ligue syndicale* with its evocation of a self-sustaining and inward-looking community. The neighbourhood as an idea has too frequently had to carry the ideological weight of *Gemeinschaft* in the face of the anonymising *Gesellschaft*. Oral evidence can magnify this nostalgia. As a former resident of Turin's Borgo San Paolo put it, 'before the First World War it was like a hamlet, a village'.[43] Yet, with its tensions and its own power relations, with its real social relations and instabilities, there was articulated in these urban neighbourhoods a structure of daily life in which a section of the petite bourgeoisie played a significant role.

This role began to decline towards the end of the nineteenth century, at least in parts of the capital cities and in the larger industrial towns of Britain, Germany and France, as more explicitly proletarian neighbourhoods emerged. The forces at work were various: increasing segregation within the town, with urban reconstruction and improving intra-urban transportation; the shift towards larger-scale industry and the emergence of an urban workforce that was less artisanal than it had once been; the consequential development of labour identities and socialist politics, which encompassed the labour movement's own institutions of retailing (consumer co-operatives) and sociability (socialist clubs, working men's clubs).[44] Small enterprise did not disappear from the more homogeneous working-class neighbourhoods but its role became more marginal. Artisanal workshops were less widespread, and small retailers less central to working-class consumption with the growth of both capitalist multiple retailing and consumer co-operation. The two processes were not unrelated, for the strength of aggressive and successful new co-operatives often lay in those parts of industrial towns dominated by large-scale factory production. The new co-operative ventures in early twentieth-century Italy were often based on single large factories, such as those based on the Pirelli, Erba and Gadda works in Milan.[45]

The speed or completeness of such a transition should not be exaggerated, and it was specific types of industrial town which were primarily affected. In many industrial towns neighbourhood petits bourgeois began to lose their influential role. The need for credit meant that small shopkeepers remained an essential element in working-class communities, but their wider social and political importance declined. In inter-war Saint-Etienne, their place in associational life was reduced and they were politically marginalised as radicalism gave way to communism in *quartier* politics.[46] In the Lancashire cotton town of Preston, a more pervasive undermining of petit-bourgeois influence accompanied the emergence of a network of institutions within the framework of the local labour movement. The petite bourgeoisie's considerable role in working-class districts was challenged there by the emergence of new neighbourhoods of council housing with distinctively labourist local institutions: its consumer life revolved around the co-operative store, weakening the credit relationship that had been fundamental to the place of the shopkeeper within the neighbourhood, while its social life came to focus on the working men's club and labour clubs. The political rise of the local Labour Party rested in part on these social changes, and made it difficult for petits bourgeois to participate in a common popular politics.[47] The loss of influence was probably most acute in such medium-sized industrial towns, and developed more gradually in large cities and capitals, yet the pattern was clear: shopkeepers and workshop masters were losing their former integral position within popular neighbourhoods.

URBAN PROPERTY

The houses and apartments owned by shopkeepers and master artisans were one facet of an attachment to local urban property which not only fixed many petits bourgeois by culture and sentiment to the town and district in which they lived, but which also influenced the parochial spirit which attracted many to the administration of local affairs. The investment habits of petits bourgeois will be explored more closely in Chapter Nine, but a continuing element was the purchase of houses and apartments to be rented by workers. In the socially diverse 1st *arrondissement* of Brussels in 1866, two social groups comprised three-quarters of all proprietors: 44 per cent were traders and artisans, and 31 per cent *rentiers*. The role of petits bourgeois in poorer housing, in which large capital had little interest, was even more substantial.[48] The typical owner of working-class housing in European cities throughout the nineteenth century was a small businessman, or a *rentier* living off investments.

In the absence of syntheses of European house-ownership patterns the evidence is unsystematic, but the picture is repeated in town after town. In the German city of Cologne, as new workers' suburbs grew beyond the walls in the early nineteenth century, it was shopkeepers and master artisans who acquired the land and built the housing, showing an entrepreneurial as well as proprietorial role which is encountered elsewhere.[49] The same pattern prevailed in Berlin at the end of century, where mortgage banks channelled loans to a landlord class of small businessmen, shopkeepers, managing clerks, widows and lesser professionals.[50] This was not an undifferentiated group, of course, for in Germany as elsewhere house-ownership was spread unevenly amongst the trades. Amongst masters in Leipzig in 1893, 41 per cent of butchers and 40 per cent of bakers owned house property, 20 per cent of joiners, but only 3 per cent of shoemakers.[51]

Larger capital appears to have been more involved in the provision of working-class housing in France. During Roubaix's growth in the first half of the nineteenth century, the merchant–manufacturers (*fabricants*) were responsible for 42 per cent of new housing, finding in house-ownership a further means to control the dispersed weavers to whom they put out work. The factories that developed from mid-century gave manufacturers more direct control over their labour force, as well as imposing new demands on their capital resources. As a consequence they withdrew from house owner-ship, and were replaced by shopkeepers and artisans, who by the end of the century owned the great mass of working-class housing.[52] This early involve-ment of large capital was unusual, and more typical was the popular Parisian artisanal district of Arts et Métiers, where many a block of workshops and apartments in mid-century was owned by a small master working and living in the same building.[53] More generally, the dominance of petits bourgeois, whether active or retired, amongst proprietors in the poorer *arrondissements* of Paris persisted, for the entry of larger-scale capital into the Parisian housing market during the Second Empire had least influence in the popular areas and the new workers' suburbs, where short leases and the demand for cheap housing offered few attractions to any other than small investors.[54]

All social groups with resources, or able to borrow them, could see the attractions of investing in housing property, and nineteenth-century house owners were therefore drawn from a wide social range, but in Britain as elsewhere it was petits bourgeois who dominated. The Royal Commission on the Poor Laws of 1834 asked parish officials to indicate who owned small houses or cottages in their district. 'For the most part small Tradespeople and persons in the middle line of life, who having made a few hundred pounds, consider it a good speculation to lay them out in building, or purchasing, houses,' was the reply for Carlisle. Town after town indicated that it was a group known as 'tradesmen'. Established landed proprietors might prevail in the older part of Manchester, but it was tradesmen, shopkeepers, publicans and mechanics who dominated in the newer districts.[55] In Salisbury, the Royal Commission learned, the owners were 'persons of small capital, generally hard-hearted, and destitute of feeling towards the tenants'.[56] Proprietors with modest incomes and resources, often unable to spare the capital to maintain the building, anxious about their rents and about the security of their property, and generally close at hand to watch over their tenants, provided a source of tension within working-class communities to which we shall return in Chapter Eight. Small house owners of this kind remained the norm throughout the century. A leading figure in the Surveyors' Institution told an inquiry in 1886 that tenements let to skilled workers were generally owned by tradesmen, such as small grocers or bakers who retired to live off the 7 per cent return offered by such property. He claimed that workers' housing was too much trouble for large capitalists, and did not offer a good enough return.[57] Personal attention was essential if such property was to prove a paying proposition, for as the financial returns became less certain, the methods of the small local proprietor became all the more necessary. The Institute of Chartered Surveyors was told in the early 1890s that large capitalists would be well advised to leave working-class weekly-tenancy property alone. It was all right for 'small capitalists,' able to control and watch over it closely for its mere 7 per cent to 8 per cent return, but such attention was needed if it were to pay.[58]

There are various explanations for this prevalence of petit-bourgeois housing proprietors. One is the way in which housing was supplied, often based not only on fragmented urban land-ownership patterns but even more frequently on a fragmented process of entrepreneurship and construction. Building craftsmen themselves became entrepreneurs in a small-scale industry, where the whole building process could be sustained on credit. In that context, small tradesmen could become entrepreneurs themselves, sub-contracting the actual building work to craftsmen, and often keeping the houses to let once complete.[59] A further factor was the character of capital markets which, away from the world of large-scale commerce and industry, were generally highly localised and personal. One contemporary attributed the speculative over-production of houses in early Victorian Sheffield to 'the petty capitalist . . . desirous of realising a handsome percentage'.[60] Small capital markets were especially localised in Great Britain, in the absence of the mortgage banks in Germany or *Crédit Foncier* in France, which mobilised more substantial capital for building development, though rarely on a scale that seriously altered the pattern of ownership.[61] A further factor explaining petit-bourgeois proprietorship was the character of working-class housing, with owner-occupation on the one hand, and provision by employers outside a small number of factory towns on the other, both rare. The mass of workers in nineteenth-century European towns lived in an apartment, a house, or a part of a house which they rented from a private landlord. To all these factors must be added the character of the petite bourgeoisie itself whose culture of investment, explored in more detail in Chapter Nine, directed them towards both the security and the visibility of local housing property.

House owners' associations emerged to represent the interests of these proprietors. As early as 1832 the *Grundeigentümerverein*, or Landlords' Association, had been formed in Hamburg, predominantly by master artisans and small tradesmen, to look after their interests in relation to tenants as well as to resist impositions by a local state from whose affairs they were effectively excluded. After constitutional reform in the city, the increased influence of small property owners made the Association a major local political force by the closing decades of the century. Other large German cities generally boasted a *Haus- und Grundbesitzer Verein*, such as that founded in Cologne in 1888, to protect property owners against the tax and improvement demands of municipal government. Although small landlords dominated the membership here, they were often led by large builders and property owners. In Vienna, the Landlords' Association (*Hausbesitzer-vereinigung*) was a significant presence in the city's affairs during the late nineteenth century.[62]

In Britain, house owners' associations emerged as petit-bourgeois interest organisations in a setting where the political voice of small enterprise was particularly muted. They can be found in the 1830s, for example with the St Helens House and Cottage Owners' Society set up to oppose legislation, unjust rates and refractory tenants.[63] These organisations grew in Britain from the 1880s, aiming to act against moonlight flits, construct lists of bad tenants, help landlords recover arrears, and act as a pressure group on municipal government. Their size suggests that they organised no more than a small proportion of the myriad of landlords.[64] The significance of house owners' associations in the representation of petit-bourgeois interests may have been a reflection of its generally weak political formation, and that limited political presence has been used to explain the ease with which petty landlords came to be marginalised in Britain, as state housing policy steadily abandoned the interests of the small landlord. Rent controls during the First World War, followed by the collectivist solution of council housing after it, left small landlords as a declining force. As housing provision and the housing market became matters of state policy, the localism of petit-bourgeois interests rendered their defence increasingly difficult.[65]

LOCAL AND MUNICIPAL GOVERNMENT

The petit-bourgeois attachment to property produced the defence of private property in general, but it also clung tightly to specific pieces of property, bound up with place, personality and family in a fashion far less marked amongst the more substantial bourgeoisie. The local standing and local relations of petits bourgeois were the basis of what success they had achieved, and of what security they had constructed. The material interests of property, credit and production were in this world bound up with moral and social relations that were often immediate and personal in character. As the nineteenth century progressed, and as larger business became increasingly impersonal in response not only to the increasing scale of enterprise and its geographical scope, but also to the bureaucratisation of the instruments of business law, so the local and personal dimensions of the petite bourgeoisie became more distinctive. They turned in on the town and neighbourhood as well as on the specific bricks and mortar of local property. This was more than merely defensive, for the owners of small business were citizens whose property and profession had in the past endowed their predecessors with rights within their communities: as burghers, bourgeois, freemen, burgesses. The historical role of these owners of small local enterprise in the communal struggles for freedom during the Middle Ages, and through the role of corporations in municipal government, had remained in no more than symbolic form in most cities by the middle of the nineteenth century, but it was a role nostalgically evoked by those lauding the social importance of the petite bourgeoisie. For the Belgian Social Catholic, Oscar Pyfferoen, the petite bourgeoisie was 'in former times the rampart of our communal liberties'.[66]

The small traditional home towns of southern Germany were the classic expression of this relationship, with their quasi-autarkic local economies, and the binding together of small enterprise, family and political life. The need to defend the local interest of these burghers in the face of increasing challenges from outside led to a belief in self-regulation and a rejection of outsiders which has been called a 'visceral xenophobia'.[67] Such towns survived in this form in Baden, Bavaria and Württemberg through to the 1860s, but they were extreme cases, protected by their very slow economic growth as much as by their constitutional autonomy. Yet they were an extreme version of an important aspect of the petite bourgeoisie's relationship to urban life: its local spirit and attachment to place, its dependence on the familiar and on personalised relationships, and the link in many places between urban property and urban rights. These characteristics found expression in the involvement of shopkeepers and master artisans in local and municipal government.

The opportunities for petit-bourgeois involvement in municipal government, as well as their actual participation, differed considerably between countries as well as between towns. In Germany, exclusion from municipal management appears to have been the rule, though local small business interests battled repeatedly for access to municipal institutions. It was a rule frequently broken, however, for the varying traditions of municipal government and autonomy in Germany coloured developments throughout the century. At one extreme stood the limited enthusiasm of Prussian burghers for the political representation established from Stein's *Städteordnung* of 1808 onwards, where citizenship was firmly associated with the ownership of property. At the other stood the fairly autonomous towns of southern Germany whose historic commitment to local autonomy left them resisting state control and bureaucratisation. On the whole, German cities experienced a developing mixture of state control and the participation of a property-owning citizenry.[68] The voting system, which attached the franchise to house-ownership and taxpaying, gave the petite bourgeoisie a limited means of access which was only partially turned into a significant role. Cities such as Hamburg, Münster and Krefeld saw old-established local elites entrenched in power, notwithstanding small-business protests against local oligarchy, but the absence of bourgeois civic enthusiasm elsewhere might lead to small businessmen being returned to local office.[69] The liberal elite generally dominated, and electoral reform towards the end of the century, as in Bremen, often left small entrepreneurs drowned in a sea of humble voters, their older urban rights slowly disappearing. In any case, the closing decades of the century saw the strengthened role of administrative officials, including mayors, who were professional appointments whose authority was buttressed by the central state and who often had few ties with the cities which had appointed them.[70]

French small businessmen and small proprietors served their apprenticeship in municipal affairs during the Revolution, entering municipal councils in large numbers during the years of the Convention. It was but a temporary role, as was much of the Revolution's democratic impetus, and the first half of the nineteenth century saw the role of petits bourgeois in municipal government, in all but small towns and communes, limited by their exclusion from the suffrage or from the right to be elected. True of Paris and the larger provincial cities under the July Monarchy, it was mirrored in the towns of a region such as the Limousin, whose municipal council rooms were occupied by lawyers, doctors, substantial *propriétaires*, with no more than an occasional prosperous retailer and rarely even a successful artisan to be seen. The notables were in control. Only in the smaller rural communes of the countryside (and France did boast 38,000 communes, each with its *mairie*) were farmers joined by small shopkeepers and artisans, especially the ubiquitous millers and blacksmiths.[71] Urban local government in France rarely operated freely, and central government restrictions on the election of councillors and of mayors, were only seriously reduced during the Third Republic.[72] In the closing decades of the century petit-bourgeois access to town councils certainly grew, not least as larger elites withdrew in search of wider horizons, but that same absence of municipal autonomy in France which made control of municipalities such a frustrating experience for early twentieth-century socialists also limited the consequences of an increasing petit-bourgeois role. Small businessmen may have entered the *Hôtels de Ville* and *Mairies* in growing numbers, but central government's continuing legislative and financial control of municipal affairs made their role of symbolic and cultural, rather than material, significance.

French municipalities could only look enviously at the degree of autonomy enjoyed by their counterparts across the Channel. The 1835 reform of municipal corporations was the beginning of unitary town councils in Britain, elected by ratepayers, but the previous multiplicity of lesser institutions of urban government did not disappear. It was at these lower levels that a town's shopkeepers and master artisans could continue to find access to the management of local affairs, even when the town council itself lay in the hands of men of greater substance. In the early nineteenth century, the vestry, police or paving commissions, and Poor Law Guardians allowed radical petits bourgeois to gain a foothold for their views and opened up oligarchic town government. The proliferation of lesser bodies continued alongside the new town councils, with health, Poor Law and later education generating their own elected authorities. In the closing decades of the century the vestries re-emerged in London as the base for resistance to centralising impulses, expressing now a petit-bourgeois concern for local popular autonomy, in the face of attempts to reform London's government. An older vestry radicalism was subtly reconstructed as a petit-bourgeois resistance to modernising liberal and socialist impulses in London's government.[73] British towns thus offered two levels of access to municipal government for smaller business, and even where the council itself remained in larger bourgeois hands, they could participate in other spheres of town administration.

The real autonomy allowed to local government in Britain, where the concept of liberty had long been bound up with the rights of local against central government, and where the nineteenth-century state encroached on that autonomy with great caution, ensured that local government remained an arena for bourgeois activity through the century. Levels of petit-bourgeois involvement nevertheless varied, before the trend of larger bourgeois with-drawal became clear towards the end of the century. Two major towns in south-west England illustrate the variation. In the port and manufacturing town of Bristol, the Council remained attractive to the city's large merchants and industrialists with its vision of 'social citizenship', and their control remained firm until the end of the century. The petit-bourgeois presence grew from 19 per cent in 1880 to 37 per cent in 1910, but the Bristol Town Council remained led by the town's elite.[74] In contrast, the traditional ecclesiastical and market centre of Exeter saw from 1835 the local clerical, banking and professional elite slowly withdraw from town government. The dominant group was within thirty years the licensed drink trade, retailers and lawyers. As early as the 1860s, the bulk of the forty-eight Town Councillors were made up of occupations such as boot and shoemakers, druggists, timber merchants, candle and soap dealers, grocers, ironmongers, builders and watchmakers.[75]

The significance of local office, the powers of local in relation to central government, the nature of the municipal franchise, and the interests of larger bourgeois in urban affairs all affected the extent of the petits bourgeois role in local government in any particular town or country. Nevertheless, what might appear mundane matters to larger businessmen and professionals could be of immediate relevance to the owners of a town's small enterprises. They could try to win municipal support for their own protection, as with Belgian shopkeepers' concern to see town councils tighten their control of itinerant traders, but most small business was anxious to avoid rather than to impose municipal regulation. Everywhere in Europe, the twin forces of municipal regulation and local taxes combined to give petits bourgeois good reason to seek a role in municipal affairs. Town councils in Britain saw the drink trade, builders concerned with building regulations, and house owners concerned with interfering public health officials all well represented. Local government throughout Europe became responsible for regulating retailers of food and drink, whether for reasons of public health or public morality. That is why innkeepers and pawnbrokers, both subject to close police scrutiny, flocked on to the Watch Committee in the Somerset town of Bridgewater in the 1850s, believing that their presence would check police activity, while publicans had themselves elected to Wolverhampton Council later in the century in order to counter the influence of Liberal temperance supporters on the licensing bench.[76] Not only did increasing public health inspection threaten the business methods and the profitability of food retailers in all countries, with butchers' abattoirs and dairies particularly threatened, but bakers' shops in most French towns were closely regulated by municipal authorities, with proprietors required to deposit reserves of flour at public depots, while matters such as the number of ovens, quality of production and hours of opening were subject to municipal control. The fact that bakers often extracted limitations on the number of shops in return for much of this regulation, until freedom of trade was introduced in 1863, only tightened the significance of municipal government for the trade.[77] Hygiene inspection of shops became a particularly sensitive political issue for Milan's food retailers at the end of the century, but inspection on account of both public health and weights and measures plagued food retailers everywhere.[78] The small shopkeepers' newspaper in Britain which attacked the excesses of local government control spoke for them all, proposing in parody of the regulations that so angered them, 'that pennyworths of treacle should be sold only on skewers duly registered and stamped'.[79] The inspection and regulation of the conditions of work in both small workshops and retail shops were the responsibility of local authorities, as were the often bitterly contested measures to limit the hours at which shops were permitted to open.

The regulatory powers accumulated by European urban government extended to that other great area of petit-bourgeois property, rented housing. As local authorities tightened building regulations in order to raise minimum standards of construction, light and sewage disposal, so house builders and others in the housing supply industry sought to control their scope and their implementation. It is not surprising that nearly one-quarter of Edinburgh Town Council in 1905 was connected to the building trades.[80] Increasing municipal regulation of housing conditions made landlord representation on the councils seem additionally relevant. As a Wolverhampton councillor commented in 1897, 'one great difficulty in dealing with the insanitary property of the town was that a large proportion of them belonged to members of the Council'. It was in this context that house owners' associations assumed a new significance in German towns such as Cologne or Düsseldorf, as those chasing the *Mittelstand* vote responded to landlord complaints about house regulation and public health requirements. Vienna's essentially petit-bourgeois Christian Social Party used its control of the city council from 1895 to block not only increases in the rent tax, but also measures concerning urban planning, housing reform, building regulations and rent controls.[81]

It was a paradox of petit-bourgeois visions of the relationship between public and private that so many who resisted municipal regulation of their own affairs were themselves ready to use the same authorities for regulation of the poor. The petit-bourgeois presence on local bodies concerned with the poor, whether elected or voluntary bodies, was as much bound up with concern to regulate those whose morality seemed a threat to the local social order as it was with any precise questions about the level of rates. The *Armenverwaltung* poor relief system in German towns was by the later nineteenth century generally controlled by small businessmen. They demanded appropriate standards of behaviour by the poor as conditions of relief. The chairmen of Hamburg's Poor Law Districts in 1902 were drawn from a broad spectrum of the city's propertied and business classes, but it was at the level of overseer (*Armenpfleger*), where relief was administered and moral standards enforced, that the master artisans and small retailers became dominant.[82] Similar concerns for moral regulation, authority in the town or parish, and the restraint of local expenditure led British petits bourgeois to play an active role as Poor Law Guardians. The composition of Boards of Guardians in London in the 1870s was very mixed, but in the old inner-north London district (places such as Holborn) the small numbers of gentlemen were overwhelmed by a varied collection of shopkeepers and small manufacturers.[83]

Finally, if none of these interests could induce a town's small businessmen to seek election to municipal authorities, there was the question of local rates and local taxes. Rent taxes in Vienna, *impôts locaux* in France, local land and income taxes in Germany, tariffs on goods entering the city such as the *dazio consumo* system in Milan, or local rates in Britain: whatever the precise system, municipal spending had a direct influence on the level of taxation, and small business was generally disproportionately affected by the levels and incidence of municipal taxes. Nowhere was the impact as great as in Britain, for rates on housing and other real property became the heart of municipal finance in a system more narrowly based than in other European countries. As a consequence, petits bourgeois found themselves carrying a disproportionate weight of local taxes, partly in volume but also as a share of their own income and business profits. Those whose income came from small business premises or from house property had a strong interest not only in ensuring that rates were low, but also in supervising valuation and collection procedures. Small business taxpayers everywhere pressed for a place in municipal councils, but rarely in as sustained a fashion as in Britain, where the ratepayers' associations which flourished from the later nineteenth century may be seen as the real political expression of petit-bourgeois interests in a context where neither political parties nor trade politics assumed that role.[84]

The owners of small enterprise often saw themselves as defending the local interests of the town and its districts against the expansive and expensive visions of the larger business and professional elite. As early as the 1850s ratepayer opposition groups were insisting that growing expenditure be restricted. The Ratepayers' Retrenchment Association in Salford was one such group in the 1850s, pressing both town council and Poor Law Guardians for economies.[85] A parliamentary inquiry was told in 1859, 'a small shopkeeper ... would most likely oppose the grant of any very large sum for a specific purpose of improvement'.[86] In many a town the owners of small business came into conflict with a bourgeois elite seeking to improve the urban infrastructure and to create a town that would embody a strong sense of bourgeois civic pride. The issue was not one of vision against self-interest, but two distinct visions and two different appreciations of self-interest, which grew from those distinct perceptions of space which this chapter has stressed. Larger bourgeois operated on an increasingly national and international scale, and their projects for the reconstruction and servicing of their cities were devised to insert them into that larger space. For petits bourgeois involved in municipal affairs, the space was the town or the neighbourhood. The most striking case of continuing conflict between these two perspectives was to be seen in Birmingham, where a Liberal nonconformist elite, with its vision of an active municipality constructing an impressive and profitable city, ran into repeated clashes with an economy-minded small-business class. The results were alternating periods of power for each tendency, and the continuing presence of Birmingham's bourgeois elite in civic affairs beyond the point at which their counterparts in other large cities had begun to withdraw.[87]

Small business interests everywhere in Europe contested municipal power in order to contain high levels of municipal spending. It was the autonomy accorded to local government in Britain, the nature of the franchise, and the frequent willingness of larger bourgeois to detach themselves from urban government, which made the petite bourgeoisie's municipal role particularly strong in Britain. Dresden, where a lower middle-class coalition kept control of the city council throughout the imperial era and pursued a policy of economy in the face of a reform-minded large business elite which they kept from power, was unusual in the German setting.[88] It is important to remember, however, that the municipal involvement of petits bourgeois throughout Europe was more than the defence of narrow interests. Their attachment to locality was an expression of their social and cultural, as much as of their economic, concerns. This was particularly true of those better-established and more prosperous petits bourgeois active in municipal affairs. These owners of the more stable and prosperous of urban small enterprises were in many ways the natural local rulers,[89] with their introspective vision, local social base, and needs defined within the town and its neighbourhoods. The space of the town was the space of their business and of their lives. Their enterprises, above all their shops, played not merely a social but also a symbolic role in the town's life. Their shutters would be ritually lowered to mark the funeral of a local worthy, while many shops would be decorated in celebration on more festive public occasions, as when the Hancocks' West Country draper's was festooned with decorations on the day of the Coronation and held a fireworks display from its balcony.[90] Notwithstanding the clear variation between different countries, it is clear that through its patterns of sociability, through its property, through its government, and through its mentalities, the town may be seen as one of those factors which created a degree of identity amongst these heterogeneous petits bourgeois.

7

POLITICS

The world of the people and the move to the right

Historians concerned with the political orientation of Europe's shopkeepers and master artisans have tended to focus on their shift to the right. A route is traced from involvement in popular radicalism in the first half of the nineteenth century, through liberalism and on to conservatism by the First World War, ending in the embrace of fascism during the inter-war years.[1] The search for the prehistory of fascism in the nineteenth century runs the risk of all teleological analysis, underestimating the role of historical contingency and neglecting the hesitations and retreats which characterise historical change and deny it a simple evolutionary path. For example, a substantial section of the German artisanat was drawn to the self-help of Schulze-Delitzsch and his credit co-operatives from the 1860s, detaching themselves from the corporatism that supposedly dominated the ideological development of German artisans. Similarly, the separation of French shopkeepers from their republican political culture was neither uniform nor unambiguous, for their support for the nationalist right in the Parisian municipal elections of 1900 was not matched by their provincial counterparts who continued to support the radical socialist party. There was certainly a trend towards the right in the decades approaching the First World War amongst petits bourgeois in western Europe, but constraints are not the same as ineluctable processes, as the comparative experience of the inter-war years makes particularly clear.[2] In any case, our categories of analysis are fluid ones, for the notion of left and right is a metaphor whose meanings varied from one country to another and from one time to another. The petits bourgeois who were drifting to the right were not conservatives adapting to the status quo, but in many ways populists protesting against the faults of existing parliamentary systems, and condemning the activities of large-scale financial and commercial capital.[3]

A revisionist literature in the last two decades has tackled a related dimension of petit-bourgeois politics, refusing to see the new levels of mobilisation behind right-wing causes as the result of manipulation from outside. Political manipulation, social pressures and economic dependence were once thought to explain the political trajectory of master artisans and small shopkeepers. They were distinguished from the larger bourgeoisie by the weakness of their cultural norms and by their unstable occupational and social itineraries, and from workers by the absence of a work experience which would generate social cohesion. As a result, dissatisfaction and volatility were seen as characterising petits bourgeois who were particularly susceptible to outside pressures. More recent studies have, however, laid less stress on petit-bourgeois responses to others, and more on their own experience, values and tradition in formulating their world picture.[4] The challenge is to relate the movements of the petite bourgeoisie itself to the larger constraints within which they took shape, for only then can the political identities and values of these owners of small enterprise be grasped. Their earlier politics was rarely distinctively petit-bourgeois, which is perhaps why historians concerned to tie political movements to social groups have neglected them before the later nineteenth century. That earlier lack of clarity – rooted in part in the social, economic and cultural ambiguities which have been a continuing thread of our interpretation – made politics of special importance in constructing a petit-bourgeois identity. Towards the end of the nineteenth century, in a good number of European countries, the distinctive pressures faced by small enterprise combined with the political and intellectual attention directed towards them to generate an assertive organisational and political presence for a vocal section of the petite bourgeoisie. The external definitional, state and party political forces which helped form petit-bourgeois identity in those years are particularly important, and they are the focus of the first part of this chapter. The second section then explores the ways in which the political activity and ideas of European petits bourgeois took shape within that framework of constraints.

WORDS AND IDENTITIES

The first of these definitional forces is the terminology and notions employed in wider discourse to situate master artisans and shopkeepers within their society. There were clear differences which went beyond the merely linguistic. The dominant term in Germany was *Mittelstand*, whereas in Britain no equivalent terminology challenged the assumption that small masters and shopkeepers were but a part of a larger middle class. The debate among late nineteenth-century observers on what to call them reveals a real terminological uncertainty. Hector Lambrechts, the workhorse of the international movement for the defence of small enterprise, later wrote of 'the fluctuating terminology at the time',[5] and the contemporary concern to define these terms is an indication of ideological as well as semantic flux. If *classes moyennes* – whether singular or plural – came to prevail in France and to a substantial extent in Belgium it was partly because of its historic resonances, drawing on an older vision which saw them as the force for liberty and independence in French and Belgian life. The term, however, now narrowed in a similar way to that of *Mittelstand* in Germany, focusing on a part of what had once been a much larger group which had stretched into the business, professional and educated bourgeoisie. The terms were attractive, emphasising in French the *moyenne* with its connotations of both middle and average, and in German both the middling and the estate (*Stand*) dimensions of the group's place in the social order. The language provided the metaphorical purchase needed for a group that was to moderate and stabilise society, an attachment whose absence in Britain emphasises the indistinct role of the petite bourgeoisie there within social and political discourse.

It is not only social groups which have a history that they carry with them, for so does language. Although in Germany the term *gewerblicher* (business) *Mittelstand* was occasionally used in the 1840s, only from the late 1870s did artisans themselves begin to lay claim to the term, a decade at least in advance of retailers. Conze has shown the importance of the *Allgemeine deutscher Handwerkerbund* (General Union of German Artisans) established at the Magdeburg artisan congress in 1882 in making *Mittelstand* 'a term in the struggle for public recognition'.[6] The concept drew on an estate rather than a class vision of society, seeing small enterprise as a buffer within an estate-based social order. The French equivalent was less contested and less aggressively employed. By 1869, a substantial literature understood *classe moyenne* to mean the world of urban and rural small enterprise, distinguished from the rich bourgeois on the one hand and the populace on the other.[7] The rhetoric of the Third Republic, however, banished the idea of class, following the republican tradition that denied the legitimacy of intermediary bodies between the citizen and national sovereignty of the kind that had bedevilled *ancien régime* France. Raymond Poincaré, conservative politican and future President, told a gathering of representatives of small business in 1910 that

> I do not much like ... this word class, which ... seems to me to be ambiguous. In a country where orders once existed and where the word class was then used to distinguish nobles, villeins and serfs, one must always fear that there is something equivocal in the use of the old term.[8]

In that context, *classe moyenne* was not used in the name of an organisation until 1907, when Social Catholics and Progressists combined in an attempt to attract petits bourgeois disillusioned with the Radical Party, but it was nonetheless used across the intellectual and political spectrum. The term *petite bourgeoisie* carried pejorative connotations in France, and was rarely used outside socialist circles.

In the first two-thirds of the nineteenth century *Mittelstand* had served to distinguish a large Third Estate from both aristocracy and populace, asserting its place as the bearer of progressive and healthy social values in German society. It claimed to represent that society's healthiest forces, those of education, enterprise and property. Only after the 1870s did the notion of *Mittelstand* narrow to the lower end of that middle, the owners of small urban and rural enterprise. The social group which the term described was now increasingly presented as a defensive and conservative force. The French term *classe moyenne* narrowed in a similar fashion, from the Orléanist discourse articulated by Guizot from the 1820s, in which the *classe moyenne* embodied the struggle of the French Third Estate (and hence of the French nation) for freedom and progress. Although its social focus was at that time indistinct, it certainly included wealthy bourgeois and professionals. As in Germany, the idea of the *classe moyenne* narrowed later in the century to centre on small enterprise, pressing similar ideological implications into a more conservative mould.

In Belgium both *petite bourgeoisie* and *classes moyennes* were employed. Gustave Francotte, Minister of Labour and Industry, made it clear to a Catholic gathering in Verviers that the terms were for him interchangeable, though the latter seemed to include more occupations.[9] Indeed, the announcement by the Belgian Royal Academy of the award of its literary prize to a collection of essays by Hector Lambrechts in 1902 moved from one term to the other without any change of meaning.[10] However, representations of small-enterprise organisations, and individual small businessmen, seem to have used *petite bourgeoisie* in preference to *classes moyennes*, which was more the language of intellectuals and politicians.[11]

In comparison with these countries, neither the terms used in Britain nor the message they purported to carry developed with any such clarity, not because of the absence of small business people, but because of their lack of an equivalent degree of social identity. The term 'lower middle class' was increasingly evident from the 1870s, signifying an attachment to the middle class as a whole, the world of clerks and managers, shopkeepers and schoolteachers (for it embraced those far beyond small enterprise) which was perceived as the lower section of a larger social group. The title of the Middle Class Defence Organisation in 1906 suggests a broader European sense of a group located between capital and labour, but it aroused little support and even its leader, L. P. Sydney, was unable to identify its social constituency, or to decide whether to call it 'lower middle class' or simply 'middle class'.[12] The language of social description in Britain continued to draw more on the categories of moral discourse than political economy, with little concern to identify artisanal or commercial occupations within the overall social order. There was thus no place for peasants, master artisans or 'petits bourgeois', all significant concepts elsewhere, in the British language of social description.[13]

Consideration of vocabulary thus reaches beyond mere nomenclature and into the construction of images and their transmission over time. The positive vision of the 'middle' embodied in the terminologies in use in Britain as much as in France and Germany in the first half of the nineteenth century identified it with morality, education, progress and intelligence. As a Germany dictionary recorded in 1838, the *Mittelstand* was 'in all civilised states the principal estate in society, the kernel of nations, on which depends their future'.[14] The belief that the middle was a force for moderation and stability had a long heritage, embracing the constitutional radicalism of Britain in the 1790s, Orléanist discourse in France and that of the reform Whigs in Britain in the 1820s and 1830s. Here was the *juste milieu*, which referred less to a social group than to a set of wholesome values that were pitted against reaction.[15] Only towards the end of the nineteenth century did the concept of the middle became attached to a section of society – the owners of small artisanal and retailing enterprise, with small farmers sometimes included. Although it now became more defensive, the idea retained its Aristotelian power, the middle which was good precisely because it eschewed the extremes. Indeed, formal reference to Aristotle became common amongst late nineteenth-century writers on small enterprise, who were often influenced by Le Playist and Social Catholic ideas.[16]

These favourable images – alongside those from socialist and Marxist ideas in which the evolution of the capitalist system was held to predict the inevitable disappearance of small enterprise – provided one setting in which petit-bourgeois politics took shape. For many petits bourgeois the idea of an unjust fate, and of the necessity for state support, were the logical conclusions which they drew from the discourse of praise and the gloomy predictions. Whether they were drawn to Conservative or Catholic Centre Party politics in Germany, the Radical Party in France, or the Catholic Party in Belgium, these images expressed a positive affirmation of the value of small enterprise. The gap between this positive image, economic predictions, and the limited nature of government responses, constituted a formative influence on petit-bourgeois politics in much of late nineteenth- and early twentieth-century Europe.

The sense of being part of the *Mittelstand* increasingly spread within German petit-bourgeois organisations. They may not have represented all, or even a majority, of small enterprise, but that exclusiveness generated a concern for demarcation which characterised petit-bourgeois movements everywhere, and nowhere more than in Germany. Defining the true *Mittelstand* or the true *classe moyenne* affirmed the ideal's moral and social values. Those who fell short of it, because they lacked the professional education or the business management skills or the level of resources deemed appropriate, were by definition excluded from the social group, for the criteria tied business success to moral standing. Itinerant traders, domestic producers, women traders or artisans, increasingly Jews in Germany, were no part of the small business *Mittelstand*. The Bremen Grocers' Association statutes of 1917 decreed that

> only Bremen residents who are owners of professionally run grocery stores and speciality shops may be members of the association . . . . The principal requirement for eligibility is that the candidate has acquired satisfactory knowledge of the business in question or has demonstrated the ability to manage a business in an orderly and efficient fashion.[17]

Associations everywhere laid stress on the superior character of their membership, and the inadequacies of those excluded. British shopkeepers giving evidence before parliamentary inquiries or intervening in local affairs habitually emphasised that they represented the 'legitimate' trade.[18] The organised movements of the French petite bourgeoisie, a mixture of national politicians and organisations of small business, increasingly acted as if they were defending a real *classe moyenne* identity that was bound up with the experiences of their members. Nowhere was this more explicit than in the evidence of shopkeepers' representatives to the Landry Inquiry of 1912–13.[19] The line of demarcation was more ideological than economic, reinforcing the image of the stable and moral small business world, in a discourse which marked them off not only from manual workers, but also from the less successful members of their own trades, cutting across a social fabric whose subtlety of gradations was denied by these artificial distinctions.

STATES AND PARTIES

State policy also influenced the cohesion and definition of the petite bourgeoisie. Taxation, the suffrage and social policy each sharpened lines of demarcation, while at the same time provoking petit-bourgeois opposition which provided a basis for cohesion amongst a section of small enterprise. Each of these fields needs attention if we are to understand the forces shaping petit-bourgeois identity and political behaviour.

Taxation was not only a domain in which petits bourgeois felt keenly the pressure of state authority, it also constructed classifications and distinctions within the petite bourgeoisie. This was particularly true with respect to the *patente* (business tax) in France, whose distribution of businesses between different formal Tables, and between those who were liable to the tax and those who were exempt from it, imposed outside distinctions upon the world of small enterprise. Financial consequences followed these distinctions, along with differences of perception. Reforms to the *patente* excluded increasing numbers of enterprises from liability – those of domestic producers, independent workers, and then family workshops. Behind these exemptions lay not only the vision of Frédéric Le Play, who saw in the family workshop a means to resolve the social crisis of mid-century, but also the belief that the development of a small family property was, in a capitalist society, a form of labour, as important as waged employment.[20] With the vote in July Monarchy France attached to the payment of specific categories of taxation, exemptions carried political consequences. More important in the long term were the ways in which the *patente* came to shape shopkeeper campaigns and organisation. In France more than anywhere else, taxation became the focus of petit-bourgeois campaigning, as organised shopkeepers saw in adjustments to this tax a means of damaging their large-scale competitors.[21]

The *dazio consumo* in Milan provides a particularly striking example of the way taxation could structure both identities and political action within the petite bourgeoisie. This local excise tax, like the classic *octrois*, was levied on goods brought into Milan for sale. The city's old Spanish walls defined the area in which the tax operated, and distinguished it from the suburban areas beyond in which most of the popular classes lived and where a different tax regime applied. Morris has shown the ramifications of this taxation division: the *dazio consumo* affected the location of retail enterprises, it provoked continuing protests from shopkeepers and workers when attempts were made to reform it, and it ensured that Milanese shopkeepers were divided by geography more emphatically than by any other criterion. Until the uniting of the tax districts in 1898, Milan's shopkeepers could find little common ground for action, and the question of the *dazio* dominated retailer politics.[22] Milan seems to have been unusual, both in the persistence of such taxation and in its consequences for shopkeeper location and politics. Taxation systems were often highly specific, and their consequences have been neglected by historians.

Conflicts over taxation were not new for it was, along with army service, the most regular point of contact between ordinary people and the early-modern state. The early nineteenth century saw a continuation of local incidents between small business and government, none more sustained than that between the Prussian state and the town of Wetzlar in Hesse. New taxation policies as the town came under Prussian rule in 1815 provoked recurrent conflict between local artisans and shopkeepers on the one hand, and the town's elite and the Prussian state on the other. The town's ruling elite chose to tax producers, notably butchers and millers, rather than the population as a whole, even if that meant anti-Prussian protests. By 1823 butchers and millers were refusing to trade, and the King's intransigent defence of the taxation regime led to violent clashes. In 1830, in the course of a campaign to stop smuggling, the son of a master baker was killed by a tax inspector. The following decade saw the conflict become one between tax inspectors and smugglers, the latter supported by the town's master artisans and traders. Heavy sentences and the intervention of armed troops inflamed the situation further. When taxes on meat and flour production were raised in 1839 and protesting guilds suspended, butchers once again went on strike and refused to trade. The matter was only resolved in 1841 when the controversial taxes were replaced by personal taxation.[23] Wetzlar provides a powerful example – if an unusually sustained and violent one – of the way in which taxation policy not only provoked conflict but also produced mobilisation and cohesion in the world of small enterprise.

From the later decades of the century, local taxation policy became an issue for mobilisation in many countries, as petits bourgeois came to assert themselves as the real tax-paying class. A Lyon retailers' newspaper in 1901, having affirmed its vigorous support for the Republic, went on to complain at 'how little concern the republican deputies have shown for the interests of

139

small shopkeepers who carry the heaviest part of taxation at both the national and municipal level'.[24] Taxation created resentment. As the shopkeepers of Vervins protested in 1912, 'the tax burden is crushing, and much higher than that applied to the same income for bonds'.[25] The incidence of business taxes and the threats of income tax produced demands at the national level, but petits bourgeois experienced fiscal pressure primarily as a local question. The municipal budget and municipal taxation were the source of frequent clashes between small enterprise and local elites, as we saw in our discussion of municipal government. Conflict need not remain primarily local. The Belgian Butchers' Federation was founded in 1878 to challenge the taxes levied to pay for compulsory abattoirs and for the appraisal of meat quality.[26] Small business was disproportionately affected by the levels and incidence of municipal taxes, but conflict over local taxation was particularly significant in Britain, where small business made its main entry into the political domain with the distinctive voice of the ratepayer.

Taxation thus played a diverse role in shaping petit-bourgeois identity, influencing both mobilisation and self-perception. On the one hand stood movements which sought fair or even punitive taxes on large-scale retailers, while on the other were the denunciations of the taxing state as leeches who made small enterprise pay for policies which benefited only others. An incipient hostility to the state was sharpened in petit-bourgeois politics. Anti-tax revolts may have largely disappeared from the arsenal of popular protest in western Europe by the middle of the nineteenth century, but the consequential historical neglect of the issue is mistaken. In a variety of ways, taxation had by the late nineteenth century become a significant source of mobilisation for Europe's shopkeepers.

Voting rights and access to public representative bodies, themselves long related to the question of taxes, constituted a second influence on the identity and mobilisation of small enterprise. The petite bourgeoisie was often excluded from national or municipal franchises for much of the nineteenth century. This was least true of Britain, where the 1832 Reform Act began a process by which an increasing proportion of urban property owners – including many of the self-employed and small employers – participated in Parliamentary elections,[27] while a ratepayer franchise was introduced for elections to municipal councils after 1835. By the second half of the century small businessmen were a major part of the urban electorate. Progress in France was much less even. The Restoration of 1815 saw virtually all artisans and shopkeepers excluded from electoral colleges by the high tax level required, and the emphasis on land taxes. After the July Revolution in 1830, this was lowered in level and widened to include payment of the *patente*, which permitted the petite bourgeoisie to enter the electoral body. The 1831 Act gave the vote for municipal elections to one-tenth of the adult male population in small communes, thus enfranchising much of the petite bourgeoisie.[28] However, not until universal manhood suffrage was introduced in 1848 were master artisans and shopkeepers fully enfranchised.

Only in 1866 in the North German Confederation and 1871 in the Empire was this level of petit-bourgeois enfranchisement reached in Germany. Even then discriminatory measures, such as those employed in Kiel and Hamburg towards the end of the nineteenth century, excluded not only workers but also the humbler sections of small enterprise from the right to vote in local and regional elections.[29] Access to the municipal vote had long been easier, at least for those of *Bürger* status, owners of a house or business, and paying taxes. The impact was greater for the electorate than for small enterprise itself. Whereas 41 per cent of the municipal electors in the town of Rheine (Westphalia) were master artisans in 1850, only 27 per cent of master artisans had the vote.[30] The importance of local politics for petits bourgeois was thus reinforced, but the electoral systems ensured that voting in Germany concerned the more prosperous of artisans and shopkeepers, while excluding until as late as 1918 the owners of smaller enterprises. In the light of Hoffmann's suggestion that obstacles to involvement in electoral politics and decision-making played a specially significant role in petit-bourgeois mobilisation,[31] the strength of autonomous movements amongst German small enterprise, in comparison with Britain and France, might derive from the limits set to their access to both national politics and municipal affairs.

Elections to Chambers of Commerce and commercial courts could in a similar fashion integrate small business into the polity, or by exclusion sharpen its distinct demands. In most countries governments consulted Chambers of Commerce as institutions speaking for the business community, often giving them formal legal powers. Access was thus a major question for small enterprise, raising questions about the very conception of a 'business community'. The issue arose most emphatically in Germany and France, in contrast to Belgium, where Chambers of Commerce had been dissolved as official institutions in 1875, the Liberal government preferring the essentially private organisations which replaced them.[32] These were similar to those in Britain, where no formal institutions of this kind existed to represent business interests or to regulate trade practices. Once such institutions exist as an official conduit for business opinion or as a regulator of the business environment, then it is in the interests of the elite of the commercial community to control them. In Germany, *Innungen* were maintained by master artisans to protect the community of the trade and its interests, following the decline or abolition of guilds. Under pressure from organised master artisans and with the support of Conservative and Centre Party politicians, these *Innungen* were given increasing powers. In 1881 they were formally recognised as public bodies, in 1884 they were given in prescribed circumstances the monopoly of training apprentices, and in 1897 not only were artisanal chambers established (*Handwerkskammern*), but *Innungen* membership became compulsory for all master artisans where a majority of the trade in a town so voted. The acceptance of artisans' role in public bodies was nowhere more visible than in Germany, but even there shopkeepers found far less sympathy for their demands for equivalent institutions.

The right to vote in elections to Chambers of Commerce and commercial courts became a live issue for small enterprise towards the end of the nineteenth century when petit-bourgeois economic and social anxieties sharpened their sense of exclusion.[33] In Hamburg, retailer protest meetings over department stores or co-operatives would usually end with a resolution demanding the establishment of a *Detaillistenkammer* (retailers' chamber) to represent their interests.[34] The granting of autonomous representation for shopkeepers was in fact most widespread in Germany, whether within Chambers of Commerce or in specific retailer chambers that were set up in the Hanseatic cities of Hamburg and Bremen where the dominance of large-scale commerce threatened to crush independent shopkeepers and their voice. In Prussia the government recognised the importance of integrating small business within existing structures, and by 1906 they had equal voting rights for over half of the country's Chambers of Commerce.[35] Rights such as these were still a matter for the more prosperous independent traders. In Bremen, the need to be a *Bürger*, a citizen of the town, restricted the electorate for the retailers' chamber set up in 1906. The logic behind this restriction was a social one. As one draper put it, 'we want the truly established retailers to be represented in the Chamber and not those who come for three months and then quit Bremen.'[36]

Pressure from below forced the expansion of voting and access to the Chambers of Commerce in Germany, but the case of St Etienne in France shows the significance of pressure from above, as the republican government, pitting itself against what it saw as *ancien régime* notables, sought to democratise both *Chambres de Commerce* and the *Tribunaux de Commerce* (commercial courts).[37] In 1883 the right to vote in elections of judges in the latter had been given to all payers of the *patente*, and pressure from both national government and local campaigns sought to extend this to the *Chambre de Commerce* itself. The political right and merchant elites led the opposition. 'In the system which the government is now proposing,' claimed one Senator in 1907, 'petty traders will drown the representatives of capital. This is dangerous.' The outcome of this opposition was to limit the vote to those who paid the higher levels of the *patente*, and left it to a local commission of representatives from the Departmental General Council, the *Chambre de Commerce* and the *Tribunal de Commerce* to establish the categories of voters in each constituency in such a way as to ensure that café-owners and grocers did not swamp large industrialists and merchants.[38]

Social policy constitutes a further way in which the state could play an important, if not always direct, role in the shaping of petit-bourgeois political identity. In comparison with the effect of the German social legislation of 1911 in demarcating the relative position of manual workers and white-collar employees, and thus contributing to the sharpening of white-collar identities,[39] the impact of social legislation on small enterprise was essentially negative, provoking resentment and opposition. Social policy throughout western Europe after the 1880s meant policy with regard to the working class. This was a common cause of complaint in petit-bourgeois movements, and amongst those speaking for the petite bourgeoisie. Social Catholics argued that the difficulties of small enterprise were exacerbated by the way those seeking to secure social stability were concerned exclusively with the wage-earning working class. Paul du Maroussem complained that the legislative and social benefits devised to help the working class only made life more difficult for small enterprise, so that 'each attempt to solve the *working-class question* serves only to deepen and to aggravate the *social question*'.[40] With the exception of pensions for workers and peasants in France, which permitted a reasonable number of master artisans and shopkeepers to insure themselves,[41] social policies imposed supplementary charges on the owners of small enterprise without any apparent benefits in their eyes. One association in Clermont-Ferrand told the Landry Inquiry in 1912 that 'the economic circumstances faced by the shopkeeper make him hostile to all social legislation', identifying child labour laws, regulation of hours of labour, and retirement pensions as particular grievances.[42]

The greatest protests concerned measures to control the opening hours and condition of labour in retailing: the weekly day off for employees, early closing days, and Sunday closing. The weekly day off, although the rule in large industrial firms and department stores, appeared to threaten the viability of small retail enterprises surviving on low labour costs.[43] A parallel conflict over attempts to strengthen compulsory Sunday closing legislation in Britain brought marginal small shopkeepers into conflict with the state and larger individual retailers, who together sought to enforce Sunday closing of shops. A flurry of organisations – such as the Shopkeepers' and Small Traders' Protection Association (1905) and local associations such as the Bradford and District Sunday Traders' Defence League (1904) – were founded to struggle on behalf of the small shopkeeper.[44]

Small enterprise everywhere argued that the costs arising from social legislation – pensions, accident compensation, and in Germany sickness and invalidity benefits, together with restrictions on the hours of labour – represented additional expenses for businesses that were already struggling to survive. Two-thirds of French shopkeepers surveyed in 1913 believed that social legislation had increased their costs.[45] Municipal Reform movements in London echoed this refrain in relation to local rates, as they tried to mobilise small businessmen against the costly policies of the progressive London County Council. They were advised that

the type of elector who should be considered is the small shopkeeper, who is hardest hit by high rates . . . . In the past too much attention has been paid to the desires of 'working men' while claims of the shop-keeping class have been neglected.[46]

The burgeoning demands of the state loomed large in the discourse of small enterprise, but they were in reality limited. In 1913 fewer than one-third of French shops were granting the *repos hebdomadaire* (weekly day off).[47] This was lower than in Germany but systematic exemptions everywhere weakened the impact of such laws. The hostility of petits bourgeois, however, was rarely assuaged.

The period beginning in the 1870s and 1880s represents a significant stage in the relationship between state institutions and the petite bourgeoisie in Europe, but a distinction must be drawn between countries where state intervention sought to organise small enterprise and develop its cohesiveness, and those where the relationship was much weaker. The first is exemplified by Germany, where the Imperial state sought to give cohesion to the *Mittelstand*, above all through corporate projects and institutions in the artisanal sector, but one can also find it in Belgium, where the Catholic government sought to establish an institutional structure and subsidies for self-help organisations as a base for collective defence amongst small enterprises. These policies of corporatism in Germany or self-defence in Belgium can rarely be found in France, and not at all in Britain.

Political needs and political conjunctures play a major part in explaining these differences, as from the 1880s political parties in various countries actively cultivated a petit-bourgeois electorate and petit-bourgeois organisations. The attention of political parties now came to play a formal role in the development of petit-bourgeois politics, as new imperatives appeared on the European political agenda. The social question, universal or extensive manhood suffrage and mass politics, and the emergence of labour and socialist movements combined in many countries to sharpen the relevance of petit-bourgeois voters. The problems of the petite bourgeoisie became involved with the continuation of the established order, and their support for that order came to be seen as an indispensable element in its stability. A competition appeared in much of Europe for petit-bourgeois votes, as parties sought to wean master artisans and shopkeepers from previous attachments to radical or popular politics, and to mobilise them in defence of the social order. As early as 1860, the liberal publicist Ludwig August von Rochau had insisted that, for all the shortcomings it had revealed in 1848, the *Mittelstand* was indispensable. 'No political idea is ready to be realised,' he wrote 'no political change has a chance to be realised and sustained without its support. The most important task of every political party is to win the *Mittelstand* for itself.'[48] It was a task which required parties that saw the petite bourgeoisie as an important part of their constituencies in a rapidly changing political situation, parties such as the Centre Party in Germany, the Catholic Party in Belgium, and the Radical Party in France. These parties, which in distinctive ways represented the existing order in their own societies, needed voters as do all parties but, more significantly, each had come to discover in the petite bourgeoisie a basis for social stability.

The confessional parties could appeal to continuing petit-bourgeois religious commitment, but they could also use corporate images to present their social ideals, identifying occupational, hierarchical and moral units within which small employers threatened by competition might hope to survive and even flourish. The political success of this vision can be seen in Belgium and Germany. After the 1893 franchise reform in Belgium, which granted universal manhood suffrage but within a plural voting system which made petit-bourgeois voters especially important, and with the rising challenge of the Belgian socialist party, there was dialogue between the Catholic Party in power, the representatives of organisations of small enterprise, and Catholic intellectuals.[49] The dialogue was part of a wider process of discovery, through which a section of Social Catholics and some followers of the French sociologist Frédéric Le Play found in small enterprise the potential for social stabilisation in a dangerously polarising society.[50] In Belgium – and in France too, though with fewer political consequences – a discourse evolved which influenced both the movements of petits bourgeois themselves, and debates on the *classes moyennes* in the decades that followed. The debate drew heavily on German writings and experience – when Hector Lambrechts was charged by the Belgian government in 1896 with setting up a service for the *classes moyennes* within the Labour Department, his first step was to tour German and Austrian towns to learn what was being done there.[51] However, few took the corporatist ambitions of German reformers as a model to follow.

Whereas French intellectuals and reformers involved in this discourse were conservatives and Catholics excluded from political power, their counterparts in Belgium had far greater influence because the Catholic Party governed without interruption from 1884 to the First World War. As a consequence it was Belgian intellectuals such as Victor Brants, Oscar Pyfferoen and Hector Lambrechts who took the lead and, although concrete government action was limited in scope, they wrote extensively and encouraged organising.[52] Intellectuals and local politicans from this milieu organised a series of international congresses of the petite bourgeoisie, the first held in Antwerp in 1899,[53] and in 1903 set up the International Institute for the Study of the Problem of the Classes Moyennes.[54] The argument was clear: the petite bourgeoisie was in crisis, its very survival was at stake, and it could be crushed beneath the wheels of the juggernaut of progress and economic concentration if a combination of self-help associations (primarily) and state support did not rescue it. A meeting in Lyon was told, 'history teaches us . . . that when, in a nation, the *classe moyenne* ceases to exist, that nation loses its vitality, and loses little time before it too disappears'.[55] The petite bourgeoisie was essential to social peace because it was the middle, the average, the *moyenne*. This metaphor of the middle came to shape perceptions of the world of small enterprise. The *classes moyennes* were the hope for mobility for ambitious workers; they acted as a buffer between the classes; they were extreme in neither ideas, wealth, nor power; their ideas were moderate and virtuous; they mixed together labour and capital, property and wealth, production and consumption, which were dangerous when concentrated yet wholesome when mixed; finally, they were the links in the social chain, the links which guaranteed social peace.

The practical results, in terms of measures of protection sought by organised small enterprise, may have been limited, but institutional structures were established which not only reinforced the sense that the petite bourgeoisie was on the political agenda, but also encouraged petit-bourgeois organisations and identity. The discourse of the middle entered the world of the organised petite bourgeoisie, as a variety of political groups drew upon it to mobilise the world of small enterprise and direct its demands. In Germany, where religious division affected political affiliation, the Catholic sections of the petite bourgeoisie tended to support the Centre Party rather than the Liberals or Conservatives, responding to its efforts to mobilise these voters to preserve its electoral position. Blackbourn writes of the Centre Party's 'demagogic exploitation of *Mittelstandspolitik* and parish-pump resentment', and Loth has described the populist wing of the Catholic Centre.[56] It was, however, the Conservatives in Germany, especially after their Tivoli Congress of 1892, who launched the most successful efforts to forge a union with the defence organisations of small enterprise, supporting their demands and sharing with them a vision of a hierarchic and organic society. They did so through concessions to their demands, through constructing neo-corporatist institutions, and through a wide-ranging policy of *Mittelstandspolitik*. The distance between rhetoric and policies remained, a distance which classic historical considerations of *Mittelstandspolitik* elide, but political attention was a powerful force shaping petit-bourgeois political identity.

In the context of France's far more fragmented party structure, republicanism and Radicals remained the heart of petit-bourgeois political allegiances through the Third Republic. In the competitive political context of the early 1890s Radicals, anxious to shore up support, engineered the setting up by the Chamber of Deputies of the Mesureur Commission to examine the problems of small enterprise and consider proposals for *patente* reform. There was a contest for petit-bourgeois votes across much of the political spectrum, to the extent that by 1900 it was hard to detect any difference between the election promises of republicans and nationalists in Paris, as both sides sought to win over the small shopkeeper.[57] The Radical Party drew the votes of petits bourgeois with a programme which envisaged the extension of private property, criticised capitalism, promised evolutionary change without conflict and without violence, and held out hopes for a society of mobility and opportunity. The defence of the petite bourgeoisie was linked to the historic struggle of the people against the rich. As Léon Bourgeois told the party's 1902 congress, he meant by the worker 'not only the wage-earner ... but the small shopkeeper, the small farmer, the small *rentier*, that is to say all those unable to participate in the skills of racketeering or the rapaciousness of speculation'.[58]

Socialist parties recruited individual master artisans and shopkeepers, but had difficulty in devising a policy directed at the petite bourgeoisie in general. The gap between their programmes and the demands of organised petits bourgeois was enormous, setting collective property against private, and an economic analysis of society against a moral vision. The German SPD opposed the reorganisation of corporate artisanal bodies in the late nineteenth century, seeing small businessmen only as future proletarians. It was keen to recruit master artisans, but on its own terms.[59] The appeal setting up the French socialist *Parti ouvrier français* had mentioned the owners of small enterprise as a potential base for the party alongside workers, but a variety of factors, including the importance of consumer co-operation to socialists from the 1890s, forced that appeal into the background. In spite of all the efforts of Jean Jaurès to present petits bourgeois as the defenders of republican values, and as the victims of large-scale capitalist exploitation, the theory of the class struggle, and the dogmatic insistence of the Guesdists within the movement, prevented the French socialists from articulating a strategy that seemed relevant to small enterprise.[60]

However much individual petits bourgeois may have joined socialist parties or voted for socialist candidates, socialist parties found it difficult to engage politically and theoretically with the defence of small enterprise. That was left to more conservative forces, as outside political parties and movements found the petite bourgeoisie an important focus for their attention. It is therefore appropriate to turn from the way in which the state, institutions, and political parties shaped petit-bourgeois politics, and look at the activities of petits bourgeois themselves.

THE POLITICS OF THE PEOPLE

The period between the later eighteenth century and the revolutionary year of 1848 was one in which master artisans and shopkeepers are to be found politically amongst the *menu peuple*, the ordinary people of employed workers, journeymen, small masters and traders, a world defined not by its economic characteristics (other than to say that none within it were rich and few who were active were very poor) but by its political and moral vision, its commitment to what has been seen as the moral economy, and its radical challenge to hierarchy and corruption. In Britain and France above all, but in any country where local and national elites were confronted from below by angry demands for reform, shopkeepers and master artisans were prominent in such movements. When historians write of working-class politics in early nineteenth-century Europe, it is really this broader popular politics that they are usually describing, and when they wrestle with the inconsistencies of early working-class ideology, it is often because of a reluctance to concede its popular rather than proletarian character.

The radical concept of the people lay at the heart of the movements: the ordinary people who were useful and productive, and who rejected the rich and the parasites who monopolised wealth and power. The radical language was less a critique of an economic system – though it might draw into itself such a critique, as happened in Chartism in Britain or co-operative socialism in France – and more a critique of a structure of power and of morality. When British radicals denounced capitalists, it was financiers and middlemen whom they were attacking rather than industrial capitalists. Here was an ideology of modest resources, hard work, and independence, one whose enemies were injustice and subordination. It took concrete shape in the writings of Tom Paine and Thelwall, in the vision of the Parisian *sans-culottes* during the French Revolution expressed in their *sections* and in their newspaper, *le Père Duchesne*, and it was developed in popular political movements throughout the first half of the nineteenth century.

The true enemies of the *menu peuple* were identified as the speculators and monopolists who were seen as manipulating structures of credit, of taxation and of influence in order to accumulate riches and power in their own hands.[61] The dependent and fragile ties of credit, and the expanding role of middlemen and merchants in craft production, reinforced the persuasiveness for the owners of small enterprise of the attack on financial speculators and unproductive middlemen. Here was an ideology which made sense of their world and the world of the ordinary people, and the economic experiences explored in other chapters would have confirmed rather than challenged its validity. The idea of the people against the rich, *le peuple* against *les gros*, was a vision which believed that material distress and inequality rested not on an economic system but on the moral dislocation of ordinary economic relationships. As European states and municipalities were seen to abandon their older role of mediating between the rich and the people, so the radicalism found new dimensions. This vision was to dominate popular movements through much of Europe in the period up to the middle of the nineteenth century, and it resonated amongst petits bourgeois far beyond those years.

Honest work and productive small property were the positive side of this vision. It conceived of property in its larger sense, one which embraced the right of an artisan to practise his trade, the right to live by one's own efforts, the right to sustain the systems of moral and economic control which defended those rights. This conception stood against the exclusively individualistic notion of property which came to prevail in nineteenth-century Europe and which saw property as limited to that which could be bought and sold, and whose defining framework was not that of older community rights but the imperatives of the market.[62] A republican newspaper – called *Le Peuple* as many were – in Limoges defined property in this way during 1848: 'Property is the right of each and everyone to satisfy their physical, intellectual and moral needs by the use, regulated by law, of each and every person's physical, intellectual and moral labour.'[63] Petit-bourgeois political relationships became bound up with these contested meanings of property. As the liberal, bourgeois milieu distanced itself from the moral connotations of property, so many petits bourgeois who refused to accept that narrowing of obligations attached themselves more firmly to the radicalism of the people. For other owners of small enterprise, their acceptance of these newer conceptions of property was one aspect of their separation from the world of waged labour.

Popular politics was at its most precocious in Britain, where from the 1750s the 'middling sort' were forming tavern societies and reading clubs to press for political change, reading radical newspapers such as the *Middlesex Journal*, and forming the bedrock support of John Wilkes, demanding that it was the electors of his constituency and not MPs who should decide on whether he should be admitted to the House of Commons. This rejection of the politics of dependence can be traced through the movements of the 1790s, to be generalised by economic hardship and increasing class tension in the explosion of radical politics from 1815 through to Chartism. Here was an expectant and optimistic politics concerned with democratic suffrage, opposition to monopolists and speculators, and support for civil and religious liberty and national education. It can be found in the efforts of shopkeepers, teachers and small manufacturers in Salford to use a variety of petty institutions to penetrate local affairs, or the activities of London's vestry radicals in the 1820s and 1830s.[64] Here was a rejection of the client economy and politics. The radical movements' concentration on 'old corruption', representative government, and the conflict between productive and unproductive provided the basis of the popular alliance which drew together workers and many petits bourgeois, and it broke down only slowly after the middle 1830s, as the older Painite radicalism splintered.[65] The Chartist movement was perhaps the turning-point for popular radicalism. Petits bourgeois were certainly involved, and many strands of the older ideas prevailed, not least the condemnation of the unproductive and concern for the democratisation of the state. New elements were coming to the fore, however, more rapidly than anywhere else in Europe, as a language of class and of working-class identity introduced a new element into radical politics, and a new style which small property-owners found less congenial. In this context the Birmingham Political Union was an effort to draw a section of the town's petits bourgeois into a reform alliance with larger business interests, using much of the language of popular radicalism but insisting on a propertied franchise.[66] The rupture of April 1848 was more symbolic than real, for petit-bourgeois radicalism did not vanish with the Chartist experience, but in that month large numbers of London's small property owners enrolled as special constables to counter the supposedly revolutionary threat posed by the great Chartist demonstration.[67]

The contrast offered by petits bourgeois in Paris probably tells us more about the nature of the regimes than it does about the owners of small enterprise. In March 1848 in Paris it was the failure of the essentially petit-bourgeois National Guard to put down the popular rising against Louis-Philippe which ensured the downfall of the elitist and narrowly-based July Monarchy. The electoral system had systematically excluded the world of small enterprise and with good reason. As one minister observed in 1844, arguing that the level of tax payment which qualified for the vote should be set so as to exclude the small *patente* payers, 'they are part of those classes who must never be allowed to join the electorate'.[68] Master artisans and shopkeepers had been central to popular movements in Paris and the larger towns from 1789 onwards. The master glazier Jacques-Louis Ménétra, like many a Parisian small master, moved without difficulty from an instinctive royalism to radical republicanism. He joined the National Guard in July 1789, stormed the Tuilleries in August 1792, and was an active member of the Bonconseil *section* in the Year 2.[69] The owners of small enterprise took a significant place on elected municipal councils not only in the larger towns, but also in rural towns and villages, where their constant relations with the population made it realistic for them to offer to represent the lower classes.[70] People such as these were prominent among the *sans-culottes*, whose radical vision was founded on the ideology of the *menu peuple* outlined above, to which was added the force of artisanal culture, and the messianic democratic commitment born out of revolutionary idealism. The *sans-culotte* vision was one of a society freed from aristocrats, priests, and externally-imposed authority – but it was not to be a society free of authority as such. The life cycle hierarchy of the workshop and the natural hierarchy of the patriarchal family were to be the sources of authority, in a world without rich or poor which would be regenerated by the morality of independence, honest work, and democracy.

This was the most radical articulation of the ideology of the *menu peuple*, but the ideas continued to colour republican movements through the opposition to repression after the July Revolution of 1830. Within months of the new regime's accession to power radical journals such as *l'Artisan* and *le Peuple* were reasserting the popular and still oppositional vision of a society where it was the useful and the productive whose interests should prevail. Petits bourgeois rallied to the republican opposition in towns all over France.[71] It was to find graphic expression in Lyon in the revolts of 1831 and 1834 when masters and journeymen silk-weavers joined together in their battle with the wealthy putting-out merchants and the political authorities who supported them.[72] Shopkeepers and master artisans were prominent in the spring of 1848, inspired by the vision of progress and democracy held out by the Revolution. For the French historian, Georges Dupeux, their belief in progress and humanity meant that the petite bourgeoisie 'more than any other class had the *quarante-huitard* (forty-eight) mentality'.[73] As a contemporary in Mulhouse observed at the time, 'the "bourgeois", that is to say the bakers, butchers, bar owners, grocers, and so on detest the factory owners. The factory owners are hated because they are rich.'[74]

The contrast between Britain and France is instructive, for it suggests that the political influence of petits bourgeois during the middle decades of the nineteenth century varied with national political structures and opportunities. The July Monarchy was willing to countenance a role in municipalities for petit-bourgeois voters and representatives, but distanced them from the national scene. It was disdainful as well as fearful of a section of society at odds with the authoritarian rule of wealth which characterised these years. It is not surprising that Louis-Philippe was advised not to carry out the annual inspection of the Paris National Guard in 1840, for his safety could not be guaranteed. An authoritarian and elitist regime set itself against those very groups who were being cultivated by wealthier bourgeois elites in Britain who, in the aftermath of parliamentary and municipal reform in the 1830s, began the process of incorporating the owners of small enterprise within a liberal political consensus. The character of British liberalism made that accommodation easier – above all its continuing critique of aristocratic privilege and the religious dissent which maintained its moral and institutional radicalism. The process was underway which progressively detached petits bourgeois from their wider popular identity.

As we move beyond industrialising western Europe information becomes sparser, as do popular movements. They were far less developed in the fragmented states of Germany during the *Vormärz* period, with opposition severely repressed (and therefore also harder to examine). Rhineland politics during these years was very much 'a politics of the notables'.[75] Master artisans were involved in food protests and in the defence of traditional rights and the moral economy, according to police reports. It is nevertheless unwise to see artisans in general as oppositional. They were as likely to be members of the militias that defended the status quo as in movements of resistance. Petits bourgeois were involved in liberal movements during these years – look at their prominent place in the Hambach demonstration for freedom of speech in 1832[76] – yet the corporatist interests of artisans and the extremely localist character of politics in the absence of effective parliamentary institutions, produced a tension with middle-class liberals that would surface in 1848. Nevertheless, the tensions should not be exaggerated by assuming that economic and political liberalism necessarily went together. Most German liberals before 1848 continued to visualise a society based on corporations, albeit reformed ones. Master artisans during 1848 could demand corporatist protections and authority in the economic sphere while holding firm to democratic and liberal political reforms.

Are the years around mid-century those when the traditions of popular politics disintegrated? Can we trace to the revolutionary experience of those years the moment when the European petite bourgeoisie abandoned its role in radical and democratic movements and turned to the defence of property and order against an increasingly assertive working class? In the long run the answer has to be yes, for the experience of 1848 signalled lasting tensions within the popular movement and even greater tensions between popular radicals and middle-class liberals, while it taught ruling elites that control required the cultivation of public opinion and the stabilising of social relations far more than it required repression. The economic and social pressures that were beginning to prise apart the working class and the owners of small enterprise received political reinforcement. These were processes, however, whose development required decades rather than the events, however dramatic, of a single spring and summer.

It is unwise to see the cleavage between small masters and journeymen in Frankfurt during 1848 itself, when they split into separate artisanal congresses, as a major social or political divide.[77] The two congresses expressed a divergence of views less in their conception of guilds than in their conception of the place of the journeyman in the master's household. For the masters this was one of subordination. In the words of a contemporary, 'the relation must be like that of children and household members to the father of the family'.[78] For the journeymen, on the other hand, they were part of a single artisanal community alongside their masters and the apprentices. The disagreement was real, but both took for granted corporate modes of thought, and both agreed on how guilds should be reformed, with the abolition of a range of abuses, and allowing masters far greater mobility in a change which would have severed the historic link between the town and the title of master. They also agreed in their rejection of freedom of competition and enterprise, and their denunciation of factory production. The different political patterns which one finds in 1848 were derived less from these matters than from local variations in relations between masters and journeymen and local political traditions. In some cases where the state strongly supported guilds, as in Bavaria or Frankfurt, masters might be prominent in conservative political associations,[79] while the appearance of workers' associations, as in Berlin and Cologne, might suggest an incipient class identity. By the autumn of 1848 the term 'worker' in political discourse in Cologne no longer included masters, who were forming *Innungen* for themselves. There were nonetheless good numbers of masters in the Cologne Workers' Association, albeit mostly small and impoverished putting-out masters.[80] Local political circumstances rather than attachment to guilds were thus central to the behaviour of masters and journeymen in 1848. Düsseldorf's master artisans were present in all the radical movements of that year, demanding democracy, civil liberties and constitutional reform, and the very same occupations whose masters were at the heart of the democratic movement were those most vociferously demanding the restoration of guilds.[81] The two sets of demands appear incompatible only because historians have absorbed the liberal world picture, and guilds could provide (as we saw in Deventer) a basis for community and mobilisation which could serve different political causes.

The defeats of 1848–49 everywhere meant that the social and political tensions, which threatened to tear apart the concept of the *menu peuple*, receded in the struggles against repression which followed. Nowhere is this more clear than in France. The June Days in Paris might be seen as the moment when the petit-bourgeois National Guard changed sides and turned its guns on the workers of the faubourg Saint-Antoine, and the fact that their opponents were disproportionately drawn from industries where workshop size was increasing might confirm the class nature of the June Days.[82] The transition was symbolic of a shift towards a more moderate petit-bourgeois republicanism through the Second Empire and into the Third Republic, and the transition was a slow one. The years of Bonapartist repression between 1849 and 1851 saw shopkeepers and artisans central to resistance in the name of the 'social and democratic republic', and then at the centre of the resistance to the Napoleonic coup of December 1851. In the department of Allier, 512 republican–democrats were charged with political crimes after the coup, of whom one-half were independent artisans and shopkeepers.[83] French shopkeepers and master artisans from then on defended a political vision that did not just place them on the left through the nineteenth century, but was also a central element in defining what the left was in France for much of the period.

THE MOVE TO THE RIGHT

The politics of petits bourgeois in the years between 1848 and the 1870s have received far less attention from historians. In spite of the political repression of the 1850s in much of Europe, these were decades of economic growth and optimism which sustained reforming movements for whom liberty, progress and justice seemed historically inevitable. Political reaction and repression paradoxically made it easier for petits bourgeois to remain attached to a progressive politics which often embraced organised workers as well as liberal bourgeois.

The consolidation of liberalism in Britain during these years saw the owners of small enterprise more firmly incorporated into the constitutional structures of liberal politics, an incorporation made easier by the contestatory nature of a liberalism that retained an anti-privilege discourse and a commitment to religious dissent. Disputes over Church Rates (or in Edinburgh the equivalent Annuity Tax) ensured that the latter remained a powerful influence.[84] Beginning in the 1840s, a political liberalism took shape at whose centre stood the fragile urban liberal community of local bourgeois, shopkeepers and small employers, and radical skilled workers. The political community developed around the often tense but viable assertion of notions of equality based on ideals that were individualistic and specifically political.[85] Far from being passively drawn into this urban liberalism, petits bourgeois helped shape its ideals, playing a significant role in the ousting of older Whig elites in places like the north-east where conflict continued into the mid-

Victorian years.[86] These were initially the more prosperous small businessmen, men like a Nottingham ironmonger whose son remembered that his dress was

> so arranged that you would have taken him for what he was, a well-to-do shopkeeper of chapel-going habits, one of the class who formed the sturdy backbone of mid-Victorian Liberalism, worshipped Lord John Russell, hated that upstart Disraeli, and conducted family prayers.[87]

Established small businessmen became the workhorses of local electoral politics, maintaining organisations, raising funds, and ensuring supporters were registered.[88] They were active in both parties, with allegiance sometimes following their trade (butchers and publicans tended to be Tory, grocers Liberal), but more commonly a variety of personal, business and religious forces.[89] For the majority of mid-Victorian petits bourgeois, these led them to liberalism.

The later nineteenth-century attachment to the corporate idea in Germany should not lead us to pass over the 1860s and 1870s as if they were uncomplicatedly a continuation of that tradition. In fact, the 1860s saw co-operative and autonomous organisations attract master artisans seeking a means to defend their independence in the face of economic change in a society where corporate and legal protections were being abandoned. It is not by chance that Hermann Schulze-Delitzsch's ideas for credit co-operatives found popularity at just this time, suggesting that corporations were not the sole point of reference for German artisans, however much the later nineteenth-century trend might suggest that they were.[90] The unfolding of liberalism in Britain and of corporatism in Germany did not constitute some single line of development, but responded to changing political circumstances and opportunities.

Many groups sought from the 1880s onwards to mobilise petits bourgeois in the cause of conservatism and stability, even in the cause of a new radicalism of the right, and it is the years between then and the First World War on which historical research has concentrated. Organisations of shopkeepers and master artisans proliferated on an unprecedented scale in these years and, although their political orientation varied between countries, and although national federations were more powerful in Germany than elsewhere, the broad process of organisation can be traced throughout industrial Europe. Associations of a single trade in a town were the most common. A small Lancashire town like Nelson in 1914 boasted associations of boot and shoe retailers, butchers, chemists, bakers, greengrocers, hairdressers, off-licence holders, painters, plumbers, newsagents, men's outfitters, and fried fish dealers. There was also a Small Traders' Association and a Tradesmen's Association, general associations which united a town's small businesses across trade boundaries.[91] The French Unions commerçants (shopkeepers' unions) were similar, established from the 1890s to represent shopkeepers to municipal authorities, watch over unlawful trading, provide miscellaneous insurance, credit and legal services for members, and apply political pressure where necessary.[92] The next level of organisation moved beyond the single town, involving representatives of local associations with an emerging stratum of professional activists in petit-bourgeois politics. These included regional and national associations of a trade, such as the Grocers' Federation in Britain founded in 1891 and the Belgian National Federation of Bakers of 1885.[93] National and regional associations recruiting across trades – amongst all retailers or all master artisans, for example – were far less common in Britain than in Germany where a more encouraging political atmosphere saw them proliferate.[94]

The Blackpool Tradesmen's Association may stand for all local single-trade or multi-trade groups in its main functions, for these differed only in emphasis between towns and between countries. Blackpool's retailers who joined the association received free legal advice; mutual plate glass insurance; a benevolent society; campaigning against illegitimate traders (such as bogus auctions); protests over municipal trading and local rates; and regular social gatherings and annual dinners.[95] In other countries there would be a greater emphasis on co-operative credit provision, and on professional and technical education, as well as collective purchasing operations. All were encouraged by those seeking to improve the condition of small enterprise through self-help, though their progress in France was a good deal less extensive than in Germany or Belgium. At the local level services and sociability prevailed, coupled with a watchful eye on the municipal authorities. Associations could form around specific campaigns, though they would often survive the waning of the initial impetus. The *Verein Bremen Ladeninhaber* was set up in Bremen in 1893 as a pressure group in relation to the weekly rest day legislation of two years earlier, while the *Gewerbe Schutzverein Hamburg* appeared in 1900 specifically to campaign against the creation of a department store in Barmbeck.[96] The town Early Closing Associations in England were a specific attempt by the more successful local shopkeepers, generally led by drapers, to cut costs and improve labour conditions by obtaining early-closing legislation that would force similar closing hours on their smaller, family-based competitors.[97]

Pressure group activity by national associations was much more explicitly political in countries where efforts were made to incorporate the *Mittelstand* or the *classes moyennes* within larger political configurations. This politicisation involved national organisations which were distant from local petits bourgeois and run by national political figures in the movement. Diverse examples include the *Ligue syndicale de travail, de l'industrie et du commerce* founded in Paris in 1888, the *Allgemeiner deutscher Handwerkerbund* established in Magdeburg in 1882, or the *Association nationale de la petite bourgeoisie* founded in Brussels in 1900. They were increasingly common after 1900 as parties and politicians manoeuvred to attract petit-bourgeois support.[98] They often drew on the other great phenomenon of petit-bourgeois – mostly shopkeeper – mobilisation in these years, the newspapers, which included specific trade journals as well as agitational and informative papers of a more wide-ranging kind, such as *La Revendication* (Paris) and *L'Alliance* (Lyon), *L'Esercente* (Milan), *The Retail Trader* (London), and *Der Detaillist* (Rhineland and Westphalia).

The economic-interest organisations and the political movements did not draw equally from all sections of small enterprise, and the development from popular radicalism to a more conservative politics can partly be explained by a shift in the centre of gravity of petit-bourgeois politics, as the poorer traders and more marginal small masters who were particularly significant in movements in the earlier nineteenth century gave way to the more stable and established petits bourgeois who dominated those from the 1880s onwards. The generalisation is nonetheless too sweeping – radical reformers in the earlier period drew support from successful small businessmen, while the owners of more marginal businesses can be found in later nineteenth-century movements. A simple change in social balance is not enough to explain the change in politics.

The new organisations did not embrace all of small enterprise. First, some trades were historically better-organised than others, such as butchers, bakers, pharmacists, and publicans, who had long faced municipal and trade regulation. It is no coincidence that grocers' and milksellers' organisations grew rapidly in Britain when these trades were subjected to new legislative and administrative interference in the 1880s. Second, organisations represented better capitalised and more stable small enterprises. If they were not all prosperous, they were less likely to be unstable and marginal. Only in occasional crises did associations appear for marginal businesses, and they were generally short-lived. An example is the Shopkeepers and Small Traders Association founded in Britain on the eve of the First World War to resist new pressures to secure Sunday closing. Even well-organised trades saw occasional flurries of opposition to domination by the owners of better enterprises. In the 1880s the *Bulletin de la Boulangerie de la Région lyonnaise* campaigned stridently against the policy of the bakers' syndicate that was dominated by the elite of the trade.[99] The organisations represented only a section of small enterprise in terms of their income and stability. It is difficult to say whether they spoke for a minority in terms of their ideas.

It was primarily shopkeepers who comprised the organised petite bourgeoisie from the 1880s in Britain, France and Belgium. In Germany, however, (as elsewhere in central Europe) the persistence of corporate institutions and the character and timing of industrialisation gave artisans a more central role in mobilisation. The corporatist framework made demands of the state a significant element in German petit-bourgeois organisations. As a memorandum from the *Zentralverband* retailer movement told the Kaiser in 1893,

to rescue the class through self-help is almost completely out of the question. Against the freedoms, which damage, even ruin, traders from fixed-selling outlets, against the superior strength of *Großital*, neither the individual nor an association can do anything; only the law can give sufficient protection.[100]

Although slight in Britain, intervention by the state entered the basket of petit-bourgeois demands to a greater or lesser extent in other countries: reform of local and professional taxes, measures to penalise department stores and retail chains; restrictions on workers' co-operatives; protection against unfair trading such as fictitious bankruptcy sales or mock auctions; restrictions on itinerant traders; suppression of employee trading and civil servants' co-operatives. The appeal for state support was particularly forceful in Germany where artisanal strength in the organised petite bourgeoisie intensified demands for the reinforcement of guild organisations to regulate the trade, limit access to mastership, control the labour force, and regulate both production and the market.[101] The reality conceded by the state – the strengthened *Innungen*, measures against department stores and co-operatives, improved tendering rights for small enterprise – was always a good deal less than the rhetoric which surrounded it, but it sustained distinctive state-oriented demands by petit-bourgeois organisations. It also helped to shape a distinctive occupational and sometimes social identity, as a group with its own institutions and values.

Corporatist projects had little appeal for small enterprise in France, where corporations were identified with the *ancien régime*, and where the Revolution had established a republican ideal which abhorred intermediary bodies between the citizen and the state. Yet the most important of petit-bourgeois organisations in these years, the *Ligue syndicale de travail, de l'industrie et du commerce* led by Léopold Christophe, developed a vision that was corporatist in many of its economic assumptions, even if it neither proposed nor even contemplated the restoration of corporations. By the end of the nineteenth century, the restoration of guilds and corporations had completed its long passage to the political right, to those who rejected the French Revolution and its attendant individualism, and throughout Europe the ideals of corporatism became bound up with Catholic reaction, conservatism, and eventually with fascist experiments. The *Ligue syndicale*, whose membership grew from some 20,000 in 1890 to 180,000 six years later (a less impressive figure than it seems, because it was mostly made up of the members of affiliated associations),[102] was not a movement of the right. The implicit corporatism which coloured its ideas was thus one that did not extend beyond the protection of enterprises to a vision of society as a whole.

At the outset the *Ligue syndicale* was aligned with the Radical Socialists, and presented a vision of a republic of small property owners, fragmentation against monopoly, and nostalgia for a past in which small enterprise provided the basis for a popular republican democracy. The ideology typifies the way in which organised shopkeepers transformed an older petit-bourgeois vision in a new political context. As petit-bourgeois politics began to move to the right, it carried with it many of its older values. The main target of the *Ligue syndicale* was the rapidly expanding department stores, those symbols of modern capitalism, speculation, and moral decline. It called for reform of the *patente* tax to load upon departments stores heavy and indeed punitive taxes, in order to undermine this 'unfair competition'. The *Ligue* vision rested on the dual forces of localism and specialisation. Small family enterprise represented both community and hierarchy, the two forces for social stability, and it existed within the local neighbourhood, which was itself being undermined by projects for urban reconstruction in Paris and other large cities. The local neighbourhood was a world in which honest folk knew each other, and in which the petits bourgeois were defended. The key to that defence was specialisation – each person should have one trade, and only one trade. It was that cardinal precept, the guarantee of decent rewards for honest endeavour, which the department stores denied. Here was an implicitly corporatist vision, the right of each to practise his own trade and to live by it, and the denial of the right to practise more than one trade. Specialism was an idea encouraged by the structure of the *patente*, in which businesses were categorised by trade. The tax thus served as a carrier of a mutant form of the corporate sense of 'the trade'. The outcome was mundane but real. As a newspaper directed at small enterprise declared in 1882 when protesting against dairymen selling potatoes and vegetables on their rounds, 'doesn't everyone have to live by their own trade?'[103] The vision of society represented by the *Ligue syndicale* was set against the world of the department store, with its plate-glass windows and grand facades, its chandeliers, its army of sales assistants, its organisation and its seductive advertising. Here was the symbol of wealth, of concentration, of urban reconstruction, whose customers were drawn from two groups anathema to the honest petit bourgeois: the idle rich of the boulevards and the army of civil servants and pen-pushers.[104] The *Ligue syndicale*'s defence of small enterprise can stand for much of the vision which moved petit-bourgeois politics in these years. It was a defence of the local community against all those forces – concentration of capital and business, idle wealth, the modern bureaucratic state – which seemed to be undermining the security of small enterprise and its social world.

Attacks on the department store as a symbol of the modernity threatening both small enterprise and the social order as a whole were made elsewhere, notably in Germany where shopkeepers demanded punitive changes in taxation. Minor *patente* reforms in France were matched by a special tax known as the *Warenhaussteuer* introduced in Bavaria in 1899, and by other taxes in Prussia, Baden, Braunschweig and Württemberg. German retailers were no more satisfied by the reforms than were their French counterparts, and the Berlin Chamber of Commerce suspected in 1905 that the demands had quite different goals. 'The tax on department stores has become a slogan in the struggle for correct economic policy. It is conceived of as one step on the path to halt the growth of large enterprise.'[105]

Hostility to department stores was voiced, in different settings and with different political resonances, wherever petit-bourgeois organisation campaigned in the decades before the First World War, even in Britain, where they were muted by the weakness of an independent petit-bourgeois political presence. British shopkeeper organisations (for master artisans were barely organised) protested against innovations which they felt to be unfair – social legislation to help workers, civil servants who set up their own co-operative societies, or the Cash on Delivery postal system which helped mail-order distribution. Yet, however much they bemoaned the competition from large-scale retailing, they demanded little from the state to help them in their supposed crisis. As a French observer noted, in England 'retailing seems to be succumbing without asking any measures of protection from the State'.[106] The solutions to the problems faced by shopkeepers appeared to rest with shopkeepers themselves, and the new retail operations were to be met by the improvement and regeneration of traditional shopkeepers. A leader of the London and Suburban Traders' Federation attacked 'those pessimistic, can't-be-done, dead-beat, rut-trailing tradesmen who consider they are born too late . . . . The world owes a living only to him who earns it.'[107]

The campaign against co-operative societies launched from St Helens in 1902 exemplifies the character of petit-bourgeois responses in Britain.[108] The aims and the tactics were limited: to persuade customers that the dividend was a fallacy and to organise a boycott by traders of all those who shopped at co-operatives. No sustained national movement followed the St Helens agitation, and no demands were made of the state for action against co-operatives. 'The enlightenment of the co-oper is really all that is wanted', argued a leading agitator in the movement in a perfect expression of rationalist liberalism.[109] The failure of the most sustained retailer campaign of the period to make any concrete demands, and its insistence on the educating of customers as the basis of a strategy for resistance, are testimony to two distinguishing features of British petit-bourgeois politics. The first was its continuing attachment to economic liberalism and the market. The second was the absence (in comparison with many other European countries) of a specific identity amongst owners of small enterprise of their special role in society or in the economy. The crisis years were no less difficult in Britain than elsewhere, but organised British petits bourgeois lacked the ideological resources with which to resist politically and with which to present themselves as the basis of a healthy moral social order. The response of all leaders of the shopkeeper movement was essentially commercial, arguing that their right to survive existed only for so long as they served an economic function.

The sense of political powerlessness in Britain was exacerbated by fears of socialism and the threat to property. Co-operation came to symbolise all that they feared. A shopkeeper in Beswick argued that the bulk of the officials [of the local co-operative society] belong to different dissenting chapels about here, where such things as Pro-Boerism, Socialism and c., are taught and applied in Jesuitical fashion in place of fear God and honour the King and love thy neighbour as thyself.[110]

The resentment, however, generated no identifiable petit-bourgeois politics. The Middle Class Defence Organisation launched in 1906 to wage an anti-socialist battle in local government, gave no special attention at all to the interests of small business.[111] Petits bourgeois drifted towards the Conservatives, as did much of the lower middle class in these years, but they travelled primarily as individual voters, without the presence of distinctive alliances such as appeared in other countries.

Petit-bourgeois politics elsewhere articulated its role between capital and proletariat, as the stabiliser of society and the guarantor of its values. Attempts at political mobilisation by parties of the centre and right, and ideological appropriation by Social Catholic writers and intellectuals, nourished these ideals. The image of being squeezed between labour and capital was increasingly pervasive. In the words of a Lyon shopkeepers' newspaper, 'the struggle is now open between two groups equally strong and equally disciplined – labour and capital – and small shopkeeping like small industry finds itself trapped between the two as between the anvil and the hammer'.[112] Whether seeking electoral bases for fragmented parties (as in France), or a bulwark against socialism (as in Germany and Belgium), political parties turned to small enterprise with promises and praise. All of this served to sharpen the consciousness amongst organised petits bourgeois that they were a special force in society. Government measures nowhere matched the rhetoric, for little would be done to restrain economic growth or limit the expansion of large business, but policies that were largely cosmetic only encouraged a sense of grievance. In all these countries the political space existed within which petit-bourgeois political identity could take shape. Its absence in Britain was one reason for the weakness there of a distinctive petit-bourgeois politics.

Autonomous petit-bourgeois parties were rare, and shopkeepers and master artisans were increasingly mobilised by movements of the political centre and, especially, right. This sometimes meant new movements in search of a political base, such as the Flemish nationalist groupings in Belgium,[113] or the later nationalist agitations in France. In the 1880s, French shopkeeper organisations were at the heart of the republican movement, but then slowly detached themselves from that milieu, as existing political groupings and their relevance to petit-bourgeois experience seemed to lose coherence. Boulangism and the Dreyfus Affair provided a mechanism for disentanglement (31 per cent of Parisians in the anti-Dreyfusard *Ligue des Patriots* were artisans and shopkeepers),[114] and by 1900 petit-bourgeois voters were the key to the shock success of the nationalists in the Paris municipal elections, and in the general elections two years later. The break between shopkeepers and socialists caused by the latters' enthusiastic espousal of the co-operative cause was one explanation for this swing to the right. Yet petit-bourgeois attachment to right-wing radical movements on the political fringe should not be exaggerated, for the nationalist success was an essentially Parisian phenomenon. Republicanism continued to flourish in the provinces. In any case, by 1905 the shopkeeper movement (and its voters) had been drawn back from the extreme right, into a more centrist conservative position, once the moderate right showed a willingness to respond to shopkeeper anxieties. The shopkeepers' movement talked less of *le peuple* and more of *les classes moyennes,* under the influence of Catholic intellectuals and politicians, and as larger business sought to win them over to mainstream conservative politics.[115] The volatility of master artisans and shopkeepers in Roubaix between 1890 and 1914 provides a case study of the diversity of petit-bourgeois political allegiances, but it was a volatility that carried them between socialist groups and Eugène Motte's local liberal, centrist *Union sociale et politique.* Many of them were members of the *Union Catholique* which backed Motte, with its slogan 'For God, small shopkeepers and liberty.'[116]

In comparative terms the shift of German petits bourgeois to the right was the most evident and the most substantial. Their demand for the restoration of guilds as obligatory organisations, and for the exclusive rights of guild masters to take apprentices and to practise the trade, stood a better chance of being met by the right or the Catholic Centre. The affinity that grew for those and other reasons led the historian Heinrich August Winkler to develop the notion of a reciprocal pact (*Rückversicherung*): to the extent that the state would support the *Mittelstand* in its struggle to survive, so master artisans and shopkeepers would help sustain the political elite in power.[117] The *Reichsdeutsche Mittelstandsverband* (Federation of the German Mittelstand), founded in 1911 in Dresden, might appear as the characteristic expression of this political alliance, for it was a party to the short-lived *Kartell der schaffenden Hände* (Cartel of the Productive Estates) alongside the representatives of large-scale farming and industry. Nevertheless, care must be taken not to overstate this trend. In 1909 the *Hansa-Bund* was organised to oppose the priority accorded to the agrarian interest and to insist on equal political recognition for all sectors of the economy, and it obtained significant support amongst the owners of small business. Furthermore, these general trends to the right and to *Mittelstand* defence organisations were weaker in southern Germany, where attachment to liberal values, which in Germany were compatible with restrictions on economic freedom and the limitation of voting rights to property owners, remained widespread. The politics of petits bourgeois was fragmented amongst three of the social milieux into which Lepsius divided German politics between 1870 and 1933: the Catholic milieu, the conservative milieu, and the bourgeois–liberal milieu.[118] The extent to which petit-bourgeois politics was rooted in the Catholic Centre[119] makes the German case close to that of Belgium, but with the fundamental difference that the Catholics in Belgium were in power while their German counterparts were in opposition, at least until 1918. The bourgeois–liberal milieu was certainly relatively weak amongst German petits bourgeois in comparison with both France and Britain, for in Germany liberalism developed in a way that kept it an essentially bourgeois project, one less capable of integrating other social groups.[120] The Geman petite bourgeoisie's links to the conservative mileu, one which contained populist movements of the right such as the Pan-German League and the Navy League,[121] may not have been the exclusive direction of the politics of master artisans and shopkeepers, but it was striking within a comparative European perspective.

This reorientation was not an inevitable process in late nineteenth-century Europe, especially where petits bourgeois had long been associated with progressive and radical politics. This was not only true of the industrial countries of western Europe, but of other countries about whose petit-bourgeois politics we know so much less. Shopkeepers in Milan had long been part of the city's anti-oligarchic Democratic bloc, but tensions grew from the start of the century as class politics came to prevail in the city, as socialist influence over the municipal administration grew, as strikes and labour organising around the new *Camera di Lavoro* (labour exchange) made small property owners fearful, and finally in 1904 as a massive general strike over the police killing of peasants in Sicily confirmed the worst fears of Milan's petits bourgeois. Under these pressures, and without the divisive influence of the *dazio consumo*, Milan's organised shopkeepers began to move firmly to the right. The drift to the more radical right was rare in Italy as it was in France, Belgium and Britain, but a shift towards more moderate and conservative politics, and to the defence of property, can be clearly seen in Milan.[122]

In Britain the petite bourgeoisie remained committed to mainstream liberal ideas and was little attracted by any of the minor movements of the radical right which flickered briefly into life. Their main political action was as ratepayers in municipal politics, and it was accompanied by a retreat into essentially trade affairs and organisations. In late nineteenth-century Leicester this meant less a shift in party allegiance than an abandonment of partisan politics, and an increasing concern for trade associations that eschewed formal political engagement.[123] The ideological distinction between the two main parties was less significant than elsewhere, and, although increasing petit-bourgeois support for the Conservative Party sustains the notion of a drift to the right, especially with the rise of the Municipal Reform movement to oppose the Progressives on the London County Council, the shift was less substantial than in some other countries. In any case, there were not the right-wing extremist or anti-parliamentary movements to seek to mobilise them, nor the anxious parties of the right seeking electoral support in a fragmented party system, or as a bulwark against socialist advance, as appeared in Britain's European neighbours. British petits bourgeois experienced similar economic problems, similar concerns, and similar anxieties over status, to their counterparts in other parts of industrial Europe. However, in a political framework which denied them groups seeking to mobilise their distinct interests, and which denied them the political space in which their demands could grow, a distinctive petit-bourgeois politics rarely surfaced in Britain.

Dupeux's judgement that 'socialism was implanted in the (French) Department of Loir-et-Cher by the petite bourgeoisie'[124] indicates one reason to qualify the generalisation of a shift to the right by shopkeepers and master artisans in the decades before the First World War even if the broad trend remains true. Owners of small enterprise remained prominent in movements of the left, even if they were no longer the major location for petit-bourgeois politics that they had once been. Small independents, drawn by both their continuing radicalism and their immersion in local working-class communities, were particularly prominent in the leadership of medium-sized industrial towns like Göttingen. whose leaders were men such as a master shoemaker and a tobacconist.[125] In Belgian industrial and mining areas, shopkeeping petits bourgeois had often been part of the working-class-oriented radical left, and were quickly drawn into the *Parti Ouvrier Belge* from its origins in 1885.[126] The French socialist movement for all its apparent ambivalence to small enterprise, found many recruits there. Shopkeepers – even excluding all bar- and café-owners – were some 12 per cent of the membership of the French socialist party in the Nord department, and equivalent or even higher proportions in departments as varied as Allier, Loire, Gard and Hérault.[127] Although some were victimised workers setting up to survive, most were shopkeepers in working-class neighbourhoods who stayed close to their customers and whose radicalism and republicanism carried them into a socialism which at the local level was heavily populist in character, and which continued to resonate with Jacobin language. Nor were all petit-bourgeois socialists to be found in working-class districts, for their affiliation often had to be concealed from customers whom it might offend. The son of a carpenter with a small business in a little town in the Ardèche recalled that 'he was on the left, my father, but in business you have to be careful'.[128]

There is a further reason to qualify this shift to the right, and that is the assumption that political behaviour and ideology can be neatly distinguished between left or right. The typology is a legacy of the French Revolution, extrapolating from a metaphor based on physical location in the National Assembly the belief in a real political continuum on which all political positions can be located, and along which individuals and groups can be seen to move. Is 'the right' a subtle enough categorisation? It meant different things in different countries: Toryism in Britain (maybe even orthodox liberalism), nationalism and *Poincarism* in France, the Catholic Party in

Belgium, or the *Kartell der schaffenden Hände* in Germany. Above all, when interpreting shifts in petit-bourgeois political ideology, it is necessary to eschew a simplistic left–right dichotomy, some automatic break between radical past and right-wing present, and ask whether this evolution towards the right nevertheless embodied real ideological continuities with earlier petit-bourgeois radicalism, maybe a continuity of interests whose expression changed with the political conjuncture.

In studying petit-bourgeois politics and movements in the decades before the First World War, one is struck by the way older radical themes recur.[129] The people against the rich was one such theme, the belief that state power was in the hands of a powerful oligarchy of wealth, and that government served not the people but the monopolists.[130] It could lead to evocations of past democratic struggles, above all in France. The grocers of Nancy called for the defence of small property in 1913: 'The revolution of 1789 was carried out with a cry of *Vive la Liberté*. Are we really going to be so spineless as to let ourselves be robbed of that liberty?'[131] A further continuing theme was mistrust of a bureaucratic, centralised state which now manifested itself in opposition to state regulation and welfare, and to that flood of civil servants labelled in France *fonctionnarisme*. The localist and democratic petit-bourgeois vision of the state was thus set against the overweening authority of the modern state with its officials, tax demands, inspectors and rubber stamps. Smaller retailers in England opposing shop hours legislation as 'an un-English practice' drew on a populist anti-state tradition that stretched back to the eighteenth century.[132] A third continuity was opposition to an organised society, one in which national and international influences would dominate, at the expense of the small-scale and the local. At its extreme it produced a denunciation of foreigners, of cosmopolitanism, hence on occasions of Jews. More generally, there was a preference for the local scale, for specialism of trades, for parochial loyalty and the ideology of neighbourhood. We find it in the *Ligue syndicale*'s vision of the economic autarky of the neighbourhood, or the belief of German independent producers that they were entitled, through the principle of *Nahrungsprinzip*, to a guaranteed stable and local clientèle.[133] There was also a continuing emphasis on morality and justice, found in denunciations of 'unfair competition' – a concept which asserts moral superiority over the pure operation of the market. The question of the quality of production was a regular theme, the traditional artisanal conception of craftsmanship which was to be guaranteed by corporate organisations in Germany, and by professional training and associations in France and Belgium. This insistence on moral values also linked private and public morality, expecting that the morality of the private world and the morality of the public could not be distinct. Finally, there was of course the persistence of corporations, or of expectations derived from a corporate past, in petit-bourgeois demands: the demands of German petits bourgeois for guild institutions, but also the more oblique corporatism of French and

Belgian retailers asserting the importance of specialism, and the right to live from their trade.

None of these themes was inherently reactionary. All recall the defence by radical petits bourgeois of the ordinary people of neighbourhoods and local communities, and they survived to colour a more defensive and conservative politics in a later period. The shift to the right from the late nineteenth century was far more than some simple capitulation to manipulation from outside, by conservatives or right-wing radicals. Indeed, their passion for independence made them hard to control. As the Belgian Social Catholic Oscar Pyfferoen tartly observed, the petite bourgeoisie are 'the people who, from an electoral point of view, are the most difficult to discipline'.[134] It was not simply the political position of petits bourgeois which was changing – so too was the political landscape itself. The location of the left was moving, as it increasingly came to mean socialism and organised labour, co-operation, and collectivism. In that context the bundle of ideas that had moved the owners of small enterprise during their more radical phase now occupied a far more ambiguous position in the political terrain. The content of petit-bourgeois political ideas had of course changed, for the framework of European politics as well as society had changed much over the century, but there were far more continuities than the simple notion of a movement to the right would allow.

The attack on department stores reminds us of one of those continuing characteristics: the need for outside symbols to attack. Symbolic targets appear to be specially prevalent in petit-bourgeois movements, as if consciousness and organisation grew more readily in response to outside threats than to internal needs. The rich and powerful, the co-operative store, the department store, the Jews, even the Eiffel Tower – petit-bourgeois movements repeatedly identified external threats, wrapped them in a symbolic representation, and used them as the basis for unity and action. The inner competitiveness of petits bourgeois made class unity awkward and their introspection made social cohesion difficult, but such responses were also a consequence of the relationship between those inside and outside worlds. The petit-bourgeois ideal was that of the family-run small enterprise, with authority and order within business and family, and their introspective world suggested that internal order at least could be realistically sought. The world outside seemed increasingly to show petits bourgeois no such order, only challenges, disharmony, and threats. The powerlessness of the owners of small enterprise meant that, unlike the wealthier and more powerful bourgeois, they could not seize control and seek to shape the disordered world that they saw around them. They could retreat into the family, as many did, but they could also respond to movements which offered to control that disordered world on their behalf. It is in this context that the denunciation of department stores, as of other symbolic enemies so common to petit-bourgeois politics, must be understood.

8

PETITS BOURGEOIS AND WORKERS

Although the owners of small enterprise were the section of the middle classes with whom working-class men and women came into the most regular contact, it is important to remember that the most enduring relationship between the petite bourgeoisie and the working class was that of family. There were the wage-earning occupations of members of many petits-bourgeois families – husband or wife where multiple occupations were needed, children where the maintenance of the next generation in small enterprise was not always possible or desirable, parents where the owner of the enterprise had come from working-class origins, as well as the occupations of brothers and sisters, uncles and aunts. For many petits bourgeois there was their own career, as they shifted between wage-earning and independence. Here were the ineluctable links that tied so many petits bourgeois to the working class. Jules Caylarde, the republican mayor of the French company town of Decazeville during the 1880s, explained the reluctance of the town's workers to use the company retail store. 'One can hardly separate the worker from the shopkeeper,' he claimed, 'because a large number [of the workers] have a son, a brother, an uncle or a cousin who is a businessman in the town.'[1] Only the upper levels of Europe's shopkeepers and master artisans could feel themselves firmly apart, and fashion more precise and distant relationships with their town's workers. If the historical analysis of class has in recent decades shown us that class identity derives from more than structural position alone, but also from dense patterns of social relations and discourses, then we need to shift attention from those forces that brought many petits bourgeois and workers close together, and explore those relationships which created distance and tension.

'With the loss of the small workshop,' Frantz Funck-Brentano told a congress in 1899, 'would go the familial relations between *patrons* and workers, the direct and personal interest of the master for his apprentice.'[2] Those defending small enterprise saw it as a haven of harmony in a world increasingly divided by class. The personal relations in workshops were contrasted with the anonymity of factory labour, the shared interests of artisanal producers with exploitation of a large-scale labour force, the

166

prospect of independence with factory workers trapped like slaves. Here was a stereotype of social relations in small enterprise which long coloured the analysis of towns such as Birmingham and Krefeld which were characterised by small units of production.[3] This stereotype assumes that working together in small units reduced the likelihood of conflict, generated an identity of interests, and produced warmth and fraternity. It was an image encouraged by the idealisation of guilds in late nineteenth-century Germany and Austria, but it flourished in France too, where the corporate memory found other channels, such as the social theories of Le Play and later Durkheim.

THE ARTISANAL WORKPLACE

The artisanal workplace was a place of interaction between petits bourgeois and workers only for those workshops where non-family labour was employed. In many trades, especially the most populous, those were a minority. It is nevertheless important to explore those relations, which developed out of the background examined in Chapter Two, where we saw how the realities of social relations in the eighteenth-century corporate trades became increasingly distant from their contemporary and subsequent ideal-isations. The harmonious relations that supposedly accompanied craft pro-duction had become the exception in large eighteenth-century cities, and the deterioration of relations between masters and journeymen was to be a common trend throughout industrialising and urbanising Europe. As cor-porations found themselves unable to regulate relations within the craft, they turned to external policing and the law to sustain labour discipline, while journeymen organisations, created primarily for mutual aid in times of hardship or while travelling, found themselves defending journeymen's interests against their masters. The forces of economic concentration and economic growth in the early nineteenth century intensified the pressures on artisanal trades, and the survival of guilds affected the form of the conflict and differentiation that this pressure produced far more than it did their existence. As a result, the early nineteenth century saw increasing pressures on artisanal trades which could not but affect the character of relations between masters and men.

Agricol Perdiguier, in the memoirs of his *tour de France* as a journeyman joiner round the workshops of provincial towns, vividly portrays the great variety of relations that existed between masters and journeymen in the 1820s. The experience of a worker was indeed structured by the larger economic forces at work, and by the customs and practices of each town, but it also depended on the personality of the master, the pattern of workshop con-viviality, and the extent to which tensions between masters and men were contained within workshop routine. 'Between employer and journeymen there was teasing, verbal abuse and jokes in poor taste.' The robust exchanges had firm limits. Of course there were 'frictions and arguments between

167

masters and workers, there could not be anything else . . . but relations were nonetheless cordial'. It is clear from Perdiguier's descriptions that two forces could damage those relations. The first was the personality of the master and the respect in which he was held by his journeymen. The description of his masters in Marseille shows how important this could be, with the real master of his craft, who was willing to learn from his own men, enjoying far better relations than the self-important *patron* whose pompous criticisms and lack of skill created repeated resentment. The personality of the master was important in determining workshop relations, but Perdiguier made his tour as the building trades were on the threshold of increased competition and structural change, and here was the second force determining relations between masters and men. Intense competition, sub-contracting, and division of labour pressurised workshop trades, and undermined such stable patterns of workplace relations as existed. Perdiguier himself saw an early expression of this in the 1827 joiners' strike in Nîmes, when intense price competition led masters to introduce wage cuts in an attempt to reduce costs.[4]

The fracturing of the craft community did not simply involve a break between masters and men, but a division amongst small masters themselves between those who sought to defend the customs and practices of the craft community as they saw it, and those who cut themselves adrift as small businessmen. The difficulties experienced by masters embedded in their trade community drew many into resistance alongside their workers. This resistance found political expression in movements such as the Owenite Grand National Consolidated Trade Union in Britain or the co-operative production workshops in Paris during the 1848 revolution, but unity between a majority of masters and their men for industrial action was less common, with the exception of trades organised under the putting-out system. In such industries, masters and men often acted in unison against the merchants whose pressures challenged them both. In the small Rhône textile town of Vienne, for example, workshop masters and their journeymen joined together in 1819 to bar the introduction of the shearing frame into the town.[5]

The silk trade of Lyon provides the most striking manifestation of such solidarity. Masters and journeymen united in the struggle for a minimum price tariff to be paid by the merchant *fabricants* to the workshop masters, a struggle which exploded in the risings of the *canuts* (silk-workers) in 1831 and 1834. The early decades of the nineteenth century had seen a steady advance in merchant control over the trade. Masters were compelled to maintain their own version of the workers' passbook, a *livret d'acquit* in which were recorded details of contracts with merchants and masters' assiduousness in carrying them out. The power of Lyon's silk merchants, and the way masters were recruited, forged a unity amongst masters and journeymen in repeated conflict with the wealthy merchants who put out the work, set the prices, and dominated the industry.[6] Tensions within the workshop were secondary to this larger struggle, as the corporate ideal of the united craft survived. As late as 1860, the *canuts* were still petitioning the Emperor for a codification of unwritten trade regulations to be enforced by the *conseil de prud'homme*.[7] One can find parallel examples of co-operation within the craft elsewhere. In the east German town of Chemnitz, the small master weavers and their journeymen in 1848 together demanded a reform of the *Innungen* (guild), as well as for a minimum wage, the establishment of arbitration bodies, and the restriction on the size of workshops to ten looms. Parallel unity during 1848 can be found in Remscheid, where the filemakers struck against merchants' refusal to concede fixed wages. Opposition to merchant capital during the revolutionary year of 1848 does in some places seem to have overcome the corporate division between masters and journeymen.[8]

Corporations had in reality rarely constituted a force for workplace cohesion, and it was only in the context of a silk trade struggling for survival, in a society where formal corporate controls no longer existed, that the corporate idiom could carry such weight in bringing together masters and men. Corporate structures had in the past been less about community and more about power, and this remained true during much of the nineteenth century in Germany and Austria, where corporate regulations recognised by the state significantly influenced relations between masters and men. These regulations allowed masters to maintain surveillance over the private life of their employees, or to be charged by the municipality with responsibility for the good management of their workers' mutual sickness societies. At work, the master need give a journeymen no more than eight days notice, while the journeymen was required to give three months to his master. Journeymen's associations were suppressed, while those of masters were tolerated and even encouraged. In the civic laws of German municipalities only the masters would be citizens. In this setting, the legal structures of corporations and municipality drove a wedge between masters and journeymen which had no parallel in Britain, France or Belgium. By the middle decades of the nineteenth century, mastership as a legal and political, as opposed to an economic, phenomenon was a particularity of Germany and central Europe.[9]

The vulnerability of small enterprise generated pressures which would outweigh the intimacy that went with a small working group. In any case, that intimacy required a continuing relationship which workplace instability made increasingly rare in large towns. The dependency of small firms on large ones, their insertion into structured capitalist relations, and intensity of price competition, introduced into workshops those conflicts over work discipline and workplace practice which we know from larger-scale manufacturing. Most reductions in costs were achieved after all not by investment in new technology but through changes in the organisation of the labour process. This is one reason why journeymen artisans were central to radical political activity and industrial conflict throughout industrialising Europe during the first half of the nineteenth century, especially those workers who faced

increasing competition through sub-contracting, increased domestic production, and the attempts of masters to break the structures and norms by
which journeymen such as tailors, furniture-makers and small metal-workers
had long defended their economic and trade position. The craft community,
where ritual and custom sustained social cohesion in spite of inequalities of
income and power, now fractured in a range of trades, above all in the larger
urban centres. The rise of masters' organisations to combat journeyman
opposition was only the most explicit expression of that fracture. As early as
1814 the Sheffield Mercantile and Manufacturing Union was formed to
oppose the journeymen's unions, and small firms were prominent amongst
its 400 members. Sheffield's small-scale cutlery and steel trades saw a
succession of masters' organisations in the first half of the nineteenth century,
such as the file forge masters whose lock-out in 1836 sought to break the
strong trade unions.[10]

The growth of trade societies in Birmingham between the 1820s and 1840s
stands witness to this fracturing of the craft community, as workshop masters
sought to withstand competition by undermining the customs of the trade.
Workplace routines, the speed of work, the number of boys and apprentices
employed, and working hours all became sources of conflict. So too did
traditional fringe benefits, such as payment for extra work, the supply of beer
in the workshop, or property in waste materials generated in production.
During peak years of trade society organising and strikes – such as 1833–35
and 1843–47 – a wide range of the town's small trades were in action, amongst
them pearl-button makers, shoemakers, tailors, cabinet-makers, edge tool-
makers, and building crafts.[11] It was not just the artisanal community which
fractured under these strains but, according to Behagg, the masters themselves. The small producer was forced to make the transition from artisanal
small master to effective small businessman, to detach himself from the
expectations of the craft and attach himself to those of a larger business world
on which he was now dependent. Those who refused to change in these ways,
or who operated in industries where few were offered the choice to do so,
often sank into the struggling class of sub-contractors and garret masters.[12]
The notion of the 'good master' now became important for journeymen
resisting change. 'My wages have not declined since [1833],' one London
journeyman tailor told Mayhew in 1849, 'because I am regularly employed,
and my master's house has not yet become one of the cheap advertising shops
– and I don't think it will in *his* time.'[13]

Most masters felt they had little choice, and conflict grew as employers
struggled to assert control of the workplace. Bitter industrial disputes in the
Sheffield cutlery trades made the town renowned for trade union conflict.
The dispute in the file-making trades in 1866, in which large and small
employers joined together in conflict with 4000 men, was ostensibly about
wages but in reality about the introduction of machinery.[14] As small
employers sought to separate journeymen from their accustomed role in the

organisation of production, conflict increasingly revolved around the question of authority in the workplace. This could involve mechanisation, speeding up, the role of supervisors, and the regularity of the working week. Disputes thus concerned practices specific to a single trade, as amongst Paris chair-makers. Faced with increasing competition from large-scale enterprises, small chair-making firms reacted by cutting costs and changing work routines. The unloading of timber, once carried out by specially employed workers, was now to be carried out by the journeymen themselves, who launched industry-wide action to oppose this breach of established customs and with it the degradation of their status as craftsmen.[15]

During the first half of the nineteenth century, conflict spread in the more pressurised trades, rooted in unstable journeymen's organisations where these were legal, but resting on the informal world of artisanal sociability even where they were not. The illegality and severe repression of journeymen's organisations in Germany before 1848 meant that sustained strikes were not a widespread form of protest, but workers in mass trades such as tailors, shoemakers and joiners were prominent in popular movements from the 1790s, as were those threatened by the competition of protoindustrial production. Elsewhere, industrial action was a more common response. More than two-thirds of strikes in July Monarchy France occurred in the artisanal and building trades.[16] In Toulouse nearly three-quarters of all strikes between 1830 and 1870 were in such trades, above all those characterised by sub-contracting (tailors, shoemakers), or by intensive competition which might include factory production (cabinet-makers, masons, smiths, printers, bakers).[17] It is hardly surprising that tailors, under pressure from sub-contracting and the growth of ready-made goods for large-scale wholesalers and retailers, should be at the forefront of working-class movements through-out industrialising Europe. Tailors defended the traditions of workshop production, resisting the decentralisation of work into the domestic setting where cheaper female labour could be more easily employed and where artisanal standards could be ignored. The politics of small-scale production assumed a gender dimension, as skilled tailors struggled to maintain the shop as a masculine and ordered world where the trade could be protected. In 1833 and 1834, and again in the early 1840s, intense waves of strikes swept over the custom tailors' shops in towns all over France.[18] Journeymen found in mutual societies and producers' co-operatives both a means of defence and an alternative artisanal form of production. The tailors and shoemakers who dominated the Icarians found in Etienne Cabet's communitarian model an alternative form of social and economic organisation.[19] It was on precisely such workers, similarly seeking to resist the transformation of their trades through a vision rooted in the social idioms of the artisan, that the Grand National Consolidated Trades Union in Britain drew during the early 1830s, fusing trade union practice with dreams derived from the shared ideals of Owenism and co-operative production.[20]

171

The use of the law by workshop masters provides further evidence of the strains within artisanal trades. In reality these legal devices had only a limited impact, for competition led masters to take on workers as they needed them irrespective of *livrets* or legal restrictions, but the attempts of small masters to obtain and to use legal processes is nonetheless revealing of the pressures which they experienced and the measures which they thought appropriate to deal with them. Laws which gave employers access to legal means of disciplining their workers were used primarily (though not exclusively) by masters in small-scale production, not only to control the behaviour of journeymen but also to hold on to them during upturns in the labour market. This was especially needed where increasing division of labour within the workshop made masters particularly vulnerable to the loss of one specialist journeyman.[21] Legal devices of this kind included the *livret* (compulsory labour book) in France from 1803, and the Master and Servants Laws in Britain until their abolition in 1875, while German masters, who between 1808 and 1829 had used the *Wanderbücher* to control journeymen migration, came subsequently to regret the loss of past regulatory powers and vociferously demanded their reintroduction in the later nineteenth century. The classic small master districts in England – such as Staffordshire, the Black Country, Birmingham and Sheffield – saw the highest numbers of prosecutions under the acts, as employers taking on sub-contracts sought the aid of the law to compensate for their market vulnerability.[22]

The image of the harmonious workshop may have become increasingly distant from any reality it once reflected, but many workshops did remain more intimate and consensual places than the previous pages might lead one to expect. The stable workforce in Marcelin's lampmaking enterprise in later nineteenth-century Nîmes generally left only when ready to set up for themselves, and the owner's son recalled that the lifestyle of master and workers remained similar, sharing an artisanal cultural and religious world in which relations with bourgeois customers and their architects contrasted with the 'more relaxed and more cordial life' they enjoyed with their workers.[23] Such relations were most common in those trades which remained relatively unchallenged by technological or organisational change; in regions where corporate traditions held strong; and in smaller urban centres serving local market functions. It was in just such a setting in the south German workshops of organ-makers that the master would each day read passages from the prayer book to his journeymen.[24] Here was the basis of the joint worker and master trade mutual associations that flourished amongst Catholic artisans in late nineteenth-century Flanders.[25] In such circumstances, pride in high quality work and skill linked to common gestures, language, and festivals to reinforce a still cohesive sense of the craft. For all the good and bad employers whom Perdiguier encountered in the 1820s, the tradition of the ball organised by the journeymen for the *patrons* and *patronnes* on the day of Saint-Anne persisted, and 'on the next day, the masters took their turn to organise a ball,

172

returning pleasure for pleasure, delight for delight'.[26] Perdiguier felt such shared trade rituals to be in decline by the 1850s. His perspective was that of an older man looking back regretfully at the more optimistic world of his youth, but such rituals of cultural identity were indeed in decline.[27] The consensual craft workplace did not disappear during the second half of the nineteenth century, but as the strains that influenced specific trades in earlier times spread more widely, it moved to the periphery of the artisanal world. By the close of the century, socialist organising and a public language of class convinced many that a harmonious workshop world had been destroyed, and a discourse about small enterprise emerged which idealised the relations that were believed once to have existed. For Pierre Du Maroussem, who organised the *Office du Travail*'s inquiries into French small enterprise in the 1890s, the political question was simply one aspect of what he idealised as traditional solidarities, and which now manifested itself in an increasing rejection of the master's authority as 'a cause of slavery and a synonym for exploitation'.[28] The idealisation of workshop relations took shape in this context of increasing distance between journeyman and master. The craft histories and museums discussed in the next chapter articulated a contemporary critique by myth-ologising older solidarities, while rituals were now emphasised at the very moment when the crafts seemed under threat. The master joiners of Liège told the Belgian National Commission in 1904 not so much of strikes, which were rare, but of a changing atmosphere which in their minds should be attributed to the social conflict of 1886 and the growth of socialism. 'On the one hand, the workers have become more demanding, more touchy, less polite. On the other, one hardly finds the pride, belief in work, concern to do better which were common in the past.'[29]

Nevertheless, the later nineteenth century saw less struggle over customary work practices and control in small enterprise, for whatever the crisis brought by depression and the pressure of large capital, conflicts over the character of artisanal productive relations had become more peripheral. The luxury sectors of certain trades provide a limited exception to this rule, such as the hatmaking and upholstery trades in Paris, which now saw increasing conflict as masters bore down on time-keeping, work routines and production schedules.[30] There was a new focus on bad working conditions which had been common in workshop trades long before late nineteenth-century social observers decided that they were a social problem. Small employers in the Sheffield cutlery trades were by the middle of the century notorious for paying low wages and maintaining the worst workplace conditions, and the *Morning Chronicle*'s travelling investigator found the same pattern when he reached the cotton town of Oldham.[31] The bakery trades everywhere were an extreme case, as traditionally difficult work conditions and exceptionally long hours were exacerbated by the intensification of competition amongst often under-capitalised bakers.[32] The gap in workplace standards was widening still further in the later nineteenth century, as regulation of factories and changing employer strategies produced real improvements in large-scale industry. Reports for both France and Germany began to denounce the long hours, low wages, appalling conditions and arbitrary supervision in small enterprise, and the labour inspectors showed how large a gap existed between small and large industrial firms.[33] Charles Booth had no doubt that in London's small-scale industry 'the small employer tends to impose harder conditions upon his workers, even though they be more irregularly enforced, than does the large employer'. The reason was clear. The small master

> often maintains a very friendly relationship with the few workers around him, but his capital is small, his business interest is concentrated, and his employees consequently become, in a more intensified form than in the case of a large employer ... the human instruments of production out of whose energy his profits most directly and most obviously come. And the strength of his interest in their labour is reflected in the force and the strenuousness of his control.

Booth concluded that 'although the small employer may more often "drive", he is also more often driven'.[34] The state regulation of workshop conditions throughout Europe not only lagged behind those in larger enterprises, it was less effectively enforced. Indeed, sub-contracting to small workshops became a means by which larger employers could bypass factory legislation. London brushmakers took strike action against just this practice in 1872.[35] The problems of enforcement were the subject of repeated complaints by trade unionists in France and Germany, who pointed out the great disparity between the number of premises which could be visited by the small number of inspectors, and the number of enterprises in existence. Inspection was not, of course, the whole question, for workers in workshops and shops were often reluctant to enter formal complaints for fear of the sack.[36]

Small-scale production now lost its once prominent position at the heart of workplace conflict. German enterprises that experienced strikes between 1904 and 1908 employed an average of forty-four workers, compared with 5 per enterprise in the occupied population as a whole.[37] Strikes in small enterprises may be partially hidden in state statistics, which found it hard to grasp the short-lived actions characteristic of small work units, and French labour inspectors repeatedly complained of their difficulties in getting information about small workplaces,[38] but the artisanal world was no longer central to the struggle for authority in the workplace. French strikes during the period between 1870 and 1913 were increasingly concentrated in the new and larger-scale sectors such as chemicals, transport and metallurgy, and while strikes in the building industry remained significant, they were weak in most artisanal sectors such as leather, clothing, wood and the food trades.[39]

Workshop relations may have become more routinised towards the end of the century, but not all artisanal trades producing for larger markets had resolved questions of customary work practices during the main period of industrialisation, and explosions could still occur in trades organised by putting-out merchants. The strike of *passementiers* (silk ribbon weavers) in Saint Etienne during the winter of 1899–1900 – explicitly concerned with payment for the process of 'setting up' the frames which preceded production itself – made explicit the growing distance between journeymen and workshop masters. Journeymen marched through the town to close workshops, smashing the windows of reluctant *chefs d'atelier*. While the journeymen now accepted the realities of wage employment and demanded more regular and defined working hours, tasks, pay and conditions, the *chefs d'atelier* who were their immediate masters sought to preserve the idiosyncrasies and informalities of production within older artisanal assumptions. The configuration of forces had changed since the 1830s when Lyon's silk-weaving masters and journeymen had united against their merchants and the government, and so too had the political and ideological terms of the debate. The *stephanois* masters, fearful of socialist threats and attracted to corporatist Catholic ideas, were drawn into co-operation with the merchants. 'The workshop masters ... are as much exploiters as are the merchants', proclaimed a journeyman in terms that had been little heard amongst the *canuts* of Lyon.[40]

If Saint-Etienne was in many ways an exception, the more general routinisation of workplace conflict did not necessarily result from the capitulation of the workforce. Many journeymen were able to keep considerable control over work processes and employment practice. A closed-shop policy and controls over the labour market of the kind practised by journeymen glassworkers in Lyon in the 1880s can be seen in many trades where skills remained high and in short supply.[41] Where forms of labour subcontracting prevailed, as in building and some metal trades, journeymen retained a substantial degree of workplace autonomy, and small masters found it hard to handle well-organised craft unions. Throughout the century, it was when the organisation of the labour process and techniques changed that employers, small as well as large, were able substantially to increase their control over their workers. In such settings, union closed shop and traditional workplace practices remained continuing sources of tension, often shifting according to the economic conjuncture, as with the carpenters of late nineteenth-century Paris.[42] Trades associations thus came to function as employers' associations. The German bakers' association, founded in 1907, was explicitly concerned with solidarity amongst masters in the face of employee strikes and boycotts.[43] Elsewhere the sense of embattled masters, as in the building trades, pervaded the reports of masters' associations.[44]

In general, however, conflict was less fundamental and probably less common than before. It found everyday expression in such institutions as the French *conseils de prud'hommes*, or the German *Gewerbegerichte*, composed of equal proportions of workers and masters, created to replace ordinary courts of law as a cheap and rapid means to resolve disputes over the employment contract between individual workers and employers. The courts tackled cases concerning insufficient notice, non-payment of wages, problems of discipline and so on. The cases were resolved routinely and often in favour of the employees.[45] Of more than five thousand cases heard before the Paris *conseil de prud'hommes* in 1910, retailing accounted for 41 per cent of cases heard, but almost all the rest were in the essentially small-scale clothing (20 per cent), metal goods (19 per cent), and building (13 per cent) trades.[46] The craft community had indeed largely fractured by the end of the century, and relations between master and journeymen had become the more routinised and conflictual relations between employer and employee.

THE SHOP AS A PLACE OF WORK

The *conseils de prud'hommes* dealt with a rapidly growing number of cases in retailing after 1907 when the law was extended to shop assistants and white-collar employees. Insecurity was the main grievance in Paris, with four-fifths of cases involving white-collar workers concerning dismissal without adequate notice.[47] An equally rapid growth in Lyon suggests that the existence of the *conseil* encouraged employees to take action against difficult employers, rather than simply to acquiesce or leave. They were drawn disproportionately from Lyon's specialist and larger-scale retail trades, whose assistants felt more confident of finding alternative employment, but small enterprises appear regularly, above all bars and cafés. Relations within shopkeeping had worsened as competition intensified, but judgements indicate that a set of unwritten trade norms prevailed, which the *conseils de prud'hommes* sought to enforce.[48]

In Britain, where employment relations lacked such arbitration courts, a similar situation existed. In London, as everywhere in Europe, the retailing workplace was both less conflictual and less close than in many workshop trades. The supposed intimacy of the relationship was still proclaimed, not least by the larger shopkeepers who opposed legal regulation of shop hours on the grounds that 'the intimate relationship existing between shopkeepers and employees at the present time is such as to warrant no such interference or intrusion'.[49] Such intimacy still existed, and the trusted assistant could still marry into both family and business, but it was an event more common in fiction than in reality.[50] The retail shop was a workplace which lacked the shared values of a craft and its history over which to tussle, where apprenticeship amounted to little even where it survived, and where the youthful workforce was shaped less by the introspective world of a workshop and more by the intrusions of customers. The workforce was young – 69 per cent of all employees in German retail trade were under 25 years of age in 1908 – and often drawn by hopes of mobility which led working-class parents to invest in unreal apprenticeships.[51] The ideal that the assistant was an embryonic shopkeeper survived and many small suburban shops were opened by those whose period as a shop assistant gave them enough knowledge and savings to hope for success.[52]

The prospects for most shop assistants were nevertheless in decline by the later nineteenth century. Munich's small retail enterprises in 1912

> employ far too many apprentices as cheap labour, without really training them; the result is to lower the general level of salaries; they merely prepare people for unemployment, offering poor work conditions, demanding unreasonably long hours of work, and they give far too short notice of dismissal.[53]

The rapid feminisation of shop employment from the 1880s reflected retailers' attempts to reduce labour costs without damaging efficiency. Women assistants remained unusual in trades with long training (such as chemists and druggists), or where wages were a relatively small element in overall costs (such as jewellers and wine merchants), or where a male clientèle expected to be served by men (such as bootmakers and gents' outfitters), but many others saw a rapid growth of young and cheap women assistants.[54]

The oversupply of labour meant that shop assistants were increasingly vulnerable, while the nature of workplace relations remained deeply personal, bound to the character of the individual shopkeeper. John Birch Thomas's memoirs of his youth in London shops in the 1870s and 1880s are in this respect reminiscent of Agricol Perdiguier's otherwise different memories of French joinery workshops half a century earlier, for the external pressures upon small enterprise were mediated through the personalities of their individual owners. In shops with small numbers of staff, such as the pawnbrokers and the china and glass shop where Thomas worked in the 1870s, the relationships were deeply personal, whatever the conflict and resentments. His daily world was bound up with that of the employer and family, their demands and personalities, their warmth or aggression.[55] Without the skill and culture that still affected the artisanal trades, relations in small shops seemed more capricious and idiosyncratic.

The classic picture of assistants living in was drawn from the authoritarian paternalism of the larger establishments, such as that of Henry Cushen's grocery shop in London's Mile End, whose assistants took meals with the family, had social evenings organised for them and, although forbidden to go to pubs, they could ask the housekeeper for beer at any time in the evenings, on condition that the privilege was not abused.[56] Here was a rule-bound paternalism which was in decline by the later nineteenth century, but finding reincarnation in the bureaucratic dormitory world of the new department stores. For most shop assistants who lived in, the environment was more strained. The six assistants of one west of England draper ate with the family, but 'this gave little chance for family or private conversation, and the talk was largely of a business nature with a few remarks about the weather or the health and inclinations of the assistants contributed by my mother'.[57] The perspective of the assistant could be even less comfortable. An apprentice with one London draper recalls the thirteen-hour working day, the kitchen which served as their sitting room, and the 'poor, down-trodden, down-at-heel company' provided by family and fellow employees. They took their meals with the family, 'and every mouthful we ate seemed to be watched and commented upon'. Only when he moved on to a shop with large numbers of employees did he find a less personal but also less oppressive atmosphere, where reasonable working hours went with better food and sleeping accommodation.[58]

Work conditions may not have seriously deteriorated in retailing during the second half of the nineteenth century, but they became a fashionable cause. There were more women employees, which created concern over conditions thought acceptable for men, and there were more of the large-scale establishments upon which reformers could focus their attention. Our picture of work conditions thus derives from the moral sensibilities of campaigners: sleeping arrangements, sanitary conditions, female and child labour, and so on.[59] Long hours, petty rules, rushed and often poor meals, and poor living conditions do nonetheless seem to have been the norm. Hours were especially long in small shops, which made their resistance to regulation the bane of early-closing campaigners everywhere. Shops in popular districts competed as much by being open at all hours as they did by price, and the differentiation between the more moderate hours of better-class and town centre shops on the one hand, and lesser and more popular shops on the other, widened towards the end of the century. So when the Belgian *Commission nationale de la petite bourgeoisie* proposed that hours of work for employees under 21 years of age be limited to sixteen for men and twelve for women, small employers insisted that such rules should not apply to those employing fewer than five assistants.[60]

These campaigns to regulate the conditions of labour of shop assistants yielded little of substance, other than tentative steps towards the regulation of hours. Belgian legislation gave some rights to Sunday as a rest day in 1905, the same year in which seats had to be provided for women assistants in the shops, a much favoured measure.[61] In 1904 local authorities in Britain were allowed to regulate closing hours where two-thirds of shopkeepers in a particular trade in a town voted for such a measure, but its effects were limited. An Act in 1911 required one half-day closing per week.[62] The French law of 1906 provided that each shop assistant was entitled to one free day per week, but this was Sunday in only 31 per cent of cases, compared with 93 per cent in artisanal trades.[63] Enforcement was once again weak everywhere. The *Ministère de Travail* had a mere 128 inspectors in 1907 to deal with over half a million enterprises.[64] In any case, salary reductions or a longer working day could be easily used to compensate for time lost through such laws. Retail employees were simply too insecure to play the role expected by those French labour inspectors who called on them to help enforce the law.[65]

The dispersed nature of the workforce, together with insecurity and the absence of organisational traditions combined to make unionisation very weak amongst Europe's shop assistants. Protest was much more likely to be individual, with an unhappy employee seeking a post elsewhere, but employment prospects were always poorer for older assistants, and they were often the most trapped. Many shop assistants' ambitions of setting up on their own increased their reluctance to confront their employers, while others merely sought a social position that set them above the working class, and the avoidance of trade unions and strikes long seemed a necessary element in that distinction.[66] A spokesman for the *Fédération des employés de France* stressed in 1901 that shop assistants could not strike. 'However powerful their union might become in the future, their action would lie in other directions, for their relations with their patrons would always remain platonic.'[67] When the assistants of the Lancashire town of St Helens joined their employers' battle against local consumer co-operatives, their chairman observed that

> he took it that the majority of shop assistants were ambitious to have a business of their own some day, but if this [the co-operatives] went on it would be mere folly for any of them ever to attempt to start in business.

Not all agreed – one assistant at the inaugural meeting argued that they should form their own association 'to look after themselves before they looked after the Masters'.[68]

Not many followed him, and shop assistants' unions remained weak in Europe before the First World War. The Belgian *Fédération nationale des sociétés de secours mutuels d'employés* was formed in 1891, but expansion was timid outside the large commercial towns of Brussels and Antwerp.[69] As in Belgium, the British National Union of Shop Assistants (1891) followed the establishment of local associations in larger provincial towns whose small assistants' organisations had broken from the employer-led early closing movement. The 7,500 members in 1900 had only grown to 21,000 ten years later, and it was only approved society status after the National Insurance Act of 1911 which saw the association's membership quadruple by 1913.[70] German associations, similarly launched in the 1890s, were even more concerned to stress the importance of co-operation with employers and distance themselves from proletarian unions, though demands over wages, pensions, hours and holidays slowly drew them towards trade-union activities.[71] In a context where European assistants were everywhere reluctant to take strike action, the increasingly conflictual relations in the Milanese retail trades from the later 1890s were exceptional. Strikes occurred in many trades from 1899, culminating in the strike of journeymen bakers in 1901, and then of 1,200 butchers' assistants in the town in 1903. The issues in the meat trades conflict concerned hours, holidays, conditions and above all the strength of the *uffici di collocamento* (labour exchanges). The struggles thus increasingly concentrated on the authority of the retailer to hire and fire in a town where the strength of the socialists and the labour movement polarised local politics.[72] Few such strikes were to be seen elsewhere. Such action as occurred in France, for example, was limited to department stores, such as the three-month strike by over two hundred delivery boys and assistants in one store in 1907–8, over the reinstatement of a dismissed employee and the restructuring of working hours.[73] Small shops remained untouched.

CREDIT, SOLIDARITY AND CONFLICT

An exploration of the relations between petits bourgeois and workers which stopped with the workplace would not only ignore the majority of owners of small enterprises who employed no labour beyond members of their own family, but it would also ignore the social interactions that concern petits bourgeois not as employers, but as owners and manipulators of petty local capital and as providers of local services. The daily sociability which embedded many shopkeepers and artisans within the wider popular community was considered in Chapter Six, as was the role of the shop as a centre for discussion, for the shaping of relations and reputations, and for the gendering of the community.[74] The interaction of shopkeepers and customers was often embedded in notions of rights. Conventional ideas about pricing are the most obvious, for they saw traditional market-place protest transferred into the shop, but these rights existed in more trivial forms such as the gifts which regular customers expected to receive. When bakers in Aachen in the crisis year of 1846 decided to discontinue the traditional practice of giving free Easter bread to regular customers, widespread rioting led to the district government ordering the bakers to reverse their decision, on the grounds that they had broken an implicit contract with their customers.[75] Efforts by Milanese shopkeepers at the end of the nineteenth century to end the practice of *regali*, the small but elegantly wrapped gifts (such as salami or nougat) which their customers were given at Christmas, failed because customers saw them as their traditional right.[76]

The Chamber of Commerce in the northern French port of Le Havre described in 1913

> the way of life of a small shopkeeper who, having much in common with his clientèle, and often sharing their life-style, as well as facing similar difficulties and hardships, sympathised with the needs of his customers and helped them in not inconsiderable ways.[77]

Credit from retailers was essential for working-class families on inadequate and fluctuating incomes, and it became even more necessary during strikes. For the shopkeeper, on the other hand, credit helped to build a clientèle and tie it to the shop, and many found that it made it easier to sell poor quality goods. An ambiguous identity of interests grew in popular neighbourhoods, but so too did tensions that grew not only out of credit, but also from petit-bourgeois ownership of working-class housing and their organisation of labour sub-contracting. So many of the difficulties of nineteenth-century working-class life were experienced in settings that brought them face to face with local shopkeepers and, to a lesser extent, master artisans that one should hardly be surprised if the relationship was an ambiguous and sometimes tense one.[78]

These ambiguities became particularly apparent during strikes. Shopkeepers in working-class areas were part of the small world in which they lived, subject to its pain and its problems. During the strikes of 1904 and 1910 in the small French mining town of Saint-Bel, the shopkeepers' association launched a subscription for the striking miners.[79] The mining company's food store threatened the livelihood of small shopkeepers, which helped attract their wholehearted support for the miners, and there was a similar tale in many company towns. The co-operation between workers and petits bourgeois in Mulhouse during the years of the Second Republic (1848–51) derived not only from a shared popular politics and hostility to the rich, but also from petit-bourgeois anger at large-scale industrialists whose setting up of *economats* (employers' shops), and whose building of workers' tenements, threatened the place of petits bourgeois in the supply of local goods and services.[80] This was one basis of the support that Decazeville's tradesmen gave to the town's workers in the 1880s, though, as in other such towns, increasing worker militancy and the establishment of worker co-operatives were to strain such alliances in the decades to come.[81]

Throughout Europe we find examples of shopkeepers giving material assistance in strikes, most often as general credit, but it could be more specific. During the 1895 shoemakers' strike in Leicester, joint committees of shopkeepers and trade unionists agreed special price tariffs for striking families.[82] Bremen shopkeepers in 1911 helped striking jute workers in very concrete ways: a woman baker gave a basket of gingerbread to their children, a draper handed out children's aprons, while a greengrocer gave a box of oranges and walnuts.[83] Even if many retailers did not like social conflict nor the violence that often accompanied strikes, community solidarity was reinforced by the knowledge that increased wages could only help their businesses. It was easier to put their name to strike subscription lists or to give a box of oranges than to advance the week-by-week credit that was the most needed, and indeed the most common, assistance. One Lancashire shopkeeper's son remembers that during the strikes of 1911,

> my mother was racked with indecision – she stood heart and soul with the strikers – but how much more food could she let go to those who, we knew, had no money to pay for it at week end. One wholesaler had stopped supplies; another threatened.[84]

Even where their support was less wholehearted, shopkeepers were realistic, as in the Leicestershire mining village of Whitestone during the 1893 strike:

The credit system ... was of infinite value to the miners during the strike. The shops which had the advantage of their regular custom were expected to continue to provide the necessaries of life, and actually did provide them to a surprising extent, although the tradespeople felt great doubts as to the likelihood of ultimate repayment. Partly, they were, no doubt, influenced by good nature and neighbourly feeling. They reckoned up the cost, however, and knowing that they stood to lose in any case by the strike, preferred to hazard present cash rather than the popularity on which future receipts would have to depend.[85]

There was another and less comfortable side to this coin, however, which saw strikers and protesters attacking shops and smashing their windows in a tradition that has persisted to the present day. At times of high food prices many towns experienced protests directed at shops rather than the traditional target of markets. In the English cathedral city of Exeter, peaks of bread prices in May 1847 and January 1854 each resulted in attacks on bakers' shops. The attacks were generally selective, as had been the older practice of *taxation populaire* in the market place, concerned with larger enterprises and with those where price increases were deemed excessive.[86] It was not always the case, for in the 1847 food crisis in Vienna, Berlin and elsewhere it seems to have been small shops which received the bulk of the attacks, as well as the large grain depots in ports.[87] Bakers attracted the greatest wrath, because of the place of bread in workers' diets as well as the significance of bread prices in traditional conceptions of rights and justice,[88] but the giving of credit and the need to sell in small quantities to poor customers made for higher prices, which ensured that small food traders were often under a permanent cloud of suspicion to which fears of adulteration only added.

In food protests hostility to shopkeepers was at least rooted in the business of shopkeeping. Far more prevalent from the second half of the nineteenth century was the smashing of shop windows during protests which seemed unconnected with the shop itself. When Chartists held a rally in the south London suburb of Camberwell in March 1848, 500 men broke away from the main demonstration, smashed windows and forced down shutters of many small shops – three shoemakers, a pawnbroker, a tailor, a clothes shop, a confectioner, a baker, and three general dealers. If the principal target was the pawnbroker, whose losses were estimated at about £900, the shoemaker who pleaded that 'I am a poor man: if you want something, don't come to me' could not prevent his shop being attacked.[89] In a more celebrated incident nearly forty years later, a section of the crowd at the demonstration by London unemployed workers in February 1886 set off down Pall Mall, attacking a variety of symbols of wealth, before turning on shops in S. Audley Street. The days that followed saw panic amongst London's shopkeepers as rumours spread through the city. Some 10,000 men were supposed to be marching on London from the suburb of Deptford, destroying the property of small traders on their way. All over south London shops were closed and their windows boarded up.[90] The fears were unrealised on that occasion, but they alert us to a threat that was always present, as much in France and Germany as in Britain. During a strike of weavers in Lavelanet (Ariège) in 1906,

> the strikers emerged in a crowd, armed with bricks, stones and axes. They made their way to the homes of their employers, to the *café Dousse* where the employers held their meetings, and to two grocery shops whose owners supported the employers' cause. Everywhere, the windows of shop fronts were smashed, the shutters and blinds taken off before being hurled inside.[91]

The disproportionate presence of foreign immigrants amongst retailers could be a contributory factor, most obviously not in the actions of workers but in the more specific pogroms where a variety of motives were woven together. These occurred several times in Germany during the *Vormärz* period, and even in 1848 itself. Artisans and retailers actually played a role in instigating these pogroms. As the government's observer noted of the riots in Heidelberg in 1819, an important factor was 'the jealousy of artisans towards those who had been given the right to trade in furniture in the town'.[92] More generally, however, racial tensions exacerbated by social conflict or poverty could lead to attacks on Jewish shops such as happened in south Wales in 1911.[93] Yet such attacks were more than the displacement of anger on to a minority group. These shopkeepers were accused of unsympathetic handling of miners' debts, whether as retailers or as the owners of workers' housing in the Valley towns. This interweaving of grievances had torn apart another south Wales town just a year earlier, when striking miners rioted in Tonypandy on 8 November 1910. They ignored the smaller back-street shops, but in the High Street spared just one chemist's shop, owned by a hero of Welsh rugby football. They attacked the premises of sixty-three shopkeepers, many of them active in local government, or owners of working-class housing, and whose attractive shop windows taunted striking workers with a consumer culture they could no longer share. Attacks on shops were simple actions that concealed a myriad of tensions. The complex web of community, dependence, and consumer aspiration was woven with fragile threads, and they could be torn apart in times of social tension.[94]

At the heart of these relations lay neither crisis nor strikes, but the daily necessities of credit. In a context where a large proportion of families was subject to irregular and low incomes and where all were vulnerable to the unpredictable incidence of ill-health, accidents or unemployment, credit was central to the survival of working-class families. It could be obtained only from smaller independent shops – the larger retailers, multiples and co-operatives insisted on cash trading only – and for a working-class family to trade in good times with shops which would afford credit in bad has rightly been seen as a form of insurance.[95] Shopkeepers in France were known as 'the bankers of the poor', while a Leicester baker in 1906 saw them as 'unofficial guardians of the poor'.[96] If the small shopkeeper disappeared, observed a small-business journal in Lyon, then at times of unemployment or sickness workers would have no option but to seek charity. 'The small shopkeeper would no longer be there to supply them with the credit without which they could not survive.'[97] Not only food was involved, for clothing and shoe retailers as well as furniture dealers used a variety of credit schemes to spread payments over time.[98] The practice of buying on credit was of course not a habit of the working class alone. One Belgian commentator observed the use of credit by 'prosperous bourgeois', and even aristocrats, a long-established practice that would have been recognised by retailers throughout Europe.[99]

Nevertheless, the relationship between credit-giving food retailers and credit-seeking working-class families is of the greatest significance here. It was sustained daily by the women of the working-class community, as they bargained for credit and as they built the household's reputation on which that bargaining rested. The shopkeeper had to take care, for the judgements could be difficult ones, well described in Robert Roberts' memories of his childhood in his mother's corner shop in Edwardian Salford. As his mother would comment, 'in the hardest times it was for me to decide who ate and who didn't'. The honesty and resources of all credit customers had to be regularly assessed, and when the poorest appealed for credit 'a shopkeeper's generosity and humanity fought with his fears for self-preservation'.[100] Helen Bosanquet decided that 'it takes someone born to the business, knowing whom to trust, and prepared to follow up defaulters, to carry on a general shop in East London'.[101] It also required a keen knowledge of the situation of all customers in order to assess the risk involved in any particular debt. It was not simply sociability which made 'gossip' such an important part of a small shop's functions – these were the basis on which character was judged, changes in health and in employment learned. When a request for credit was made, Mrs Roberts

> would make an anxious appraisal, economic and social – how many mouths had the woman to feed? Was the husband ailing? . . . Did the male partner drink heavily? Was he a bad timekeeper at work? Did they patronise the pawnshop? If so, how far were they committed? Were their relations known good payers?[102]

Shopkeepers in this way could play a major role in defining local respectability.

Credit was above all a means of building a regular clientèle, in competition with markets and with other shops. As one Welsh grocer observed, 'the tradesman favours the credit system because it has a tendency to keep his customers under an obligation to deal with him',[103] and its importance grew in the later nineteenth century as new forms of retailing insisted on cash payments. The danger was always that the independent trader only obtained credit trade, while in good times his customers were lost to the co-op and the multiples, but it was always wise for a household to become a loyal customer of a shop which could offer credit in times of need. Shopkeepers had their own debts to pay, and for these they required a regular flow of cash, which explains why *The Grocer* observed bleakly in 1904 that 'the greatest cause of failure seems to be the credit system'.[104] A wine merchant in Second Empire Paris spoke for a myriad of others like him.

> I have suffered considerable losses as the result of the credit that is indispensable in all sectors of retail trade. In addition, the low retail price at which one can sell, in comparison with the cost of the wines, leaves me with only the most modest of profits. These would have been sufficient to cover my costs ... had it not been for the ruinous credit which I have allowed.[105]

This is the explanation for the various schemes which emerged at the start of the twentieth century, such as the *Rabatt* scheme in Germany, to give rebates on purchases to cash customers.

The need to secure repayment of debts could lead to more formal retailer action. The closing decades of the nineteenth century saw the emergence of local debt-collecting associations in many countries, like the *Ligue du commerce et de l'industrie* which was set up in Ghent in 1878 to gather information about debts and to pursue those clients who did not pay.[106] Legal action for debt recovery also grew. As early as 1825 the establishment in Scotland of the Sheriff Small Debt Courts provided a machinery by which small debts could be recovered directly from wages, and the procedure was used above all by shopkeepers and landlords.[107] The Courts of Requests and, from 1847, the County Courts enabled small creditors in England and Wales to pursue debtors through legal action, and local traders overwhelmingly dominated the ranks of plaintiffs.[108] In the Paris working-class suburb of Belleville actions by shopkeepers to obtain such payments had by 1910 become the second largest source of cases brought before the Justice of the Peace courts, after rents.[109]

The most insistent source of distrust was perhaps neither the tussle for credit itself, nor the legal actions for debt recovery, but the fact that the tying of working-class customers to a shop through credit permitted higher prices, lower quality, and the adulteration of products. It was claimed in 1856 that bad and diseased meat in Manchester went to 'small shopkeepers who give credit to the poor'.[110] The adulteration of food became of increasing public and official concern in many countries from mid-century. Milk was the most notorious of adulterated products: it has been estimated that London's milk before 1872 on average contained 25 per cent of added water after one-third of the cream had been removed, while flour, carrot juice and chalk were added

185

to restore the character lost in this process of dilution.[111] Legislation made such practices illegal, but the dairymen felt they had been completely normal. At a large meeting to agree a price rise in 1873, one remarked that all they were doing was restoring the price they had been in reality getting for their milk before the government prevented them adding water.[112] Grocers agreed that if all goods were pure, they would be priced out of the reach of the poor.[113] The adulteration of food and drink products to make them go further or to improve their appearance was normal in mid-nineteenth-century European cities, and only slowly declined in the face of government legislation and municipal inspection.[114] The result was increased shopkeeper hostility towards the state. Many a shopkeepers' association in Britain was launched to defend traders against municipal officials harassing them over adulteration, false weights, and so on.[115] Anxieties of this kind became even more acute when socialist influence led to tighter regulation. In Vierzon-Village (Cher) in 1892, the socialists on the municipal council secured the purchase of a machine which would check the quality of milk, and insisted upon commissions to check the weight of bread and the hygienic conditions in which meat was sold.[116] Weights and prices were old concerns, but the demand for quality became increasingly important during the later nineteenth century. It was one of the driving forces behind European consumer cooperation. 'The member in purchasing at the Store is conscious that what he so obtains will be of the best quality, free from adulteration, and produced under the best conditions of sanitation and labour', wrote a leading cooperator in Woolwich, in outer South-East London.[117] The tensions surrounding credit and quality could not destroy the other solidarities of community and mutual dependency that bound many shopkeepers to their working-class clientèle, but they complicated those solidarities and provided the basis for the labour and socialist attacks which were to sour relations further towards the end of the century.

PETITS BOURGEOIS AS LOCAL INTERMEDIARIES

The role of petits bourgeois (and especially shopkeepers) as owners of petty local capital and as intermediaries in the local economy further complicated their relationships with working-class families. They frequently acted as intermediaries in local labour markets, certainly in Britain where petits bourgeois were active in organising at a secondary level the widespread putting-out system. Their rental of frames to knitters in the Nottingham hosiery industry was a *rentier* investment not unlike that in houses.[118] 'Foggers' was the Black Country name for those shopkeepers and publicans who acted as middlemen – notably in nail-making – and often paid partly in kind through their pubs and shops.[119] They can be found organising sections of the furniture trades, such as the chair-makers around High Wycombe in the 1870s.[120] The 'lumpers' on the London docks, and the Thames coalwhippers, were similarly organised by publicans and chandlers acting as sub-contractors of labour gangs.[121] These systems proliferated where workers were employed for irregular or small-scale tasks, and where intermediaries could create order in essentially unstructured labour markets. They often organised payment so as to increase the money spent in their own shops and public houses.

The most pervasive of such relationships flowed from petit-bourgeois ownership of working-class housing, which is why a Birmingham tenants' organisation seeking to take action in 1867 against landlords could call for a boycott of the shops of those landlords who were also retailers.[122] Irregular incomes meant that many working-class tenants struggled to pay their rent, especially poorer families because there was an inverse relationship between the size of income and the proportion of it devoted to rent. On the other side stood the landlords, who sought both the income and the sense of investment security which attracted them to house-ownership. Landlord and tenant thus often intersected at a point of maximum anxiety for each, and the resulting tensions should come as no surprise. These small landlords were generally judged by contemporaries to be the worst, for they could barely afford to maintain their property in a satisfactory condition, and where they did so the costs involved increased their determination to ensure that the tenants behaved properly within it.[123]

As a consequence, landlords often closely supervised their tenants, especially as they frequently lived in the same neighbourhood. In the 1830s, the small proprietors of Derby 'invest their money in running up rows of little tenements, the rents of which they rigidly collect every Monday'.[124] The same point was made half a century later of those small house proprietors in Bristol who 'look very sharply after their tenants', and like to collect their rents personally.[125] The interfering local landlord was commented upon wherever petit-bourgeois ownership of small rental property prevailed, even in Paris. By the years of the Second Empire more substantial capital was moving in to this sector, but in the poorest *quartiers*, such as Gros-Caillou and la Sorbonne in the old centre and the *faubourgs* on the periphery, local proprietors were renowned for their regular interference.[126] Arrears of rent were, like shop-keeper credit, essential to the domestic economy of much of the working class, and property owners were compelled in just the same way as shop-keepers to decide who might accumulate arrears during hard times. A good tenant, like a good customer, was worth keeping, and arrears often served the landlord's best interests. Decisions were nonetheless finely balanced, and made in a context in which both sides felt vulnerable. In Saint-Etienne, for example, the butchers, wine merchants and other such tradesmen repeatedly clashed with tenants before the police tribunal over non-payment of rent, rents levels, midnight flits, and agreements that were all too often merely verbal.[127] Legal procedures introduced in most countries to allow easier eviction of recalcitrant tenants and the seizure of property from those who owed money, produced the most acute and often violent conflict.[128] The Scottish right of hypothec allowed landlords to sequester tenants' possessions even before they went into rent arrears. It is not surprising that landlordism became such a strong political issue in early twentieth-century Scotland.[129]

Although it was less common for conflict to extend beyond the legal to the political sphere, the years surrounding the First World War did see the politicisation of the rent question in many countries. As early as 1848 the opportunities offered by the Revolution saw tenants in the Paris suburb of Belleville openly leaving without paying their rent yet insisting on receiving the *quittances* from their landlord without which new accommodation was hard to secure. Any resistance from the landlord saw the black flag hoisted above his property.[130] Anti-landlord feeling was at its most political where larger capital had replaced petty proprietors in control of much working-class housing, as in Paris by the end of the century, but the rise of more limited tenants' organisations to deal with smaller landlords was a broader feature of those years, and one which served to increase the sense of embattlement felt by many petits bourgeois in the face of increasingly vocal labour movements.[131]

THE GROWTH OF SOCIAL DISTANCE

The emergence of landlords and tenants organisations in the later nineteenth century signifies the distance that seems to have been emerging between petits bourgeois and workers during those years. One reason for this was changes in the character of the working class itself in western European industrial economies, as male employment shifted its centre of gravity from the artisanal trades towards heavy and factory-based industry. The increasing cultural distance this generated was reinforced by the emergence of distinctly proletarian housing areas in more rapidly segregating large cities. This 'proletarianisation' of the working class was accompanied by a slow shift in the character of its politics to make it a less congenial home for petit-bourgeois radicalism. The German Social Democratic Party, for example, became increasingly hostile to an independent artisanat, willing to appeal to it on questions such as social policy where they shared common ground, but unprepared to attend to the specific problems of artisans.[132] The petite bourgeoisie does not disappear from popular political movements in these years, as we have seen, but the decline of popular radical ideology as trade unionism, labourism and socialism came to dominate, provided a style and a rhetoric that it found less welcoming. When Milanese shopkeepers were treated as any other bourgeois during the general strike of 1904 to protest against a police massacre in Sicily, their relationship to the growing labour movement with which they had once co-operated became clearer.[133] It was a clarification that affected much of small enterprise in these years.

Socialist denunciations of the independent retailer alienated many who were barely touched by the competition of consumer co-operatives, creating the fear among shopkeepers and independent artisans alike that small enterprise had little to hope for from labour politics and a good deal to fear. Artisans might also feel challenged, as they were in France, by socialist calls for technological innovation to modernise industry. As Hector Lambrechts, the Belgian bureaucrat of the international petit-bourgeois movement, explained, 'the disappearance of the petite bourgeoisie is one of the indispensable stages in the approach of the collectivist system'.[134] The need to draw a firm line between proletarians and others was particularly strong amongst French socialists in these years, but it can be seen everywhere that labour movements saw in co-operation both an element in working-class emancipation and a basis for building a strong movement. Jules Guesde commented that French shopkeeper organisations 'can whine, petition, and start newspapers; they will continue to be devoured, one after another'.[135] Socialist leaders did indeed make efforts to cultivate petit-bourgeois support, especially in defence of Republican order, but for small shopkeepers everywhere the combination of socialist discourse and co-operative presence seemed to tell a simpler tale. Mere predictions of the death of small traders were enough. 'They did not wish to keep out the small shopkeeper,' one Scottish co-operator wrote during the St Helens boycott, 'but like the handloom he would have to go.'[136] In the eyes of many shopkeepers, co-operation became identified with a wider demonology of all that would destroy the good social order in which they believed.[137] As one Belgian baker explained, the consequence of co-operation was to 'deepen the ditch that separated the petite bourgeoisie from the working class to the point where it had become a chasm'.[138] The co-operative store offered an alternative vision of the daily relations of retailing, and as such not only challenged shopkeepers' income but also their place within the neighbourhood. For an increasing number of petits bourgeois, society appeared to be polarising between two great classes, and in that context they felt threatened and isolated. A south London shopkeeper, who had sunk a small inheritance into a picture-framers' and fancy-goods shop, captured the fears and the anger:

> It makes me positively ill to hear the blatant cant that is talked about the working man, meaning journeymen and labourers only. The small London suburban shopkeeper toils far harder than any of them, is preyed upon by them to an extent which must be incredible to those who don't know, is taxed almost out of existence to support them in the schemes continually being propounded for their benefit by their representatives on the Borough Councils, and is quoted in radical newspapers as the bitter enemy of the working classes.[139]

Defenders of the petite bourgeoisie complained that only the workers seemed to matter now. As the working class became subject to the political attentions and social policies of governments, so a sense of neglect and embattlement was expressed by an increasing proportion of petits bourgeois, initially in France and Belgium, although this atmosphere grew strongly in Germany primarily after 1918. Campaigns to reform working conditions in small enterprise only sharpened those grievances.[140] A sense of distance and superiority in relation to the working class was one dimension of the petit-bourgeois identity which took cultural, associational and political shape in these years. Joseph Brown, the small Birmingham toolmaker, spoke in a somewhat contemptuous manner of his workmen – their drinking, gambling, and wasting of good wages. His craft pride did not mean that he felt any real identity with those whom he employed. De Rousiers commented that Brown had a 'poor opinion of men who find it hard to make a living for themselves and their families in a trade where he has been able to raise himself and his family to a good position'.[141] The petit-bourgeois witnesses to the Belgian national enquiry in the early years of the twentieth century contained a number who genuinely sought to grasp the material problems of the working class, but the majority presented a hostile and negative image. The workers were dirty, dishonest, drunken, susceptible to socialists, bad payers and through their co-operatives destroying the very rungs of the ladder up which they might one day hope to climb. The petite bourgeoisie, by implicit contrast, represented the reverse of these vices.[142] These were the voices of ordinary local artisans and tradesmen, but they may have been using a discourse which they believed that the Commissioners wanted to hear. Artisans and shopkeepers in everyday contact with working-class men and women may well have behaved somewhat differently, and differentiated more closely within a working class which was represented in unrealistically homogeneous terms in public speeches. Yet there was indeed a change of tone in the later nineteenth century which indicates something real: not the severing of once close ties, but a growing sense of distance in a relationship that had always been ambiguous.

9

CULTURE AND SOCIABILITY

The prevailing image of the cultural practices of the European petite bourgeoisie is unambiguous. As we turn from contemporary novels and cartoons to the image in historical writings, we find the petite bourgeoisie presented as an essentially imitative social group. The Marxist literary critic Christopher Caudwell felt that the petite bourgeoisie 'has no traditions of its own and it does not adopt those of the workers, which it hates, but those of the bourgeois, which are without virtue for it did not help to create them'.[1] In the more recent words of the French sociologist Pierre Bourdieu, 'with his petty cares and petty needs, the petit bourgeois is indeed a bourgeois "writ small" . . . a man who has to make himself small to pass through the strait gate which leads to the bourgeoisie'.[2] It is a powerful image, with small businessmen, minor civil servants and office-workers driven by a combination of anxiety and aspirations to imitate a bourgeois culture whose substance they could rarely grasp, and that is why petit-bourgeois lifestyle has been the subject of so many humorous novels and cartoons. The literary image is nonetheless more difficult to sustain once we explore the realities of petit-bourgeois life.

Pierre-Louis Marcelin was a tinsmith and lampmaker employing a handful of journeymen in Nîmes during the second half of the nineteenth century. We would know as little about his culture as we do of that of his fellow petits bourgeois, had his son not become a prominent member of the rationalist movement, and contributed a memoir of his youth to a rationalist periodical. He provides an insight into the complexities of petit-bourgeois culture, one that is particularly valuable given our dependence on simplistic stereotypes and fragmentary research.[3] His parents were never prosperous, though a life of hard work meant that by their latter years they could enjoy a degree of comfort, or at least security, that was not granted to the town's wage-earners. The security came from property, the *mazets nîmois*, small plots of land with a rough cottage which most of the town's artisans had occupied legally or semi-legally in the countryside a few kilometres out, and to which they fled on Sundays to relax and to raise some vines or olive trees. The Marcelins were embedded in the town's artisanal culture, where differences between crafts, or within a craft, were less important than the larger distinctions between artisans and labourers, or between artisans and bourgeois. Pierre-Louis enjoyed the traditional celebrations and the dialect jokes and stories, but he continued to display the ferocious individualism characteristic of most of the town's master craftsmen, whose internal competition for trade meant that economic or cultural associations were hard to sustain. The formal culture of art and literature was shared with journeymen, for in most Nîmois crafts the difference between masters and their employees was often one of life-cycle stage. This culture was rooted in the locality but it reached beyond. The master plumber who had read most of the novels of Dumas and could declaim *Cyrano de Bergerac* from memory had gone further than most, but in general they were 'great lovers of *belcanto*: in the workshop or on the building site one could hear the great arias' from Halévy's *La Juive*, Gounod's *Faust* or the *Huguenots* by Meyerbeer. 'The atmosphere was both popular and free.' Old local cultures enlarged by newer national ones? The reality was less straightforward, because that traditional Nîmois culture, with its mixture of *patois* and French, was itself reinvigorated by the publication of traditional poems and fables by Bigot, a Protestant poet who was a leading Nîmois merchant, and whose resurrection of those traditions found particular favour with the town's petits bourgeois.

There was little place for art in Pierre-Louis's world, though he admired the rather conventional reproductions in *Le Magasin Pittoresque*, a Saint-Simonian periodical to which he became so attached that he set about collecting a complete set, back to its foundation in 1835. The appeal to this earnest Protestant small employer was not Saint-Simonian ideology but the systematic exposition of knowledge. After the evening meal, the family would read of the science, industry, art, history and customs of the different countries of the world. It was learning – more precisely it was knowledge – that Pierre-Louis felt that he lacked. In the middle of the century he had become attached to the works of the patriotic, populist and even vulgar Pierre Jean de Béranger, whose best-selling books of songs and poems were especially popular amongst artisans and shopkeepers.[4] By the 1860s and 1870s his purchases were more sober: the writings of the American social reformer William Ellery Channing, *Robinson Crusoe* and *Don Quixote*, along with the tragedies of Racine. One wonders whether he read them. The newspapers taken regularly were the local *Foyer Protestant*, and the anti-clerical *Le Petit Méridional*, for Protestantism and republicanism were fundamental to the Marcelins. This combination of artisanal culture, respect for learning, Protestantism and republicanism produced for Pierre-Louis at one and the same time a commitment to change and a rejection of social conflict: charity, savings banks and *jardins ouvriers* (allotments) were for him the way to achieve the progress of the working class.

192

OPPOSITION, DISTINCTION AND THE CULTURE OF WORK

An analysis of the traditions, values and cultural practices of the petite bourgeoisie is hardly possible in the current state of research, and in this chapter the emphasis will be placed on two central dimensions of that culture. First, what might be termed petit-bourgeois mentality, concentrating on the distinctive themes of family, localism and property. Second, cultural practice, looking at books and music, artefacts and possessions, sociability and associations. The sensitive memoir by Paul Marcelin points towards some of the essential themes: the extent to which the petite bourgeoisie detached itself from a wider popular culture; the role of formal literary and artistic culture in a milieu that allowed little time for such activities yet increasingly valued them; the importance of property in petit-bourgeois identity; the localism of the cultural and social world, but a localism that was being redefined along with the traditions that sustained it; and the extent to which social and cultural associations were inhibited by an individualistic ethos, as well as being rendered difficult by the intensive demands of the enterprise. Not every European petit-bourgeois was a Protestant Nîmois tinsmith, for sure, but the issues raised by the Marcelin memoir recur as these questions are explored, and as we ask how far cultural practice and characteristics provide evidence of a social group taking shape within the diverse and layered world of the European petite bourgeoisie.

The Marcelin biography suggests a culture that was not only more complex than the stereotype of imitation would lead us to expect, but also more argumentative. Contest and innovation within sections of the petite bour-geoisie are characteristics that have been too frequently ignored. Aggressive religious dissent was often important in sustaining political radicalism, as it did with Marcelin and others in Protestant areas of France, but it was especially important in Britain where nonconformist dissent and Methodism allowed the idea of independence to be maintained in a petite bourgeoisie for whom its economic connotations were in retreat. It enmeshed with an antagonism to the centralised state, or to the dominant church, or to both; and for some it produced an anti-clericalism and secularism within which petits bourgeois were active.[5] They were active in the movement for civic burials which built up in France from the 1880s – the movement in Reims, for example, rested on the town's weavers on the one hand, and its small shopkeepers and master artisans on the other.[6]

A contestatory independence had long marked out the role of village shopkeepers and artisans within the rural community, and not only in those agrarian regions such as eastern England and the Paris basin where large landowners and farmers allowed less scope for independent action by agricultural workers. In the villages and small rural towns of Limousin they were vital to the dissemination of radical culture and ideas through the July

Monarchy and the Second Empire, and Margadant has shown how the links between radical petits bourgeois in countryside and market towns explain the geography of the 1851 insurrection in rural France.[7] These rural craftsmen and retailers, in Britain as much as in France, were more geographically mobile, more likely to have been born or to marry in other communities.[8] They distributed ideas as well as goods in the countryside – even as apparently minor an aspect of culture as forenames. In the communes around Niort in western France, where traditional saints' names had long been the rule amongst peasants and labourers, it was shopkeepers and artisans who introduced the fashionable names from outside, such as Alix and Georgine.[9] Their greater education, diversity of contacts, and partial distance from the suffocating pressure of the rural power structure, gave them a role as political and religious independents, and as the animators and organisers of rural associational life. Rural nonconformity in nineteenth-century England rested on just this stratum of craftsmen, tradesmen and small owner-occupying farmers.[10] Michael Home wrote of his father, a bricklayer and carpenter with a small plot of land in a Lincolnshire village towards the end of the nineteenth century: he was a leading Oddfellow, a Methodist steward and an uncompromising radical. That is why the village shopkeepers and master artisans were so important to the birth of agricultural trade unions in Britain during the 1870s: men like George Rix, a grocer and general dealer in Norfolk who was a Primitive Methodist preacher, an active radical, and secretary of the local branch of the National Agricultural Labourers' Union.[11]

The innovativeness of the petite bourgeoisie was less apparent in the towns, however, as the century wore on. The urban setting was becoming more difficult as economic and social pressures forced many petits bourgeois towards a limited emulation of the larger bourgeoisie. Theodor Fontane, whose novels chronicle imperial German society, portrayed in *Frau Jenny Treibel* a grocer's daughter who had succeeded in marrying a *Kommerzienrat*, a title of honour and rank signifying a significant position and usually held by wealthy businessmen.

> In effect her mother, Frau Bürstenbinder, who knew well how to show her little doll to advantage in her orange shop, had used all her feminine wiles in planning her coup. Her little doll had now become a *Kommerzienrätin* and could present herself as a model bourgeois woman.[12]

They turned as well towards the protections offered by family privacy and cultural conformity. In exploring some of the features of that urban culture, it is important to recall the aspirations to survive or to advance in business, the concern for education as a family resource, the involvement in popular and neighbourhood sociability, and the prevailing localism. There was above all the increasing tendency to turn in upon family life which characterised much of the petite bourgeoisie in the second half of the century. Even the Marcelins, embedded in a wider artisanal culture of neighbourhood and

194

mazet, invited into their home only members of the larger family, and then only for meals on religious feasts.[13] The conventional image thus reappears, hardened by a literature entranced by the apparent introspection and smallness of petit-bourgeois life – one thinks of the novels of Arnold Bennett and George Gissing in England, of Emile Leclercq in Belgium, or autobiographical writings such as that of Oscar Walcker in Germany – but it does indeed represent an increasingly significant dimension of this culture. Binding all these characteristics together were the ambiguous social situation of petits bourgeois as the century progressed, and the realities of work, business and political contest. The characteristics of petit-bourgeois culture cannot therefore be separated from the other themes of this book.

Nor can they be separated from the question of distinction,[14] and the extent to which through mentalities, cultural practices and artefacts, as well as through sociability and associations, sections of the petite bourgeoisie developed an identity that cannot simply be seen as the result of later nineteenth-century political mobilisations. The need for distinction can be more readily found in the rapidly expanding white-collar strata with whom others increasingly associated these older petits bourgeois. From the late nineteenth century, white-collar workers throughout Europe, sharing with the working class a form of labour and unable to claim an even notional economic independence, sought to assert their non-working-class identity. This most often took the form of seeking to imitate what they saw as bourgeois culture.[15] This process of cultural aspiration was less evident in the world of small enterprise, though it was certainly found in those sections of the petite bourgeoisie for whom access to the larger bourgeoisie by association and culture, if not by personal mobility, remained a real goal. It was, however, harder to achieve than for white-collar employees. The nature of small enterprise and the close attachment of workplace to home allowed no equivalent of the segregated lower-middle-class residential districts where a white-collar lifestyle developed, with its suburban pattern of associations and leisure. The constraints of distance and geography inhibited petit-bourgeois cultural imitation, but so too did the constraints of other resources, above all time in a sector where long hours and attachment to the workplace characterised all but the most successful of businesses. It is therefore essential to distinguish between different sections of the petite bourgeoisie. One level of differentiation follows size and stability of enterprise, with an elite of shopkeepers and masters merging with a wealthier urban bourgeoisie in their associations and *cercles*, while the owners of a myriad of marginal enterprises were culturally bound up with the popular milieux of which they were a part. Nevertheless, even if the culture described here was often attached most clearly to the more stable and more prosperous sections of small enterprise, the contours of that culture were apparent throughout the petit-bourgeois world. The importance of family, the nature of the attachment to an enterprise conceived in moral as much as financial terms, and the localism of horizons were pervasive characteristics of the petite bourgeoisie as a whole.

An exploration of petit-bourgeois culture must also distinguish between artisans and shopkeepers. While artisans – including artisan retailers such as bakers and butchers – could draw upon an evolving trade culture that might be rooted in a corporate past, retailers generally lacked such traditions. From the later nineteenth century efforts were made to create them, with the publications of books glorifying the history and traditions of specific retail trades, so as to sharpen the idea of the 'legitimate trader'.[16] Master artisans could draw on firmer work-based cultures. In its classic idealised form the unifying culture embraced the succession from journeyman to master which represented the movement through an individual life cycle, though we have seen this traditional culture weakening in the eighteenth century, and fragmenting in the nineteenth. The culture of these crafts remained important even as it broke apart. Elements of journeyman culture entered working-class culture in the nineteenth century, often in fact constituted that culture, and while Sewell has stressed the way in which the artisanal ideological frame came to shape workers' movements in July Monarchy France, equivalent processes were at work in Britain. The notions of the rights of the trade, of the moral force of customary practices, of the right to practise one's time-served occupation, and of the obligation on the trade community to defend itself, all gave early working-class movements their core ideals and practices, perhaps more so than in Germany where the masters clung longer to the ideal of the craft corporation and its moral imperatives, and where the break with the language of the past occurred first amongst journeymen.[17]

The artisanal past is therefore central to any understanding of working-class development,[18] but what entered a wider petit-bourgeois culture? From the middle of the nineteenth century a combination of economic pressures and the emergence of working-class movements saw the process of separation between masters and journeymen spreading, though the speed varied greatly with both trade and place. The result was a very differentiated appropriation of the artisanal past. In some cases the craft memory rested on a surviving moral community of the trade which bound masters and journeymen together – the Marcelin family firm provides one such example. In other cases the craft memory had to be recovered from a period of slow decline, which at an extreme produced an idealisation of a past which had barely existed. By the late nineteenth century, the combination of social reformers seeking to distance artisans from socialist and labour movements, journeymen and masters confronted by circumstances less and less receptive to the unifying force of tradition, and masters proud of their craft past, all served to encourage the reconstruction of artisan traditions and their appropriation by the masters. As the actual practice of the craft culture declined, so it was memory which best survived to play an increasingly important part in master artisans' culture. The end of the century saw the reconstruction of artisanal culture as myth.[19]

The now fashionable craft museums sometimes represented the intervention of larger urban bourgeois interests, insisting on an artisanal culture that was non-proletarian. Yet, as with the *Kunstgewerbe* movement in Germany which extracted money from large-scale industry to found institutions such as the Düsseldorf craft museum, the process was appropriated and used by sections of the petite bourgeoisie.[20] There was a more indigenous process in the later nineteenth century, with the embellishment of artisanal 'traditions', as small artisanal businessmen affirmed ritual identities derived from an often imagined past. Handicraft traditions were romanticised in Vienna, where master bakers spent money on organising their guild archive and on publishing books on the bakers' past. Their festival processions, with traditional costume and the old guild banners, mirrored activities elsewhere. For the leader of the Viennese carpenters, the anti-Semitic Christian social activist Johann Jedlicka, this was part of attempts to restore the old guild system, but for most it was tied more broadly to the search for historical roots and legitimations. This new sense of the 'corporation' was accompanied by a new emphasis on the unifying and historical role of the *fêtes patronales*, now more elaborately celebrated. The Lyon bakers celebrated Saint-Honoré on an ever grander scale – Henri Béraud remembered the mass (attended primarily by the wives while the men drank in a café close by), the dinner, the speeches, the songs, and the dancing. Local civic dignitaries now participated, as the corporation reasserted itself. The banquet itself – with its *table d'honneur* and speeches – was an expression of the hierarchy of that corporation.[21] These movements to resurrect or mythologise past traditions were not necessarily in tension with business modernisation. Indeed, they often went together. The Swedish craft organisations, along with the General Trading Association of Sweden, launched museums and craft histories after 1895. They were anxious not just to glorify the past but also to demonstrate their role in economic progress in the future.[22] It was generally the better-off petits bourgeois who used their organisations to generate a new historical consciousness, and they were often those in the forefront of technical modernisation. Their activities were a bid for status in urban cultural competition, rather than a cry of protest from those in decline. They also served to demarcate those not at the appropriate level, and to establish a new scale of occupational values. Museums and traditions might constitute a critique of the present, idealising corporate harmony in the face of liberal individualism, but it was a superficial critique that did not represent the voice of those most threatened, and which was frequently turned against them.

History and traditions may evoke a nostalgic and often invented dimension of artisanal conceptions of production, but they were rooted in the reality of work which was an inescapable part of master artisans' identity. Artisans were in this respect closer to workers than were shopkeepers, for manual labour and skill were fundamental to their daily lives: they sweated, they became dirty, they roughened their hands. This culture of manual labour distinguished master artisans from other bourgeois groups – from the work routines and exhaustion of the baker who rose in the early hours of the morning to prepare and knead the dough to the craft commitment of the joiner as he turned a newel. As relatively prosperous a small master as Joseph Brown, the Birmingham toolmaker, 'still flatters himself that no smith in Birmingham can turn out better or quicker work'.[23]

FAMILY, LOCALISM AND PROPERTY

A group of common themes gave shape to petit-bourgeois culture through the nineteenth century. As culture, far from being a residual category, is both rooted in other experiences and a means of organising them, these themes recur throughout the book: family, home and privacy, localism and property. The first of these provided the most significant element in petit-bourgeois lifestyle and culture. An increasing family introspection and concern for privacy prevailed not so much in spite of the limitations of most petit-bourgeois homes, but because of them. Schlumbohm has pointed to the contrast in late eighteenth-century German towns between an upper bourgeoisie closed in on a privatised family world, and an artisanal lower bourgeoisie whose daily life was shaped by the public world of the street.[24] The shift of lifestyle in the century that followed, into the more privatised setting and values of the home, is one point of convergence between petits bourgeois and the larger bourgeoisie, one aspect of detachment from the popular world. Even at lower levels of small enterprise we found attempts to restrict children's street contacts and to limit entry to the home, which became an expression of family unity and values. Privacy was a form of defence present in all social classes in the nineteenth century, but the increasing rejection of the street by most petits bourgeois living in popular neighbourhoods, and restricted access to the formal sociability of bourgeois institutions, combined to render that privacy particularly acute and limiting, especially for children and for those women not actively engaged in the enterprise. A common result was a rigid imitation of bourgeois rituals, such as table manners. One organ-builder remembered that 'at the table the children had to remain silent, while the father and mother would speak'.[25] The increasing importance of the private family influenced petit-bourgeois political values, as private and personal moralities were transposed on to the economic and political spheres. We have seen this manifest itself in various ways: the concern that workplace relations should reflect that of the harmonious family, and the claim that this characterised small enterprise; the insistence on the personal nature of economic relations as the basis for economic justice, and with it the rooting of the just economy in the virtual autarky of local relations; the moralistic conception of 'fairness' in economic and fiscal matters; the attack on idleness and waste, whether represented by financiers on the one hand or state bureaucrats on the other; and in Germany, according to Blackbourn, a vision of the state as a stern paterfamilias insisting on fairness.[26] The moral critique within petit-bourgeois protest – the attack on department stores is the best example – was one repeatedly defined by the moral ideals of the family.

Localism represented a further dimension of petit-bourgeois culture. More exactly, it was an aspect of urban petit-bourgeois culture for in smaller rural communities craftsmen and retailers often represented the opening to a wider world. As the urban structure developed, so the mentalities and the defences of the small town, and of the small neighbourhoods within larger towns, came to be increasingly identified with the petite bourgeoisie. Localism embraces complex pattern of characteristics, one aspect of which was the protection offered by the reassurance of predictability in a familiar world. From the serialised stories in Le Journal, a newspaper successfully directed at the French petite bourgeoisie in the 1890s, emerges a world rooted in daily routine and in which readers could find themselves in 'familiar surroundings'.[27]

Localism had a variety of dimensions. The first was economic, both in nostalgia and in demands, as retailers and craftsmen sought to restore the protections that the growth of larger markets and mercantile activity had denied them. The growth of regional, national and international competition, spreading at different speeds through different trades, had most effectively stripped small enterprise of its traditional defences, and it is not surprising that the ideals of a localised economy should seem increasingly attractive to petits bourgeois under pressure. As larger capital came to reshape both the city and the market in which petits bourgeois operated, so the ideology of localism became a prominent political response: local markets, local customers and traders, the honesty, familiarity, and interdependence of the local economy, all came to represent not just the economic defence of small retailers and artisans, but the defence of their moral values as well. The ideal was most clearly articulated in the French Ligue syndicale, with its almost autarkic vision of local economic interdependence,[28] but it was an underlying theme of most petit-bourgeois defence organisations from the late nineteenth century, as they presented the localist alternative to the challenge of large-scale capital and the bureaucratic state. Even in Britain, where localist ideology had a more limited influence on shopkeeper movements, it appeared in less formal ways. A 'Local Trader' in Kent wrote a series of letters to his town newspaper in 1894, calling for a consumer boycott of department stores and retail chains in favour of buying from local tradesmen and keeping profits in local circulation, arguing that here was the basis for a thriving local community.[29] Localism as defence nonetheless was matched by increasing regional and national organisation, particularly so in Germany where the influence of localism may have begun to wane.

The second dimension of localism was the concrete importance for small businessmen of specific towns and specific districts. Their business interests were rooted there, and municipal rather than central state authorities most affected them. The route of a tramway, the location of a market hall, or the inspection of shop conditions seemed far more important to them than did decisions of central government. Their property had a specificity of place alien to the inherently mobile large-scale capital. Property becomes a distinguishing feature of petit-bourgeois identity, but their belief in the rights of property became bound up – both morally and economically – in a specific piece of property. Petit-bourgeois capital and property, in contrast to that of the larger bourgeoisie, remained essentially immobile in practice. Cardiff councillors protested in 1880 against the threat that the town's shipping elite could simply shift to docks elsewhere, arguing that 'to the Cardiff Chamber of Commerce the Cardiff Docks are a convenient and economical means of carrying on their business. To the ratepayers of the town they are an absolute necessity of existence.'[30] The implication was clear. While the wealthy elite could operate their business elsewhere, the interests of Cardiff's small enterprise were tied to property that was both specific and local. It became an increasingly distinctive characteristic of the petite bourgeoisie as the horizons of the larger bourgeoisie widened, with economic interests increasingly national and international, integration into national political and institutional structures, and the broadening of larger bourgeois investment beyond the local sphere. The withdrawal of the larger business and professional bourgeoisie from urban affairs was a characteristic of the fifty years before World War One, though it advanced more rapidly in Britain and France than in Germany. The local sphere now mattered far less, whether it was the control of municipal government, the day-to-day domination of the town's working class, or the mastery of the local stage on which the drama of status and influence was played out. Lequin has called this process 'the delocalisation of the bourgeoisie'.[31] Localism was culturally and materially tied into petit-bourgeois daily lives precisely because it distinguished them from other sections of the middle class. In smaller towns shopkeepers and masters increasingly presented themselves as the leading social group. Their mode of life and economic organisation were presented as all that was best in small communities, a world that was self-regulating, ordered, and honest. This was most deeply rooted where guilds provided the historic basis of local municipal freedoms, as in Te Brake's Deventer or Mack Walker's German home towns, but this model was perhaps prevalent throughout small-town Europe.[32] As Mack Walker wrote of the home-town small businessman, 'there and only there he was a Bürger. Outside he was nobody.'[33]

There was, finally, the role of small businessmen in creating the culture of local traditions. Historians of nineteenth-century Europe have become increasingly interested in the attempts to root social and cultural legitimacy in the embellishment and often invention of what were presented as historic traditions.[34] Local patriotism, the defiance of outsiders, the dreams of restoring the organic communities in which master artisans and retailers had once felt secure, were responses to bureaucratic state building and increasing economic scale that were particularly intense in Germany's small towns, and older ideals were transfigured into an almost utopian traditionalism. Petits bourgeois in most towns, however, assumed a major part in animating localist traditions. Neighbourhood associations in the German town of Boppard mythologised their historic origins, representing the response of petit-bourgeois natives to the wider horizons of bourgeois associations. The same can be seen in *Mittelstand* attachment to Bochum's *Maifest* (May festival) or Düsseldorf's carnival in the later nineteenth century.[35] *Heimat* (homeland) associations in the Rhenish Palatinate saw a movement led by substantial notables at the regional level resting on a mass of local associations, pre-dominantly small business and white-collar in character, concerned with the celebration of local traditions: town history, the restoration of a castle, the revival of a folk festival or of local dialect poetry. One is reminded of the reconstruction of local *patois* literature in Pierre-Louis Marcelin's Nîmes. A study of a Tokyo community during the present century provides an instructive non-European parallel to this development of localist traditions: as a rapid influx of office workers threatened local social relations, so the neighbourhood's small businessmen organised local festivals and rituals which they presented as the continuation or resurrection of older practices.[36] The locality was emphasised not just because it was their economic terrain, but because it represented a world in which prestige and status were defined by criteria that they could understand. Nevertheless, in formal public presentations of local society, petits bourgeois would be expected to take their correct place in processions – after the notables but before the workers – as in the German town of Detwold during the inauguration of the Hermann monument.[37]

If family and localism are two defining characteristics of petit-bourgeois culture, a third is property. Given the importance of manual labour for master artisans and some retailers, and their close daily relations with employees, it was property above all which marked them off from the working class in general and from their own workers in particular. The ownership of property within petit-bourgeois culture, far more than amongst the larger bourgeoisie, was an end in itself as much as a means to an end.

Property was a concept whose changing meanings helped to define petit-bourgeois identity. The shift from perceptions of property bound up with corporate and community rights and guarantees, towards more individualistic and exclusive senses of the term, was never entirely complete. Yet there was a shift of emphasis which, in attaching these owners of small business more firmly to liberal bourgeois meanings of property, was fundamental in the construction of a petite bourgeoisie and of a distinctive petit-bourgeois identity. Within the eighteenth-century world of small-scale production and trading, property was coloured by its corporate and moral meanings. Masters' ownership of their property was constrained by a structure of non-economic rights, duties and moral requirements which themselves constituted a form of property. The abolition of guilds did not instantly transform the ideological frame within which property was perceived, for much petit-bourgeois radicalism in nineteenth-century Europe carried a continuing moral conception of property, but a shift of emphasis occurred. Even in Britain the effective absence of guilds does not mean that individualistic market ideas had prevailed amongst small enterprise. Indeed, the notion of 'the trade' which was so important in the eighteenth- and early nineteenth-century artisanal world was a corporate ideal that existed without the legal and institutional structure of corporations. Here was an alternative definition of the rights of property to that proposed by political economy, embracing the right to work at one's trade, and to defend its customs and privileges, whether as a master or journeyman. 'The trade' was a moral community which fractured under the pressure of changing productive relations in the first half of the nineteenth century.[38] In Britain and France, masters detached themselves from those restrictions of the older ideal of property which they had once seen as their right and their defence, as the idea of property became leaner and more individualistic. Property owners were now to be free to use their own property in whatever way they chose, to enter the market as free individuals. In a context where individualistic property was coming to define civic and political rights (not least in *censitaire* and propertied definitions of full voting citizenship), that distinct sense of property came to demarcate social divisions, to elevate the group now known as the owners of property. As those ideas entered the changing world of master artisans and shopkeepers, we can see one element in petit-bourgeois identity.

Property was never completely shorn of its moral and social significance, never simply identified with its neutral market meaning. In the discourse of later petit-bourgeois movements, small property and small enterprise were vested with Jacobin or Jeffersonian republican virtues, or with moral superiority in the defence of a healthy social order. It retained the symbolic meanings which were generally absent from the world of the larger bourgeoisie, especially the belief that property was an expression of stability rather than a tool for expansion and growth. Property, for much of the petite bourgeoisie, came to represent independence, autonomy and security.[39] Pernoud sees this as the implication in France of the term *fonds de commerce* which was first used in 1872. The word *fonds* was originally used to describe landed property alone, and its extension to small businesses he sees as imbuing it with a stable landed rather than a mobile connotation.[40] Property was now a witness to personal merits, expressing a growing individualism in petit-bourgeois culture. A survey of London social life in 1904 noticed shopkeepers' religion of stern individualism and their belief that every man should stand or fall by his own efforts.[41] As the Birmingham toolmaker Joseph

Brown saw it, 'each man's life is a problem of which he must find the solution'.[42] Property came to represent the success of those endeavours.

The actual composition of petit-bourgeois wealth and investment clarifies these cultural dimensions of property. The general characteristics recur across different European societies, but the sources available to historians are unfortunately uneven. The most extensive data exist for France, where notarial archives provide detailed information on property-holdings at death. Neither Britain nor Germany can offer such rich sources, and we are left dependent on more anecdotal evidence. Savings and acquisitions, for those petits bourgeois to whom they were available, served diverse purposes: the development of the business, security for times of difficulty, the creation of a patrimony to pass on to children, investments that might allow a *rentier* retirement, and of course the display of status or achievement. It is difficult for the historian to read intentions into data as specific as the composition of fortune at death, especially as we know too little about life-cycle property patterns, but we can agree with the French historian Jean-Pierre Chaline that in the property people accumulate, 'there is a choice of investments and sources of income that is heavy with social implications and which are often extremely revealing about deeply-rooted mentalities'.[43]

Shopkeepers and master artisans preferred real property (land and build-ings) to personal property (investments in business, shares, loans, bank accounts, and so on). At a time when the composition of middle-class wealth in general was showing a strong and continuing trend towards what Pierre Léon called 'the triumph of mobile capital', here was the most striking characteristic of petit-bourgeois property.[44] Although part of petit-bourgeois wealth was tied up in the business itself, this was generally a smaller proportion than for the more substantial bourgeoisie: for example, 39 per cent of shopkeeper wealth at death in July Monarchy Paris, compared with nearly 70 per cent of that of merchants and industrialists.[45] Profits and income were frequently turned into more secure investments, and that meant buildings and land. Throughout Europe we see the attractions of security and the status of being a proprietor drawing petits bourgeois to real property in a way that was declining amongst other wealth-leaving groups. These investments could be used to guarantee credit and loans, but the attractions were more than practical. In July Monarchy Paris (as in German cities), petits bourgeois were acquiring real property even when they had to go into debt to do so. Bankrupts will often have held on to their acquisitions far too long, rather than discharging the debt and the accompanying burden of interest pay-ments.[46] The evidence of this attachment to *immobilier* (real property) right through to the end of the nineteenth century can be seen not only from a wide range of French towns – Lyon, Paris, Lille, Bordeaux, Rouen – but elsewhere in Europe as well. Amsterdam's shopkeepers and artisans dying between 1855 and 1875 left 40 per cent of their wealth in real estate, at a time when all other middle-class groups left less than 20 per cent, shunning in the process the growing trend towards stocks, bonds and shareholding investments.[47]

This real property might include the building in which the home and enterprise were located, but house ownership went further, as we have already seen. Residential housing for rental not only itself seemed secure, it also afforded individual security in the face of possible disaster, whether business decline, illness, or the death of the owner.[48] Except where rural property had been inherited, the bulk of this petit-bourgeois investment was urban and local. Rural investment continued – and was increasing amongst Lyonnais retailers for whom a little vineyard, field or tiny house remained a continuing attraction – but even in France rural property was less attractive than urban, especially so amongst master artisans.[49] Houses in Lyon itself accounted for only 36 per cent of the real property held by the town's butchers in the 1860s, but this had risen to 92 per cent by the early years of this century.[50] Urban housing, as amongst the small businessmen of late nineteenth-century Cardiff, attracted less for its rate of return than for the security it offered of local bricks and mortar.[51] Here was a desire not just for security, but for the direct and personal control of one's own wealth. One had to know one's property.

Personal knowledge and control were alien to the new world of private stock-market investment that was burgeoning throughout industrial Europe in the second half of the nineteenth century and petits bourgeois participated in these markets far less than other middle-class groups. The world of government stocks, shares in public companies and debenture stocks which dominated large bourgeois fortunes by the end of the century, took second place to the attractions of real property on the one hand, and personal credits and loans to neighbours and family on the other.[52] The increasing importance of life-assurance investment indicated the recurrent concern for security, as did that of savings bank deposits.[53] The local nature of these savings banks was one of their attractions – savings in Cologne's mostly petit-bourgeois savings bank actually peaked in the crisis year of 1847, as local artisans and shopkeepers put their trust in the security of a municipal institution in contrast to the unreliability of the larger state that had so often failed them.[54] Shopkeepers and master artisans did not eschew stock-market investments, but they approached them less enthusiastically than other groups. While 36 per cent of the wealth of the liberal professions in Lille in 1908, and 22 per cent of that of industrialists, was tied up in industrial, financial and railway shares, the figure for petits bourgeois was a mere 4 per cent.[55] When such investments were made, there was a tendency to choose secure and often local institutions, such as railway companies, or local water and gas companies. They continued to be regarded with suspicion, but provided a reserve that might be more productive than the savings bank.[56] Public utilities and banks dominated the shareholding investments of Glasgow small businessmen in 1861, and the pattern is well illustrated by the small but increasingly prosperous South Wales draper David Morgan in the 1860s and 1870s. By the time he made the move to a more ambitious shop in Cardiff from the small town of Pontlottyn, he could boast of the leasehold ownership of four shops and twenty-four cottages in Pontlottyn, shares in a range of local gas and water companies, shares in the local iron company, and a farm let to tenants.[57] As investment became increasingly anonymous in nineteenth-century industrial Europe, petits bourgeois clung to an older and more personal perception of their property. Even when they shared in anonymous investments, market considerations might yield to more subjective ones, as witnessed by the deep reluctance of Rouennais petits bourgeois to invest in German stocks in the later nineteenth century, even though they had been drawn into Russian investment.[58] Suspicion of international investments could be used politically, as when the founding appeal of the *Reichsdeutscher Mittelstandsverband* in 1911 declared that 'the *Mittelstand* has two great international enemies. The one enemy is the golden international, the other the red international.'[59]

BOOKS AND THINGS

Family, locality and property provide three motifs of petit-bourgeois mentality, but as we move into more detailed aspects of the culture – such as sociability, leisure, reading and music – the paucity of evidence at the historian's disposal makes conclusions only tentative. The larger bourgeoisie left personal records and memoirs as well as institutional archives to guide us, while fear of the urban working class stimulated the surveys of popular lifestyle which are now so invaluable to the historian. The petite bourgeoisie falls between the two stools, neither substantial enough to leave evidence of these matters nor threatening enough to persuade others to do so. Nonetheless, the constraints which operated on petit-bourgeois cultural and leisure activities provided a clear context. In comparison with the more substantial bourgeoisie, they suffered the constraints of money, domestic space, and, above all, time. In comparison with the urban working class, most longer-term shopkeepers and master artisans probably enjoyed more money and education, but the increasingly formalised division between working and non-working time for a growing proportion of workers during the last decades of the nineteenth century was of limited relevance to all but the better-off owners of small enterprise. This inhibited the development of a leisure-based and associative culture.

The importance of family within the petit-bourgeois world is once again confirmed, and the Marcelins reading together *Le Magasin Pittoresque* is one example of the way in which much improvement was turned in on a domestic setting. Improvement, in the nineteenth-century sense, was increasingly present amongst petits bourgeois, especially amongst those artisans whose trade cultures contained a strong ethic of improvement.[60] However, as masters and men separated within the social world of artisanal production, the significance of workplace cultures declined for small masters. Improvement

205

was not exclusively centred on the home. Educational organisations for the working class came to be used – sometimes even colonised – by petits bourgeois and white-collar employees. This was the context in which Josiah Chater, building his tailoring and outfitting business in mid-century Cambridge, attended the YMCA and the Working Men's College (where he studied German and Latin as well as history and mechanical drawing). In those middle decades of the century, shopkeepers, master craftsmen and petty traders were prominent in Mechanics' Institutes. Indeed, they dominated the audience for lectures on great authors, geology, and experimental physics, and were the main users of the library and museums of the Mechanics' Institute in mid-Victorian Lewes.[61] Manual workers were never more than a minority of those using the popular libraries established in France as part of a strategy to moralise the working class during the second half of the century. These libraries acted 'as a means to incorporate not so much the working class as the petite bourgeoisie within the dominant literary culture of nineteenth-century France'.[62]

Were books common in petit-bourgeois homes? The answer depends in part upon the size of enterprise, and of course on the level of education and literacy which should not be taken for granted in the first half of the nineteenth century. A Colchester grocer who died in 1815 and left household effects worth £474 was clearly at the prosperous end of the retailing world, but his library was nonetheless impressive: Ossian's Poems, Gil Blas, Homer's Iliad, Dryden's translation of Virgil, the poetry of Dryden and Swift, Shakespeare, Gulliver's Travels, a group of fashionable eighteenth-century novels including Pamela, Amelia and Tom Jones, works by Ovid and Milton, and a sundry collection of other books and magazines.[63] Here was a fairly prosperous grocer embedded in the intellectual life of his town, though one still wonders how many of these books were read. On the other hand, shopkeepers in Paris in the first half of the nineteenth century hardly appear as keen book purchasers. Only 6 per cent had what might be called a library – that is more than a handful of volumes – compared with 36 per cent of merchants, 60 per cent of professions, 37 per cent of state employees. Nor were petits bourgeois in the small town of Niort likely to have more than a handful of books through the middle decades of the century, though a quarter possessed at least some, with prizes given to children at school, dictionaries, and one or two books of travel or trade volumes the most common.[64] Amongst sixty-five inventories of ribbon-weavers in the east German region of Lausitz, only twenty record the ownership of books. Religious works such as bibles and prayer books dominate, as they do in the south of Germany. Books here were about piety and religious standing far more than discovery and knowledge.[65] Here was a traditional relationship to books that still prevailed in the mid-nineteenth-century Swedish town of Härnosand, where one-third of artisans had books and where they were almost entirely religious in character.[66]

Petit-bourgeois diaries and autobiographies rarely mention reading, and it does not appear that petits bourgeois were generally regular book purchasers. A handful of volumes was the most that the majority would have, like the Croix Rousse baker who died in 1857 possessing a several volume *History of Napoleon*, or the baker who died in 1847 leaving volumes by Voltaire and the four-volume *History of the French Revolution* by Thiers.[67] Alongside Henri Martin's multi-volume *History of France*, the Parisian master locksmith who was surveyed in 1897 had Victor Hugo's *Notre Dame de Paris*, *Napoléon le Petit*, and *93*, together with fifty-six instalments of Hugo's complete works.[68] A taste for history and a taste for Hugo are a common thread in the few petit-bourgeois book collections of which we know, but the former was probably true of all who acquired books in the nineteenth century.

Voltaire, Napoleon, Thiers, Hugo – the presence of such books hints at a radical commitment expressed through literature, but we have no more than hints. Most access to books was, in any case, not through purchase, even late in the century when new production and distribution techniques brought cheap editions to the market. Commercial libraries – such as the *cabinets de lecture* that flourished in France, the German *Leihbibliotheken*, or local subscription libraries in England – were a more common means of demo-cratising the middle-class reading public. The mostly small *cabinets de lecture* provided novels, literature and newspapers which could be on the spot or, more usefully for those with businesses to attend to, borrowed on sub-scription. Here we see petits bourgeois as creators and animators of culture and not simply its consumers, for a good proportion of Parisian *cabinets* were opened by master artisans and shopkeepers alongside their existing business. Their location suggests a clientèle that, in the first half of the century at least, was made up of bourgeois, servants, students, and, above all, artisans and shopkeepers.[69] By the later nineteenth century French petits-bourgeois readers were enjoying books that had been fashionable some couple of decades earlier, such as Scott, Fenimore Cooper, George Sand, Alexandre Dumas. As one librarian at Pau observed, 'the shopkeepers know the name of only one author, Alexandre Dumas'.[70] The majority would not have read even those, though it is interesting that in England good books for their children seem to have been more important than reading for themselves.[71] The real impact on petit-bourgeois reading came perhaps with the new mass daily newspapers and weekly reviews that spread from the 1880s – the *Daily Mail* and *Tit-Bits* in England, *Le Journal* and *Le Petit Parisien* in France, or *Gartenlaube* in Germany.

On other aspects of petit-bourgeois cultural activity we know little more. The ability to massproduce good piano mechanisms cheaply by the 1880s, assisted by new methods of distribution on credit, encouraged the spread of pianos into the petit-bourgeois home. Here was a piece of furniture that could be used as well as displayed, a means to improve oneself and above all one's children, as well as a means of family music-making. There was a huge expansion of sales of sheet music – in England a diverse range of music hall songs, parlour songs, Gilbert and Sullivan, and light classics.[72] The importance of the piano for domestic music-making can be seen in *La Conquête*, a Lyonnais shopkeepers' newspaper which on the eve of the Great War carried in every issue a piece of music, generally written or transcribed for piano, often a song with piano accompaniment devised for domestic performance.[73] The piano was thus bound up with family leisure and family status. In some German artisanal families the children's piano practice was closely watched over by the parents.[74] It could be abandoned if unsuccessful, however, as when one Berlin family gave up the piano lessons for a clearly ungifted son and diverted the money into a more intensive school education.[75]

The culture was thus an increasingly domestic one, and we know too little about domestic acquisitions and lifestyle, not just the objects but the means of appropriating and living with them. Descriptions are rare, and even inventories are too vague when it comes to personal possessions, furniture and the uses of domestic space. The model of the bourgeois sitting room and its furnishings spread after 1850 amongst German petit-bourgeois households. Nevertheless, the three-roomed apartment of a Munich engraver in 1907 reveals a modest comfort and only limited decoration. The sitting room contained a divan, table and bed, three cupboards, several chairs, a sewing machine, and a few decorations on the walls. The size of the apartment suggests a modest prosperity that was reflected in the furniture.[76] By the later nineteenth century Lyon bakers were more sharply distinguishing family space from business space in terms of the names of rooms, while they were also furnishing them with a view to style as well as comfort, with sofas, armchairs, and desks.[77]

Given the paucity of detailed descriptions, Paul de Rousiers' visit to Joseph Brown's Birmingham home that adjoined his toolmaking workshop is particularly valuable, presenting the home of a solid but not prosperous master in late nineteenth-century England. The house was comfortable, but without great attention to fashion. De Rousiers wrote only of 'good family furniture', though there was some effort to display possessions in the parlour, while family life centred on the sitting room where they also ate their meals. The parlour revealed that display certainly mattered. Brown had spent six guineas on a marble chimney 'to beautify the parlour', in which a table was covered with books and albums, and on whose walls were indifferent prints and the photographs that were by now ubiquitous in petit-bourgeois homes. The fact that the piano was in the sitting room suggests that it was played. Here was a solidly equipped home, concerned with value and efficiency more than with consumer expenditure and fashion.[78] As in most petit-bourgeois homes, constraints of space were more acute than amongst others with equivalent incomes. The development of home-based conspicuous consumption at the lower end of the middle class, an innovation in European consumption patterns that was spread during the later nineteenth century by department stores and women's magazines, concerned the expanding white-collar lower middle class much more than it did small business.[79]

SOCIABILITY AND ASSOCIATIONS

There was leisure activity outside the home. From the middle of the nineteenth century theatres in larger French towns began to attract socially distinct audiences, with establishments such as *Le Vaudeville* in Paris or *le Théâtre français* in Rouen offering drama and comedy to the small business and white-collar *classes moyennes*.[80] Yet music hall, *café-concerts*, and light theatre played everywhere to strikingly mixed audiences through the middle decades of the century, even if the larger establishments segregated by price within the theatre, until petits bourgeois withdrew from what were pre-dominantly working-class entertainments.[81]

The more informal daily sociability of the street, the café and pub, remained significant during the first half of the nineteenth century, though subject to the constraints we have already discussed. One feature of detachment from that milieu, linked to increasing distance from journeymen and the demon-stration of respectability needed for business reputation, was a decline in master involvement in the culture of drinking. It had always been more than a merely voluntaristic sociability of drink, for the pub or tavern served as the locus for trade information and labour recruitment, even dealing for cash.[82] The withdrawal of masters from this broader artisanal sociability was uneven in chronology and in industry. Agricol Perdiguier described the masters' society in early nineteenth-century Marseille which met in a garden outside the town to play boules, cards and so on. Journeymen would join them, and 'there was general gaiety there; singing was the order of the day'.[83] Perdiguier noted even then that many masters were absent from the daily life of the workshop and from the artisan sociability outside it. This trend became widespread as the century went on.

Did there then emerge a distinctively petit-bourgeois pattern of formal and informal sociability? The limited degree of residential concentration made that unlikely – small-business petits bourgeois were less residentially segreg-ated within the nineteenth-century town than any other major social group. They were dispersed and their territory was shared with others, while the socially specific sociability which emerged in working-class neighbourhoods or white-collar suburbs towards the end of the nineteenth century was never a possibility. Any distinctive informal sociability lay in the centrality of the enterprise itself to the social relations of petits bourgeois. If many a small enterprise was a focus for popular sociability, then by the same token it served as the setting for social contact, certainly for shopkeepers but also for a range of artisans. The small grocers who added a drinks licence and bar to encourage the sociability essential for trade, the Parisian artisans who attached a reading room to their workshop, were at the same time building the social world of their daily life. A woman who grew up in a Chatham greengrocer's shop at the beginning of this century remembered that 'I don't remember we ever got fed up with running the shop. We enjoyed the company. We enjoyed seeing people, and we learned to mix with everybody, whatever class they were.'[84] This was not only true of those who dealt with a working-class clientèle. Middle-class customers would expect to spend a long time in the shops, particularly in clothing and drapery shops. One West of England draper would provide a full sit-down lunch for clients on market day, at which family, assistants and invited clients would dine together.[85] For many petits bourgeois a large part of their non-family sociability was bound up with the enterprise.

What though of the role of the petite bourgeoisie in the more formal sociability which was a significant innovation of nineteenth-century bourgeois society?[86] Associations in general – voluntary societies, cercles, Vereine – were each in their distinct way characteristic of bourgeois sociability and forms of action in Europe during the middle decades of the nineteenth century. They were crucial to the articulation of a middle-class presence in public life, of particular importance in Germany where associations created a public sphere independent of the state. It was not simply larger bourgeois organisations, but also the petit-bourgeois choral, savings and insurance, and similar associations which played that role in Vormärz Württemberg.[87] The distinction between charitable and interventionist associations on the one hand, and those concerned more with leisure and sociability amongst members on the other, is not necessarily helpful, for the reality was less distinct. The committees, dinners and weekly activities of a local society concerned with administering charitable relief to the poor, for example, would also provide the forum in which middle-class men, and to a lesser extent women, would meet socially. This was true of predominantly petit-bourgeois associations such as the Société Royale de chant in Brussels, where artisans gathered in the 1850s to give concerts in order to raise money for a pension fund. Providence and entertainment could go together.[88]

The extent to which members of the local elite and petits bourgeois were drawn together in voluntary associations made the British case distinctive. The years of social crisis and class formation between the 1820s and 1840s saw the emergence of voluntary societies led by members of a town's middle-class elite, often primarily directed at the moralising of the working class, but whose goals included the incorporation of a radical petite bourgeoisie. A great variety of voluntary societies in Britain either had a petit-bourgeois audience (many cultural institutions) or allocated to petits bourgeois a major organisational and administrative role (charities, savings banks, relief funds).[89] Here was a petit-bourgeois associational activity which points towards the ambiguous attachment of many shopkeepers and master artisans to a larger bourgeois world and a larger bourgeois culture. The process by which small businessmen and women were incorporated in a bourgeois ideological world was complex and incomplete, and other chapters have indicated the forces at work – amongst them commercial ties, webs of credit, dependency, and political anxieties. Associations which embraced different levels of the middle class were central to that process, and nowhere more so than in Britain. These were not so much learned and literary societies – the Literary and Philosophical Societies in Britain, the *Académies des sciences, belles lettres et arts* in France, or the *Gelehrten Gesellschaften* in Germany – whose high subscriptions or social exclusivity kept out small businessmen. It was much more the charitable and religious associations, the educational and temperance societies, that were directed at the working class.[90]

Urban elites and political authorities needed to detach an often radical petite bourgeoisie from popular social and political milieux, and on this basis even separate associations were welcomed in the tense social conditions of France during the later years of the July Monarchy. The Prefect of Hérault, for example, was pleased in 1846 to receive an application for the formation of a *Société des Arts* for shopkeepers and artisans, hoping that it might help develop a social distance between them and the workers.[91] Specifically petit-bourgeois leisure and cultural associations were generally hard to establish or sustain in the first half of the century. The Leeds Literary Institution in Britain's woollen textile centre provides a good example. Founded in the 1840s as a radical cultural alternative to elite-led institutions such as the Philosophical and Literary Society, this non-hierarchical association represented 'the culture of the shopkeepers, lesser employers and substantial master tradesmen, the better-paid white-collar workers, and the professional men who found themselves outside the elite'.[92] In France and Germany such associations would have been stifled by the state. In Britain it was financial difficulties and a more diffuse elite hostility that all too often prevented such ventures from being sustained. The effect was the same – a low level of independent petit-bourgeois associations during the first half of the nineteenth century.

The extent of petit-bourgeois clubs and associations should not be exaggerated, and involvement in institutions with a socially less exclusive membership remained common right through to the Great War. The years after mid-century did nonetheless see the beginnings of a more specifically petit-bourgeois associational life. In France shopkeepers, master artisans, and lesser professionals adopted the once more exclusive model of the *cercle*, an essentially social institution meeting in the private room of an inn or café, sometimes even in its own premises. The early years of the Third Republic saw a rush of such clubs in Paris, above all in the city's outer districts. The membership of the *Cercle de Bercy-Bel*, for example, in the 12th *arrondissement*, comprised 33 per cent artisans, 13 per cent shopkeepers, 33 per cent white-collar employees.[93] Smaller businessmen set up *cercles* in small towns and bourgs all over France, often Republican in character as in Berry, but usually directed at no more than the pleasures of meeting, drinking, playing games, talking.[94] Artisans' societies emerged in a similar fashion in Germany from the 1850s, to organise dances, hear lectures, and above all to enjoy each other's company every Sunday. The large number of beekeeping associations that grew there in the 1850s have been interpreted as a means for petits bourgeois, anxious about the threat from below and feeling increasingly distant from the larger bourgeoisie above, to assert a distinctive social identity.[95]

These Westphalian beekeeping associations are an example of the apparently single-purpose cultural and sporting societies, in which we see petits bourgeois becoming involved. The overwhelming domination of the Edinburgh Bowling Club by small businessmen and white-collar employees throughout the second half of the century is but one example amongst many.[96] Shooting clubs, gymnastic associations, choirs and brass bands – whatever the national variations which, for example, saw the first two insignificant in Britain – represented a world of leisure activities that grew rapidly from the 1860s and saw substantial petit-bourgeois participation. Shopkeepers and master artisans might form their own associations: consider their domination of the musical societies and, with the peasantry, the sporting societies of Saône et Loire in France, or their dominant role in many of the gymnastic and shooting associations that spread rapidly in Third Republic France.[97] Others saw petits bourgeois playing a leading role in societies with a strong skilled working-class involvement – this is especially the case with bands and choirs, orphéons and harmonies. The Fanfare des enfants d'Olympe, founded in Lyon's 3rd arrondissement in 1866 is one example of this kind of mixed club, the Orphéon de Villefranche in 1875 another.[98] The popular sporting clubs in the towns of Saône et Loire were organised by local shopkeepers and artisans, though workers formed the bulk of the membership.[99] They would often dominate a gymnastic society in Germany. The Dresden gymnastic club in which Walter Hofmann's engraver father was active through the 1850s and 1860s was composed of masters and journeymen artisans, minor civil servants and small businessmen.[100] The brass band movement that flourished in Britain from mid-century was solidly rooted in working-class industrial communities, but most required a local organising committee of shopkeepers and other small businessmen to act as trustees, to administer activities, to raise funds.[101] For aspirant petits bourgeois here was an alternative sociability, providing social networks and purposeful spare-time activities, while giving them the kind of local social importance that larger-scale philanthropy and organisations provided for the towns' elites.

Associations could also be more broadly lower middle class, drawing together small business petits bourgeois, white-collar employees and lesser professions. The Société la Gaîté Lyonnaise was founded in 1885 to give 'concerts and family soirées. The programme will contain ballads, light songs, operettas, vaudeville and dance.' Half the members were white-collar employees, the other made up of a variety of small businessmen such as a café owner, joiner, locksmith, butcher, ironmonger and baker. The choral societies and amateur orchestras, rooted in an older and more informal lower middle class and artisanal choral tradition, that flourished in England from the middle decades of the century reveal a similar social base.[102] Here was a social mixing which drew the small business petite bourgeoisie away from associations formed with workers and towards those they shared with white-collar employees. A more broadly-based lower middle class does appear to have been taking shape.

This associational sociability was almost exclusively masculine, with female associations rare and women's role in male associations highly circumscribed: as guests at dinners (the Lyon bakers were proud when they began to invite *les boulangères* to the Saint Honoré feast in the 1890s) or as audiences at concerts. Choral societies were inevitably more mixed, in membership if not in management, but it is rare to find explicitly female petit-bourgeois associations such as the secular and republican *Société Protectrice des Infortunes*, founded in Lyon in 1879 to bring charitable and moral improvement to poor families whose children attended lay schools. The President, Mme Rousset, ran a family business producing pasta, while the other members were made up of women with a variety of small enterprises: a grocer, dressmakers, florists, fruiterers, the owner of a joinery firm.[103]

There was one form of associational sociability which was exclusively petit-bourgeois: the increasingly important social life grafted on to trade organisations. Some were set up with that in mind, forming a kind of trade-based *cercle*, as was common in Belgium towards the end of the nineteenth century. The Master Pâtissiers of Brussels set up a society in 1887 'to get together from time to time, to see each other and to talk over the past', as well as to discuss matters of concern to the trade. In 1881 the *Cercle de la Treille* was founded in a backroom of a restaurant in the Parisian district of Bercy by a group of wine and spirit retailers who, as they expressed it when seeking authorisation, 'after having spent the whole day in the same occupations, gather together in the evenings in the same place, without having to leave this rather out-of-the-way part of the capital'. The *cercle* formed by master joiners in Lyon in 1867 combined trade and social goals more openly – 'with a view to establishing regular and friendly relations between the master joiners; to tighten amongst themselves ties of fraternity; and to associate for the progress of their trade'.[104] The dinners and festivals, or the conviviality of monthly tradesmen's meetings, were less explicit, and this form of sociability was the norm in Britain, where the *cercle* and such social clubs had few roots. The sociability of small town and suburban tradesmen sustained the growth of retailer organisations in Britain before 1914. The tradesmen in the London suburb of Fulham, for example, dined together at a local hotel once a year, but a sense of dissatisfaction at the level of cohesion produced by these dinners led to the setting up of a Fulham Tradesmen's Association which supplemented its

business concerns with social activities. The Leicester Scotch Drapers Association held regular smoking concerts, the town's chemists organised their own
Social Union, and trade associations offered whist drives, summer family
excursions, and so on. There was even a Leicester Tradesmen's Cricket Club
in 1900.[105]

Finally, there was the continuing importance of religious activity and
associations, above all in Britain where nonconformist chapels throughout
the century drew on a continuing core of petit-bourgeois support. By the end
of the nineteenth century the Booth inquiry concluded that shopkeepers
living above their shop were vital to the survival of these inner-London
suburbs where nonconformist congregations remained strong.[106] Throughout the century, democratic nonconformist religious congregations, with
their substantial role for lay people, their commitment to forceful and
intellectual preaching, and their plethora of meetings and charities, constructed a social world for large numbers of petits bourgeois, one in which
wealthier elites were less and less involved and in which they could construct
their own patterns of religious-based leisure and their own involvement in
working-class improvement. As Knox concluded for Edinburgh, 'the religious community was often at the centre of the petit-bourgeois world'.[107]
This dissenting Protestantism opposed to the aristocratic state and the
established Church not only deepened the individualistic and moralistic
character of petit-bourgeois culture, it also maintained a radical edge within
a culture which in other respects might be seen as becoming more conservative and conformist. Not only in Britain – look at the distinctiveness of
his Protestantism for the values and culture of Pierre-Louis Marcelin – but
its importance was certainly at its greatest there both in constructing an
associational world and in reinforcing a specific set of values. Elsewhere, the
picture looks less clear. Not only was there the small-town Catholic
conservatism which made the Centre Party such a force in south-western
Germany during the Wilhelmine years, but also the vigorous denouncers of
the clergy amongst the Republican, Masonic, anti-clerical petits bourgeois of
late nineteenth-century French towns.[108] There was a diversity of petit-
bourgeois religion which research is only now beginning to explore.

The social world of the petite bourgeoisie was more rooted in family, home
and enterprise than that of other social groups, and it is doubtful whether the
more formal associational sociability seen here ever involved more than a
minority of petits bourgeois – probably the more stable and successful of
small businessmen. The diversity of petit-bourgeois sociability is clear. Some
were involved in predominantly working-class associations, though less so
from the middle of the nineteenth century; others were drawn into subaltern
roles in organisations founded by wealthier urban elites, though that too
declined from mid-century; distinctively petit-bourgeois associations
emerged as associations in general became more specialised, and there were
signs of social overlap with the white-collar lower middle class. Taken with

the cultural characteristics considered above, the contours of a distinctively petit-bourgeois social world emerge. Substantially more research is needed not only to fill out the detailed picture, and not only to pinpoint national variations beyond those indicated here, but also to explore the variations between different types of town. Was their cohesion greatest in larger towns which exposed them to daily relations and regular conflict with other social groups? Or was it in the smaller towns that shopkeepers and artisans had their most cohesive social identity, sharpened as it could be by personal acquaintance? The diaries kept between the 1850s and 1880s by Thomas Skarratt, a draper in the small town of Kington on the Welsh borders, suggests that that might be the case. Although his business is barely mentioned, for this was a personal diary, his identification with the town's shopkeepers and small businesses is clear – news about these tradesmen, their marriages and deaths, fills its pages. When the first sod was to be ceremonially cut for the town's new railway, crowds turned out to watch the procession. The children of the local schools were at the head, followed by flag bearers, four navvies with a symbolic wheelbarrow, the members of two local friendly societies in their regalia, and then at the rear 'the Tradesmen of Kington', and the local aristocrats in a carriage. These tradesmen were not only Thomas Skarratt's social group, their identity within the town was a real one.[109]

10

CONCLUSION
Into the twentieth century

This book began by asking about the class character of the petite bourgeoisie during the long nineteenth century. A good number of social observers and sociologists had little doubt that the petite bourgeoisie could indeed be seen as a class at the end of that period. Max Weber identified four social classes in the German Empire, each uniting those with similar relations to the market and with real social connections, and the petite bourgeoisie was one of them.[1] In France and Belgium in the same years, the debate about the *classes moyennes* placed the owners of small independent retail and productive enterprises at the heart of society, the literally crucial element in the social structure whose capacity and identity would provide the moral basis for a harmonious social order.[2] The concept remained tied to small enterprise, for the debate around a new conception of the *classes moyennes* began only on the eve of the First World War, a conception which gave increasing priority to white-collar employees, teachers, minor professionals, and managers.

Those writing round the turn of the century, all with their own theoretical perspectives, could draw upon a range of economic, social and political evidence. In spite of all the economic changes of the nineteenth century, master artisans, workshop owners and shopkeepers had kept their distinguishing economic character. They combined the formal ownership of their means of production, their own personal labour, and family enterprises. The petite bourgeoisie certainly experienced a range of pressures: the closure of enterprises, subordination to commercial and industrial capital, and for artisans a shift towards sub-contracting and dependency and a host of consequent difficulties. Yet through all of this there was also a feverish and continuing creation of new firms. The retail trades were perhaps less troubled than the artisanat, at least for a large part of the period, but whole sectors of the mass-consumption artisanal trades (especially tailors, shoemakers, and cabinet-makers) were reduced to defending their meagre independence by concentrating on repairing, or more commonly succumbing to the minute division of labour and sweating within which independence was at the most a pretence. The economic experiences of small enterprise varied according to the trade, the sector, often also the country or the region. It certainly varied

216

between town and country. As a result, the world of small enterprise dissolves under close inspection – as it must always do when the historian focuses on differentiation and individual experiences – into a multitude of specific occupational trajectories, each shaped by the distinctive conditions of the trade, the locality, the country. Recent studies have tried to examine the structure of classes not by ignoring the individuality of these lifetime experiences but by working with them.[3]

This pattern is not peculiar to the petite bourgeoisie, but is common to all class analysis. Thus Jürgen Kocka differentiated, within 'the victorious advance of wage labour' in Germany between 1800 and 1870, between the distinctive situations of servants and agricultural workers, domestic producers and artisans, railwaymen, metal workers, miners and factory workers.[4] In a similar way, Jean-Pierre Chaline's study of the bourgeoisie of Rouen distinguished between a variety of divergent professional situations – *rentiers*, merchants, industrialists, liberal professions, civil servants – while nevertheless concluding that a certain unity embraced them all.[5] As R. J. Morris's exploration of the Leeds middle class in its formative years makes clear, class is what unites people whom other forces and experiences might seem to divide.[6] This book has sought not only to understand the different experiences within the petite bourgeoisie, but also to explore the sources of common experience which might constitute the basis for identity. In the study of social classes and social groups the question is not one of unity or differentiation, but the extent to which the two can co-exist.

Master artisans and shopkeepers across Western Europe – Eastern Europe has largely remained outside the scope of this analysis for reasons that relate both to the linguistic skills of the authors and to the state of research on the petite bourgeoisie in those countries – lived through the transition from *ancien régime* societies. The process involved not simply the disappearance of guilds and corporations, which themselves left tangible traces of their importance in countries such as Germany, but also the changing physiognomy of towns which altered the place of small independents in the urban fabric, the emergence of modern bureaucracies and mass politics, and the often rapid transformation of work and employment. In the face of changes such as these, related to the very differentiated pressures of capitalist industrialisation, petits bourgeois developed a specific identity in relation to the key class groups of nineteenth-century societies: the workers and peasants on the one hand, larger bourgeois and aristocrats on the other. What were the bases of that common position and identity?

In spite of their economic heterogeneity, and their dispersal over different sectors of both production and distribution, master artisans and shopkeepers faced analogous situations with the dissolution of their corporate defences. Their independence was fragile, due not only to a level of capitalisation that was generally inadequate, but also to their dependence on markets over which their control was minimal and to whose fluctuations small enterprise was more vulnerable than was large. In Max Weber's terms, petits bourgeois did not have that control of one of the factors of production which would have assured them an influential position in the market, because their 'market situation' was weak. The need for finance and supplies, and the terms on which they obtained them, made petits bourgeois dependent on merchants and industrialists. At the other end of the chain stood their customers, which for artisans producing for local consumption and for all shopkeepers meant a clientele whose purchasing power and taste fluctuated, and the majority of whom did not see their disposable income significantly rise until the late nineteenth century. As a result, structural instability and a submissive relationship to the market were characteristics of the great majority of artisans and shopkeepers. For all but a small elite amongst their numbers, they were those who felt themselves as *petits* (little) before they thought of themselves as *bourgeois*.[7]

In the absence of adequate resources with which to control this uncertainty a majority, though not all, petits bourgeois were closer to working-class experience than to bourgeois prosperity. Relations with workers may not always have been cordial, and the differences between employer and employee in small enterprise exploded into conflict throughout the century, but the inequality of power between employer and worker was completely unlike that in large-scale businesses. Tension and conflict could exist alongside conviviality and solidarity in the face of large-scale capital. This was not some feature of early industrial society that was destined to disappear: consider the small employers in France who took on workers sacked for their militancy from large car factories.[8] Neither the model of *patronage* and employer social policy which characterised large-scale employment in some countries towards the end of the nineteenth century, nor that of class struggle in the workplace, can capture the ambiguous and complex relations which we have seen to have existed between small employers and their workforce.

Nowhere did artisanal enterprise succumb to the triumphant advance of industrial concentration, for it continued to find a place in these developing economies: sometimes economically marginal, sometimes subordinated to large enterprises, and sometimes retaining a real autonomy. The flexibility and fluidity of this sector have historically been the causes of its fragility, but they are also precisely the reasons for the adaptability and responsiveness which has enabled small enterprise to survive all predictions of its demise. There is indeed a danger that historians accept too readily small enterprise's self-image of decline, above all with respect to the artisanat. The public face of artisanal enterprise has frequently wallowed in nostalgia, setting up an idealised past against which the present might be judged. Historians must avoid that nostalgic trap and resist the assumption that things must have been better for artisans in the period immediately before that being studied. Artisanal organisations, together with those who supported them in the later nineteenth century, inspired new interest in the history of artisanship. The outcome was the revival of artisanal traditions and myths which we encountered in the last chapter, and its museums, histories and rituals reinforced the sense of loss. Many artisans were indeed suffering from a declining position, but to accept the myth gives us only a partial view of the artisanat, whose narrow vision excludes its recurrent regeneration with new trades, new techniques, new markets. This was particularly true from the later nineteenth century. Examples abound, as in metal production, with bicycle manufacturers and shops, and with early car production, and as in the food trades, with the invention of the fish and chip shop in England.[9] Paul Marcelin shifted the emphasis of the family tinsmith's business to a new range of plumbing skills at the end of the nineteenth century, to take advantage of the growing demand for domestic bathrooms.[10] It was not only the shopkeeping sector which was responsive to market innovation.

Social analysis of the petite bourgeoisie reveals the same variation of experience and situation as one finds amongst the nobility, the bourgeoisie or the working class. Through variables such as business turnover, individual wealth, and longevity of enterprise we can distinguish the different levels of the petite bourgeoisie. Trades that required a high level of technical skill and substantial capital display a much greater stability than those needing small initial capital and only rudimentary training. It was therefore amongst drapers and ironmongers, rather than general shopkeepers or greengrocers, that one found the elite of the retail sector, not only in wealth and stability but also in their public and organisational role. Stability increased as one climbed the hierarchy of a trade, but that did not prevent the average experience of small enterprise being that of movement and flux. Fear of instability and of failure, and the need to struggle to avoid it, were the experience of small enterprise as a whole, one which characterised even better businesses.

Faced with this endemic instability, the owners of small enterprise adopted two kinds of strategy. On the one hand there were those masters and shopkeepers who turned in on themselves and their families, seeking to root their survival in their own resources. The declared aim of many petits bourgeois was thus to assure the passage of the workshop or the shop to the next generation, although this goal was never easy to achieve. As the century progressed, other strategies emerged. The petite bourgeoisie might appear at times as a transit class into which only a minority was born, and which one entered less in the hope of real independence than to find a more stable livelihood and a more assured income. The search for stability by turning in on family resources was fundamental to petit-bourgeois social strategy, and it was accompanied by a desire for property whose goal was security rather than wealth. Against that stood the second strategy, and one which became increasingly important from the last third of the century: the placing of their children in careers outside small enterprise. The growth of white-collar employment in both the private and public sectors, and of newly expanding minor professions such as schoolteachers and vets, created a range of new occupations with which master artisans and shopkeepers had increasing social contact. Insofar as marriage patterns, sociability and occupational choice help define class position, then one can see the traditional petite bourgeoisie turning to this larger range of class contacts from the 1870s, a process which accelerated after the First World War. Petit-bourgeois deriding of pen-pushers, and their contempt for the government clerks who staffed oppressive regulatory bureaucracies, did little to stem the flow of their children into occupations which came to be seen as new lower middle class, *nouvelle classe moyenne*.

Social Catholics, and others who saw in independent small enterprise a force for morality and social stability, doubted that the new *classe moyenne* could fill that role, at least until the more urgent attempts to construct a conceptual unity during the interwar period. Without heredity and independ-ence it was felt that there could be no real reconstruction of the *classe moyenne*.[11] For such commentators, the fact that the children of shopkeepers and small masters flocked to these posts was a sign of their pessimism and degradation. In the words of one, 'they are forced by necessity to seek not a trade but a career.'[12] The distinction mattered. But flock they did, in what was to become the most striking manifestation from the late nineteenth century of the petite bourgeoisie's character as a world in movement.

A context such as this poses an immediate question: can we find specific social or cultural characteristics which might distinguish the petite bour-geoisie from other social classes? Can one identify, beyond the wider flux, elements of stability, of structures and of social functions which might permit us to talk of a social identity? The preceding chapters have responded with a cautious yes, with respect to at least a section of the owners of small enterprise, those whose enterprises survived over time but also those whose aspirations for stability kept them socially tied to those whose ranks they could only intermittently join. The combination of individual instability and aspirations to security was not some obstacle to social identity for the petite bourgeoisie, but one of its defining characteristics. The principal sources of social identity, however, were traced to the role of petits bourgeois in their urban and social settings.

The owners of small enterprise were, from the beginning of the nineteenth century, amongst those urban social groups most closely interested in the management of municipal affairs. Even if they were in many countries long excluded from a direct role in urban government, they formed and joined a range of associations which watched closely over the urban business world and which shaped the social relations of many urban neighbourhoods. It was rare to see a 'shopocracy' play a major role in urban government outside Britain, where a more prosperous and stable stratum of the petite bourgeoisie was able to contest for power in local affairs. In general, however, the social weight and influence of the owners of small enterprise were too weak for them to be able to impose themselves politically in the face of powerful urban elites and bureaucratic states. That was just one reason why the smaller towns which they could dominate provided a more comfortable social world for shopkeepers and master artisans. They may have been excluded from the urban patriciat in the larger towns, but they constituted a popular elite that repeatedly manifested itself in political affairs and in neighbourhood society, until the late nineteenth-century popular movement's ideological stress on labour and strategic stress on co-operatives drove most petits bourgeois from its midst. In the neighbourhood, however, the shops of grocers and bakers, the workshops of shoemakers and blacksmiths, and the convivial premises of café and bar owners, provided the framework of daily life and the tissue of daily relations. Their premises were permanent even when their proprietors were not, and those who did secure a degree of stability sunk deep roots into local communities that survived real differences of lifestyle.

The petite bourgeoisie has occupied a specific place in the urban social structure. The German sociologist Georg Simmel concluded that the extent to which the petite bourgeoisie allowed a fluidity of movement within society played a major role in assuring the stability of society and its protection against insurrectionary and revolutionary upheavals. Simmel may have drawn his criteria for social stability too narrowly from Anglo-Saxon experience, but he underlined an important factor in the analysis of the petite bourgeoisie. Its specificity flowed from the broad social space which it occupied, within which mobility and change of occupation were permitted by the absence of those mechanisms of exclusion provided by professionalisation or cultural capital. The more societies accepted and permitted this fluidity in a large and open *classe moyenne*, according to Simmel, the more they would achieve stability and social cohesion.[13] In Austria and Germany, however, state legislation and corporatist barriers limited access to the milieu of workshop masters and, to a lesser degree, that of shopkeepers. These barriers in the social landscape may indeed have served to prevent the petite bourgeoisie from playing a full role in social movement and social promotion, and they certainly structured the ideology of ambition and of exclusion in such a way as to increase perceptions of social inequality. The comparison with Britain, France, Belgium and Italy appears in this light striking, though the paucity of comparative social mobility studies makes it unclear how far the different cultures of opportunity mirrored different levels of mobility. As the larger bourgeoisie drew in on itself from the middle of the nineteenth century, so the world of small enterprise became increasingly important for perceptions of opportunity in European societies, the social space in which workers' dreams of social promotion might be realised. However, the notion of social promotion was not necessarily that dreamed of by students of social mobility. Not all – indeed maybe not even most – movement in and out of small enterprise was experienced as social mobility. Nevertheless, as a space for social movement, interpreted at times as social promotion, the petite bourgeoisie occupied a significant and strategic place in the social structure. The

221

enlargement of the world of the petite bourgeoisie towards the new service and administrative sectors towards the end of the nineteenth century altered but did not remove this social role.

This study has also stressed the importance of common values and cultural practices, as well as political activity, in shaping a petit-bourgeois identity. There was clearly no unanimity of culture or practice in these fields common to the world of small enterprise, yet in spite of the diversity which we have found in the way businesses were run, following differences of period as well as of sector and geographical location, it has been suggested that petits bourgeois in general shared a certain community of ideas and values. There was a persistent localism of perspective as well as of interest in comparison with the national and international scale; there was the specific significance of family for the business, way of life, and values; there was a distinctive conception of property, both in the strategies of petits bourgeois and in their identities; and there were particular perceptions of morality and justice which flowed from all of these. These values changed over time and place, yet they remain recognisable points of continuity, and even those shopkeepers and artisans with a more transitory hold on petit-bourgeois status might share them, for they were not exclusively dependent on stability nor on any particular cultural practice. We cannot speak with confidence as to how far the values spread. Our evidence in these matters is too dependent on the one hand on autobiographies concerned to reconstruct their authors' past by describing it, and on the other on the statements of petit-bourgeois defence organisations similarly concerned to reconstruct their members' present by describing it. A section of the owners of small enterprise will have remained distant from such cultural practices and values, forming their own distinct identities or sharing those of other social groups, in the same way as amongst any social class. Nevertheless, we have argued that the values of localism, family and property, bound together with a perception of independence, were anchors in the economic and social experiences of petits bourgeois, reinforced by those experiences while also providing the cultural apparatus with which to interpret them.

The *embourgeoisement* of the petite bourgeoisie, the adopting and the adaptation of bourgeois practices and values, certainly existed. It can be seen in the style of both dress and furnishing, as well as in the efforts to achieve a certain lifestyle marked by privacy and correct behaviour. It can perhaps be seen, in specific countries at least, in certain kinds of religious adherence and practice. An analysis attentive to Pierre Bourdieu's notion of 'distinction' would uncover similarities and influences amongst at least a section of the petite bourgeoisie.[14] The book has nevertheless stressed the values that seem particular to the world of the petite bourgeoisie, as well as to underline the very real material, economic and social constraints that made it difficult and often inappropriate, to adopt the values and practices of more substantial bourgeois. The ideal of domesticity, of the wife at home, is the most striking of these.

Politics constituted a further sphere in which petits bourgeois could acquire a sense of identity and unity. There were exclusions from the suffrage, official legal descriptions, statistical categories and tax structures, all of which shaped the framework within which people identified themselves. These forces were at work everywhere, nowhere more strongly than in Germany where state legislation expressed a strategy, both symbolic and effective, to forge a united *Mittelstand* set apart from the working class. These forces could only accentuate that sense of the petite bourgeoisie as a *classe objet*, a class whose identity was bestowed from outside attention more than from inner cohesion.[15] Theoretical discussion of the petite bourgeoisie has often focused on this lack of autonomy, on a class manipulated and buffeted from one political position to another. Here is the classic vision of petit-bourgeois politics, of a class waiting to be mobilised and whose consequent volatility drew it to the political extremes. This vision is at least partially contradicted by the great panoply of organisations established by shopkeepers and master artisans, initially at the local level but from the 1880s increasingly linked regionally and nationally. This capacity for self-organisation was at its strongest in countries with a surviving corporate tradition.

Mobilisation from outside and autonomous action from within are not mutually exclusive explanations of petit-bourgeois politics. The petite bourgeoisie's evident capacity for self-organisation forces us to think again about interpretations which rest on manipulation, but it is important to recognise the role of outside discourse interacting with these organised owners of small enterprise. The proponents of *Mittelstandspolitik*, the Social Catholics and Le Playists, from another direction the French Radicals, all proposed discourses and engaged in dialogue with the owners of small enterprise, and in so doing they helped shape the language, values and ideas articulated by the organised petite bourgeoisie itself. The absence of such a distinctive external discourse in Britain cannot have simply been a result of the weak presence of the petite bourgeoisie within visions of the social order – it was also a significant cause of it. Different European countries can be distinguished according to the degree of organisation of petits bourgeois, and the extent to which those organisations could influence the legislative, executive and symbolic work of the state. One of the major problems of interwar western Europe seems to have been that the place of the petite bourgeoisie in representations of the political and social system had changed, and that shopkeepers and master artisans felt themselves set apart from political systems which were increasingly concentrated on the relation between organised capital and labour unions.

There were also political values and icons which had a remarkable durability throughout the nineteenth century, defining a political culture that was a continuing thread of petit-bourgeois distinctiveness. In addition to the judgements of political and economic life that link to the concept of the 'moral economy', one finds also those passionate defences: of the small against the large, the concrete against the abstract, the local against the national and international, the personal against the anonymous, and the individual against the structure. These ideas recur unceasingly in the discourses of petit-bourgeois politics. These motifs find their counterparts in peasant ideas, and to a lesser extent those of white-collar occupations, but by the middle of the nineteenth century they were not part of the normal arsenal of bourgeois debate nor of working-class movements. They gave expression to real experiences in the economic and social existence of small business owners, but their meanings varied with the political and ideological context in which they were used. Petit-bourgeois populism could find expression in the Radical Party in France, whereas in Germany it took shape within an organicist and conservative vision of the social order.

Finally, although the political engagement of all classes responds to outside stimuli, this was a particularly strong characteristic of the petite bourgeoisie, whose political organisation seemed especially dependent on periods of crisis and especially difficult to sustain in calmer times. Petit-bourgeois organisations were not constructed to conquer or to defend political power, but rather to defend their trades and maintain a degree of regulation within them. Pressure groups therefore played a greater role than political parties in the world of small enterprise, though if the conquest of power was not ideologically on the agenda of petit-bourgeois movements, the imposition of a special social vision was.[16]

Does all of this point towards some natural inclination towards extremist political ideas and to support for movements hostile to the existing political order? The answer for a long time could only be affirmative, for interest in the petite bourgeoisie was primarily motivated by its presumed link to interwar fascism. Our examination of petit-bourgeois politics sought to undermine the inevitability of that link, by stressing not only the real national variations in the character of petit-bourgeois political engagement, but also the ideological ambiguities of the move to the right. Fascism remains the great political question for students of the inter-war petite bourgeoisie, a question which even a challenging recent collection of essays on the period cannot dislodge from prominence.[17] It is unfortunate that we still know so little about the social, economic and cultural dimensions of petit-bourgeois life during that period.[18]

As early as July 1929, the liberal German newspaper *Vossische Zeitung* proclaimed that the National Socialists represented 'the petty bourgeois gone mad'.[19] For many, at the time and since, fascism has indeed been seen as an intrinsically petit-bourgeois disorder. The German sociologist Theodor Geiger, writing in 1930, diagnosed a 'panic in the *Mittelstand*' that had been produced by economic crisis and whose outcome was the electoral success of the Nazi Party.[20] The philosopher Ernst Bloch wrote of *Ungleichzeitigkeit*, a time-lag between the lived experience of petits bourgeois and their mental framework, to explain that romanticism and irrationality in their culture of which he saw a taste for fascism as no more than the culmination.[21] In the post-war period, the American sociologist S. M. Lipset identified an 'extremism of the middle', with the petite bourgeoisie trapped between other classes, as explaining the success of Nazism.[22] The petite bourgeoisie became interesting precisely when writers sought to explain its attraction to fascism. A vision of the petite bourgeoisie flowed from that, as this literature extrapolated social characteristics and cultural tendencies from the politics of the class. In this light, fascism was the anxious voice of those displaced and threatened by the growth of modern society: by economic scale, class and mass consumption. Their politics was seen as little more than a cry of anti-modernist anguish.

There are serious problems with arguments such as these which propose some close and even privileged link between petits bourgeois and fascist movements. The first is the teleological vision of the historical process which proceeds to write the history of the petite bourgeoisie as if it had but one ending, ignoring the alternative possibilities and the complex character of petit-bourgeois experience and ideas. Second, it is an argument with an apologetic bias, shifting responsibility for fascism from contemporary or post-war ruling elites, and placing the guilt firmly on the shoulders of the owners of small enterprise. Industrialists and bureaucrats, landowners and merchants, even workers slip from view, as a partial perspective of the socio–political roots of fascism comes to prevail. Finally, there is a problem central to the social history of politics: the belief that once one has empirically tied fascist support to its social base, one has explained it. To be precise, that one identifies the social base of fascist support, looks inside the economic and social experiences of that group, and finds in them the explanation of fascism's success and of its character. The problem is not simply that the empirical evidence for linking the petite bourgeoisie to fascism in this way is ambiguous, but also that the connection between the social and the political becomes too neat, with far too little autonomy allowed to politics itself.[23]

There is a further problem, which is that the argument is essentially built upon the German case. As Koshar has observed, a single national study is thus turned into a social science law.[24] There is certainly a good deal of evidence to support the argument for Germany where the owners of small retail and artisanal enterprises were over-represented in the Nazi movement, and where the organisations of artisans and especially shopkeepers had been substantially infiltrated by the Nazi Party by the end of the Weimar Republic. Local and regional studies seem to corroborate this affinity between the Nazis and the petite bourgeoisie, interpreted as the final stage of the passage of petits bourgeois from democratic and liberal parties at the start of the Weimar Republic, through right-wing parties and on to the NSDAP. In Bavaria the non-peasant self-employed made up 21 per cent of Nazi Party members in 1933, and the white-collar/civil servant lower middle class 28 per cent. Each was about twice as strongly represented in the Party as in the occupied population as a whole. Nevertheless, only about 2 per cent of these groups joined the NSDAP in Bavaria.[25] Although the lower middle class as a whole – old small business groups and new white-collar and professional – did join the NSDAP in disproportionate numbers, the vast mass of them did not do so. The same position prevailed when the Nazis were in power. The white-collar/professional/civil servant group made up 34 per cent of membership, the working class 32 per cent, and petits bourgeois 20 per cent, with the small business group the most over-represented in relation to its place in the population. Throughout the period of large-scale membership of the NSDAP, the lower middle-class element was strong, but the white-collar and professional group was the most important of these, and amongst small enterprise retailers played a much greater role than master artisans, whose presence was often less than their role in the local population.[26]

Studies in electoral sociology suggest that the Nazis did indeed attract votes disproportionately from petits bourgeois, but the picture is by no means as clear as once was thought. The picture has certainly become more differentiated, with shopkeepers more attracted to voting for the NSDAP than artisans, and greater Nazi voting in the north than south, in Protestant areas than Catholic ones.[27] Hamilton's massive study is the most concerted attack on the notion that the urban lower middle class was exceptional in its degree of voting for the NSDAP, arguing that late-Weimar election results do not confirm that votes came essentially from a lower middle class in crisis. Though many historians are reluctant to accept the firmness of his conclusions, it is clear that the lower middle class base for fascism is not as self-evident as contemporary comment and later analysis suggested.[28]

The sociology of fascism has been less intensively studied for other countries, and conclusions become even harder to draw than for Germany. Italian fascism did seek in the 1920s to build itself as a movement supported by the middling classes with an ideology based upon a radical critique of socialism. The Italian lower middle classes were certainly attached to fascism from an early stage. Petit-bourgeois membership, however, was no greater at the end of 1921 than that which the role of small enterprise in the occupational structure would have led one to expect, and it became less significant rather than more so over the subsequent decade. Fascist support in Italy came above all from an educated lower middle class of teachers, civil servants and white-collar employees who, it is argued, turned to the rhetorical ideals of the nation to deny the existence of a class struggle which frightened them.[29] In Belgium we know that petit-bourgeois politics in the 1920s and 1930s saw movements that were anti-tax and anti-labour, calling for support for small business which was increasingly frustrated by its lack of a role in a political structure where capital and labour were incorporated within the framework of state decision-making. Fascist movements developed in the 1930s and by 1936 the Rexist movement in French-speaking Belgium and the Flemish Nationalists elsewhere won nearly 20 per cent of the vote, much of it from a petite bourgeoisie whose anger was fuelled by both political exclusion and economic crisis.[30] Thus it was that in the Brussels commune of St. Josse, 28 per cent of the members of the Rexist party were shopkeepers and 15 per cent white-collar employees.[31]

The fact that the social basis of fascist parties changed with the conjuncture suggests that historians need to add a sensitive comparative chronology to the analysis of fascist movements. The shopkeepers who in 1936 flooded to support Rexist candidates had deserted the movement three years later. Snapshot data on membership or voting can be misleading. There was a difference, for example, between supporting the NSDAP in its very early days; supporting it after 1928 when power seemed feasible and the party was directing specific propaganda at small enterprise;[32] and supporting it after it had come to power and before the emptiness of many of its promises to small business had become clear. Consider the case of Bremen, where the NSDAP had long made efforts to get influence in the *Kleinhandelskammer* (Chamber of Small Retail Trade) but was only successful after the Nazi victory at the national level. Of those in high office in the Chamber in August 1933, 70 per cent were new and had not been elected in the last proper elections the year before. There were plenty of reasons for Bremen's retailers to feel discontented in the 1920s, as they felt deserted by the main political parties and the state while experiencing increasing competition. Right-wing parties sought their support, but the Nazis received little until after they had come to power.[33] Petit-bourgeois support for Nazism was in any case a variable phenomenon. If in Belgium as in Germany it was synonymous with a protest against political exclusion, it could be nourished by anti-socialist and anti-Bolshevik sentiment, as was particularly the case in France and Italy. Egalitarian ideas themselves entered as a factor, as in Germany where the attachment of at least some petits bourgeois to the NSDAP can be interpreted as a protest against traditional notables dominating petit-bourgeois defence organisations and local life.[34]

There were many meanings to support for fascism, and it is difficult to explain its success primarily through its petit-bourgeois character. Research has increasingly come to stress the omnibus character of the NSDAP, attracting votes from such a diverse social and ideological constituency that one can, as Childers has observed, plausibly call the party a *Volkspartei* (People's Party) by 1932, a claim made by most parties at the time but realised more successfully by the Nazis than by any other.[35] As Mühlberger noted, it was 'a party which effectively transcended the class divide'.[36] It could draw on the votes of larger bourgeois, white-collar employees, civil servants and teachers, as well as workers from the smaller artisanal manufacturing towns. Small farmers, shopkeepers and independent artisans may have been the most stable part of the Nazi constituency in the years up to 1932, but they were part of a movement extremely wide-ranging in its support.[37] Fascist parties throughout Europe developed policies to attract petit-bourgeois support, but these were a minor element in a broader politics of the defence of private property, the crushing of the power of organised labour, the uprooting of socialism and communism, and the systematic use of violence to destroy existing parliamentary regimes. It was a declaration of war on bourgeois and liberal democracy, as well as on socialist and communist ideas, which could attract petits bourgeois in large numbers for a time, but substantial attachment to fascist movements was not easy to sustain. Increasing hostility was hard to display in the Third Reich, but by 1937 it was claimed that the business petite bourgeoisie was the most discontented section of the population in Bavaria.[38]

Elsewhere, petit-bourgeois support for fascism could rapidly be undermined by mainstream responses from within the political system. Belgium's strong democratic party politics united rapidly against the Rexist threat in 1936. The leading parties of left and right combined to respond to petit-bourgeois demands, with measures that included a Retailing Commission, a separate government department for the *classes moyennes*, and the Padlock Law of 1937 under which stores with more than one branch of trade and over five employees needed ministerial authorisation before they could be opened or enlarged. Here was a concerted strategy by the orthodox parties of left and right in a stable parliamentary system to draw the petite bourgeoisie into a corporatist state system from which they felt politically excluded.[39] The result was the rapid decline of support for the Rexists who dwindled into insignificance. In France, petits bourgeois remained faithful to radicals and conservatives, especially when these responded after 1936 to their demands and to their fears of communism. As Zdatny has shown, French artisans may have suffered less acutely in the economic crisis of the interwar period than their counterparts in some other countries, but their problems and complaints were familiar. There was certainly a corporatist wing of the French artisanal movement whose ideas mirrored aspects of fascist thought, seeking to defend the trade, family, and moral conservatism, attacking the emergence of mass society, and rejecting political corruption. The fascists, however, were able to sustain no mass support in the petite bourgeoisie, their temporary success resting primarily on fears of communism. The French political system was alert to the problems of small enterprise, conceding tax advantages, incorporating them on public bodies, using legislation to constrain competition. In Zdatny's words, the artisanal movement 'enjoyed an intimate, if not wholly satisfactory, relationship with the institutions of the state'.[40] Furthermore, the depth of the democratic political culture in France, and the populist rather than anti-democratic nature of petit-bourgeois movements, created a climate in which it was hard for fascism to build a strong base in the world of small enterprise.

Interwar Europe certainly saw a move to the right by the owners of small retailing and artisanal enterprises, as anxieties grew and with it the feeling that

228

action was needed. Those anxieties were expressed, however, in a wide variety of political forms. Fascism was but one of those options, and its success depended on political structures and political context, an observation graphically illustrated by the striking weakness of fascist parties in Britain. Germany (and with it Austria) are in this light special cases rather than the norm, and it is unwise to build a theory of petit-bourgeois politics upon them. A comparative analysis makes it clear how important were political opportunities and conjunctures for petit-bourgeois attachment to fascist movements. It is a conclusion that emerges from chronological as well as national comparisons. In Germany the disintegration of the parties of the centre through the 1920s made the Nazis look increasingly attractive to petits bourgeois as the alternatives withered. As Baldwin has observed, such an argument does not reject social factors, but directs attention at the longer-term social processes which had destabilised German politics.[41] The comparative perspective on political opportunities and conjunctures highlights their importance in explaining not only fascist success, but the respective roles of petits bourgeois within it, in countries such as Germany and Austria where fascism was strong, in those like Belgium where its brief flourish was rapidly dealt with, and in those like Britain and France where it made little headway in the world of small enterprise.

The degree of petit-bourgeois support for fascism which can be observed, even if related to political opportunities and conjunctures, was no accident, for the meanings of fascism could be related to older themes of petit-bourgeois politics and culture. There was the recurrent concern to cleanse politics of corruption and self-interest; the challenge to entrenched elites whose riches and power crushed the ordinary people; distrust of large-scale enterprise and organised labour; the creation of a harmonious social order which had once existed before being torn apart by the forces of corruption and class; the resting of that harmony on a people moralised by the forces of family, authority and hard work; and the attachment to the local sphere, to the honest traditions of local daily life whose harmony and personal relations contrasted with the national battles of parties and classes. These forces of the local were in Germany embraced by the concept of *Heimat*, whose concept of home territory did not stand in opposition to the conception of the German nation that took root from the Wilhelmine era but rather enhanced it: the German nation was to be the harmonious and personal *Heimat* writ large.[42] These are all concerns familiar to the student of the nineteenth-century petite bourgeoisie. To the extent that the discourse of fascism appeared to address these concerns, it provides a further explanation for the petit-bourgeois responses to fascism in some countries, and one that is perhaps more fruitful than conceptions of a disordered personality or a natural predisposition to irrational politics.

Although this book's concern with the petite bourgeoisie did not begin with fascism, the relationship between the two in interwar Europe provides one measure of the value of the results presented here. First of all, the stress on the heterogeneity of the milieu renders plausible the proposition that no one unanimous or largely unanimous political option would emerge from the petite bourgeoisie, and that diversity of experience – whether cultural, economic or social – would find expression in a diversity of politics. Heterogeneity enables us to understand the very different repercussions of economic crisis within this milieu. Where instability constituted the average experience of small masters and shopkeepers, acute crisis could be perceived not so much as a trauma but as an aggravated form of normality. On the other hand, whole sections of small enterprise with stable and comfortable positions survived the depression years. Economic deprivation and fascism do not in this light appear necessarily linked. The economic development during the long nineteenth century also draws attention to the different chronologies under which small enterprise was exposed to large-scale capital: the threats of mass production to the artisanat in the second half of the nineteenth century were accompanied by only a slow growth of large-scale retailing. Mass retailing was a phenomenon which spread most extensively in these interwar years, which may explain the greater shopkeeper support for fascism, though this needs also to be interpreted as a function of shopkeepers' greater isolation and detachment from the community of workshop and trade. The experience of the interwar years also shows that in those countries where the state had actively sought to forge a petit-bourgeois identity as a form of social and political defence, as in Germany and Belgium, the development of a politics more concerned with large capital and organised labour could create a sense of isolation and neglect amongst petits bourgeois. Movements for the defence of the *Mittelstand* and Nazi voting in Germany during the 1920s, and support for Rexism and Flemish nationalism in Belgium during the middle years of the 1930s, can be seen as an attempt to recover influence and press their distinctive demands. There was little that was irrational about such a political choice. The interwar experience does, above all, confirm our argument that political activity, attention and mobilisation were of unusual importance in petit-bourgeois formation and identity.

In the absence of detailed studies of the interwar social and economic experiences of small enterprise, without the detailed exploration of the culture of urban life and of the place of petits bourgeois within it or of the character of business and personal instability, in the absence of detailed monographic studies of specific trades, it is the politics of the petite bourgeoisie which dominates as a historical problem. Yet, if the approach that underpins this book is valid, we can understand neither the social group nor its politics without them. If social history is to investigate shopkeepers and master artisans through the archives of their organisations, and that remains a favoured path for historians, then it is through social and cultural associations and *Vereine* that the group may be sought, far more effectively than through its pressure groups and formal professional organisations. Historians of

Britain have perhaps made the least headway in exploring these groups for the interwar period – for historians can be as influenced by the perceived significance of a social group as were contemporary commentators – and when George Orwell or the Mass-Observation studies engaged with the culture and sociology of the middle strata in interwar Britain it was the new white-collar and professional occupations which drew attention rather than the still numerous world of small enterprise.[43] Their concern may have reflected a particular view of the middling classes, but it was one repeated throughout the 1930s in European sociological and intellectual debate. Academic sociologists now joined a field once left to Social Catholics in attempts to reconceptualise the middle strata of society, and the consequent debates sought to define these sections of the social structure whose centre of gravity was increasingly moving towards the white-collar, civil servant and professional occupations and away from small enterprise.[44] A debate which had stalled before the First World War now assumed considerable significance, and this turning to the new *classes moyennes* further marginalised the petite bourgeoisie. Efforts to mobilise concepts such as 'patrimony' or 'technique', as unifying features of a middle which contained both small business and the new occupations, constituted an attempt to save a social idea that was disintegrating in the face of rapid changes in the occupational structure.[45] Henceforth, except when small enterprise could once again force itself upon the political stage in movements such as Poujadism,[46] societies' concern for the middle focused on the new world of offices, civil servants, engineers, teachers and professionals.[47]

If this conclusion has consciously left many questions open, for it is a well-established convention that one ends one book by pointing towards others while refusing to leave the reader with the comforting illusion that all the main problems have been resolved, we would prefer to close with some firmer methodological conclusions. Our common work on the petite bourgeoisie began in the years before the linguistic turn became such a powerful force in social history, and it started with the analysis of economic structures, social relations, the experiences of daily life and the strategies for survival, and in general with the relationship between larger processes and structural change on the one hand, and the particularities of the petite bourgeoisie on the other. The transition from corporations, urbanisation, industrialisation have thus been explored in their relationship to the petite bourgeoisie, alongside the family, mobility, the stages of political activity and cultural practice. However, an increasing attention to questions of language and of discourse, to the way in which the group presented itself and the way in which it was represented by others, has come to inform what is a work of social history – for we are social historians and shall so remain. It has pushed the analysis to accentuate the tension between the structures and activities which we have studied and contemporary perceptions, discovering that the perceptions themselves have structural consequences. The discussion of these questions of perception and discourse, of the forces which define and shape identity, has informed our recurrent concern to probe the class character of the petite bourgeoisie, to explore the ways in which the experience of social position and social opportunity drew on contemporary images of the social system to shape identities. It has not, however, been necessary in our view to abandon the firm terrain of social history in order to draw upon the valuable insights provided by recent historical debates.

The value of comparative analysis constitutes our second conclusion. The uneven spread of research in what remains an under-explored field has made it difficult to build systematic comparisons throughout the book, whether between the same countries, the same towns or the same regions. In certain chapters, formal and systematic comparison has necessarily ceded place to a gathering of evidence from a range of different countries or settings. Indeed, one of our conclusions from a study of the petite bourgeoisie has something of a Janus-like quality, on the one hand stressing the value of comparative analysis while, on the other, urging the inadequacy of always constructing those comparisons at the level of the nation state. Yet comparative history so commonly does just that. It uses quantitative data organised according to the structure of the states whose statistical services gathered the figures, rather than following any geographical divisions imposed by the historian's analysis. The national state comparisons work well in certain fields – for the study of political formations and strategies, for corporations and juridical structures. Even here the excessive attachment to juridical certainties can hide the social commonalities within different legal settings. Our comparison of artisanal experience and ideas in eighteenth-century France and Britain makes such a point clear, with many parallels which transcend the simplicities of a picture according to which one country had strong guilds and the other virtually no guilds at all. Once we approach those aspects of the petite bourgeoisie in which national boundaries present less relevant demarcations, the national state comparisons have less to offer. It is indeed difficult to compare at the level of countries when one considers such subjects as the family, the place of petits bourgeois in the town, social relations and conflict, culture and sociability. The national context does of course play a role, but as one moves into spheres where the state's role was less direct and defining, so one finds that issues such as rural social structure, type of town, or religious character-istics become more significant, issues which are rarely susceptible to compar-ison at the national level. There are real difficulties in assuming that the most appropriate unit of analysis is that of the nation state, except where state-defined phenomena, such as politics or social policy, are the issue. The existence of national societies and national economies are too often taken for granted by comparative historical analyses which take data produced on the national level and assume that these represent some underlying national phenomena – for example, census data representing a national society for social historians, or national accounts data a national economy for economic historians.[48]

This study has ended with generalisations about the study of social history, which is an uneasy way to end a book on the petite bourgeoisie. The shopkeepers and master artisans with whom this book has been concerned were rarely comfortable with generalisation, preferring the security of the precise and the personal to a world in which generalities and breadth of vision held sway. Petits bourgeois had their visions, and the plural is as necessary as with any social group, because petits bourgeois were especially shaped by the particularities of their own world and their own circumstances. Shopkeepers and master artisans were ever more at home with the particular, defending their own property rather than conceptualising property in general, sustaining their own family rather than preaching the importance of family as a social phenomenon, introspectively concerned for their own enterprise and its demands in a way that hindered their capacity for collective action, and moved by perceptions of independence which became a general idea in the mouths of those who pretended to defend them far more than in their own vision of their world. There are many points of entry to the petite bourgeoisie during the long nineteenth century, of which the ambiguous concepts of enterprise, family and independence presented in the book's title are of particular importance. It is to be hoped that the combination of research and synthesis presented here will help sustain a revival of interest which will advance our understanding of a group critical to the analysis of nineteenth-century European society.

NOTES

Unless otherwise stated, the place of publication of all English-language books is London, and of all French-language books is Paris. See Abbreviations, p.xi.

1 INTRODUCTION

1 M. Turmann, 'Un aspect du problème des classes moyennes', *La chronique sociale de France*, 18 (1909), p. 461.
2 J. Rancière, *The Nights of Labour: The Workers' Dream in Nineteenth-Century France*, 1989.
3 A. Saur, 'Die Organisationen der Bremer Kleinhändler von 1914 und ihre soziale Basis', in H.-G. Haupt (ed.) *Der Bremer Kleinhandel um 1900*, Bremen, 1983, pp. 64–5.
4 K. Marx, 'The Class Struggles in France: 1848–1850', in K. Marx and F. Engels, *Selected Works*, Moscow, 1962, vol. 1, pp. 139–242; K. Marx, 'The Eighteenth Brumaire of Louis Bonaparte', in ibid., pp. 257–344.
5 K. Marx, 'Critique of the Gotha Programme', in ibid., vol. 2, pp. 18–37.
6 E. Bernstein, *Evolutionary Socialism: A Criticism and an Affirmation*, 1909 (first published in German, 1899).
7 L. Gall and R. Koch (eds) *Der europäische Liberalismus im 19. Jahrhundert*, Frankfurt, 1981, vol. 4, p. 74.
8 W.H. Riehl, *Die bürgerliche Gesellschaft*, Frankfurt, 1976 edn, p. 194.
9 H. Lambrechts, 'La concentration, commun dénominateur de la question sociale', *Revue sociale catholique*, 17 (1912–13), p. 186.
10 See W. Küttler, G. Lozek and H.-U. Wehler in J. Kocka (ed.) *Max Weber, der Historiker*, Göttingen, 1986, pp. 173–203; M. Weber, *Wirtschaft und Gesellschaft*, Cologne, 1964 edn, pp. 224 ff., 678 ff., 995–6.
11 T. Geiger, *Die soziale Schichtung des deutschen Volkes*, Stuttgart, 1967 edn; E. Bloch, *Erbschaft dieser Zeit*, Frankfurt, 1935.
12 N. Poulantzas, *Classes in Contemporary Capitalism*, 1978; E.O. Wright, *Classes*, 1985.
13 See for example C. Baudelot, R. Establet and J. Malemort, *La petite bourgeoisie en France*, 1974. For the division between small business, state cadres and private-sector cadres, see p. 253 ff.
14 In addition to *Classes*, op. cit., see E.O. Wright, *et al.*, *The Debate on Classes*, 1989. For a brief but useful survey of recent theoretical approaches, see R. Scase, 'The petty bourgeoisie and modern capitalism: a consideration of recent theories', in A. Giddens and G. MacKenzie (eds) *Social Class and the Division of Labour*, Cambridge, 1982, pp. 148–61.

15 F. Bechhofer and B. Elliott, 'Persistence and change: the petite bourgeoisie in industrial society', *European Journal of Sociology*, 17 (1976), p. 75. This article offers an important historical sketch of the development of the British petite bourgeoisie as a context for their later sociological research, one which at a number of points is confirmed by the conclusions of this book.

16 F. Bechhofer and B. Elliott, 'The petite bourgeoisie in late capitalism', *Annual Review of Sociology*, 11 (1985), p. 204.

17 Ibid., p. 181.

18 See also F. Bechhofer and B. Elliott (eds) *The Petite Bourgeoisie: Comparative Studies of the Uneasy Stratum*, 1981; F. Bechhofer, B. Elliott, and D. McCrone, 'Structure, consciousness and action: a sociological profile of the British middle class', *British Journal of Sociology*, 29 (1978), pp. 410–36; R. Bland, B. Elliott and F. Bechhofer, 'Social mobility in the petite bourgeoisie', *Acta Sociologica*, 21 (1978), pp. 229–48.

19 A.J. Mayer, 'The lower middle class as a historical problem', *Journal of Modern History*, 47, 1975, p. 436.

20 Et. Martin Saint-Léon, 'L'organisation corporative des classes moyennes', *la Réforme sociale*, 60 (1910), p. 205.

21 D. Denecke and G. Shaw, 'Traditional retail systems in Germany', in J. Benson and G. Shaw (eds), *The Evolution of Retail Systems c. 1800–1914*, Leicester, 1992, p. 85; B. Angleraud, 'Les boulangers lyonnais aux XIXe – XXe siècles (1836 à 1914). Une étude sur la petite bourgeoisie boutiquière', Thèse de doctorat, University of Lyon 2, 1993, vol. 2, p. 388.

22 H.-G. Haupt, 'Kleinhändler und Arbeiter in Bremen zwischen 1890 und 1914', *Archiv für Sozialgeschichte*, 22 (1982), pp. 113–17.

23 See the important discussion by Bechhofer and Elliott, 'Persistence and change', op. cit., pp. 76–8. See also A. Cottereau's introduction to D. Poulot, *Le sublime*, 1980, p. 63ff.

24 H. de Balzac, *César Birotteau*, Livre de Poche edn, 1972, p. 285.

25 Compare A. Leppert-Fögen, *Die deklassierte Klasse. Studien zur Geschichte und Ideologie des Kleinbürgertums*, Frankfurt, 1974, pp. 39–70.

26 The relation between the petite bourgeoisie and fascism in historical inquiry is considered in the Conclusion (Chapter Ten).

27 H.A. Winkler, *Mittelstand, Demokratie und Nationalsozialismus. Die politische Entwicklung von Handwerk und Kleinhandel in der Weimarer Republik*, Cologne/Berlin, 1972; R. Gellately, *The Politics of Economic Despair: Shopkeepers and German Politics 1890–1914*, 1974; S. Volkov, *The Rise of Popular Antimodernism in Germany: The Urban Master Artisans, 1873–1896*, Princeton, 1978.

28 Mayer, op. cit.; G. Crossick (ed.) *The Lower Middle Class in Britain 1870–1914*, 1977, and J. Kocka (ed.) *Angestellte im europäischen Vergleich*, Göttingen, 1981 are collections that seek to do this primarily with regard to the then neglected historical field of white-collar employees.

29 *Commission Internationale*.

30 The Research Group was organised by Geoffrey Crossick, Heinz-Gerhard Haupt, Ginette Kurgan-van Hentenryk and Philippe Vigier.

31 Selected papers from the Round Tables were published in two special issues of the French social and labour history journal, *le mouvement social*, 108 (1979) and 114 (1981), and in *Crossick and Haupt*. The most significant studies seeking to divorce the political history of the petite bourgeoisie from its teleological framework were D. Blackbourn, *Class, Religion and Local Politics in Wilhelmine Germany: The Centre Party in Württemberg before 1914*, New Haven, 1980, and P. Nord, *Paris Shopkeepers and the Politics of Resentment*, Princeton, 1986.

32 The major publications produced over this period can be found in the Further Reading, at the end of which the key theses are also listed.

33 See the discussion in Chapter Three.

34 For a fuller discussion see G. Crossick, 'L'histoire comparée et la petite bourgeoisie', *Bulletin du Centre Pierre Léon d'histoire économique et sociale*, June (1992), pp. 13–25.

35 G. Crossick, 'From gentlemen to the residuum: languages of social description in Victorian Britain', in P.J. Corfield (ed.) *Language, Class and History*, 1991, esp. pp. 167–9, 171–2.

36 See H.-G. Haupt, 'La petite bourgeoisie en France et en Allemagne dans l'entre-deux-guerres', in H. Möller *et al.* (ed.) *Gefährdete Mitte? Mittelschichten und politische Kultur zwischen den Weltkriegen: Italien, Frankreich und Deutschland*, Sigmaringen, 1993, pp. 35–55.

2 THE TRANSITION FROM CORPORATIONS

1 J. Revel, 'Corps et communautés d'ancien régime: présentation', *Annales E.S.C.*, 43 (1988), p. 295.

2 Cited in ibid., p. 296.

3 Two books in recent years have stressed the need to approach guilds and corporations from directions other than the merely economic: R. Mackenney, *Tradesmen and Traders: The World of the Guilds in Venice and Europe c. 1250 – c. 1650*, 1987; S. Cerutti, *La ville et les métiers. Naissance d'un langage corporatif (Turin, 17e-18e siècles)*, 1990.

4 For an important study of the interlocking functions of traditional corporations see J. Bergmann, *Das Berliner Handwerk in den Frühphasen der Industrial-isierung*, Berlin, 1973; for France, see the masterly study by J.-C. Perrot, *Genèse d'une ville moderne. Caen au XVIIIe siècle*, Paris, 1975, pp. 321–80.

5 D. Garrioch, *Neighbourhood and Community in Paris 1740–1790*, Cambridge, 1986, p. 113.

6 E.C. Musgrave, 'Women in the male world of work: the building industries of eighteenth-century Brittany', *French History*, 7 (1993), pp. 46–9.

7 The terms guild and corporation will here be used interchangeably.

8 On this last point see Garrioch, op. cit., p. 98 ff.; J.R. Farr, 'Popular religious solidarity in sixteenth-century Dijon', *French Historical Studies*, 14 (1985–86), p. 203; W. Fischer, *Handwerksrecht und Handwerkswirtschaft um 1800*, Berlin, 1955; M. Stürmer (ed.), *Herbst des alten Handwerks*, Munich, 1986; R.S. Elkar (ed.) *Deutsches Handwerk in Spätmittelalter und früher Neuzeit*, Göttingen, 1973.

9 Cited by C. Eisenberg, *Deutsche und englische Gewerkschaften. Entstehung und Entwicklung bis 1878 im Vergleich*, Göttingen, 1986 p. 290.

10 B. Supple, 'The nature of enterprise', in *Cambridge Economic History of Europe*, vol. 5, Cambridge, 1977, p. 437.

11 C. Poni, 'Norms and disputes: the shoemakers' guild in eighteenth-century Bologna', *Past and Present*, 123 (1989), pp. 80–108, provides a good case study.

12 W. Te Brake, *Regents and Rebels: The Revolutionary World of an Eighteenth-Century Dutch City*, Oxford, 1989, passim. The petitions statistic is from p. 78, and the quotation from p. 127.

13 J.M. Diefendorf, *Businessmen and Politics in the Rhineland, 1789–1834*, Princeton, 1980, p. 24.

14 F. Lenger, *Sozialgeschichte der deutschen Handwerker seit 1800*, Frankfurt, 1988, p. 18 ff.

15 K.H. Kaufhold, 'Das deutsche Gewerbe am Ende des 18. Jahrhunderts. Handwerk,

Verlag, und Manufaktur', in H. Berding and H.P. Ullmann (eds), *Deutschland zwischen Revolution und Restauration*, Königstein, 1981, pp. 311–14; H. U. Wehler, *Deutsche Gesellschaftsgeschichte, 1700–1815*, vol. 1, Munich, 1987, p. 189.

16 A. Kraus, *Die Unterschichten Hamburgs in der ersten Hälfte des 19. Jahrhunderts*, Stuttgart, 1965, p. 21.

17 J.J. Sheehan, *German History 1770–1866*, Oxford, 1989, p. 112.

18 M. Walker, *German Home Towns: Community, State, and General Estate 1648–1871*, Ithaca, 1971.

19 Lenger, op. cit., p. 30.

20 H. Schultz, 'Die Herkunft der Berliner Handwerker im 18. Jahrhundert', in *Internationales Handwerksgeschichtliches Symposium*, Veszprem, 1983, pp. 49–62; A.R. Benscheid, *Kleinbürgerlicher Besitz. Nürtinger Handwerkerinventare, 1660–1840*, Münster, 1985, p. 142; K.H. Kaufhold, *Das Handwerk der Stadt Hildesheim im 18. Jahrhundert. Eine Wirtschaftsgeschichtliche Studie*, Göttingen, 1982, p. 143; R. Reith, *Arbeits- und Lebensweise im Städtischen Handwerk. Zur Sozialgeschichte Augsburger Handwerksgesellen im 18. Jahrhundert (1700–1806)*, Göttingen, 1988, pp. 101–64, 207–11, 239–45.

21 Reith, op. cit., pp. 178–9, 227–30; A. Griessinger, *Das symbolische Kapital der Ehr. Streikbewegungen und kollektives Bewußtsein deutscher Handwerksgesellen im 18. Jahrhundert*, Frankfurt, 1987; A. Herzig, *Unterschichtenprotest in Deutschland 1790–1870*, Göttingen, 1988.

22 J. Kocka, 'Craft traditions and the labour movement in nineteenth-century Germany', in P. Thane, G. Crossick and R. Floud (eds), *The Power of the Past: Essays for Eric Hobsbawm*, Cambridge, 1984, pp. 110–12.

23 Walker, op. cit., p. 136.

24 Cf J. Bergmann, 'Das Zunftwesen nach der Einführung der Gewerbefreiheit', in B. Vogel (ed.), *Preußische Reformen 1807–1820*, Königstein, 1980, pp. 150–67; B. Vogel, *Allgemeine Gewerbefreiheit. Die Reformpolitik des preußischen Staatskanzlers Hardenberg (1810–1820)*, Göttingen, 1983; A. Herzig, 'Kontinuität und Wandel der politischen und sozialen Vorstellungen Hamburger Handwerker 1790–1870', in U. Engelhardt (ed.), *Handwerker in der Industrialisierung*, Stuttgart, 1984, pp. 294–319.

25 C. Lipp, 'Württembergische Handwerker und Handwerkerinnen im Vormärz und in der Revolution 1848/49', in ibid., pp. 347–80.

26 R.J. Bazillion, 'Liberalism, modernization, and the social question in the Kingdom of Saxony, 1830–90', in K.H. Jarausch and L.E. Jones (eds), *In Search of a Liberal Germany. Studies in the History of German Liberalism from 1789 to the Present*, New York, 1990, p. 100–1.

27 H. Sedatis, *Liberalismus und Handwerk in Südwestdeutschland*, Stuttgart, 1979.

28 F.W. Henning, 'Die Einführung der Gewerbefreiheit und ihre Auswirkungen auf das Handwerk im Deutschland', in W. Abel *et al.* (eds), *Handwerksgeschichte in neuer Sicht*, Göttingen, 1978, pp. 142–72; K.H. Kaufhold, 'Gewerbefreiheit und gewerbliche Entwicklung im 19. Jahrhundert', in *Blätter für deutsche Landesgeschichte*, 118 (1982), pp. 73–114.

29 G. Unwin, *Industrial Organization in the Sixteenth and Seventeenth Centuries*, 1904 (1963 edn), p. 16.

30 F.J. Fisher, 'Some experiments in company organisation in the early seventeenth century', *Economic History Review*, 4 (1933), pp. 177–94; D.M. Palliser, 'The trade guilds of Tudor York', in P. Clark and P. Slack (eds), *Crisis and Order in English Towns 1500–1700*, 1972, pp. 86–116.

31 Unwin, op.cit., pp. 196 ff.

32 On apprenticeship, see J. Rule, *The Experience of Labour in Eighteenth-Century Industry*, 1981, pp. 95–123; on the 1814 repeal, T.K. Derry, 'The repeal of the

apprenticeship clauses of the statute of artificers', *Economic History Review*, 3 (1931), pp. 67–87.

33 C.R. Dobson, *Masters and Journeymen: A Prehistory of Industrial Relations 1717–1800*, 1980, p. 50, pp. 127–9.

34 G. Unwin, *The Gilds and Companies of London*, 1908, pp. 342–51.

35 J.R. Kellett, 'The breakdown of gild and corporation control over the handicraft and retail trade in London', *Economic History Review*, New Series, 10 (1957–58), pp. 381–94.

36 A. Plummer, *The London Weavers' Company 1600–1970*, 1972, pp. 289, 354–5.

37 Quoted in Dobson, op. cit., p. 53.

38 G. Rudé, *Hanoverian London 1714–1808*, 1971, pp. 183–204; R.W. Malcolmson, 'Workers' combinations in eighteenth-century England', in M. Jacob and J. Jacob, (eds) *The Origins of Anglo-American Radicalism*, 1984, pp. 149–61; Dobson, op. cit.; F.W. Galton, *Selected Documents Illustrating the History of Trade Unionism: (i) The Tailoring Trades*, 1896.

39 Rule, op. cit., pp. 198–9.

40 Quoted by Malcolmson, op. cit., p. 157.

41 I. Prothero, *Artisans and Politics in Early Nineteenth-Century London: John Gast and his Times*, 1979, p. 37.

42 M. Agulhon, *La vie sociale en Provence intérieure au lendemain de la Révolution*, 1970, pp. 150–1; for a similar pattern in the woollen town of Bédarieux: C. Johnson, 'Artisans vs fabricants: urban protoindustrialization and the evolution of work culture in Lodève and Bédarieux, 1740–1830', European University Institute Working Paper 85/137, n.d., p. 19.

43 D. Roche (ed.) *Journal de ma vie. Jacques-Louis Ménétra. Compagnon vitrier au 18ème siècle*, 1982, p. 350.

44 For a detailed study of masters' responses, see S.L. Kaplan, 'Social classification and representation in the corporate world of eighteenth-century France: Turgot's "Carnival"', in S.L. Kaplan and C.J. Koepp, (eds), *Work in France: Representations, Meaning, Organization, and Practices*, Ithaca, 1986, pp. 176–228.

45 G. Martin, *Les associations ouvrières au XVIIIe siècle (1700–1792)*, 1900, p. 21.

46 M. Sonenscher, 'Work and wages in Paris in the eighteenth century', in M. Berg, P. Hudson and M. Sonenscher (eds), *Manufacture in Town and Country before the Factory*, Cambridge, 1983, pp. 147–72; M. Sonenscher, *Work and Wages: Natural Law, Politics and the Eighteenth-Century French Trades*, Cambridge, 1989. For parallel processes of sub-division in many London trades see M.D. George, *London Life in the Eighteenth Century*, 1925, pp. 158–212.

47 S.L. Kaplan, 'Les corporations, les "faux ouvriers" et le faubourg Saint-Antoine au XVIIIe siècle', *Annales E.S.C.*, 43 (1988), pp. 353–78.

48 Garrioch, op. cit., pp. 105–7.

49 S.L. Kaplan, 'The character and implications of strife among the masters inside the guilds of eighteenth-century Paris', *Journal of Social History*, 19 (1986), pp. 635–7.

50 G. Bossenga, *The Politics of Privilege: Old Regime and Revolution in Lille*, Cambridge, 1991, esp. ch. 7, pp. 131–67; G. Bossenga, 'Protecting merchants: guilds and commercial capitalism in eighteenth-century France', *French Historical Studies*, 15 (1988), pp. 702–3.

51 O.H. Hufton, *Bayeux in the Late Eighteenth Century*, Oxford, 1967, pp. 9–10. For a study showing that mobility need not be antagonistic to guilds, see E.J. Shepherd Jr., 'Social and geographical mobility of the eighteenth-century guild artisan: an analysis of guild receptions in Dijon 1700–1790', in Kaplan and Koepp, op. cit., pp. 97–130.

52 C.M. Truant, 'Independent and insolent: journeymen and their "rites" in the Old

Regime workplace', in ibid., pp. 137–8; S. Kaplan, 'Réflexions sur la police du monde du travail 1700–1815', *Revue historique*, 261 (1979), pp. 17–77.

53 Garrioch, op. cit., pp. 103–4; for details of conflicts over wages, hours and placement see Martin, op. cit., pp. 132–47.

54 Truant, op. cit., pp. 131–73.

55 For placement as a source of conflict, Martin, op. cit., pp. 149–62. The issue was a recurrent source of tension in guild production systems: L. Edgren, 'Crafts in transformation?: masters, journeymen, and apprentices in a Swedish town, 1800–1850', *Continuity and Change*, 1 (1986), pp. 376–7.

56 R. Darnton, 'Workers revolt: the Great Cat Massacre of the Rue Saint-Séverin', in his *The Great Cat Massacre and other Episodes in French Cultural History*, New York, 1984, pp. 79–104.

57 D. Garrioch and M. Sonenscher, '*Compagnonnages*, confraternities and associations of journeymen in eighteenth-century Paris', *European History Quarterly*, 16 (1986), pp. 25–45.

58 Quoted in A. Cotta, *Le corporatisme*, 1984, p. 19.

59 B.F. Hyslop, 'French gild opinion in 1789', *American Historical Review*, 44 (1939), pp. 252–71.

60 G. Lefebvre, *Etudes Orléanaises. (1) Contributions à l'étude des structures sociales à la fin du XVIIIe siècle*, 1962, p. 134.

61 J.-P. Hirsch, *Les deux rêves du commerce. Entreprise et institution dans la région lilloise, 1780–1860*, 1991, pp. 237–62.

62 M.D. Sibalis, 'Corporatism after the corporations: the debate on restoring the guilds under Napoleon I and the Restoration', *French Historical Studies*, 15 (1988), pp. 718–30.

63 E. Levasseur, 'La Corporation sous le Consulat, l'Empire et la Restauration', *la Réforme sociale*, 43 (1902), pp. 148–9; M.H. Elbow, *French Corporative Theory 1789–1948: A Chapter in the History of Ideas*, New York, 1953, p. 17.

64 A. Chatelain, 'Pour une histoire du petit commerce de détail en France. Lutte entre colporteurs et boutiquiers en France pendant la première moitié du XIXe siècle', *Revue d'Histoire Economique et Sociale*, 49 (1971), p. 370.

65 For a detailed case study of bakers, Y. Le Brun, 'La liberté de la boulangerie à Rennes sous le IIe Empire', *Annales de Brétagne*, (1987) pp. 167–84, 303–24.

66 H.-G. Haupt, 'Zur gesellschaftlichen Bedeutung des Kleinbürgertum in westeuropäischen Gesellschaften des 19. Jahrhunderts', *Geschichte und Gesellschaft*, 16 (1990), pp. 290–317.

67 Cited in Bossenga, op. cit., p. 410.

68 J.-J. Heirwegh, 'Les corporations dans les Pays-Bas autrichiens (1738–1784)', Doctoral Thesis, Université Libre de Bruxelles, 1980–81 is an impressively full exploration of attempts to reform Belgian corporations under Habsburg rule.

69 J.W. Boyer, *Political Radicalism in Late Imperial Vienna: Origins of the Christian Social Movement 1848–1897*, Chicago, 1981, pp. 54–67.

70 P. Ayçoberry, 'Histoire sociale de la ville de Cologne (1815–1875)', Thèse d'Etat, University of Paris 1, 1977, p. 317.

71 P.H. Noyes, *Organisation and Revolution: Working-Class Associations in the German Revolutions of 1848–49*, Princeton, 1966, pp. 163–91.

72 Ayçoberry, op. cit., pp. 434–5; F. Lenger, *Zwischen Kleinbürgertum und Proletariat. Studien zur Sozialgeschichte des Düsseldorfer Handwerker 1816–1878*, Göttingen, 1986, pp. 179–82.

73 Ibid., pp. 150–87.

74 S. Volkov, *The Rise of Popular Antimodernism in Germany: The Urban Master Artisans, 1873–1896*, Princeton, 1978, pp. 178–91, 237–65.

75 M.J. Neufeld, *The Skilled Metalworkers of Nuremberg: Craft and Class in the Industrial Revolution*, New Brunswick, 1989, p. 115.

76 T. Hampke, 'Die Innungsentwicklung in Preußen', *Schmollers Jahrbuch*, 18 (1984), pp. 195–228; W. Stieda, 'Die Innungs-Enquête', *Jahrbücher für National-ökonomie und Statistik*, 67 (1896), pp. 1–35; H.-G. Haupt (ed.), *Die radikale Mitte. Lebensweise und Politik von Handwerkern und Kleinhändelern in Deutschland*, Munich, 1985, pp. 174–5.

77 Though Kocka has nonetheless stressed elements of continuity between a corporatist anti-capitalist tradition and the socialism of the early labour movement: Kocka, 'Craft traditions', op. cit., p. 102.

78 J. Briquet, 'Signification sociale des compagnonnages', *Revue d'histoire économique et sociale*, 33 (1956), pp. 321–36.

79 A. Faure, 'Introduction' in A. Perdiguier, *Mémoire d'un compagnon*, 1983, p. 3 ff.; C.M. Truant, 'Solidarity and symbolism among journeyman artisans: the case of "compagnonnage"', *Comparative Studies in Society and History*, 21 (1979), pp. 214–26; W.H. Sewell, Jr., *Work and Revolution in France: The Language of Labor from the Old Regime to 1848*, Cambridge, 1980, p. 167 ff.

80 J. Rancière, *La nuit des prolétaires. Archives du rêve ouvrier*, 1981; C. Johnson, *Utopian Communism in France: Cabet and the Icarians 1839–1851*, Ithaca, 1974; R. Gossez, *Les ouvriers de Paris*, La Roche-dur-Yon, 1967; D. Poulot, *Le sublime, ou le travailleur comme il est en 1870, et ce qu'il peut être*, (introd. by A. Cottereau), 1980 (originally published 1870); R. Aminzade, 'The transformation of social solidarities in nineteenth-century Toulouse', in J.M. Merriman (ed.), *Consciousness and Class Experience in Nineteenth-Century Europe*, New York, 1979, pp. 85–105.

81 B.H. Moss, *The Origins of the French Labor Movement: The Socialism of Skilled Workers, 1830–1914*, Berkeley, 1976.

82 W.H. Sewell, Jr., op. cit.

83 L. Hunt and G. Sheridan, 'Corporatism, associationism, and the language of labor in France, 1750–1850', *Journal of Modern History*, 58 (1986), pp. 815–20; Johnson, 'Artisans vs fabricants', op. cit.

84 V. de Clercq, *L'Organisation professionnelle de la petite bourgeoisie en Belgique*, Lille/Paris 1904, p. 10.

85 J.-L. Pinol, *Les mobilités de la grande ville. Lyon fin XIXe – début XXe*, 1991, pp. 365–71.

86 Y. Lequin, 'Apprenticeship in nineteenth-century France: a continuing tradition or a break with the past?', in Kaplan and Koepp, op. cit., pp. 457–74. For a comparison with Germany, see A. Grießinger and R. Reith, 'Lehrlinge im deutschen Handwerk des ausgehenden 18. Jahrhunderts. Arbeitsorganisation, Sozialbeziehungen und alltägliche Konflikte', *Zeitschrift für Historische Forschung*, 13 (1986), pp. 149–99; K. Abraham, *Der Strukturwandel im Handwerk in der ersten Hälfte des 19. Jahrhunderts und seine Bedeutung für die Berufserziehung*, Vienna, 1955. A comparison of the book trades reveals a marked difference between the structure and practices (training, apprenticeship, occupational inheritance) that were maintained in Germany but progressively disappearing in France: F. Barbier, 'Livre, économie et société industrielle en Allemagne et en France au XIXe siècle', Thèse d'Etat, University of Paris 4, 1988.

87 On the *Ligue syndicale*, see P. Nord, *Paris Shopkeepers and the Politics of Resentment*, Princeton, 1986.

88 M. Hubert-Valleroux, 'Les charges fiscales du petit commerce et de la petite industrie', *La Réforme sociale*, 60 (1910), p. 371. The Mayor of Lille in 1804 had certainly seen the *patente* as a type of maîtrise that gave its owner the right to be protected: Bossenga, *Politics of Privilege*, op. cit., p. 413.

89 P. Nord, 'The shopkeepers' movement and politics in France, 1888–1914', in *Crossick and Haupt*, pp. 175–94.
90 For French corporatist theory after 1870, see Elbow, op. cit. For the refounding of the corporate ideal by Belgian Social Catholics, see the case study of a Louvain guild which significantly lacked any role in industrial regulation, but nonetheless embraced masters and journeymen alike, mutual institutions, masters' *chefs d'œuvre*, and a ritual place in town affairs: V. Brants, 'La gilde des métiers et négoces de Louvain. Corporation chrétienne de la petite industrie', *la Réforme sociale*, 26 (1893), pp. 473–88. On Social Catholics and small enterprise, G. Crossick, 'Metaphors of the middle: the discovery of the petite bourgeoisie 1880–1914', *Transactions of the Royal Historical Society 1994*, 6th series, 4 (1995), pp. 251–79.
91 C. Behagg, *Politics and Production in the Early Nineteenth Century*, 1990, passim.
92 S. Pollard, *A History of Labour in Sheffield*, Liverpool, 1959, pp. 65–7, 152.

3 SMALL ENTERPRISE: SURVIVAL OR DECLINE?

1 'Manifesto of the Communist Party', in K. Marx and F. Engels, *Selected Works*, vol. 1, Moscow 1962, p. 41.
2 *Schriften des Vereins für Sozialpolitik*, vol. 62–70, vol. 72: *Berichte und Referate über die Generalversammlung des Vereins für Sozialpolitik*, Cologne, 1897; W. Stieda, *Die Lebensfähigkeit des deutschen Handwerks*, Rostock, 1897; O. Thissen, *Beiträge zur Geschichte des Handwerks in Preussen*, Tübingen, 1901.
3 Quoted by W. Walton, 'Political economists and specialized industrialization during the Second French Republic, 1848–52', *French History*, 3 (1989), p. 306.
4 G. Schmoller, 'Reform der Gewerbe-Ordnung', *Schriften des Vereins für Sozialpolitik*, 13 (1877), p. 193.
5 A. Faure, 'Note sur la petite entreprise en France au XIXe siècle. Représentations d'Etat et réalités', in *Entreprises et entrepreneurs XIX–XXème siècles. Congrès de l'Association française des Historiens Economistes Mars 1980*, 1983, pp. 204ff.
6 G. Kurgan-van Hentenryk and G. Viré, 'Les registres des patentables, source de l'histoire de Bruxelles à la fin du XIXe siècle', *Acta Historica Bruxellensia*, 4 (1981), p. 390.
7 A. Desrosières and L.Thévenot, 'Les mots et les chiffres: les nomenclatures socioprofessionnelles', *Economie et Statistique*, 110 (1979), pp. 49–65; E. Higgs, 'The struggle for the occupational census, 1841–1911', in R. MacLeod (ed.), *Government and Expertise: Specialists, Administrators and Professionals, 1860–1919*, Cambridge, 1988, pp. 73–86; A. Oberschall, *Empirical Social Research in Germany, 1845–1914*, Paris, 1965.
8 J. Kocka, *Arbeitsverhältnisse und Arbeiterexistenzen. Grundlagen der Klassenbildung im 19. Jahrhundert*, Bonn, 1990, pp. 299–302.
9 1851 Census Report, Great Britain. *PP* 1852–53, lxxxviii – Part 1, p. lxxviii.
10 Faure, op. cit., p. 201ff.
11 A. Desrosières and L. Thévenot, *Les catégories socioprofessionnelles*, Paris, 1989.
12 Faure, op. cit., pp. 209–12. For Germany, see K.H. Kaufhold, 'Erwerbstätigkeit und soziale Schichtung im Deutschen Reich um 1900. Quantitative Aspekte nach den Berufszählungen von 1895 und 1907', in H. Henning *et al.* (eds), *Wirtschafts- und Sozialgeschichtliche Forschungen und Probleme*, St Katherinen, 1987, p. 212ff.
13 H.-G. Haupt, 'Zur ökonomischen Entwicklung und Struktur des Kleinhandels in Frankreich zu Beginn des 20. Jahrhunderts', in H.-G. Haupt (ed.), '*Bourgeois und Volk zugleich?' Zur Geschichte des Kleinbürgertums im 19. und 20. Jahrhundert*, Frankfurt/New York, 1978, p. 120ff.

14 F. Caron, *An Economic History of Modern France*, 1979, p. 164.
15 G. Hohorst *et al.*, *Sozialgeschichtliches Arbeitsbuch*, vol. 2, Munich, 1975, p. 75; F. Lenger, *Sozialgeschichte der deutschen Handwerker seit 1800*, Frankfurt, 1988, p. 115.
16 J. Bouvier, 'Une démarche révisioniste', in P. Fridenson and A. Straus (eds), *Le capitalisme français 19e–20e siècle. Blocages et dynamismes d'une croissance*, 1987, pp. 11–30. See also R. Roehl, 'French industrialization: a reconsideration', *Explorations in Economic History*, 13 (1976), pp. 233–81.
17 D. Crew, *Town in the Ruhr: A Social History of Bochum 1860–1914*, New York, 1979, p. 17.
18 G. Kurgan-van Hentenryk, 'A forgotten class: the petite bourgeoisie in Belgium, 1850–1914', in *Crossick and Haupt*, pp. 121–2.
19 A.E. Musson, 'Industrial motive power in the UK, 1800–1870', *Economic History Review*, 29 (1976), pp. 415–39.
20 N.F.R. Crafts, *British Economic Growth during the Industrial Revolution*, Oxford, 1985; R. Cameron, 'A new view of European industrialization', *Economic History Review*, 38 (1985), pp. 1–23; P.K. O'Brien, 'Do we have a typology for the study of European industrialization in the XIXth century?', *Journal of European Economic History*, 15 (1986), pp. 291–333. On national and regional perspectives, see S. Pollard, 'Industrialisation and the European economy', *Economic History Review*, 26 (1973), pp. 636–48; S. Pollard (ed.), *Region and Industrialisation: Studies on the Role of the Region in the Economic History of the Last Two Centuries*, Göttingen, 1980.
21 P. Kriedte *et al.*, 'Sozialgeschichte in der Erweiterung – Proto-Industrialisierung in der Verengung?', *Geschichte und Gesellschaft*, 18 (1992), pp. 243–55.
22 See C. Behagg, *Politics and Production in the Early Nineteenth Century*, 1990, especially Chapter 1, pp. 20–70.
23 G.I.H. Lloyd, *The Cutlery Trades: An Historical Essay in the Economics of Small-scale Production*, 1913, p. 206; J. Gaillard, *Paris, la Ville (1852–1870)*. Lille 1976, p. 462.
24 For two successful establishments in Paris, see 'La société des immeubles industriels et l'usine de force Louyot', in *Les classes moyennes dans le commerce et l'industrie*, XXIXe congrès de la Société internationale d'économie sociale, 1910, pp. 109–16.
25 A. Julin, 'L'outillage mécanique de l'atelier familial', *La Revue sociale Catholique*, 9 (1904–05), pp. 290–5; U. Wengenroth, 'Motoren für den Kleinbetrieb. Soziale Utopien, technische Entwicklung und Absatzstrategien bei der Motorisierung des Kleingewerbes im Kaiserreich', in U. Wengenroth (ed.) *Prekäre Selbständigkeit. Zur Standortbestimmung von Handwerk, Hausindustrie und Kleingewerbe im Industrialisierungsprozess*, Stuttgart, 1989 pp. 183–9.
26 J. Scott, 'Men and women in the Parisian garment trades: discussions of family and work in the 1830s and 1840s', in P. Thane, G. Crossick and R. Floud (eds), *The Power of the Past*, 1984, pp. 67–93; C.H. Johnson, 'Patterns of proletarianization: Parisian tailors and Lodève woolens workers', in J. Merriman (ed.), *Consciousness and Class Experience in Nineteenth-Century Europe*, New York, 1979, pp. 65–84; F. Lenger, 'Handwerk, Handel, Industrie: Zur Lebensfähigkeit des Düsseldorfer Schneiderhandwerks in der zweiten Hälfte des neunzehnten Jahrhunderts', in U. Wengenroth (ed.), op. cit., pp. 71–92.
27 P. du Maroussem, *La petite industrie*, vol. 2, 'Le vêtement à Paris', 1896; R. Beier, *Frauenarbeit und Frauenalltag im Deutschen Kaiserreich. Heimarbeiterinnen in der Berliner Bekleidungsindustrie 1880–1914*, Frankfurt, 1983, pp. 26–40.
28 For the Midlands industries, see G.C. Allen, *The Industrial Development of Birmingham and the Black Country 1860–1927*, 1929 (reprinted 1966).

29 For a contemporary perception of this advantage, see A. Julin, 'Les industries à domicile et les moteurs électriques', *la Réforme sociale*, xliv (1902), pp. 322–4.

30 F. Le Play, *Les ouvriers européens. Etudes sur les travaux, la vie doméstique et la condition morale des populations ouvrières de l'Europe*, 1855, p. 152.

31 Allen, op. cit, pp. 116–19; M.J. Wise, 'On the evolution of the jewellery and gun quarters in Birmingham', Institute of British Geographers, *Transactions*, 15 (1951), pp. 57–72. For other case studies see J.R. Bailey, 'The struggle for survival in the Coventry ribbon and watch trades 1865–1914', *Midland History*, vii (1982), pp. 142–8; H. Zwahr, 'Zum Gestaltwandel von gewerblichen Unternehmern und kapitalabhängigen Produzenten', in J*ahrbuch für Geschichte*, 32 (1985), pp. 9–64.

32 Gaillard, op. cit., p. 438.

33 M.D. George, *London Life in the XVIIIth Century*, 1925, pp. 176–7; M. Sonenscher, 'Work and wages in Paris in the eighteenth century', in M. Berg, P. Hudson and M. Sonenscher (eds) *Manufacture in Town and Country before the Factory*, Cambridge, 1983, p. 155.

34 A point made by in a pioneering article by F. Bechhofer and B. Elliott, 'Persistence and change: the petite bourgeoisie in industrial society', *European Journal of Sociology*, 17 (1976), p. 91.

35 C. Erickson, *British Industrialists: Steel and Hosiery 1850–1950*, Cambridge, 1959, pp. 94–102, 124.

36 K.H. Brooker, 'The transformation of the small economy in the boot and shoe industry 1880–1914, with special reference to Northampton', PhD thesis, University of Hull, 1986.

37 Gaillard, op. cit., p. 438; L.S. Weissbach, 'Artisanal responses to artistic decline: the cabinet makers of Paris in the era of industrialisation', *Journal of Social History*, 16 (1982), pp. 67–82.

38 K.H. Kaufhold, 'Das Handwerk zwischen Anpassung und Verdrängung', in H. Pohl (ed.), *Sozialgeschichtliche Probleme in der Zeit der Hochindustrialisierung (1870–1914)*, Paderborn, 1979, p. 136.

39 C. Sabel and J. Zeitlin, 'Historical alternatives to mass production: politics, markets and technology in nineteenth-century industrialization', *Past and Present*, 108 (1985), p. 147; D. van Lente, 'The crafts in industrial society: ideals and policy in the Netherlands, 1890–1930', *Economic and Social History in the Netherlands*, 2 (1991), p. 102; J.H. Clapham, *An Economic History of Britain*, vol. 3, 1964 edn, pp. 193–5.

40 Wengenroth, op. cit., p. 180; *Bulletin de l'Institut des Classes Moyennes*, 1, August 1905; van Lente, op. cit., p. 106.

41 A. Beltran, 'Du luxe au cœur du système. Electricité et société dans la région parisienne (1880- 1939)', *Annales E.S.C.*, 1989, p. 1113–16; Wengenroth, op. cit.

42 Et. Martin Saint-Léon, 'Le problème des classes moyennes en France', *Congrès International des Classes Moyennes urbaines et rurales (Liège 1905)*, Brussels, 1906, p. 6.

43 P. Kropotkin, *Fields, Factories and Workshops*, 1912 edn, p. 281.

44 Clapham, op. cit., vol. 3, p. 183.

45 M. Lévy-Leboyer, 'Le patronat français a-t-il été malthusien?', *le mouvement social*, 89 (1974), p. 15.

46 Allen, op. cit., pp. 127, 136.

47 P. Ayçoberry, 'Histoire sociale de la ville de Cologne (1815–1875)', Thèse d'Etat. University of Paris 1, 1977. Lille, 1980, pp. 626–7.

48 E. Knox, 'Between capital and labour: the petite bourgeoisie in Victorian Edinburgh', PhD thesis, University of Edinburgh, 1986, ch. 5; R.A. Aminzade, *Class, Politics, and Early Industrial Capitalism: A Study of Mid-Nineteenth Century Toulouse, France*, Albany, 1981; for Austria, see G. Otruba, 'Handwerk

und Industrialisierung in Österreich im 19. und am Beginn des 20. Jahrhunderts', in K. Roth (ed.), *Handwerk in Mittel- und Südosteuropa. Mobilität, Vermittlung und Wandel im Handwerk des 18. bis 20. Jahrhunderts*, Munich, 1986, pp. 195–216.

49 T. Koditschek, *Class Formation and Urban Industrial Society: Bradford 1750–1850*, Cambridge, 1990, pp. 115–17.

50 Gaillard, op. cit.; F. Bourillon, 'La rénovation de Paris sous le Second Empire: étude d'un quartier', *Revue historique*, 278 (1987), pp. 135–60.

51 Quoted by A. Armengaud, *Les populations de l'Est-Aquitain au début de l'époque contemporaine. Recherches sur une région moins développée (vers 1845-vers 1871)*, 1961, p. 252.

52 Aminzade, op. cit., p. 23.

53 G. Kurgan-van Hentenryk, 'Les patentables à Bruxelles au XIXe siècle', *le mouvement social*, 108 (1979), p.72.

54 H. Aubin and W. Zorn (eds), *Handbuch der deutschen Wirtschafts- und Sozialgeschichte*, Stuttgart, 1973, vol. 2, pp. 616 and 625.

55 I. Mitchell, 'Retailing in eighteenth- and early nineteenth-century Cheshire', *Transactions of Historic Society of Lancashire and Cheshire*, 130 (1981), pp. 37–60. For a recent study of eighteenth-century retailing, see H.-C. and L. H. Mui, *Shops and Shopkeeping in Eighteenth-Century England*, 1989.

56 G. Shaw and M. Wild, 'Retail patterns in the Victorian city', Institute of British Geographers, *Transactions*, 4 (1979), p. 280.

57 D. Denecke and G. Shaw, 'Traditional retail systems in Germany', in J. Benson and G. Shaw (eds), *The Evolution of Retail Systems, c.1800–1914*, Leicester, 1992, pp. 82–6.

58 Ayçoberry, op. cit., pp. 603–4; Kurgan-van Hentenryk, 'Les patentables', pp. 83–6; J. Morris, *The Political Economy of Shopkeeping in Milan 1886–1922*, Cambridge, 1993, pp. 12–35; M. Boyer, 'Les métiers de la viande à Lyons de 1860 à 1914. Une étude sur la petite bourgeoisie', Thèse de cycle, University of Lyon 2, 1985, pp. 60–1.

59 *Statistik des Deutschen Reiches*, 211, p. 113; 418, p. 89 'the number of employees in retailing increased more rapidly than the population as a whole'.

60 Morris, op. cit., pp. 32–4.

61 A. Faure, 'The grocery trade in nineteenth-century Paris: a fragmented corporation', in *Crossick and Haupt*, pp. 155–74; H.-G. Haupt, 'Kleinhändler und Arbeiter in Bremen zwischen 1890 und 1914', *Archiv für Sozialgeschichte*, 1982, pp. 95–134.

62 Morris, op. cit., pp. 64–88.

63 B. Defaudon, 'Bourg-en-Bresse: aperçu d'une société urbaine au début du XIXe siècle 1815–1848', Mémoire de Maîtrise, University of Lyon 2, 1976, pp. 220–3.

64 M.B. Miller, *The Bon Marché: Bourgeois Culture and the Department Store, 1869–1920*, Princeton, 1981.

65 P. Moride, *Les Maisons à succursales multiples en France et à l'étranger*, Paris, 1913, p. 63; R. de Boyer-Montégut, 'Enquête sur la situation des classes moyennes. Toulouse et la Haute-Garonne', *la Réforme sociale*, lx (1910), pp. 230–6. On Britain, H.W. Macrosty, *The Trust Movement in British Industry: A Study of Business Organisation*, 1907, p. 235.

66 G. Tietz, *Hermann Tietz. Geschichte einer Familie und ihrer Warenhäuser*, Stuttgart, 1965; J. Wernicke, *Kapitalismus und Mittelstandspolitik*, Jena, 1907.

67 E. Demolins, 'La question des grands magasins', *la Science sociale*, 9 (1890), pp. 294–303; R. Gellately, 'An der Schwelle der Moderne. Warenhäuser und ihre Feinde in Deutschland,' in G. Brunn (ed.) *Im Banne der Metropole*, Göttingen, 1992.

68 E. Zola, *Au bonheur des dames*, 1883.
69 J. Bernard and L. Hoffmann, 'Le petit commerce et les grands magasins', *la Réforme sociale*, lxi (1911), p. 301.
70 J.B. Jefferys, *Retail Trading in Britain 1850–1950*, Cambridge, 1954, pp. 16–18.
71 Gellately, op. cit., pp. 38–9.
72 M. Purvis, 'The development of co-operative retailing in England and Wales, 1851–1901: a geographical study', *Journal of Historical Geography*, 16 (1990), pp. 314–31; D. Köhn and C. Niermann, 'Konsumvereine als Konkurrenten des Kleinhandels in Bremen vor 1914', in H.-G. Haupt (ed.), *Der Bremer Kleinhandel um 1900*, Bremen, 1983, pp. 257–82.
73 Jefferys, op. cit., pp. 22–3.
74 P. Matthias examines several important chains in the food trade in his *Retailing Revolution: A History of Multiple Retailing in the Food Trades based upon the Allied Suppliers Group of Companies*, 1967. On Camberwell, H.J. Dyos, *Victorian Suburb: A Study of the Growth of Camberwell*, Leicester, 1966, pp. 151–2.
75 Moride, op. cit., pp. 71–94; Matthias, op. cit., 120, p. 171; S. Jaumain, 'Les petits commerçants belges face à la modernité (1880–1914)', Doctoral thesis, Université libre de Bruxelles, 1991, vol. 3, Table VII.
76 For German itinerant traders, see W. Conze in Aubin and Zorn, op. cit., II, p. 627, and the excellent case study in C. Niermann, '"Gewerbe im Umherziehen" – Hausierer und Wanderlager in Bremen vor 1914', in Haupt (ed.), *Kleinhandel*, op. cit., pp. 207–56. On Belgium, Jaumain, op. cit., vol. 1, p. 225ff.
77 Jefferys, op. cit., p. 29; Conze, op. cit., p. 626.
78 C.P. Hosgood, 'Shopkeepers and society: domestic and principal shopkeepers in Leicester, 1860–1914', PhD thesis, University of Manitoba, 1987, pp. 79–80.
79 *Bexley Heath and Bexley Observer*, 6 October 1911.
80 E. Labrousse (ed.), *Aspects de la crise et de la dépression de l'économie française au milieu du XIXe siècle, 1846–51*, 1966.
81 A. Daumard, *La bourgeoisie parisienne de 1815 à 1848*, 1963, pp. 434–40.
82 J. Le Yaouanq, 'Les effets de la crise de 1848–1851 sur le monde boutiquier parisien', unpublished paper to *4th Round Table*, 1984.
83 Behagg, op. cit., pp. 143–4.
84 J. Gaillard, 'La petite entreprise entre la droite et la gauche', in G. Levau, G. Grunberg and N. Mayer (eds), *L'univers politique des classes moyennes*, 1983, p. 65; A. Offer, *Property and Politics 1870–1914: Landownership, Law, Ideology and Urban Development in England*, Cambridge, 1981, pp. 288–9.
85 H. Sedatis, *Liberalismus und Handwerk in Südwestdeutschland. Wirtschafts- und Gesellschaftskonzeption des Liberalismus und die Krise des Handwerks im 19. Jahrhundert*, Stuttgart, 1979.
86 Allen, op. cit., pp. 210–30.
87 J. Ehmer, 'Small-scale production and the Great Depression: some arguments based on Austrian data', unpublished paper to *4th Round Table*, 1984.
88 J. Bergmann, *Wirtschaftskrise und Revolution. Handwerker und Arbeiter 1848/49*, Berlin, 1986, p. 971.
89 Ayçoberry, op. cit., pp. 140–1.
90 Sedatis, op. cit.
91 Lloyd, op. cit., p. 193. H. Mayhew, *London Labour and the London Poor*, vol. 3, 1861, pp. 228–9.
92 Figures from P. Bairoch, *Cities and Economic Development*, 1988, p. 221.
93 Faure, op. cit., p. 213; Lenger, *Sozialgeschichte*, op. cit., p. 118.
94 H. Harnisch, 'Kapitalistische Agrarreform und industrielle Revolution. Agrarhistorische Untersuchungen über die Zusammenhänge zwischen den kapitalistischen Agrarreformen und der Herausbildung des Inneren Marktes als

Voraussetzung für die Industrielle Revolution', Diss. B., University of Rostock, 1978, pp. 313–25.
95 A. Moulin, *Les paysans dans la société française*, 1988, p. 84.
96 H. Schultz, 'Landhandwerker und ländliche Sozialstruktur um 1800', *Jahrbuch für Wirtschaftsgeschichte*, 1981, II, pp. 11–49.
97 Le Play, op. cit., p. 260ff.
98 R. Hubscher, 'La petite exploitation en France, XIXe-XXe siècle', *Annales E.S.C.*, 1985, pp. 14–16; R. Hubscher, 'La pluriactivité: un imperatif ou un style de vie? L'exemple des paysans ouvriers du département de la Loire au XIXe siècle', in Association des Ruralistes Français, *La pluriactivité dans les familles agricoles*, 1984, pp. 75–85.
99 J.-C. Farcy, 'Les limites de la pluriactivité des familles agricoles dans une région de grande culture. L'exemple de la Beauce au XIXe siècle', in ibid., pp. 87–97.
100 Lenger, *Sozialgeschichte*, op. cit., p. 118ff.
101 G. Schmoller, *Zur Geschichte der deutschen Kleingewerbe im 19. Jahrhundert. Statistische und nationalökonomische Untersuchungen*, Halle, 1870, p. 316.
102 For this neglected theme in English rural history, see M. Reed, 'Nineteenth-century rural England: a case for "Peasant Studies"', *Journal of Peasant Studies*, 14 (1986), pp. 87–8; B.A. Holderness, 'Rural tradesmen, 1660–1850. A regional study in Lindsey', *Lincolnshire History and Archaeology*, 7 (1972), p. 77.
103 C. Hallas, 'Craft occupations in the late nineteenth century: some local considerations', *Local Population Studies*, 44 (1990), p. 26.
104 J.M. Martin, 'Village traders and the emergence of a proletariat in south Warwickshire, 1750–1851', *Agricultural History Review*, 32 (1984), pp. 179–88.
105 M.F. Davies, *Life in an English Village: An Economic and Historical Survey of the Parish of Corsley in Wiltshire*, 1909, pp. 105–9; see also G.F. Eyre, 'The small holdings of Far Forest, Worcestershire', *Economic Review*, xii, 1902, pp. 158–71.
106 Royal Commission on Labour (Agricultural Labour), 'General Report by Mr WC Little', *PP* 1893–94, xxxvii.2, p. 139; Royal Commission on the Agricultural Depression, *PP* 1894, xvi.1, Q. 552.
107 P. Pinchemel, *Structures sociales et dépopulation rurale dans les campagnes picardes de 1836 à 1936*, 1957, pp. 129–40.
108 G. Dupeux, *Aspects de l'histoire sociale et politique du Loir-et-Cher 1848–1914*, 1962, p. 121.
109 C. Montez, 'Aspects du vignoble au Pays de Condrieu, 1800–1914', Mémoire de maîtrise, University of Lyon 2, 1990.
110 J.A. Chartres, 'Country tradesmen', in G.E. Mingay (ed.) *The Victorian Countryside*, 1981, pp. 302–3.
111 P.A. Graham, *The Rural Exodus*, 1892, p. 39.
112 Royal Commission on the Agricultural Depression, op. cit., xvi.1, Q. 39,366 and 41,250.
113 R.J. Olney, *Rural Society and County Government in Nineteenth-Century Lincolnshire*, Lincoln, 1979, p. 65; J. Saville, *Rural Depopulation in England and Wales, 1851–1951*, 1957, pp. 74, 211–12.
114 B.J. Davey, *Ashwell 1830–1914: The Decline of a Village Community*, Leicester, 1980, pp. 55–7.
115 Davies, op. cit., p. 128; A. Jessop *Arcady: For Better for Worse*, 1887, pp. 12–13; F. Gresswell, *Bright Boots*, 1956, pp. 98–103.
116 W. Kaschuba and C. Lipp, *Dörfliches Überleben. Zur Geschichte materieller und sozialer Reproduktion ländlicher Gesellschaft im 19. und frühen 20. Jahrhundert*, Tübingen, 1982, pp. 167–9.
117 Y. Rinaudo, 'Un travail en plus: les paysans d'un métier à l'autre (vers 1830 – vers 1950)', *Annales E.S.C*, 42 (1987), pp. 283–302.

118 Moulin, op. cit., p. 148.
119 J.-C. Farcy, 'L'artisanat rural et la crise des années 1880–1890: le cas de l'Eure-et-Loir et de la Beauce', paper to *4th Round Table*, 1984.
120 T. Hardy, 'The Dorsetshire labourer', *Longman's Magazine*, 2 (1883), pp. 268–9.
121 For early recognition of how the petite bourgeoisie was trapped and made vulnerable by its dependence on credit, notes, and debts, see K. Marx, *The Class Struggles in France: 1848–1850*, in D. Fernbach (ed.) *Karl Marx: Surveys from Exile*, Harmondsworth, 1973, pp. 65–7.
122 Behagg, op. cit., pp. 38–9, 52–9.
123 See the comments of the Belgian government official who found the wood trades of Ath completely dependent on timber merchants in 1904: G. Malherbes, 'La petite industrie de bois à Ath', Commission nationale de la petite bourgeoisie, *Enquêtes Ecrites. Monographies*, vol. 1, 1904, p. 251.
124 R.M. Springthorpe, 'The brush manufactures, 1880–1910: a study in small enterprise', unpublished B.A. Dissertation, University of Essex, 1990.
125 V. Brants, *La petite industrie contemporaine*, 1902, p. 124.
126 Ayçoberry, op. cit., pp. 147–9.
127 Quoted in Behagg, op. cit., p. 55.
128 F.C. Huber, *Warenhaus und Kleinhandel*, Berlin, 1899, p. 7.
129 H. Fode, 'The urban lower middle class in crisis. Craftsmen and small-scale retailers during the 1880s', paper to *4th Round Table*, 1984.
130 J. Burnett, 'The baking industry in the nineteenth century', *Business History*, 5 (1962), pp. 100- 1; B. Angleraud, 'Les boulangers lyonnais aux XIXe–XXe siècles (1836 à 1914). Une étude sur la petite bourgeoisie boutiquière', Thèse de doctorat, University of Lyon 2, 1993, vol 1, pp. 94–9.
131 For example, H. Lambrechts, *Le crédit des classes moyennes en Belgique*, Brussels, 1908; H. Faucherre, *Die Händler-Rabattsparvereine. Studie über die praktischen Probleme der Mittelstandsbewegung*, Jena, 1912.
132 *Rapport . . . sur la situation du commerce en France* (Rapport Landry), Chambre des Deputés, 10ème Législature 1914, 85, impression 3432, pp. 134–6; Wernicke, op. cit; B. Ahuis, 'Sozialpolitische Probleme des oldenburgischen Handwerks im 19. und frühen 20. Jahrhundert', in *Oldenburg um 1900*, Oldenburg, 1975, p. 131.
133 R. Roberts, *The Classic Slum: Salford Life in the First Quarter of the Century*, Harmondsworth, 1973, pp. 82–3.
134 Hosgood, op. cit., pp. 32–5.
135 A.J. Giles, Secretary of Metropolitan Grocers' Federation. Booth Collection, B134 ff 2–3. In Paris it was increasingly common for a retailer in difficulties to make over the business to the main creditor as a surety for the debt: *Bulletin de l'Institut international des Classes Moyennes*, August 1906.
136 E. Porter, *Victorian Cambridge: Josiah Chater's Diaries*, 1975, p. 63.
137 Select Committee on Shops Hours Regulation, *PP* 1886, xii, Q. 274–82.
138 Moride, op. cit., pp. 43–5, 52–3.
139 J.C. Martin, 'Le commerçant, la faillite et l'historien', *Annales E.S.C.*, 35 (1980), p. 1262. For an Italian case, D.L. Caglioti, 'I fallimenti del Tribunale di Commercio di Napoli: una fonte per lo studio del piccolo e medio commercio cittadino', *Società e Storia*, XII (1989), pp. 443–53.
140 Behagg, op. cit., pp. 59–66.

4 A WORLD IN MOVEMENT

1 *Compte Rendu Sténographique du Congrès International de la Petite Bourgeoisie, tenu à Anvers les 17 et 18 Septembre 1899*, Bruxelles, 1900, p. 94.

NOTES

2 *Congrès des œuvres sociales de Liège 1886*, cited by P. Delfosse, 'La petite bourgeoisie en crise et l'Etat: le cas belge (1890–1914)', *le mouvement social*, 114 (1981), p. 89.
3 M. Garden, 'The urban trades: social analysis and representation', in S.L. Kaplan and C.J. Koepp (eds), *Work in France: Representations, Meaning, Organization, and Practices*, Ithaca, 1986, pp. 287–96.
4 *AN* C. 7461.
5 H. Lambrechts, *Le problème social de la petite bourgeoisie en Belgique*, 1901, p. 33.
6 H.-G. Haupt, 'Zur ökonomischen Entwicklung und Struktur des Kleinhandels in Frankreich zu Beginn des 20. Jahrhunderts', in H.-G. Haupt (ed.), *Bourgeois und Volk zugleich? Zur Geschichte des Kleinbürgertums im 19. und 20. Jahrhundert*, Frankfurt/New York, 1978, p. 127.
7 Booth Collection, B133 f 8 (British Library of Political and Economic Science).
8 C. Colson, *Cours d'économie politique*, 1903, vol. 2, p. 564.
9 J.-C. Martin, 'Le commerçant, la faillite et l'historien', *Annales, E.S.C.*, 35 (1980), p. 1257.
10 K. Brooker, 'The changing position of the small owner in the English shoemaking industry 1860–1914', unpublished paper to *2nd Round Table*, Bremen, 1980.
11 Calculated from *Statistique de la Ville de Paris*, 1906–13.
12 A. Faure, 'The grocery trade in nineteenth-century Paris: a fragmented corporation', in *Crossick and Haupt*, p. 171.
13 F. Lenger, *Zwischen Kleinbürgertum und Proletariat. Studien zur Sozialgeschichte der Düsseldorfer Handwerker 1816–1878*, Göttingen, 1986, pp. 88–93; J.-L. Pinol, *Le monde des villes au XIXème siècle*, 1991, p. 151 ff.
14 H.-G. Haupt, 'Kleinhändler und Arbeiter in Bremen zwischen 1890 und 1914', *Archiv für Sozialgeschichte*, 22 (1982), p. 110.
15 *Kolonialwaren-Kleinhandel und Konsumvereine. Untersuchungen unter Mitwirkung der Handelskammern Brandenburg, Magdeburg, Nordhausen, Hildesheim und Hildburgshausen, herausgegeben von der Handelskammer für das Herzogthum Braunschweig*, Leipzig, 1901, pp. 43–68.
16 E. Knox, 'Between capital and labour: the petite bourgeoisie in Victorian Edinburgh', PhD Thesis, University of Edinburgh, 1986, pp. 10–13.
17 L. Edgren, *Lärling, gesäl, mästare. Hantwerk och hantverkare i Malmö 1750–1847*, Lund, 1987, p. 400.
18 D. Cagliotti, 'Petites bourgeoisies napolitaines du XIXe siècle. Mobilités géographiques et sociales', *Bulletin du Centre Pierre Léon*, 1993, pp. 5–14.
19 Calculated from figures in S. Jaumain, 'Les petits commerçants belges face à la modernité (1880–1914)', Thèse de doctorat, Université Libre de Bruxelles, 1991, vol. 3, Table XIX.i.
20 F. Lenger, *Sozialgeschichte der deutschen Handwerker seit 1800*, Frankfurt, 1988, p. 115; K.H. Kaufhold, 'Das Handwerk zwischen Anpassung und Verdrängung', in H. Pohl (ed.), *Sozialgeschichtliche Probleme der Hochindustrialisierung 1870–1914*, Paderborn, 1979, pp. 109–10.
21 J. Benson, *The Penny Capitalists: A Study of Nineteenth-Century Working-Class Entrepreneurs*, Dublin, 1983.
22 Select Committee on Shops (Early Closing) Bill, *PP* 1895, xii, Q. 4153.
23 Select Committee on Sunday Trading, *PP* 1906, xiii, Q. 3365.
24 P. Ayçoberry, 'Histoire sociale de la ville de Cologne (1815–1875)', Thèse d'Etat, University of Paris 1 (1977), pp. 671–2.
25 *AN* C 7462.
26 *1851 Census Sample*.
27 C. Niermann, 'Die Bedeutung und sozialökonomische Lage Bremer Klein-

händlerinnen zwischen 1890 und 1914', in H.-G. Haupt (ed.), *Der Bremer Kleinhandel um 1900*, Bremen, 1983, p. 96.

28 D. Hervier, *Cafés et cabarets en Berry de 1851 à 1914*, Chateauroux, 1980, pp. 45–8.

29 J.E. Williams, *The Derbyshire Miners: A Study in Industrial and Social History*, 1962, p. 216. See the bizarre case of the followers of the millenarian Jezreelite movement in the 1880s, which spawned a network of small enterprises to support its members in the Kent towns of Chatham and Gillingham: P.G. Rogers, *The Sixth Trumpeter: The Story of Jezreel and his Tower*, 1963, pp. 33–5.

30 J. Michel, 'Le mouvement ouvrier chez les mineurs d'Europe occidentale. Etude comparative des années 1880 à 1914', Thèse d'Etat, University of Lyon 2, 1987, pp. 581–3.

31 Booth Collection, B133 f 45.

32 R.Q. Gray, *The Labour Aristocracy in Victorian Edinburgh*, Oxford, 1976, pp. 131–3. German research has similarly stressed the way turnover varied with the capital and labour intensity of different crafts – see Lenger, *Sozialgeschichte*; J. Kocka, *Lohnarbeit und Klassenbildung. Arbeiterbewegung in Deutschland 1800–1875*, Bonn, 1991.

33 C. Hosgood, 'Shopkeepers and society: domestic and principal shopkeepers in Leicester, 1860–1914', PhD thesis, University of Manitoba, 1987, p. 103.

34 V.S. Pritchett, *A Cab at the Door*, 1970, p. 6.

35 Faure, op. cit., pp. 168–70.

36 B. Angleraud, 'Les boulangers lyonnais aux XIXe-XXe siècles (1836 à 1914). Une étude sur la petite bourgeoisie boutiquière', Thèse de doctorat, University of Lyon 2, 1993, vol. 1, pp. 136–45.

37 *Les etudes fiscales et sociales. Troisième Congrès Annuel (nov. 1910)*, Limoges, 1911, p. 175.

38 Syndicat industriel et commercial de l'arrondissement d'Alençon, *AN* C 7466.

39 A. Daumard, *Les bourgeois de Paris au XIXe siècle*, 1970, p. 131.

40 C. Booth, *Life and Labour of the People in London*, 1902 edn, Second Series, vol. 3, p. 250.

41 F.W. Bullen, *Confessions of a Tradesman*, 1908, p. 156.

42 J. Bernard, 'Du mouvement d'organisation et de défense du petit commerce français', Thèse de droit, University of Paris, 1906, p. 34.

43 Daumard, op. cit., p. 126; Faure, op. cit., p. 170; J. Le Yaouanq, 'Aspects de l'immigration departementale à Paris au XIXe siècle: les commerçants et artisans ligeriens', *Cahiers de l'Institut d'Histoire de la Presse et de l'Opinion*, 3, 1974–75; G. Désert, 'Immigration et ségrégation à Caen', in M. Garden and Y. Lequin (eds), *Habiter la Ville. XVe – XXe siècle*, Lyon, 1984, p. 180; Angleraud, op. cit., p. 111. For the importance of shopkeeping for migrants to both Amiens and Nîmes, see L.P. Moch and L.A. Tilly, 'Joining the urban world: occupation, family and migration in three French cities', *Comparative Studies in Society and History*, 27 (1985), p. 44.

44 Le Yaouanq, op. cit., pp. 12–18.

45 *1851 Census Sample*; 1851 Census *PP* 1852–53, lxxxviii, p. 31.

46 J.D. Marshall and J.K. Walton, *The Lake Counties from 1830 to the mid-twentieth century*, 1981, pp. 90–1; D. Jenkins, *The Agricultural Community in South-West Wales at the Turn of the Twentieth Century*, 1971, p. 251.

47 P. Mathias, *Retailing Revolution: A History of Multiple Retailing in the Food Trades based upon the Allied Suppliers Group of Companies*, 1967, pp. 40–4.

48 F. Raison-Jourde, *La colonie auvergnate de Paris au XIXe siècle*, 1976, pp. 121–60.

49 J. Le Yaouanq, 'Trajectoires sociales à Paris au XIXe siècle: le monde de la boutique', *Bulletin du Centre Pierre Léon*, 1993, pp. 25–4; Faure, op. cit., p. 170.

50 Raison-Jourde, op. cit.
51 S. Schraut, *Sozialer Wandel in Industrialisierungsprozeß. Esslingen 1800–1870*, Sigmaringen, 1989, pp. 226–7.
52 W.R. Lambert, 'Drink and work-discipline in industrial south Wales, c. 1800–1870', *Welsh History Review*, 7 (1975), p. 298.
53 Booth, op. cit., first series, vol. 1, p. 34.
54 *1851 Census Sample.*
55 H.-G. Haupt, 'Kleinhändler und Arbeiter in Bremen zwischen 1890 und 1914', *Archiv für Sozialgeschichte*, 22 (1982), p. 105 ff.
56 Select Committee on Shop (Early Closing) Bill, *PP* 1895 xii, Q 3979–4004. For the movement for early closing and the relationship between large and small shopkeepers, see G. Crossick, 'Shopkeepers and the state in Britain 1870–1914', in *Crossick and Haupt*, pp. 252–6.
57 J. Lorçin, 'Histoire sociale et attitudes mentales. Les archives de la Chambre de Commerce de Saint-Etienne,' *Actes du 89e Congrès national des sociétés savantes*, Lyon, 1964, vol. 2, pp. 793–809; A. Saur, 'Die Organisationen der Bremer Kleinhändler vor 1914 und ihre soziale Basis', in H.-G. Haupt (ed.), *Der Bremer Kleinhändler um 1900*, Bremen, 1982, p. 48.
58 See the evidence to the Select Committee on Shop Hours' Regulation Bill, *PP* 1886 xii; and to the Select Committee on Shop (Early Closing) Bill, op. cit.
59 Knox, op. cit., pp. 406–7.
60 A. Daumard (ed.), *Les fortunes françaises au XIXe siècle*, 1973, pp. 216–21. The figure for workers' fortunes is from Daumard, *Les bourgeois*, op. cit., pp. 364–5. For parallel figures for Lyon, see P. Léon, *Géographie de la fortune et structures sociales à Lyon au XIXe siècle (1815–1914)*, Lyon, 1974, pp. 150–1.
61 Schraut, op. cit., p. 227.
62 Hosgood. op. cit., pp. 22–5. Policies insured both stock and household property.
63 B. Defaudon, 'Bourg-en-Bresse: aperçu d'une société urbaine au debut du XIXe siècle 1815–1848', Mémoire de maîtrise, University of Lyon 2, 1976, pp. 207–9, pp. 220–2.
64 A. Noll, *Socio-ökonomischer Strukturwandel des Handwerks in der zweiten Phase der Industrialisierung unter besonderer Berücksichtigung der Regierungsbezirke Arnsberg und Münster*, Göttingen, 1975, p. 69.
65 *1851 Census Sample.*
66 C. Niermann, op. cit., pp. 93, 100.
67 On patrimony as the motor for strategies of petit-bourgeois accumulation in the present day, see J. Capdeville, *Le fétichisme du patrimoine. Essai sur un fondement de la classe moyenne*, 1986.
68 Faure, op. cit., p. 169.
69 Kurgan-van Hentenryk, *Commission Internationale*, p. 195; M. Boyer, 'Les métiers de la viande à Lyon de 1860 à 1914', Thèse de 3e cycle, University of Lyon 2, 1985; J. Merriman, *The Red City: Limoges and the French Nineteenth Century*, New York, 1985, pp. 147–51; H.-G. Haupt's analysis of TRA sample of *actes de mariage*. For details of the TRA sample, see J. Dupâquier and D. Kessler, *La société française au XIXe siècle. Tradition, transition, transformations*, 1992, pp. 23–61.
70 H. Henning, 'Handwerk und Industriegesellschaft. Zur sozialen Verflechtung, westfälischer Handwerksmeister, 1870–1914', in K. Düwell and W. Köllmann (eds), *Rheinland-Westfalen im Industriezeitalter*, Wuppertal, 1984, vol. 2, p. 178 ff.
71 Select Committee on Shop Hours Regulation Bill, op. cit., Q. 321–3, Q. 2698–9.
72 Saur, op. cit., pp. 46–50.
73 Schraut, op. cit., pp. 226–49; Lenger, *Düsseldorf*, op. cit., pp. 33, 41.
74 Schraut, op. cit., p. 238 ff.

75 P. Ayçoberry, 'Histoire sociale de la ville de Cologne (1815–1875)', Thèse d'Etat, University of Paris 1 (1977), pp. 606–7; Lenger, *Düsseldorf*, op. cit., pp. 106–9 (the figures are for those whose occupations were known).

76 F. Galton, *Hereditary Genius: An Inquiry into its Laws and Consequences*, 1869; L. Thévenot 'La politique des statistiques: les origines sociales des enquêtes de mobilité sociale', *Annales E.S.C.*, 1990, pp. 1275–300; J.H. Goldthorpe, 'Soziale Mobilität und Klassenbildung. Zur Erneuerung einer Tradition soziologischer Forschung', in H. Strasse and J.H. Goldthorpe (eds), *Die Analyse sozialer Ungleichheit. Kontinuität, Erneuerung, Innovation*, Opladen, 1985, pp. 174–204.

77 For recent questioning of some of these assumptions see the special issue of *Annales E.S.C.*, nov-déc 1990; R. Kreckel, 'Klasse und Geschlecht. Die Geschlechtsindifferenz der soziologischen Implikationen', *Leviathan*, 17 (1989), pp. 305–21.

78 G. Crossick, *An Artisan Elite in Victorian Society: Kentish London 1840–1880*, 1978, p. 114.

79 Quoted from a 1874 police report by G. Jacquemet, *Belleville au XIXe. Du faubourg à la ville*, 1984, p. 317.

80 W. Renzsch, *Handwerker und Lohnarbeiter in der frühe Arbeiterbewegung. Zur sozialen Basis von Gewerkschaftsbewegung und Sozialdemokratie im Reichsgründungsjahrzehnt*, Göttingen, 1980, pp. 75 ff.; Lenger, *Sozialgeschichte*, op. cit., p. 150.

81 R.Q. Gray, op. cit., p. 132.

82 D. Crew, *Town in the Ruhr: A Social History of Bochum 1860–1914*, New York, 1979, pp. 82–3.

83 M. Gribaudi and A. Blum, 'Des categories aux liens individuels: l'analyse statistique de l'espace social', *Annales E.S.C.*, 1990, pp. 1365–402.

84 W.H. Sewell Jr., *Structure and Mobility: The men and women of Marseille, 1820–1870*, Cambridge, 1985; Crossick, *Artisan Elite*, op. cit., chapter 6, pp. 105–33.

85 R. Girod and Y. Fricker, 'Mobilité séquentielle', *Revue française de sociologie*, xii (1971), pp. 1–18.

86 See, for example, W.R. Hubbard, 'Social mobility and social structure in Graz 1857–1910', *Journal of Social History*, 17 (1984), pp. 455–7.

87 *1851 Census Sample*; *PP* 1852–3, lxxxviii. Pt I, p. 6 .

88 Sewell, op. cit., p. 236.

89 *1851 Census Sample*; *PP* 1852–3, lxxxviii. Pt I, pp. 6–15.

90 Analysis of 838 marriages in the parochial archives of ten parishes in Braunschweig: H.-G. Haupt, *Kleinhändler*, op. cit.

91 A.-M. Morier, 'Structures familiales des commerçants de Givors (1851–1914)', Mémoire de Maîtrise, University of Lyon 2, 1977–78, p. 40.

92 H. Béraud, *La Gerbe d'Or*, 1928, p. 187.

93 Le Yaouanq, 'Trajectoires sociales', op. cit., p. 12.

94 Faure, op. cit., p. 167.

95 Booth, op. cit., 2nd series, vol. 3, pp. 79–80.

96 W.H. Hubbard, 'Aspects of social mobility in Graz, 1857–1880', *Historical Social Research*, 14 (1980), pp. 11–12.

97 S. Schötz, 'On the recruitment of the Leipzig middle strata from the working class, 1830–1870', in G. Iggers (ed.), *Marxist Historiography in Transformation: East German Social History in the 1980s*, New York/Oxford, 1991, pp. 95–113.

98 Knox, op. cit., pp. 423–35.

99 Pinol, op. cit., p. 313.

100 J. Le Yaouanq, verbal communication.

101 Calculated from data in B. Preston, *Occupations of Father and Son in Mid-Victorian England*, University of Reading Geographical Papers no. 56, 1977.
102 Hosgood, op. cit., p. 224.
103 R. Aminzade and R. Hodson, 'Social mobility in a mid-nineteenth century French city', *American Sociological Review*, 47 (1982), pp. 450–1.
104 J. Le Yaouanq, 'La mobilité sociale dans le milieu boutiquier parisien au XIXe siècle', *le mouvement social*, 108 (1979), pp. 103–7.
105 A. Miles, 'Lower middle class mobility in England, 1839–1914', unpublished paper to Colloquium Trajectoires et mobilités dans les classes moyennes urbaines en Europe aux 19e et 20e siècles, Florence, 1990.
106 Schraut, op. cit., pp. 226 ff.; Lenger, *Düsseldorf*, op. cit., pp. 112–15.
107 Henning, op. cit. Henning's sample was skewed towards the upper reaches of the artisanat.
108 G. Hohorst, J. Kocka and G.A. Ritter (eds), *Sozialgeschichtliches Arbeitsbuch. Materialen zur Statistik des Kaiserreichs 1870–1914*, Munich, 1978, pp. 126–7.
109 J.P. Chaline, 'Les contrats de mariage à Rouen au XIXe siècle. Etude d'après l'enregistrement des actes civils publics', *Revue d'histoire économique et sociale*, 48 (1970), p. 260 ff.; A. Daumard, *Les bourgeois et la bourgeoisie en France depuis 1815*, 1987; P. Guillaume, *La population de Bordeaux au XIXe siècle. Essai d'histoire sociale*, 1972; F.P. Codaccioni, *De l'inégalité sociale dans une grande ville industrielle. Le drame de Lille de 1850 à 1914*, Lille, 1976, vol. 1, p. 676 ff.
110 Mathias, op. cit., pp. 40–4.
111 J.-P. Chaline, *Les bourgeois de Rouen. Une élite urbaine au XIXe siècle*, 1982, p. 67.
112 P. Lundgren, M. Kraul and K. Ditt, *Bildungschancen und soziale Mobilität in der ständischen Gesellschaft des 19. Jahrhunderts*, Göttingen, 1988, p. 150.
113 E. Wahrann in *Bulletin de l'Institut International des Classes Moyennes*, September, 1905.
114 F. Gresle, *L'univers de la boutique. Les petits patrons du Nord (1920–1975)*, Lille, 1981, pp. 84–90.
115 P. Bourdieu, L. Boltanski and M. de Saint-Martin, 'Les stratégies de reconversion. Les classes sociales et le système d'enseignement', *Information sur les Sciences Sociales*, 12 (1973), pp. 61–113.
116 Gaillard, *Paris, la Ville (1852–1870)*, Lille, 1976, p. 404.
117 Quoted by D. Blackbourn, 'Between resignation and volatility: the German petite bourgeoisie in the nineteenth century', in *Crossick and Haupt*, p. 45.
118 N. Hancock, *An Innocent Grows Up*, 1947, pp. 110–14.
119 Report of the Schools Inquiry Commission, *PP* 1867–68, xxviii; B. Heeney, *Mission to the Middle Classes: The Woodard Schools 1848–1891*, 1969.
120 Lundgren, Kraul and Ditt, op. cit.
121 Crew, op. cit., pp. 93–4.
122 Lundgren, Kraul and Ditt, op. cit., pp. 120–1.
123 J.-P. Briand and J.-M. Chapoulie, 'La IIIe République crée un réseau d'écoles: les débuts de l'enseignement primaire supérieur,' *Revue Historique*, cclxxxiii (1990), p. 81.
124 R. Gildea, 'Education and the classes moyennes in the nineteenth century', in D.N. Baker and P.J. Harrigan (eds), *The Making of Frenchmen: Current Directions in the History of Education in France, 1679–1979*, Waterloo, Ontario, 1980, pp. 275–99.
125 P.J. Harrigan, *Mobility, Elites and Education in French Society of the Second Empire*, Waterloo, Ontario, 1980, pp. 25–8.
126 Hosgood, op. cit., p. 224. For the expansion of white-collar employment in

Britain, see G. Crossick (ed.) *The Lower Middle Class in Britain 1870–1914*, 1976.

127 F.G. D'Aeth, 'Present tendencies of class differentiation', *Sociological Review*, iii (1910), p. 271.

128 G. Vincent, 'Les professeurs du second degré au début du XXème siècle: essai sur la mobilité sociale et la mobilité géographique', *le mouvement social*, 55 (1966), pp. 47–73.

129 G. Duplat, *La classe moyenne. Son rôle social. Son action politique. Sa situation économique. Les réformes urgentes*, Brussels, 1914, p. 301.

130 Departmental Committee on the Pupil–Teacher System, *PP* 1898, xxvi.

131 P.J. Harrigan, 'Secondary education and the professions in France during the Second Empire', *Comparative Studies in Society and History*, 17 (1975), p. 365.

132 T. Geiger, *Die soziale Schichtung des deutschen Volkes. Soziographischer Versuch auf statistischer Grundlage*, Darmstadt, 1967, pp. 106–38.

133 Goldthorpe, op. cit.

5 THE FAMILY: IMAGES AND NECESSITIES

1 A. Goodyn, *Le mouvement coopératif*, Gand, 1896, pp. 14–15.

2 M. Segalen, *Mari et femme dans la société paysanne*, 1980, p. 121.

3 *1851 London Census Sample*. Reference to London shopkeeper households and families in 1851 is derived from an analysis of an 1851 London Census Sample. The sample was made up of all the London enumeration districts (fifty-one in total) which had been included in the 1851 Census National Sample project organised by Professor Michael Anderson at the University of Edinburgh and funded by the Economic and Social Research Council. Further work on the London clusters data set was funded by an additional grant from the ESRC, for which Geoffrey Crossick is grateful. W. Ogle, 'On marriage-rates and marriage-ages, with special reference to the growth of population', *Journal of the Royal Statistical Society*, LIII (1890), p. 276.

4 S. Volkov, *The Rise of Popular Antimodernism in Germany: The Urban Master Artisans 1873–1896*, Princeton, 1978, pp. 27–8.

5 R. Reith, *Arbeits- und Lebensweise im städtischen Handwerk. Zur Sozial-geschichte Augsburger Handwerksgesellen im 18. Jahrhundert (1700–1806)*, Göttingen, 1988, pp. 132ff. For the same phenomenon in the following century, see J. Ehmer, *Heiratsverhalten, Sozialstruktur, ökonomischer Wandel. England und Mitteleuropa in der Formationsperiode des Kapitalismus*, Göttingen, 1991.

6 R. Sieder, *Sozialgeschichte der Familie*, Frankfurt, 1987, pp. 103–24; S. Schraut, *Sozialer Wandel im Industrialisierungsprozeß. Esslingen 1800–1870*, Esslingen, 1989, pp. 92–100.

7 J. Ehmer, 'The artisan family in nineteenth-century Austria: embourgeoisement of the petite bourgeoisie?', in *Crossick and Haupt*, pp. 195–218.

8 E. Lunander, *Borgaren blir foretagare. Studier kring ekonomiska, sociala och politiska forhallanden i forandringens Orebro under 1800-talet*, Stockholm, 1988, p. 151.

9 D. Garrioch, *Neighbourhood and Community in Paris 1740–1790*, Cambridge, 1986, p. 62.

10 M. Mitterauer and R. Sieder, *The European Family: Patriarchy to Partnership from the Middle Ages to the Present*, Oxford, 1982, pp. 80–1.

11 K.J. Bade, 'Altes Handwerker, Wanderzwang und Gute Policey: Gesellen-wanderung zwischen Zunftökonomie und Gewerbereform', *Vierteljahrschrift für Sozial- und Wirtschaftsgeschichte*, 69 (1987), pp. 32ff.

12 S. Cerutti, *La ville et les métiers. Naissance d'un langage corporatif (Turin, 17e-18e siècles)*, 1990, p. 170.
13 Schraut, op. cit., p. 238ff.
14 M.H. Darrow, *Revolution in the House: Family, Class and Inheritance in Southern France, 1775–1825*, Princeton, 1989.
15 Schraut, op. cit., p. 254.
16 L. Strumingher, 'The artisan family: traditions and transitions in nineteenth-century Lyon', *Journal of Family History*, 2 (1977), pp. 211–22.
17 N. Hancock, *An Innocent Grows Up*, 1947, p. 95.
18 For Germany, see H. Möller, *Die kleinbürgerliche Familie im 18. Jahrhundert. Verhalten und Gruppenkultur*, Berlin, 1969; H. Rosenbaum (ed.), *Seminar: Familie und Gesellschaftsstruktur*, Frankfurt, 1973. On social segregation, F. Lenger, *Zwischen Kleinbürgertum und Proletariat. Studien zur Sozialgeschichte der Düsseldorfer Handwerker 1816–1878*, Göttingen, 1986, p. 133.
19 P. de Rousiers, *The Labour Question in Britain*, 1896, p. 4.
20 G.C. Allen, *The Industrial Development of Birmingham and the Black Country 1860–1927*, 1966 edn, pp. 114–15; M. Lardière, 'Les faillites des ferblantiers à Lyon de 1850 à 1914', Mémoire de Maîtrise, University of Lyon 2, 1989, p. 42.
21 Schraut, op. cit., p. 253ff.
22 H. Mayhew, *London Labour and the London Poor*, 1861–2, vol. 3, p. 223; J.-C. Martin, 'Commerce et commerçants à Niort au XIXe siècle. Les faillites', *Bulletin de la Société Historique et Scientifique des Deux-Sèvres*, 13 (1980), p. 398.
23 Strumingher, op. cit., p. 213; Flora Tristan, *Le Tour de France: journal inédit 1843–44*, 1973 edn, p. 92.
24 Naples during the second half of the nineteenth century provides a rare exception. Although artisan businesses remained attached to the home, 61 per cent of retailers lived in a different neighbourhood from that of their business. This did not, however, stop family members playing an essential role in the enterprise. D. Cagliotti, 'Petites bourgeoisies napolitaines du XIXe siècle. Mobilités géographiques et sociales', *Bulletin du Centre Pierre Léon*, 1993, pp. 9–11.
25 D. Alexander, *Retailing in England during the Industrial Revolution*, 1970, p. 185; L. Davidoff and C. Hall, *Family Fortunes: Men and Women of the English Middle Class 1780–1850*, 1987, p. 231; H.J. Dyos, *Victorian Suburb: A Study of the Growth of Camberwell*, Leicester, 1961, p. 152.
26 Mrs D. Greig, *My Life and Times*, Bungay, 1940, pp. 16–19.
27 Quoted in J. Benson, *The Penny Capitalists*, Dublin, 1983, p. 121.
28 Martin, op. cit., p. 397.
29 Hancock, op. cit., p.23.
30 Mile End Vestry: Deed 5094. Tower Hamlets Library, London.
31 *Rapport fait au nom de la commission du commerce et de l'industrie chargé de procéder à une enquête sur la situation du commerce en France et, notamment, sur la condition actuelle du petit commerce*, Chambre des Députés (France), 10ème Législature, 1914, vol. 85, Impression no. 3432, p. 223.
32 C. Booth (ed.) *Life and Labour of the People in London*, 1896, vol. vii, 'Population Classified by Trades (Continued)', pp. 256–7.
33 C. Niermann, 'Die Bedeutung und sozialökonomische Lage. Bremer Klein-händlerinnen zwischen 1890 und 1914', in H.-G. Haupt (ed.), *Der Bremer Kleinhandel um 1900*, Bremen, 1983, p. 89.
34 S. D'Cruze, 'To acquaint the ladies: women traders in Colchester 1750–1800', *Local Historian*, 1986, pp. 158–61.
35 Niermann, op. cit., p. 93.
36 The justification was provided in the Census Report, *PP*, 1852–53, lxxxviii. Pt 1,

p. lxxxviii; J.D. Milne, *Industrial and Social Position of Women in the Middle and Lower Ranks*, 1857, p. 178.

37 Young has stressed the role of women in the business rather than the production side of artisanal enterprises in rural Scotland. C. Young, 'Women's work, family and the rural trades in nineteenth-century Scotland', *Review of Scottish Culture*, 7 (1991), pp. 54–6.

38 G.J. Sheridan, 'Family and enterprise in the silk shops of Lyon: the place of labor in the domestic weaving economy, 1840–1870', in *Research in Economic History*, Supplement 3 (1984), pp. 33–60.

39 D. Roche (ed.), *Journal de ma vie. Jacques-Louis Ménétra. Compagnon vitrier au 18e siècle*, 1982.

40 J.P. Burdy, M. Dubesset and M. Zancarini Fournel, 'Rôles, travaux et métiers de femmes dans une ville industrielle: Saint-Etienne 1900–1950', *le mouvement social*, 140 (1987) pp. 27–53.

41 J. Scott, 'Men and women in the Parisian garment trades: discussions of family and work in the 1830s and 1840s', in P. Thane, G. Crossick and R. Floud (eds), *The Power of the Past: Essays for Eric Hobsbawm*, Cambridge, 1984, pp. 70–1.

42 Select Committee on Sunday Trading. *PP* 1847, Q. 341–2.

43 This applied to half the butchers' shops in Lyon in both 1866 and 1906. M. Boyer, 'Les métiers de la viande à Lyon de 1860 à 1914', Thèse 3e Cycle, University of Lyon 2, 1985, p. 56.

44 D. Bertaux and I. Bertaux-Wiame, 'Artisanal bakery in France: how it lives and why it survives', in F. Bechhofer and B. Elliott (eds), *The Petite Bourgeoisie: Comparative Studies of the Uneasy Stratum*, 1981, pp. 155–81.

45 B. Angleraud, 'Les boulangers lyonnais aux XIXe-XXe siècles (1836 à 1914). Une étude sur la petite bourgeoisie boutiquière', Thèse de doctorat, University of Lyon 2, 1993, vol. 1, p. 148.

46 R. Barjavel, *La charrette bleu*, 1980, pp. 25–6.

47 A. Faure, 'The grocery trade in nineteenth-century Paris: a fragmented corporation', in *Crossick and Haupt*, p. 169.

48 Quoted in H.-G. Haupt (ed.), *Die radikale Mitte. Lebensweise und Politik von Handwerkern und Kleinhändlern in Deutschland seit 1848*, Munich, 1985, p. 89.

49 D. Cagliotti, 'Il guadagno difficile. Commercianti e artigiani napoletani nella seconda metà dell'800', PhD dissertation, EUI Florence, 1992, p. 113.

50 L. Edgren, 'Crafts in transformation? Masters, journeymen and apprentices in a Swedish town 1800–1850', *Continuity and Change*, 1 (1986), pp. 365–8.

51 D. Dessertine, *Divorcer à Lyon. Sous la Révolution et l'Empire*, Lyon, 1981, p. 276.

52 de Rousiers, op. cit., p. 35.

53 A. Daumard, *Les bourgeois de Paris au XIXe siècle*, 1970, p. 132.

54 See Geoffrey Crossick's forthcoming study of shopkeepers and photographs in turn of the century Britain and France.

55 F. Weber-Kellermann, *Die deutsche Familie*, Frankfurt, 1989, p. 82. See also J. Ehmer, *Familienstruktur und Arbeitsorganisation im frühindustriellen Wien*, Vienna, 1980, pp. 108–14.

56 Niermann, op. cit., p. 100 ff.

57 For the example of Naples, see Cagliotti, 'Il guadagno difficile', op. cit., p. 109.

58 Davidoff and Hall, op. cit., pp. 198–228.

59 Will of Thomas Carr, Old Kent Road. Proved 1876. General Register Office, Somerset House, London.

60 Milne, op. cit., p. 17.

61 Davidoff and Hall, op. cit., p. 286.

62 T.K. Hareven, 'The house and the family in historical perspective', in *Social Research*, 58 (1991), pp. 253–8.

63 T. Vigne and A. Howkins, 'The small shopkeeper in industrial and market towns', in G. Crossick, (ed.) *The Lower Middle Class in Britain 1870–1914*, 1976, pp. 197–206.

64 A. Muscetta, *Memorie di un commerciante*, Avellino, 1984, p. 59; M. Serao, *Il paese di cuccagno* (1890), Milan, 1981, p. 259. There was the same concern for bourgeois domesticity amongst later nineteenth-century German artisans: see the passage from *Meister Theodor*, published originally in *Deutscher Handwerks-kalender aus dem Jahr 1883*, Osnabruck, 1883, pp. 70–4.

65 G.J. Sheridan Jr, 'Household and craft in an industrializing economy: the case of the silk weavers of Lyons', in J.M. Merriman (ed.), *Consciousness and Class Experience in Nineteenth-Century Europe*, 1979, pp. 111–12; C. Charmettant, 'La petite industrie à Lyon', *la Réforme sociale*, III (1882), pp. 78–83.

66 Volkov, op. cit., pp. 73–4.

67 A.L. Rowse, *A Cornish Childhood*, 1942, p. 83.

68 Roche, op. cit., p. 303.

69 See Mile End Vestry, Harford Street Improvement Papers 1888, in Tower Hamlets Library, London.

70 de Rousiers, op. cit., p. 20.

71 *Statistik des Deutschen Reichs* 213, p.39ff.

72 Select Committee on Shop Hours Regulation Bill, *PP* 1886, xii, Q.1692–7.

73 M. Garden, 'Deux siècles de malthusianisme à la française', in Y. Lequin (ed.), *Histoire des français. XIXe–XXe siècles*, 1984, vol. 1, p. 191.

74 M. Garden, 'Lyon et les lyonnais au XVIIIe siècle', Thèse d'Etat, University of Lyon, 1969, pp. 167–70, 236–40. A high use of wet-nurses among the small *patronat* of eighteenth-century Paris has been observed in D. Roche, *The People of Paris: An Essay in Popular Culture in the 18th Century*, Leamington Spa, 1987, p. 240.

75 M. Livi-Bacci, 'Social-group forerunners of fertility control in Europe', in A.J. Coale and S.C. Watkins (eds), *The Decline of Fertility in Europe*, Princeton, 1986, pp. 196–8.

76 Garden, 'Lyon et les lyonnais', op. cit., pp. 169–70.

77 For some of the methodological and source problems involved in linking demographic behaviour to the characteristics of individuals, see M.S. Teitelbaum, *The British Fertility Decline: Demographic Transition in the Crucible of the Industrial Revolution*, Princeton, 1984, pp. 6–10; for an international study of mining and heavy industrial occupations and fertility, see M. Haines, *Fertility and Occupation: Population Patterns in Industrialisation*, 1979.

78 For recent discussion of these issues, see J.R. Gillis, L.A. Tilly and D. Levine (eds), *The European Experience of Declining Fertility 1850–1970: The Quiet Revolution*, Oxford, 1992.

79 For a contemporary judgement that the *classes moyennes* led the way in low natality, see H. Morel-Journel, 'Le réveil des classes moyennes en France', in La Société d'économie politique et d'économie sociale de Lyon, *Compte rendu analytique des séances de l'année 1910–1911*, Lyon, 1911, p. 77.

80 Garden, 'Deux siècles', p. 213.

81 E. Accampo, *Industrialisation, Family Life and Class Relations: Saint-Chamond 1815–1914*, Berkeley, 1989, pp. 57–8, 121.

82 Schraut, op. cit., p. 250.

83 R. Spree, 'The German petite bourgeoisie and the decline of fertility: some statistical evidence from the late 19th and early 20th centuries', unpublished paper to *3rd Round Table*, Paris, 1981; similar suggestions for the early twentieth century

can be found in J.E. Knodel, *The Decline of Fertility in Germany 1871–1939*, Princeton, 1974, pp. 119–25.
84 R.I. Woods, 'Approaches to the fertility transition in Victorian England', *Population Studies*, 41 (1987), pp. 289–90.
85 J.W. Innes, *Class Fertility Trends in England and Wales 1876–1934*, Princeton, 1938, pp. 42–3.
86 C.W. Smith, 'Class and the decline of fertility in nineteenth-century England', PhD thesis, University of Sheffield, 1982, esp. pp. 375–6, 392–402, 498–9. See also R. Woods and C.W. Smith, 'The decline of marital fertility in the late nineteenth century: the case of England and Wales', *Population Studies*, 37 (1983), pp. 216–25.
87 Ehmer, op. cit., p. 207.
88 S. Nenadic, 'The structure, values and influence of the Scottish urban middle class: Glasgow 1800 to 1870', PhD thesis, University of Glasgow, 1986, p.82.
89 L. Niethammer and F. Brüggemeier, 'Wie wohnten die Arbeiter im Kaiserreich', in *Archiv für Sozialgeschichte*, 16 (1975) pp. 61–134; J. Ehmer, 'Wohnen ohne eigene Wohnung. Zur sozialen Stellung von Untermietern und Bettgehern', in L. Niethammer (ed.), *Wohnen im Wandel*, Wuppertal, 1979, pp. 132–50.
90 Lunander, op. cit., p. 147.
91 R. Schaub, 'Familienformen in Oldenburg', in W. Conze (ed.), *Sozialgeschichte der Familie in der Neuzeit Europas*, Stuttgart, 1976; H. Schiekel, 'Zur Sozialstruktur der Stadt Oldenburg um 1900', in *Oldenberg um 1900. Beiträge zur wirtschaftlichen, sozialen und kulturellen Situation des Herzogtums Oldenburg im Übergang zum industriellen Zeitalter*, Oldenburg, 1975, pp. 205–20.
92 Volkov, op. cit., pp. 110–11. This can be seen from the middle of the century in Nurenberg: M.J. Neufeld, *The Skilled Metalworkers of Nurenberg: Craft and Class in the Industrial Revolution*, New Brunswick, 1989, pp. 40–1.
93 Lunander, op. cit., pp. 155–7.
94 J.W. Boyer, *Political Radicalism in Late Imperial Vienna: Origins of the Christian Social Movement 1848–1897*, Chicago, 1981, p. 110.
95 E. Knox, 'Between capital and labour: The petite bourgeoisie in Victorian Edinburgh', PhD thesis, University of Edinburgh, 1986, pp. 462–3.
96 Boyer, 'Métiers de viande', op. cit., pp. 56–7.
97 Booth Collection B133 ff. 16, 20–1 (Library of Political and Economic Science, London).
98 C. Niermann, A. Saur, P. Schöttler, and E. Sinner, 'Petit commerce et apprentissage à Brême au début du XXe siècle', *le mouvement social*, 108 (1979), pp. 136–7.
99 M. Anderson, 'The social implications of demographic change', in F.M.L. Thompson (ed.), *The Cambridge Social History of Britain 1750–1950*, Cambridge, 1990, vol. 2, p. 64; E. Higgs, *Domestic Servants and Households in Rochdale 1851–1871*, New York, 1986, pp. 124–6.
100 Schaub, op. cit.
101 Higgs, op. cit.
102 Boyer, 'Métiers de viande', op. cit., pp. 296–7.
103 Quoted in M. Winstanley, *The Shopkeeper's World 1830–1914*, p. 147.
104 Select Committee on Sunday Trading in the Metropolis, *PP* 1847, ix, Q.2364.
105 Higgs, op. cit., p. 101.
106 Nenadic, op. cit., pp. 101–4.
107 See for example A. Janssens, 'Industrialisation without family change? The extended family and the life cycle in a Dutch industrial town 1880–1920', *Journal of Family History* 11 (1986), pp. 25–42.
108 Anderson, op. cit., p. 61.
109 A.-M. Morier, 'Structures familiales des commerçants de Givors (1851–1914)', Mémoire de Maîtrise, University of Lyon 2, 1977–78, p. 29.

110 Nenadic, op. cit., p. 82.
111 Segalen, op. cit., p. 69.
112 On urban households changing over the life cycle, see D.S. Reher, 'Old issues and new perspectives: household and family within an urban context in 19th-century Spain', *Continuity and Change*, 2 (1987), pp. 103–43.
113 A. Janssens, *Family and Social Change: The Household as a Process in an Industrializing Community*, Cambridge, 1993, pp. 123–4, 156. See also for Givors, Morier, op. cit., p. 49.
114 A. Delor, 'La corporation des bouchers de Limoges', *la Réforme sociale*, X (1885), pp. 454–9; J.M. Merriman 'Incident at the statue of the Virgin Mary. The conflict of old and new in nineteenth-century Limoges', in J.M. Merriman (ed.), *Consciousness and Class Experience*, op. cit., pp. 129–48.
115 A.N. Morgan, *David Morgan 1833–1919: The Life and Times of a Master Draper in South Wales*, Risca, 1977, p. 58.
116 J.-C. Martin, 'Le commerçant, la faillite et l'historien', *Annales E.S.C.*, 35 (1980), p. 1262.
117 F. Raison-Jourde, *La colonie auvergnate de Paris au XIXe siècle*, 1976, p. 140.
118 N. Hancock, *An Innocent Grows Up*, 1947, p. 79.
119 Barjavel, op. cit., p. 13.
120 See for example the considerable number of shopkeepers and artisans amongst the amateur photographers gathered in *Mémoire de l'Oubli. La photographie populaire en Charente 1880–1920*, Musée Municipal d'Angoulême, 1983.
121 Hancock, op. cit., p. 176.
122 Raison-Jourde, op. cit., p. 360.
123 H. Corke, *In Our Infancy: An Autobiography, Part 1 1882–1912*, 1975, pp. 38, 44–5.
124 P. Thompson, *The Edwardians*, 1977, pp. 125–6.
125 D. Blackbourn, 'Between resignation and volatility: the German petite bourgeoisie in the nineteenth century', in *Crossick and Haupt*, p. 49; A. Leppert-Fögen, *Die deklassierte Klasse. Studien zur Geschichte und Ideologie des Kleinbürgertums*, Frankfurt, 1974, Ch. 3.
126 H. Vouters, *Le petit commerce contre les grands magasins et les coopératives de consommation*, 1910, p. 28.
127 R. Becker, 'La cordonnerie à Louvain', Commission Nationale de la Petite Bourgeoisie, *Enquêtes Ecrites, Monographies*, vol. 1 (1904), p. 284–6.
128 'Hego' (Hector Lambrechts), 'Pour les dames', *La Métropole*, 15 June 1901.
129 Et. Martin Saint-Léon, *Le petit commerce français. Sa lutte pour la Vie*, 1911, pp. 97–8.
130 G. Levy, 'Les conditions de travail des employés', *Le mouvement socialiste*, sept-oct 1911, p. 188.
131 See for example F. Le Play, *Les ouvriers européens*, 1855, pp. 258–9.
132 Volkov, op. cit., p. 110.
133 M.B. Miller, *The Bon Marché: Bourgeois Culture and the Department Store 1869–1920*, Princeton, 1981, pp. 209–11.
134 *L'Alliance*, November 1902.
135 *Premier Congrès International du Travail au Domicile*, Louvain, 1911, cited by A. Beltran, 'Du luxe au cœur du système. Electricité et société dans la région parisienne (1880–1939)', *Annales E.S.C.*, 1989, p. 1117.

6 THE PETITE BOURGEOISIE AND THE TOWN

1 G. Duplat, 'L'action communale et les classes moyennes', *Revue sociale catholique*, 17 (1912–13), p. 265.

2   E. Vierhaus (ed.) *Bürger und Bürgerlichkeit im Zeichen der Aufklärung*, Heidelberg, 1981; B. Roeck, *Lebenswelt und Kultur des Bürgertums in der frühen Neuzeit*, Munich, 1991.

3   C. Poni, 'Norms and disputes: the Shoemakers' Guild in eighteenth-century Bologna', *Past and Present*, 123 (1989), p. 84ff.

4   F. Braudel, *Les structures du quotidien. Civilisation matérielle, économie et capitalisme*, 1979, p. 421.

5   G. Duplat, *La classe moyenne. Son rôle social. Son action politique. Sa situation économique. Les réformes urgentes*, Brussels, 1914, p. 47.

6   F. Engels in *Marx/Engels Werke*, Berlin, 1957–68, vol. 4, p. 45.

7   M. Walker, *German Home Towns: Community, State and General Estate 1648–1871*, Ithaca, 1971; W. Te Brake, *Regents and Rebels: The Revolutionary World of an Eighteenth-Century Dutch City*, Oxford, 1989.

8   G. Dupeux, *Aspects de l'histoire sociale et politique du Loir-et-Cher 1848–1914*, 1962, pp. 131–3. Artisans and shopkeepers were community leaders in the small towns and villages in the rural Var in the early nineteenth century: M. Agulhon, *La vie sociale en Provence intérieure au lendemain de la Révolution*, 1970, pp. 303–4.

9   See G. Jacquemet, *Belleville au XIXe. Du faubourg à la ville*, 1984, p. 94; E. Accampo, *Industrialization, Family Life, and Class Relations: Saint Chamond 1815–1914*, Berkeley, 1989; H. Kaiser, *Handwerk und Kleinstadt. Das Beispiel Theine/Westf.*, Munster, 1979, p. 55.

10 D. Garrioch, *Neighbourhood and Community in Paris 1740–1790*, Cambridge, 1986.

11 Historians are faced with the paradox of substantial geographical and residential instability of workers alongside real social and occupational identities. The role of institutions – whether of the neighbourhood, workgroup, or others – in providing modes of incorporation and identity for at least some of the mobile population is one means by which this apparent paradox can be resolved. See the approach of C. Stephenson, 'A gathering of strangers? Mobility, social structure, and political participation in the formation of nineteenth-century American working-class culture', in M. Cantor (ed.), *American Working-Class Culture: Explorations in American Labor and Social History*, Westport, 1979, pp. 31–60.

12 For general approaches to the urban neighbourhood, see C. Lis and H. Soly, 'Neighbourhood social change in western European cities. Sixteenth to Nineteenth Centuries', *International Review of Social History*, 38 (1993), pp. 1–30; the special issue of *le mouvement social*, 118 (1982) edited by Y. Lequin on 'Ouvriers dans la ville'; S. Bleeck, *Quartierbildung in der Urbanisierung. Das Münchener Westend 1890–1933*, Munich, 1991.

13 D Saalfeld, 'Gottinger Miet- und Sozialverhaltnisse im zweiten Drittel des 19. Jahrhunderts', in H. Matzerath (ed.), *Stadtewachstum und innerstadtische Strukturveranderungen*, Stuttgart, 1984, p. 144.

14 J. Morris, *The Political Economy of Shopkeeping in Milan 1886–1922*, Cambridge, 1993, pp. 64- 88.

15 In Lyon, from the late nineteenth century, they had the lowest index of segregation of any of the occupational groups: J.-L. Pinol, *Les mobilités de la grande ville. Lyon fin XIXe – début XXe*, 1991, p. 163.

16 C.F.G. Masterman, 'The problem of South London', in R. Mudie-Smith, (ed.), *The Religious Life of London*, 1904, p. 192.

17 T. Vigne and A. Howkins, 'The small shopkeeper in industrial and market towns', in G. Crossick (ed.), *The Lower Middle Class in Britain 1870–1914*, 1977, p. 190–1; R. Roberts, *The Classic Slum: Salford Life in the First Quarter of the Century*, Harmondsworth, 1973, pp. 17–18.

18 J. Behnken *et al.*, *Stadtgeschichte als Kindheitsgeschichte*, Opladen, 1989.

19 E. Accampo, 'Entre la classe sociale et la cité: identité et intégration chez les ouvriers de Saint-Chamond, 1815–1880', *le mouvement social*, 118 (1982), p. 52.

20 Quoted in P. Thompson, *The Edwardians*, 1977 edn, pp. 125–8.

21 H.J. Schwippe and C. Zeidler, 'Die Dimension der raumlichen Differenzierung in Berlin und Hamburg im Industrialisierungsprozeß des 19. Jahrhunderts', in Matzerath, op. cit., p. 225.

22 Jalla took the words quoted from Procacci. D. Jalla, 'Le quartier comme territoire et comme représentation: les "barrières" ouvrières de Turin au début du Xxe siècle', *le mouvement social*, 118 (1982), pp. 94–5.

23 A. Burguière, *Bretons de Plozévet*, 1977, esp. pp. 146ff.; F. Gresswell, *Bright Boots*, 1956, p. 102 for the shoemaker's shop in a Lincolnshire village; D. Buchan, 'The expressive culture of nineteenth-century Scottish farm servants', in T.M. Devine (ed.), *Farm Servants and Labour in Lowland Scotland 1770–1914*, Edinburgh, 1984, p. 228.

24 Roberts, op. cit., p. 25. Edwin Pugh's short story, 'A Small Talk Exchange', in his *A Street in Suburbia*, 1895, pp. 79–89 describe the endless conversation in just such a a general provisions shop.

25 P. Ayçoberry, 'Histoire sociale de la ville de Cologne (1815–1875)', Thèse d'Etat, University of Paris 1, 1977, 2 vols, p. 330.

26 B. Angleraud, 'Les boulangers lyonnais aux XIXe – XXe siècles (1836 à 1914). Une étude sur la petite bourgeoisie boutiquière', Thèse de doctorat, University of Lyon 2, 1993, vol. 1, pp. 289–90; H. Béraud, *La Gerbe d'Or*, 1928, p. 86.

27 N. Griffith, *Shop Book: Brighton 1900–30*, Brighton, n.d., p. 66.

28 The historical contrast between café and pub warrants further attention. M. Crubellier and M. Agulhon, 'Les citadins et leurs cultures', in G. Duby (ed.), *Histoire de la France urbaine*, vol. 4 'La ville de l'âge industriel', 1983, pp. 436–40. On the role of *Kneipen* in the working-class districts of Hamburg, see R.J. Evans (ed.), *Kneipengespräche im Kaiserreich. Stimmungsberichte der Hamburger Politischen Polizei 1892–1914*, Hamburg, 1989, p. 21 ff.

29 E.J. Hobsbawm and J.W. Scott, 'Political shoemakers', *Past and Present*, 89 (1980), pp. 104–5; A. Foley, *A Bolton Childhood*, Manchester, 1973, p. 19.

30 Quoted in T.W. Margadant, *French Peasants in Revolt: The Insurrection of 1851*, Princeton, 1979, p. 174.

31 Burguière, op. cit., pp. 148–9.

32 See M. Miller, *The Bon Marché: Bourgeois Culture and the Department Store, 1869–1920*, Princeton, 1981.

33 A. Sherwell, *Life in West London: A Study and a Contrast*, 1901, p. 126. For a fine fictional picture of the pub as the base for illicit betting, see George Moore, *Esther Waters*, 1894.

34 M. Agulhon, *Le cercle dans la France bourgeoise 1810–1848*, 1977, pp. 39–40, 55–6; Crubellier and Agulhon, op. cit., pp. 437–8.

35 On the latter, see for example T. Owen, *Personal Reminiscences of Oswestry Fifty Years Ago*, Oswestry, 1904, pp. 30, 58, 72.

36 C. Hosgood, 'The "Pigmies of Commerce" and the working-class community: small shopkeepers in England, 1870–1914', *Journal of Social History*, 33 (1989), pp. 447–8.

37 J.-P. Burdy, *Le Soleil noir. Un quartier de Saint-Etienne 1840–1940*, Lyon, 1989, pp. 155–76; E. Ross, 'Survival networks: women's neighbourhood sharing in London before World War 1', *History Workshop Journal*, 15 (1983), pp. 4–27.

38 J. Paton, *Proletarian Pilgrimage: An Autobiography*, 1935, p. 92; F. Zonabend, *La mémoire longue. Temps et histoires au village*, 1980, p. 278; Pinol, op. cit., p. 95.

39 Garrioch, op. cit., p. 28.

40 Foley, op. cit., passim.

41 F. Lenger, *Zwischen Kleinbürgertum und Proletariat. Studien zur Sozialgeschichte der Düsseldorfer Handwerker 1816–1878*, Göttingen, 1986, pp. 133–49.

42 A. Faure, 'Les racines de la mobilité populaire à Paris au XIXe siècle', in O. Benoit-Guilbot (ed.), *Changer de région, de métier, changer de quartier. Recherches en région parisienne*, 1982, pp. 112–13, 119; Pinol, op. cit., p. 224; M. Boyer, 'Les métiers de la viande à Lyon de 1860 à 1914. Une étude sur la petite bourgeoisie', Thèse de 3e cycle, University of Lyon 2, 1985, pp. 178–83.

43 Jalla, op. cit., p. 84.

44 Particularly useful for these developments are M. Savage, *The Dynamics of Working-Class Politics: The Labour Movement in Preston, 1880–1940*, Cambridge, 1987, and M. Rebérioux, 'Les socialistes français et le petit commerce au tournant du siècle', *le mouvement social*, 114 (1981), pp. 57–70.

45 Morris, op. cit., pp. 215–16.

46 Burdy, op. cit., especially chs 7 and 8, pp. 177–232.

47 Savage, op. cit., pp. 101–33.

48 P. van den Eeckhout, 'Brussels', in M. Daunton (ed.), *Housing the Workers, 1850–1914: A Comparative Perspective*, Leicester, 1990, pp. 78–9.

49 P. Ayçoberry, 'Au-delà des remparts: "vrais Colonais" et banlieusards au milieu du XIXe siècle', *le mouvement social*, 118 (1982), p. 31.

50 N. Bullock, 'Berlin', in Daunton, *Housing the Workers*, op. cit., p. 203.

51 K. Bücher, 'Eigentumsverhältnisse der Leipziger Handwerker', in Schriften des Vereins für Socialpolitik 67, *Untersuchungen über die Lage des Handwerks*, vol. 6, Leipzig, 1897, pp. 699–705.

52 P. Deyon, 'Roubaix dans la première moitié du XIXe siècle', in M. Garden and Y. Lequin (eds), *Construire la Ville XVIIIe – XXe siècles*, Lyon, 1983, pp. 117–29.

53 F. Bourillon, 'Etude de la sociabilité dans un milieu pré et post-Haussmannien. Le quartier des Arts et Métiers à Paris entre 1850 et 1880', Thèse de troisième cycle, University of Paris X – Nanterre, 1985, p. 582.

54 A. Daumard, *Maisons de Paris et propriétaires parisiens au XIXe siècle*, 1965, pp. 237–42; J. Gaillard, *Paris, la Ville (1852–1870)*, Lille, 1976, pp. 37–8.

55 Royal Commission on the Poor Laws, *PP*, 1834, xxxvi, Appendix B2, pp. 26, 68. For London cases see ibid., pp. 87, 95, 98.

56 Ibid., p. 246.

57 Select Committee on Town Holdings, *PP*, 1886, xii, Q. 7875, 7905–6.

58 H. Griffin, 'Weekly property as an investment', in The Surveyors' Institution, *Transactions*, xxvi (1893–94), pp. 331–76.

59 See for example T. Hinchcliffe, *North Oxford*, 1992, p. 51. On the small-scale character of the housebuilding industry in London, see H.J. Dyos, 'The speculative builders and developers of Victorian London', *Victorian Studies*, 11 (1968), pp. 641–90, and G. Crossick, *An Artisan Elite in Victorian Society: Kentish London 1840–1880*, 1978, pp. 55–8; in Berlin and Vienna, see Daunton, *Housing the Workers*, op. cit., pp. 81 and 119.

60 D.J. Olsen, 'House upon House', in H.J. Dyos and M. Wolff (eds), *The Victorian City: Images and Reality*, 1973, vol. 1, p. 335.

61 N. Bullock and J. Read, *The Movement for Housing Reform in Germany and France 1840–1914*, Cambridge, 1985, pp. 299–300.

62 R.J. Evans, *Death in Hamburg: Society and Politics in the Cholera Years 1830–1910*, Harmondsworth, 1990, pp. 42–3; B. Ladd, *Urban Planning and Civic Order in Germany, 1860–1914*, 1990, p. 158; R. Banik-Schweitzer, 'Vienna', in Daunton, *Housing the Workers*, op. cit., p. 137.

63 T.C. Barker and J.R. Harris, *A Merseyside Town in the Industrial Revolution: St Helens 1750–1900*, 1959, pp. 290–1.

64 D. Englander, *Landlord and Tenant in Urban Britain 1838–1918*, Oxford, 1983, pp. 51–81.

65 See ibid., especially p. 75ff; D. McCrone and B. Elliott, 'The decline of landlordism: property rights and relationships in Edinburgh', in R. Rodger (ed.), *Scottish Housing in the Twentieth Century*, Leicester, 1989, pp. 223–8. In German towns, house-ownership increasingly became a burden as the state sought increased finance from proprietors during the inter-war period, and it was an increasingly significant source of conflict from 1929: H.-G. Haupt, 'Mittelstand und Kleinbürgertum in der Weimarer Republik. Zu Problemen und Perspektiven ihrer Erforschung', in *Archiv für Sozialgeschichte*, 26 (1986), pp. 217–38.

66 O. Pyfferoen, 'La petite bourgeoisie d'après une enquête officielle à Gand (1)', *La Réforme sociale*, xxxvii (1899), p. 292.

67 The words, in a critique of what he sees as an idealisation in Mack Walker's book, are those of Et. François, in M. Garden and Y. Lequin (eds), *Habiter la Ville. XVe – XXe*, Lyon, 1984, p. 39.

68 See the summary in J.J. Sheehan, *German History 1770–1866*, Oxford, 1989, pp. 487–500. For the diversity of local situations, see H. Naunin (ed.), *Städteordnungen des 19. Jahrhunderts. Beiträge zur Kommunalgeschichte Mittel- und Westeuropas*, Cologne, 1984.

69 J.J. Sheehan, *German Liberalism in the Nineteenth Century*, Chicago, 1978, p. 22. See also L. Gall, '". . . ich wünschte ein Bürger zu sein". Zum Selbstverständnis des deutschen Bürgertums im 19. Jahrhundert', *Historische Zeitschrift*, 245 (1987), pp. 601–23; L. Gall (ed.), *Stadt und Bürgertum im 19. Jahrhundert*, Munich, 1990.

70 P. Marschalk, 'Der Erwerb des bremischen Bürgerrechts und die Zuwanderung nach Bremen um die Mitte des 19. Jahrhundert', *Bremisches Jahrbuch*, 66 (1988), p. 295ff.; B. Ladd, *Urban Planning and Civic Order in Germany, 1860–1914*, 1990, pp. 15–17; W. Hoffmann, *Die Bielefelder Stadtverordneten. Ein Beitrag zu bürgerlicher Selbstverwaltung und sozialem Wandeln 1850–1914*, Lübeck/Hamburg, 1964; W.R. Krabbe, *Die deutsche Stadt im 19. und 20. Jahrhundert*, Göttingen, c. 1989, pp. 54–68.

71 A. Corbin, *Archaïsme et modernité en Limousin au XIXe siècle (1845–1880)*, 1975, pp. 804–7; A. Daumard, *Les bourgeois de Paris au XIXe siècle*, 1970, pp. 285–6.

72 For a sketch of French municipal government and elections, see J.-L. Pinol, 'L'exercise du pouvoir', in Y. Lequin (ed.), *Histoire des Français. XIXe – XXe siècles*, vol. 3, 'Les citoyens et la démocratie', 1984, pp. 75–92.

73 On the vestries see J. Davis, *Reforming London: The London Government Problem 1855–1900*, Oxford, 1988, pp. 22–3; E. Marino, 'Small traders and the vestries in nineteenth-century London', MA dissertation, University of Essex, 1993.

74 H.E. Meller, *Leisure and the Changing City, 1870–1914*, 1976, p. 87.

75 R. Newton, 'Society and politics in Exeter, 1837–1914', in H.J. Dyos (ed.), *The Pursuit of Urban History*, 1968, pp. 310–11.

76 Select Committee on Small Tenements Acts, *PP*, 1859.2, vii, Q. 138–9; G.W. Jones, *Borough Politics: A Study of the Wolverhampton Town Council, 1888–1964*, 1969, pp. 121ff.

77 Angleraud, op. cit., pp. 74–90; Y. Le Brun, 'La liberté de la boulangerie à Rennes sous le IIe Empire', *Annales de Brétagne*, 1987, pp. 167–84, 303–24.

78 Morris, op. cit., pp. 114–16.

79 *Small Trader and Shopkeeper*, January 1915.

80 B. Elliott, D. McCrone and V. Skelton, 'Property and political power: Edinburgh 1875–1975', in J. Garrard (ed.), *The Middle Class in Politics*, Farnborough, n.d. (*c.* 1978), p. 107.

81 Jones, op. cit., p. 131; Ladd, op. cit., pp. 163–4; Banik-Schweitzer, op. cit., p. 137.

82 Evans, op. cit., pp. 99–100. See also D. Crew, *Town in the Ruhr: A Social History of Bochum, 1860–1914*, New York, 1979, pp. 119–23.

83 Return of Poor Law Guardians, Metropolis, *PP*, 1871, lix, p. 465 ff.

84 On the importance of rates, see E.P. Hennock, 'Finance and politics in urban local government in England, 1835–1900', *Historical Journal*, vi (1963), pp. 212–25; A. Offer, *Property and Politics 1870–1914: Landownership, Law, Ideology and Urban Development in England*, Cambridge, 1981, pp. 288–9.

85 J. Garrard, *Leaders and Politics in Nineteenth-Century Salford: A Historical Analysis of Urban Political Power*, Salford, n.d., pp. 64–5.

86 Select Committee on Small Tenements Act, op. cit., Q. 1098.

87 On Birmingham see E.P. Hennock, *Fit and Proper Persons: Ideal and Reality in Nineteenth-century Local Government*, 1973. On other towns, Elliott, McCrone and Skelton, op. cit., p. 107; M.J. Daunton, *Coal Metropolis: Cardiff 1870–1914*, Leicester, 1977, pp. 114–23; Garrard, *Leaders and Politics*, op. cit., p. 36. The trend towards a greater petit-bourgeois role in municipal affairs was not uniform. Hosgood found a decline in shopkeeper presence on Leicester town council by the later nineteenth century, as the extension of the town's boundaries shifted the focus of power to the suburbs, in whose politics they had little involvement, C. Hosgood, 'Shopkeepers and society: domestic and principal shopkeepers in Leicester, 1860–1914', PhD thesis, University of Manitoba, 1987, pp. 334–44.

88 Ladd, op. cit., p. 31.

89 On this point see Daunton, *Coal Metropolis*, op. cit., p.150.

90 N. Hancock, *An Innocent Grows Up*, 1947, pp. 17–19.

7 POLITICS: THE WORLD OF THE PEOPLE AND THE MOVE TO THE RIGHT

1 A sophisticated version of this orthodoxy is H.A. Winkler, *Mittelstand, Demokratie und Nationalsozialismus. Die politische Entwicklung von Handwerk und Kleinhandel in der Weimarer Republik*, Cologne/Berlin, 1972; H.A. Winkler, 'From social protectionism to National Socialism: the German small-business movement in comparative perspective', *Journal of Modern History*, 48 (1976), pp. 1–18; R. Gellately, *The Politics of Economic Despair: Shopkeepers and German Politics 1890–1914*, 1974; S. Volkov, *The Rise of Popular Antimodernism in Germany: The Urban Master Artisans 1873–1896*, Princeton, 1978.

2 See the Conclusion (Chapter Ten) for some consideration of this theme, and an important recent collection of essays: R. Koshar (ed.), *Splintered Classes: Politics and the Lower Middle Classes in Interwar Europe*, New York, 1990.

3 On the populism of petit-bourgeois movements, see P. Nord, 'Les mouvements de petits propriétaires et la politique (des années 1880 à la première guerre mondiale)', *Revue historique*, 558 (1986), pp. 407–33.

4 D. Blackbourn, *Class, Religion and Local Politics in Wilhelmine Germany: The Centre Party in Württemberg before 1914*, New Haven, 1980; G. Eley, *Reshaping the German Right: Radical Nationalism and Political Change after Bismarck*, New Haven, 1980; F. Lenger, *Sozialgeschichte der deutschen Handwerker seit 1800*, Frankfurt, 1988.

5 H. Lambrechts, *Trente années au service des Classes Moyennes*, Dison, 1931, p. 316.

6 W. Conze, 'Mittelstand', in O. Brunner, W. Conze and R. Koselleck (eds), *Geschichtliche Grundbegriffe*, Stuttgart, 1978, vol. 4, p. 84.

7 J. Dubois, *Le vocabulaire politique et social en France de 1869 à 1872*, 1962, p. 14ff.

8 *Les études fiscales et sociales*, April 1910, p. 10.

9 *Bulletin de l'Institut International pour l'Étude du Problème des Classes Moyennes*, June 1906, pp. 4–5.

10 H. Lambrechts, *Le problème social de la petite bourgeoisie envisagé au point de vue belge*, Brussels, 1902, pp. vii–viii.

11 G. Kurgan-van Hentenryk, 'A la recherche de la petite bourgeoisie: l'Enquête orale de 1902–1904', *Revue belge d'histoire contemporaine*, 14 (1983), pp. 294–8; S. Jaumain, 'Les petits commerçants belges face à la modernité (1880–1914)', Thèse de doctorat, Université Libre de Bruxelles, 1991, p. 68ff.

12 G. Crossick, 'From gentlemen to the residuum: languages of social description in Victorian Britain', in P. Corfield (ed.), *Language, History and Class*, 1990, pp. 173–4. See Sydney's speech to the Association de Défense des Classes Moyennes, in *Les études fiscales et sociales. Troisième congrès annuel (nov. 1910)*, Limoges, 1911, pp. 117–19.

13 See Crossick, 'Gentlemen to the Residuum', op. cit.

14 Quoted in Conze, op. cit., p. 62.

15 D. Wahrman, 'Virtual representation: parliamentary reporting and languages of class in the 1790s', *Past and Present*, 136 (1992), pp. 83–113; V.E. Starzinger, *Middlingness: Juste Milieu Political Theory in France and England, 1815–1848*, Charlottesville, 1965; K.-P. Sick, 'Le concept de classes moyennes. Notion sociologique ou slogan politique?', *Vingtième siècle*, 37 (1993), pp. 16–18.

16 This was not surprising, given the neo-Thomist revival in Social Catholic thought. The classic statement in Aristotle's own writings is in *The Politics*, Book 4, Chapter 11.

17 Staatsarchiv Bremen 4,75/7 – VR 235.

18 C. Hosgood, 'A "Brave and Daring Folk"? Shopkeepers and trade associational life in Victorian and Edwardian England', *Journal of Social History*, 36 (1992), pp. 291–2. For France, see J.M. Gourden, 'Les petits métiers parisiens et leurs fonctions au XIXème siècle. L'exemple des marchands de quatre saisons', Thèse de 3ème cycle, University of Paris VII, 1983, pp. 335–8.

19 See H.-G. Haupt, 'The petite bourgeoisie in France, 1850–1914: in search of the *juste milieu*?', in *Crossick and Haupt*, pp. 108–9; P. Nord, 'The small shopkeepers' movement and politics in France, 1888–1914', in ibid., pp. 175–94.

20 A. Faure, 'Note sur la petite entreprise en France au XIXe siècle. Représentations d'Etat et réalités', in *Entreprises et entrepreneurs en France au XIXe-XXe siècles. Congrès de l'Association française des Historiens Economistes Mars 1980*, 1983, p. 205.

21 For a summary of shopkeeper demands for *patente* reform in the early twentieth century, see Et. Martin Saint-Léon, *Le petit commerce français. Sa lutte pour la vie*, 1911, pp. 119–31.

22 J. Morris, *The Political Economy of Shopkeeping in Milan 1886–1922*, Cambridge, 1993. See R. Laurent, *L'octroi de Dijon au XIXe siècle*, 1960, for parallel taxation systems with less striking political consequences.

23 H.W. Hahn, 'Zunftproteste gegen den modernen Steuerstaat. Die Wetzlar Auseinandersetzungen um die preußische Mahl- und Schlachtsteuer 1820–1840', *Nassauische Annalen*, 98 (1987), pp. 173–98.

24 *L'Alliance*, January 1901.

25 *AN* C 7460.

26 Jaumain, op. cit., pp. 234–6.

27 For evidence of their place in one small borough before the 1867 Reform Act, see C.E. Brent, 'The immediate impact of the Second Reform Act on a southern county town: voting patterns in Lewes Borough in 1865 and 1868', *Southern History*, 2 (1980), p.146.

28 P. Vigier, *La monarchie de Juillet*, 1962, p. 77ff.

29 J. Reulecke, *Geschichte der Urbanisierung in Deutschland*, Frankfurt, 1985, p. 133.

30 H. Kaiser, *Handwerk und Kleinstadt. Das Beispiel Rheine/Westfalen*, Münster, 1978, p. 106ff.

31 S. Hoffmann, *Le mouvement Poujade*, 1956, pp. 387–402.

32 J.J. Boddewyn, *Belgian Public Policy towards Retailing since 1789: The Socio-Politics of Distribution*, East Lansing, 1971, p. 23.

33 Not only in Germany. See the protests in Lyon at the way in which the Chambre de Commerce was dominated by notables to the exclusion of the mass of small business. *La tribune lyonnaise*, 9 December 1882. For later French demands, Martin Saint-Léon, op. cit., p. 163ff. and J. Bernard, 'Du mouvement d'organisation et de défense du petit commerce français', Thèse de Droit, University of Paris, 1906, pp. 181–2.

34 Gellately, op. cit., pp. 97–108.

35 Ibid., pp. 83–110. See also K. van Eyll, *Die Geschichte einer Handelskammer, dargestellt am Beispiel der Handelskammer Essen 1840–1910*, Cologne, 1964.

36 *Verhandlungen zwischen Bürgerschaft und Senat*, Bremen, 1906, p. 200.

37 For a valuable local study of a *tribunal de commerce*, see J.-C. Martin, 'Hiérarchie et structure de la société commerçante: les listes d'électeurs au tribunal de commerce de Niort en 1864 et 1874', *le mouvement social*, 112 (1980), pp. 57–77.

38 J. Lorcin, 'Les archives de la chambre de commerce de Saint-Etienne', in *Actes du 89e Congrès national des sociétés savantes*, Lyon, 1964, Section d'histoire moderne et contemporaine, vol. 2, 1965, pp. 793–806. Quotation on p. 805.

39 J. Kocka, *Die Angestellten in der deutschen Geschichte 1850–1980. Vom Privat-beamten zum angestellten Arbeitnehmer*, Göttingen, 1981, pp. 116–40.

40 P. du Maroussem, *La question ouvrière. vol. 3: le jouet parisien. Grands magasins. 'Sweating-system'*, 1894, pp. 202–3. Emphasis in original.

41 For the position immediately after the War, see l'Office du Travail, *Rapport sur l'application de la loi des retraites ouvrières et paysannes en 1923 et 1924*, 1926.

42 *AN* C 7466.

43 For France, see H.-G. Haupt, 'Les petits commerçants et la politique sociale: l'exemple de la loi sur le repos hebdomadaire', *Bulletin du Centre d'histoire de la France contemporaine*, 8 (1987), pp. 7–34.

44 G. Crossick, 'Shopkeepers and the state in Britain, 1870–1914', in *Crossick and Haupt*, pp. 254–6; *The Shopkeeper* from 1905 onwards; Joint Committee on Sunday Trading, *PP*, 1906, xiii.

45 A. Landry, *Rapport fait au nom de la commission du commerce et de l'industrie chargé de procéder à une enquête sur la situation du commerce en France et, notamment, sur la condition actuelle du petit commerce*, Chambre des Députés (France), 10ème Législature, 1914, vol. 85, Impression no. 3432. Calculation based on responses to the inquiry.

46 *Morning Post*, 2 December 1912, quoted in K. Young, *London Politics and the Rise of Party*, Leicester, 1975, p. 102.

47 *Bulletin de l'Office du Travail*, 1913, p. 1085.

48 Quoted in J.J. Sheehan, *German Liberalism in the Nineteenth Century*, Chicago, 1978, p. 89.

49 Jaumain, 'Les petits commerçants', op. cit., p. 397ff.; P. Delfosse, 'La petite bourgeoisie en crise et l'Etat: le cas belge', *le mouvement social*, 114 (1981), pp. 85–103.

50 G. Crossick, 'Metaphors of the middle: the discovery of the petite bourgeoisie 1880–1914', *Transactions of the Royal Historical Society 1994*, 6th series, 4 (1995), pp. 251–79; Jaumain, 'Les petits commerçants', op. cit., pp. 395–406.

51 Lambrechts, *Trente Années*, op. cit., p. xiv.

52 The best source of publications in this field are the journals *la Réforme sociale* in France and *le Revue social catholique* in Belgium. The most important writings

include V. Brants, *La petite industrie contemporaine*, 1902; H. Lambrechts, *Le problème social*, op. cit.; G. Duplat, *La classe moyenne. Son rôle social. Son action politique. Sa situation économique. Les réformes urgentes*, Brussels, 1914.

53 *Compte Rendu Sténographique du Congrès International de la Petite Bourgeoisie, tenu à Anvers le 17 et 18 septembre 1899*, Brussels, 1900.

54 The activities of the International Institute were reported in its monthly *Bulletin* which began publication in 1905.

55 M. Turmann, 'Un aspect du problème des classes moyennes', *La Chronique sociale du France*, xviii (1909), p. 461.

56 D. Blackbourn, *Class, Religion and Local Politics in Wilhelmine Germany: The Centre Party in Württemberg before 1914*, New Haven, 1980, p. 140; W. Loth, *Katholiken im Kaiserreich. Der politische Katholizismus in der Krise des wilhelmin-ischen Deutschland*, Düsseldorf, 1984.

57 P. Sorlin, *Waldeck-Rousseau*, 1966, pp. 421–2. For the politics of small shop-keepers in Paris, and the political attention directed at them, see P. Nord, *Paris Shopkeepers and the Politics of Resentment*, Princeton, 1986.

58 *L'Alliance*, January 1902. For the way the Radical Party found an ideological as well as an electoral base in the *classes moyennes*, see S. Berstein, 'L'enracinement de la République au sein des classes moyennes au début du XXe siècle', in P. Isoart and C. Bidegaray (eds), *Des Républiques françaises*, 1988, pp. 261–83.

59 E. Sinner, 'La politique de la social-démocratie allemande vis-à-vis de l'artisanat à la fin du XIXe siècle', *le mouvement social*, 114 (1981), pp. 105–23.

60 C. Willard, *Les Guesdistes. Le mouvement socialiste en France (1893–1905)*, 1965, pp. 362–6; M. Rebérioux, 'Les socialistes français et le petit commerce au tournant du siècle', *le mouvement social*, 114 (1981), pp. 57–70.

61 For eighteenth-century radicalism in England in this light, see J. Brewer, 'Commercialization and politics', in N. McKendrick, J. Brewer and J.H. Plumb, *The Birth of a Consumer Society: The Commercialization of 18th-Century England*, 1982, pp. 197–262.

62 For a discussion of this theme see W.H. Sewell, Jr., *Work and Revolution in France: The Language of Labor from the Old Regime to 1848*, Cambridge, 1980, pp. 92–113.

63 A. Corbin, *Archaïsme et modernité en Limousin au XIXe siècle 1845–1880*, 1975, p. 800.

64 J. Garrard, *Leaders and Politics in Nineteenth-Century Salford: A Historical Analysis of Urban Political Power*, Salford, n.d., pp. 55–7; J.Epstein, *The Lion of Freedom: Feargus O'Connor and the Chartist Movement 1832–1842*, 1982, pp. 24ff. See also T.J. Nossiter, 'Shopkeeper radicalism in the nineteenth century', in T.J. Nossiter (ed), *Imagination and Precision in the Social Sciences*, 1972, p. 425.

65 For an excellent analysis of this radicalism in London, see I. Prothero, *Artisans and Politics in Early Nineteenth-Century London: John Gast and his Times*, Folkestone, 1979.

66 C. Behagg, *Politics and Production in the Early Nineteenth Century*, 1990.

67 D. Goodway, *London Chartism*, Cambridge, 1982, pp. 74–8.

68 Quoted in Gaillard, *Commission Internationale*, vol. 1, pp. 150–1.

69 D. Roche (ed.) *Journal de ma vie. Jacques-Louis Ménétra. Compagnon vitrier au 18e siècle*, 1982, pp. 394–6.

70 L. Hunt, *Politics, Culture and Class in the French Revolution*, 1986, pp. 149–212; W.D. Edmonds, *Jacobinism and the Revolt of Lyon 1789–1793*, Oxford, 1990, pp. 86–97.

71 See the case of Caen: G. Désert (ed.), *Histoire de Caen*, Toulouse, 1981, p. 214.

72 R.J. Bezucha, *The Lyon Uprising of 1834: Social and Political Conflict in the Early*

NOTES

July Monarchy, Cambridge, Mass., 1974; F. Rude, *Les révoltes des canuts 1831–1834*, 1982.

73 G. Dupeux, *Aspects de l'histoire sociale et politique du Loir-et-Cher 1848–1914*, 1962, p. 122.
74 Quoted in A. Borghese, 'Industrial paternalism and lower-class agitation: the case of Mulhouse, 1848–1851', *Histoire sociale/Social History*, 13 (1980), p. 81.
75 J. Sperber, *Rhineland Radicals: The Democratic Movement and the Revolution of 1848–1849*, Princeton, 1991, p. 109.
76 Sheehan, op. cit., pp. 22–3.
77 Cf. P.H. Noyes, *Organization and Revolution: Working-Class Associations in the German Revolutions of 1848–1849*, Princeton, 1966, pp. 163–220.
78 Quoted in F. Lenger, 'Handwerk, Handel, Industrie. Zur Lebensfähigkeit des Düsseldorfer Schneiderhandwerks in der zweiten Hälfte des neunzehnten Jahrhunderts', in U. Wengenroth (ed.), *Prekäre Selbständigkeit. Zur Standortbestimmung von Handwerk, Hausindustrie und Kleingewerbe im Industrialisierungsprozess*, Stuttgart, 1989, p. 78.
79 Sperber, op. cit., p. 483.
80 P. Ayçoberry, 'Histoire sociale de la ville de Cologne (1815–1875)', Thèse d'Etat, University of Paris 1, 1977, pp. 433–5.
81 F. Lenger, *Zwischen Kleinbürgertum und Proletariat. Studien zur Sozialgeschichte der Düsseldorfer Handwerker 1816–1878*, Göttingen, 1986, pp. 133–87.
82 C. Tilly and L.H. Lees, 'The people of June, 1848', in R. Price (ed.), *Revolution and Reaction: 1848 and the Second French Republic*, 1975, pp. 170–209.
83 Others were primarily *propriétaires–rentiers* and peasants: J.-P. Geay, 'Les "Républicains-Démocrates" dans l'Allier, 1848–1851', Mémoire de Maîtrise, Université Blaise Pascal Clermont-Ferrand, 1988, pp. 141–5. On resistance in general see T.W. Margadant, *French Peasants in Revolt: The Insurrection of 1851*, Princeton, 1979.
84 See, for example, Brent, op. cit., p. 139; E. Knox, 'Between capital and labour: the petite bourgeoisie in Victorian Edinburgh', PhD thesis, University of Edinburgh, 1986, pp. 303–5.
85 J.R. Vincent, *The Formation of the British Liberal Party*, 1966.
86 T.J. Nossiter, 'The social basis of radicalism: politics and the shopocracy in the North-East, 1832–1860', in his *Influence, Opinion and Political Idiom in Reformed England*, Hassocks, 1975, pp. 144–61.
87 L.P. Jacks, *The Confession of an Octogenarian*, 1942, p. 33.
88 P. Joyce, *Work, Society and Politics: The Culture of the Factory in Later Victorian England*, Brighton, 1980, pp. 268–9. See also C. Hosgood, 'Shopkeepers and society: domestic and principal shopkeepers in Leicester, 1860–1914', PhD thesis, University of Manitoba, 1987, p. 320ff.
89 R.J. Morris, *Class, Sect and Party: The Making of the British Middle Class: Leeds, 1820–1850*, Manchester, 1990, pp. 143–6; J.R. Vincent, *Pollbooks: How Victorians Voted*, Cambridge, 1967.
90 H.-G. Haupt and F. Lenger, 'Liberalismus und Handwerk in Frankreich und Deutschland um die Mitte des 19. Jahrhunderts', in D. Langewiesche (ed.), *Liberalismus im 19. Jahrhundert. Deutschland im europäischen Vergleich*, Göttingen, 1988, pp. 309–12; D. Georges, 'Zwischen Reaktion und Liberalismus. Die Organisation handwerklicher Interessen zwischen 1849 und 1869', in H.J. Puhle (ed.), *Bürger in der Gesellschaft der Neuzeit*, Göttingen, 1991, pp. 223–37.
91 'Report on the proposed general early closing order under the Shops Act, 1912, for the Borough of Nelson, by Samuel Pope', *PP*, 1914–16, xxxv, pp. 757–8.
92 Bernard, op. cit., p. 90ff.
93 For a full exploration of retailers' organisations in Belgium, see Jaumain, op. cit.,

pp. 473–526. For case studies of two trades in Belgium, see the essays by R. Ankaert on café owners (pp. 29–68) and D. Vasquez Martinez on pharmacists (pp. 69–100), in G. Kurgan-van Hentenryk and S. Jaumain, (eds), *Aux Frontières des Classes Moyennes. La petite bourgeoisie belge avant 1914*, Brussels, 1992.

94 Gellately, op. cit., pp. 112–47.

95 *The Retail Trader*, September 1911.

96 A. Saur, 'Die Organisationen der Bremer Kleinhändler vor 1914', in H.-G. Haupt (ed.), *Der Bremer Kleinhändler um 1900*, Bremen, 1983, pp. 42–54; Gellately, op. cit., pp. 87–8.

97 Crossick, 'Shopkeepers and the state', op. cit., pp. 254–6, and the contemporary sources referred to there. For the movement, see W.B. Whitaker, *Victorian and Edwardian Shopworkers: The Struggle to Obtain Better Conditions and a Half-holiday*, Newton Abbot, 1973, who fails to recognise the divisions amongst retailers; Hosgood, 'Shopkeepers and society', op. cit., pp. 185–219.

98 There is no space to explore these movements in any detail. The most relevant sources for further information are the works by Gellately and Jaumain already referred to, alongside such contemporary surveys as those by Martin Saint-Léon and Bernard. See also Volkov, op. cit.; and Nord, *Paris Shopkeepers*, op. cit.

99 B. Angleraud, 'Les boulangers lyonnais aux XIXe–XXe siècles (1836 à 1914). Une étude sur la petite bourgeoisie boutiquière', Thèse de doctorat, University of Lyon 2, 1993, p. 526.

100 Quoted in Gellately, op. cit., p. 122.

101 See Volkov, op. cit., for an indispensable study of the early stages of this movement.

102 Nord, 'The small shopkeepers' movement', op. cit., p. 191.

103 *La Tribune lyonnaise*, 29 April 1882.

104 This picture of the *Ligue syndicale* draws heavily on Nord, *Paris Shopkeepers*, op. cit., together with the contemporary works by Martin Saint-Léon and Bernard referred to already.

105 *Mitteilungen der Handelskammer zu Berlin*, 3 Jg., No. 1, January 1905.

106 Bernard, op. cit., p. 73.

107 *Retailer and Associated Trader*, January 1914.

108 For more on the St Helens movement and its consequences see Crossick, 'Shopkeepers and the state', op. cit., pp. 248–51.

109 F.M. Bussey, editor of *Tradesman and Shopkeeper*, 20 September 1902.

110 *Tradesman and Shopkeeper*, 30 August 1902.

111 See the interview with L. P. Sydney in *Tradesman and Shopkeeper*, 24 March 1906; G. R. Sims, *The Referee*, 4 March 1906; and the general programme in *The Elector*, March 1909.

112 *L'Alliance*, January 1901.

113 E. Witte and J. Craeybeckx, *La Belgique politique de 1830 à nos jours. Les tensions d'une démocratie bourgeoise*, Brussels, 1987, pp. 91ff., 135ff.

114 Z. Sternhell, *La droite révolutionnaire: les origines françaises du fascisme*, 1978, p. 125.

115 Nord, *Paris Shopkeepers*, op. cit., pp. 351–464.

116 D. Gordon, 'Liberalism and socialism in the Nord: Eugène Motte and republican politics in Roubaix, 1898–1912', *French History*, 3 (1989), pp. 312–41. Quotation pp. 222–3.

117 Winkler, *Mittelstand, Demokratie*, op. cit.

118 R.M. Lepsius, 'Parteisystem und Sozialstruktur: zum Problem der Demokratisierung der deutschen Gesellschaft', in G.A. Ritter (ed.), *Die deutschen Parteien vor 1918*, Cologne, 1973, pp. 56–80.

119 Blackbourn, *Class, Religion and Local Politics*, op. cit. For the Centre Party's efforts to attract petit-bourgeois support, see p. 77ff.
120 On the attitude of German liberals to the petite bourgeoisie, see D. Langewiesche, *Liberalismus in Deutschland*, Frankfurt, 1988, p. 128ff.
121 Eley, op. cit. for the Navy League; R. Chickering, *We Men Who Feel Most German: A Cultural Study of the Pan-German League, 1886–1914*, 1984.
122 J. Morris, op. cit., pp. 225–64.
123 Hosgood, 'Shopkeepers and society', op. cit., pp. 314–73.
124 Dupeux, op. cit., p. 608.
125 A. von Saldern, *Auf dem Wege zum Arbeiter-Reformismus. Parteialltag in sozialdemokratischer Göttingen (1870–1920)*, Frankfurt, 1984, pp. 299–300.
126 J. Michel, 'Le mouvement ouvrier chez les mineurs d'Europe occidentale. Etude comparative des années 1880 à 1914', Thèse de Doctorat d'Etat, University of Lyon 2, 1987, pp. 759–60.
127 Willard, op. cit., pp. 240–1, 266, 278, 293. For England, see the presence of owners of small enterprises in the Independent Labour Party in Lancashire during the 1890s: D. Howell, *British Workers and the Independent Labour Party 1888–1906*, Manchester, 1983, p. 332.
128 A.M. Thiesse, *Le roman du quotidien. Lecteurs et lectures populaires à la Belle Epoque*, 1984, p. 63.
129 On the question of such continuities see the essays by Crossick and Haupt, and Nord in *Crossick and Haupt*; also, Nord, 'Mouvements des petits propriétaires', op. cit.; and the discussion in F. Bechhofer and B. Elliott, 'Persistence and change: the petite bourgeoisie in industrial society', *European Journal of Sociology*, 17 (1970), pp. 84–5.
130 For the continuing power of this theme in French politics see P. Birnbaum, *Le peuple et les gros. Histoire d'un mythe*, 1979.
131 *AN* C 7465.
132 Resolution from the North Staffordshire Traders' Association, *Tradesman and Shopkeeper*, 11 April 1903.
133 Nord, 'The small shopkeepers' movement', op. cit., pp. 176–7; Blackbourn, *Class, Religion and Local Politics*, op. cit., p. 66.
134 O. Pyfferoen, 'La formation technique des classes moyennes', *la Réforme sociale*, 50 (1905), p. 838.

8 PETITS BOURGEOIS AND WORKERS

1 Quoted in D. Reid, *The Miners of Decazeville: A Genealogy of Deindiustrialization*, Cambridge, Mass., 1985, pp. 84–5.
2 *Compte Rendu Sténographique du Congrès International de la Petite Bourgeoisie, tenu à Anvers les 17 et 18 septembre 1899*, Brussels, 1900, p. 88.
3 For the classic picture see the discussions of Birmingham in A. Briggs, 'Social structure and politics in Birmingham and Lyons (1825–1848)', *British Journal of Sociology*, 1 (1950), pp. 67–80; T.R. Tholfsen, 'The artisan and the culture of early Victorian Birmingham', *University of Birmingham Historical Journal*, 4 (1954), pp. 144–66. For a critique of this position see C. Behagg, 'Myths of cohesion: capital and compromise in the historiography of nineteenth-century Birmingham', *Social History*, 11 (1986), pp. 375–84.
4 A. Perdiguier, *Mémoires d'un compagnon*, 1964 edn, pp. 75–8, 193–6, 241–3.
5 P. McPhee, *A Social History of France 1780–1880*, 1992, p. 131.
6 R.J. Bezucha, *The Lyon Uprising of 1834: Social and Political Conflict in a Nineteenth-Century City*, Cambridge, Mass., 1974; F. Rude, *Le mouvement*

ouvrier à Lyon de 1827 à 1832, 1944; F. Rude, *Les révoltes des canuts 1831–1834*, 1982.

7 G.J. Sheridan, 'The political economy of artisan industry: government and the people in the silk trade of Lyon, 1830–1880', *French Historical Studies*, 11 (1979–80), pp. 226–7.

8 R. Boch, 'Zunfttradition und frühe Arbeiterbewegung. Ein Beitrag zu einer beginnenden Diskussion mit besonderer Berücksichtigung des Handwerks im Verlagssystem', in U. Wengenroth (ed.), *Prekäre Selbständigkeit. Zur Standortbestimmung von Handwerk, Hausindustrie und Kleingewerbe im Industrialisierungsprozess*, Stuttgart, 1989, pp. 61, 65.

9 J. Kocka, *Arbeitsverhältnisse und Arbeiterexistenzen. Grundlagen der Klassenbildung im 19. Jahrhundert*, Bonn, 1990, pp. 342–58.

10 G.I.H. Lloyd, *The Cutlery Trades. An Historical Essay in the Economics of Small-scale Production*, 1913, pp. 251, 313

11 C. Behagg, *Politics and Production in the Early Nineteenth Century*, 1990, pp. 112–15.

12 For a contemporary description of London's sub-contracting cabinet-makers, see E.P. Thompson and E. Yeo (eds), *The Unknown Mayhew: Selections from the Morning Chronicle 1849–1850*, 1971, pp. 388–9.

13 Ibid., pp. 189–90.

14 S.Pollard, *A History of Labour in Sheffield*, Liverpool, 1959, p. 140.

15 E. Bédé, *Un ouvrier en 1820*, 1984.

16 D.W. Giesselmann, *'Die Manie der Revolte'. Protest unter der Französischen Julimonarchie (1830–1848)*, Munich, 1993, vol. 2, pp. 599–622; J.P. Aguet, *Contribution à l'étude de mouvement ouvrier français. Les grèves sous la monarchie de juillet (1830–1847)*, Lausanne, 1954. On Germany, M. Gailus, *Straße und Brot. Sozialer Protest in deutschen Städten unter besonderer Berücksichtigung Preußens, 1847–1849*, Göttingen, 1990, pp. 153–8.

17 R. Aminzade, *Class, Politics and Early Industrial Capitalism: A Study of Mid-Nineteenth Century Toulouse, France*, Albany, 1981, pp. 77–9.

18 J.W. Scott, 'Men and women in the Parisian garment trades: discussions of family and work in the 1830s and 1840s', in P. Thane, G. Crossick and R. Floud (eds), *The Power of the Past: Essays for Eric Hobsbawm*, Cambridge, 1984, pp. 67–93; C.H. Johnson, 'Patterns of proletarianisation: Parisian tailors and Lodève woolens workers', in J. Merriman (ed.), *Consciousness and Class Experience in Nineteenth-Century Europe*, New York 1979, p. 70 ff.

19 On the Icarians, see C.H. Johnson, *Utopian Communism in France: Cabet and the Icarians, 1839–1851*, Ithaca, 1974.

20 M.J. Haynes, 'Class and class conflict in the early nineteenth century: Northampton and the Grand National Consolidated Trades' Union', *Literature and History*, 5, (1977), pp. 73–94.

21 Select Committee on Master and Servant, *PP*, 1886, xiii, Q. 1372–81.

22 R.J. Bezucha, 'The "preindustrial" worker movement: the canuts of Lyon', in R.J. Bezucha (ed.) *Modern European Social History*, 1972, p. 98; D. Simon, 'Master and Servant', in J. Saville, (ed.), *Democracy and the Labour Movement: Essays in Honour of Dona Torr*, 1954, pp. 160–200; D.C. Woods, 'The operation of the Master and Servants Acts in the Black Country, 1858–1875', *Midland History*, vii (1982), pp. 93–115; S. Volkov, *The Rise of Popular Antimodernism in Germany: The Urban Master Artisans, 1873–1896*, Princeton, 1978, pp. 119–21.

23 P. Marcelin, 'Souvenirs d'un passé artisanal', *Les cahiers rationalistes*, 253 (1968), p. 53.

24 O. Walcker, *Erinnerungen eines Orgelbauers*, Kassel, 1948, p. 12.

25 G. Kurgan-van Hentenryk, 'Belgique. La petite entreprise de la fin de l'ancien régime à nos jours', in *Commission Internationale*, vol. 1, p. 207.

26 Perdiguier, op. cit., p. 195.

27 For the breaking apart of *patrons* and journeymen in the Lyon bakery trade in 1890, each organising a separate Saint Honoré celebration, see B. Angleraud, 'Les boulangers lyonnais aux XIXe-XXe siècles (1836 à 1914). Une étude sur la petite bourgeoisie boutiquière', Thèse de doctorat, University of Lyon 2, 1993, vol. 2, pp. 490–1.

28 P. du Maroussem, *La question ouvrière. vol. 4: Halles centrales de Paris*, 1994, p. 33.

29 *Commission nationale de la petite bourgeoisie* (Belgium), Enquête écrite. Monographies, vol. 1, 1904, p. 198.

30 L.R. Berlanstein, *The Working People of Paris 1871–1914*, Baltimore, 1984, pp. 79–84.

31 Lloyd, op. cit., pp. 195–203; P.E. Razzell and R.W. Wainwright (eds), *The Victorian Working Class: Selections from letters to the Morning Chronicle*, 1973, pp. 192–3.

32 I. McKay, 'Bondage in the bakehouse? The strange case of the journeymen bakers, 1840–1880', in R. Harrison and J. Zeitlin (eds), *Divisions of Labour. Skilled Workers and Technological Change in Nineteenth-Century Britain*, Brighton, 1985, pp. 47–86; E. Dubois, 'Une enquête sur les ouvriers boulangers et pâtissiers allemands', *la Réforme sociale*, 27 (1894), pp. 477–9; B.S. Frykman, 'Industrial working conditions – the future dream of journeymen bakers', *Ethnologia Scandinavica*, 1986, pp. 56–71.

33 See for example F. and M. Pelloutier, *La vie ouvrière en France*, 1900, and L. and M. Bonneff, *La vie tragique de travailleurs. Enquête sur la condition économique et morale des ouvriers et ouvrières d'industrie*, 1911.

34 C. Booth, *Life and Labour of the People in London*, 1902 edn, second series, vol. 5, pp. 117–18. This could be recognised by friends of small enterprise, as in V. Brants, *La petite industrie contemporaine*, 1902, pp. 158–66.

35 R.M. Springthorpe, 'The brush manufactures, 1880–1910: a study in small enterprise', BA Dissertation, University of Essex, 1990, p. 25. According to one study of London, state factory regulation served to encourage the growth of sweated workshop labour: J.A. Schmiechen, *Sweated Industries and Sweated Labour: The London Clothing Trades 1860–1914*, 1984, pp. 134–60.

36 H.-G. Haupt, 'Les petits commerçants et la politique sociale: l'exemple de la loi sur le repos hebdomadaire', *Bulletin du Centre d'Histoire de la France contemporaine*, 8 (1987), pp. 7–34.

37 H. Volkmann, 'Modernisierung des Arbeitskampfes? Zum Formwandel von Streik und Aussperrung in Deutschland 1864–1975', in H. Kaelble *et al.*, *Probleme der Modernisierung in Deutschland. Sozialhistorische Studien zum 19. und 20. Jahrhundert*, Opladen, 1978, pp. 130–3.

38 *AN* F22 390, Inspecteur Zacon to his superior, 14 February 1909.

39 M. Perrot, *Les ouvriers en grève, France (1871–1890)*, 2 vols, 1974; E. Shorter and C. Tilly, *Strikes in France 1830–1968*, 1974.

40 J. Lorçin, 'Un essai de stratigraphie sociale: chefs d'atelier et compagnons dans la grève des passementiers de Saint-Etienne en 1900', *Cahiers d'Histoire*, 13 (1968), pp. 179–92. The quotation is on p. 189.

41 Y. Lequin, 'Mobilité géographique et organisations ouvrières, 1840–1880', *le mouvement social*, 99 (1977), pp. 53–62.

42 P. du Maroussem, *La question ouvrière: vol. 1. Charpentiers de Paris. Compagnons et Indépendants*, 1891.

43 *Bulletin de l'Institut internationale des classes moyennes,* June 1907.
44 Ibid., December 1907, for details of the Bavarian Master Joiners' Association formed for mutual support in strikes.
45 M. Kieffer, 'La législation prud'homale de 1806 à 1907', *le mouvement social,* 141 (1987), pp. 20–3.
46 *Annuaire statistique de la ville de Paris, 1900,* 1900, p. 358.
47 Berlanstein, op. cit., p. 110; *Annuaire statistique de la ville de Paris,* 1908 and following years.
48 H.-G. Haupt, 'Les employés lyonnais devant le Conseil de prud'hommes du commerce (1910–1914)', *le mouvement social,* 141 (1987), pp. 81–99.
49 Henry Cushen, grocer, in evidence to the Select Committee on the Shop Hours Regulation Bill, *PP* 1886, xii, Q 3301.
50 See Arnold Bennett, *The Old Wives' Tale,* 1908.
51 A. Rost, *Die wirtschaftliche Lage der deutschen Handlungsgehilfen im Jahre 1908,* Hamburg, 1910, p. 131; C. Niermann, A. Saur, P. Schöttler and E. Sinner, 'Petit commerce et apprentissage à Brême au début du XXe siècle', *le mouvement social,* 108 (1979), pp. 131–49; M.J. Winstanley, *The Shopkeeper's World 1830–1914,* Manchester, 1983, p. 69.
52 See the determination of one young assistant in the 1870s and 1880s, son of a grocer, to learn a retail trade, almost any retail trade, which would enable him to set up on his own, in J.B. Thomas, *Shop Boy: An Autobiography,* 1983.
53 K. Mende, *Münchener jugendliche Ladnerinnen zu Hause und im Beruf,* Munich, 1912, p. xvi.
54 L. Holcombe, *Victorian Ladies at Work: Middle-Class Working Women in England and Wales, 1850–1914,* Newton Abbot, 1973, p. 107.
55 Thomas, op. cit.
56 Booth Collection (British Library of Political Science, London School of Economics), B133 f 9.
57 N. Hancock, *An Innocent Grows Up,* 1947, p.21.
58 W.F. Fish, *The Autobiography of a Counter Jumper,* 1929, pp. 30–1, 47–51, 60–6. For the variety of shop living-in conditions, see M. Bondfield, 'Conditions under which shop assistants work', *Economic Journal,* ix (1899), pp. 277–86.
59 For such evidence of conditions, see W.B. Whitaker, *Victorian and Edwardian Shopworkers: The Struggle to Obtain Better Conditions and a Half-holiday,* Newton Abbot, 1973, p. 17.
60 S. Jaumain, 'Les petits commerçants belges face à la modernité (1880–1914)', Thèse de doctorat, Université Libre de Bruxelles, 1991, p. 327.
61 Ibid., pp. 577–8.
62 Whitaker, op. cit., pp. 159–60.
63 *Bulletin de l'Office du Travail,* 1913, p. 1085.
64 J.A. Tournerie, *Le Ministère du Travail. Origines et premiers développements,* 1967, p. 198.
65 *AN*: F22 390, note from the *Ministre de Travail,* 18.10.1913; F22 391, *Inspecteur général de Toulouse* to the *Ministre de Travail,* 25.7.1909. For the question as a whole, see H.-G. Haupt, 'Les petits commerçants et la politique sociale: l'exemple de la loi sur le repos hebdomadaire', *Bulletin du Centre d'Histoire de la France contemporaine,* 8 (1987), pp. 7–34.
66 G. Crossick, 'The emergence of the lower middle class in Britain', in G. Crossick, (ed.), *The Lower Middle Class in Britain 1870–1914,* 1977, pp. 24–7.
67 *AN* F22 368.
68 *St Helens Newspaper and Advertiser,* 15 August 1902.
69 G. Moreau, 'Entre classe ouvrière et petite bourgeoisie: les premières tentatives de syndicalisation des employés', in G. Kurgan-van Hentenryk and S. Jaumain,

(eds), *Aux Frontières des Classes Moyennes. La petite bourgeoisie belge avant 1914*, Brussels, 1992, pp. 123–30.

70 H.A. Clegg, A. Fox and A.F. Thompson (eds), *A History of British Trade Unionism since 1889*, vol. 1, 1889–1910, Oxford, 1964, pp. 226–7, 453; Holcombe, op. cit., p. 120.

71 R. Gellately, *The Politics of Economic Despair: Shopkeepers and German Politics 1890–1914*, 1974, pp. 53–7.

72 J. Morris, *The Political Economy of Shopkeeping in Milan 1886–1922*, Cambridge, 1993, p. 246ff.

73 *Statistique des grèves et du recours à l'arbitrage*, 1907, p. 124ff.

74 For a valuable exploration of these themes for one English provincial town, see C. Hosgood, 'The "Pigmies of Commerce" and the working-class community: small shopkeepers in England, 1870–1914', *Journal of Social History*, 33 (1989), pp. 439–60.

75 J. Sperber, *Rhineland Radicals: The Democratic Movement and the Revolution of 1848–1849*, Princeton, 1991, pp. 141–2.

76 Morris, op. cit., pp. 124–5. *Étrennes* were given by Belgian bakers and tobacconists; *Congrès international de la Boulangerie, 28 and 29 août 1910*, Louvain, 1910, p. 66.

77 *AN* C 74672.

78 On the multiplicity of relations between petits bourgeois and workers, see B. Elliott and D. McCrone, 'Landlords in Edinburgh: some preliminary findings', *Sociological Review*, 23 (1975), p. 542.

79 We are grateful to Annie Grange for this information drawn from her research on Saint-Bel.

80 A. Borghese, 'Industrialist paternalism and lower-class agitation: the case of Mulhouse, 1848–51', *Histoire sociale/Social History*, xiii (1980), pp. 55–84.

81 D. Reid, op. cit., 1985, pp. 72–113.

82 C. Hosgood, 'Shopkeepers and society: domestic and principal shopkeepers in Leicester, 1860–1914', PhD thesis, University of Manitoba, 1987, pp. 442–3.

83 M. Ellerkamp, *Industriearbeit, Krankheit und Geschlecht. Zu den sozialen Kosten der Industrialisierung: Bremer Textilarbeiterinnen, 1870–1914*, Göttingen, 1991, p. 232.

84 R. Roberts, *The Classic Slum: Salford Life in the First Quarter of the Century*, Harmondsworth, 1973, p. 96.

85 Economic Club, *Family Budgets: Being the Income and Expenses of Twenty-eight British Households, 1891–94*, 1896, p. 55.

86 R. Swift, 'Food riots in mid-Victorian Exeter, 1846–67', *Southern History*, 2 (1980), pp. 101–28.

87 A. Herzig, *Unterschichtenprotest in Deutschland 1790–1870*, Göttingen, 1988, p. 55.

88 On the moral economy of food prices, see the classic article by E.P. Thompson, 'The moral economy of the English crowd in the eighteenth century', *Past and Present*, 50 (1971), pp. 76–136.

89 D. Goodway, *London Chartism, 1838–1848*, Cambridge, 1982, pp. 114–16.

90 G. Stedman Jones, *Outcast London: A Study of the Social Relations between Classes in Victorian Society*, Oxford, 1971, pp. 291–4.

91 *AN* F 22167, Procureur général before the Cour d'Appel de Toulouse au Garde de Sceaux, 21 April 1906.

92 A. Herzig, op. cit., p. 60; M. Gailus, op. cit., pp. 154–6.

93 G. Alderman, 'The Anti-Jewish Riots of August 1911 in South Wales', *Welsh Historical Review*, 6 (1972), pp. 190–200. See also M.J. Daunton, 'Jack ashore:

seamen in Cardiff before 1914', *Welsh Historical Review*, 9 (1978), p. 194 for attacks on Chinese laundries.

94 D. Smith, 'Tonypandy 1910: definitions of community', *Past and Present*, 87 (1980), pp. 158–84.

95 P. Johnson, *Saving and Spending: The Working-Class Economy in Britain 1870–1939*, Oxford, 1985, pp. 144–8.

96 The exact origin of this term is unclear. It was used by H. Morel-Journal, 'Le réveil des classes moyennes en France', in Société d'Economie politique et d'Economie sociale de Lyon, *Compte Rendu Analytique des Séances de l'Année 1910–1911*, Lyon, 1911, p. 73. The Leicester baker is quoted by Hosgood, 'Shopkeepers and society', op. cit., p. 239.

97 *La defense commerciale et industrielle*, Lyon, January 1913.

98 Johnson, op. cit., pp. 150–7.

99 Compte Rendu Sténographique du Congrès International, 1899, op. cit., pp. 440–1. For the use of very extended credit by eighteenth-century French aristocrats in Paris, see N. Coquery, 'De l'hôtel aristocratique aux ministères: habitat, mouvement, espace à Paris au XVIIIe siècle', Thèse de doctorat, University of Paris 1, 1995, pp. 189–219.

100 Roberts, op. cit., p. 81.

101 H. Bosanquet, 'The burden of small debts', *Economic Journal*, vi (1896), p. 219.

102 Roberts, op. cit., pp. 81–2.

103 *The Grocer*, 6 March 1909. For the cash trades' tendency to gravitate towards street markets, see J. White, *Rothschild Building: Life in an East End Tenement Block, 1887–1920*, 1980, pp. 108–18.

104 *The Grocer*, 28 May 1904.

105 F. Raison-Jourde, *La colonie auvergnate de Paris au XIXe siècle*, 1976, p. 167.

106 H. Lambrechts, *Le problème social de la petite bourgeoisie en Belgique*, 1901, p. 18.

107 D. Englander, 'Wage arrestment in Victorian Scotland', *Scottish Historical Review*, lx (1981), pp. 68–75.

108 M. Finn, 'Debts and credit in Bath's Court of Requests, 1829–39', *Urban History*, 21 (1994), pp. 211–36; P. Johnson, 'Small debts and economic distress in England and Wales, 1857–1913', *Economic History Review*, 46 (1993), pp. 66–8.

109 G. Jacquemet, 'Belleville ouvrier à la Belle Epoque', *le mouvement social*, 118 (1982), p. 67.

110 Select Committee on the Adulteration of Food, *PP*, 1856, viii, Q 2163.

111 P.J. Atkins, 'Sophistication detected: or the adulteration of the milk supply, 1850–1914', *Social History*, 16 (1991), pp. 320–3.

112 *National Chamber of Trade Circular*, 1 October 1873.

113 Ibid., 1 November 1873.

114 J. Burnett, *Plenty and Want: A Social History of Diet in England from 1815 to the Present Day*, Harmondsworth 1968, pp. 99–120.

115 Examples are the South London Grocers' Association; *National Chamber of Trade Circular*, 1 July 1873; and the Sheffield and District United Tradesmen's Association; *Tradesman and Shopkeeper*, 11 June 1904.

116 M. Pigennet, 'Les ouvriers du Cher (fin XVIIIe siècle – 1914): travail, espace et conscience sociale', Thèse de doctorat, University of Paris 5, 1987, p. 324.

117 T.G. Arnold, *The Benefits of Co-Operation, By Mr T. George Arnold of Woolwich*, Manchester, 1900, p. 6. For co-operation in south-east London, see G. Crossick, *An Artisan Elite in Victorian Society: Kentish London 1840–1880*, 1978, pp. 165–73.

118 Report of the Truck Commissioners, *PP*, 1871, xxiii, p. xxviii.

119 G.C. Allen, *The Industrial Development of Birmingham and the Black Country 1860–1927*, (1929), 1966 edn, p. 128.

120 J.R. Oliver, *The Development and Structure of the Furniture Industry*, Oxford, 1966, p. 70; H. Mayhew, *London Labour and the London Poor*, 1961 (Dover edn 1968), vol. 3, p. 223.

121 Ibid. pp. 235–42, 290–2; Razzell and Wainwright, op. cit., p. 255.

122 D. Englander, *Landlord and Tenant in Urban Britain 1838–1914*, Oxford, 1983, p. 88. Englander provides an excellent survey of the difficulties bound up in the rent relationship in the first three chapters of this book, pp. 1–50.

123 Royal Commission on the Housing of the Working Classes, *PP*, 1884–85, xxx, Q 6813–16; Select Committee on Town Holdings, 1886, xii, Q 7906.

124 Royal Commission on the Poor Laws, *PP*, 1834, xxxvi, p. 31.

125 Royal Commission on the Housing of the Working Classes, op. cit., Q 6801–4.

126 J. Gaillard, *Paris, la Ville (1852–1870)*, Lille, 1976, p. 132.

127 J.-P. Burdy, 'Commerçants et artisans dans un quartier prolétaire: le Soleil, à Saint-Etienne, 1840–1940', unpublished paper to *5th Round Table*, Bad Homburg, 1987.

128 M.J. Daunton (ed.), *Housing the Workers: 1850–1914. A Comparative Perspective*, Leicester, 1990: for such measures in Britain see p. 20; Brussels p. 82; Vienna pp. 138–9. See also Englander, op. cit., pp. 12–21.

129 D. McCrone and B. Elliott, 'The decline of landlordism: property rights and relationships in Edinburgh', in R. Rodger (ed.), *Scottish Housing in the Twentieth Century*, Leicester, 1989, pp. 219–20.

130 G. Jacquemet, 'Belleville aux XIXᵉ et XXᵉ siècles: une methode d'analyse de la croissance urbaine à Paris', *Annales E.S.C.*, 30, 1975, p. 837.

131 M.J. Daunton, 'Introduction', in Daunton, op. cit., pp. 19–20; Englander, op. cit., pp. 143–9 for the Wolverhampton rent strike of 1913.

132 E. Sinner, 'La politique de la social-démocratie allemande vis-à-vis de l'artisanat à la fin du XIXe siècle', *le mouvement social*, 114 (1981), pp. 105–23.

133 Morris, op. cit., pp. 259–63.

134 'Hego' [H. Lambrechts], 'La petite bourgeoisie. Petit commerçants', *La Métropole* (Antwerp), 29 March 1897.

135 Cited by M. Rebérioux, 'Les socialistes français et le petit commerce au tournant du siècle', *le mouvement social*, 114 (1981), p. 60.

136 *St Helens Newspaper and Advertiser*, 10 October 1902.

137 See the quotation at the top of p. 160.

138 *Congrès international de la Boulangerie 28 & 29 août 1910*, Louvain, 1910, p. 54.

139 F.T. Bullen, *Confessions of a Tradesman*, 1908, p. 158.

140 See for example the very defensive speech by the representative of the Brussels bakers to the *Congrès international de la Boulangerie*, op. cit., pp. 78–96.

141 P. de Rousiers, *The Labour Question in Britain*, 1896, pp. 6–8.

142 S. Jaumain, 'Les petits commerçants et la frontière entre petite bourgeoisie et classe ouvrière (1880–1914)', in Kurgan-van Hentenryk and Jaumain, op. cit., pp. 101–13.

9 CULTURE AND SOCIABILITY

1 C. Caudwell, *Studies in a Dying Culture*, 1938, p. 77.

2 P. Bourdieu, *Distinction: A Social Critique of the Judgement of Taste*, 1984, p. 338.

3 The following draws upon P. Marcelin, 'Souvenirs d'un passé artisanal', *Les cahiers rationalistes*, 253 (1968), pp. 33–72.

4 On Béranger's popularity, see M. Lyons, *Le triomphe du livre. Une histoire sociologique de la lecture dans la France du XIXe siècle*, 1987, p. 94.

5 An example from France is A. Corbin, *Archaïsme et modernité en Limousin au XIXe siècle, 1845–1880*, 1975, p. 791.

6 M. Crubellier and M. Agulhon, 'Les citadins et leurs cultures', in G. Duby (ed.), *Histoire de la France Urbaine*, vol. 4, 'La ville de l'âge industriel', 1983, p. 452.

7 Corbin, op. cit., p. 794; T.W. Margadant, *French Peasants in Revolt: The Insurrection of 1851*, Princeton, 1979.

8 J. Robin, *Elmdon: Continuity and Change in a North-West Essex Village 1861–1964*, Cambridge, 1980, pp. 110–11,148–9; M.F. Davies, *Life in an English Village: An Economic and Historical Survey of the Parish of Corsley in Wiltshire*, 1909, pp. 264–5.

9 J.-C. Martin, 'La famille: mode d'être des petits bourgeois ruraux', unpublished paper to *3rd Round Table*, Paris, 1981.

10 P.A. Graham, *The Rural Exodus: The Problem of the Village and the Town*, 1992, pp. 50–60; D.R. Mills and B.M. Short, 'Social change and social conflict in 19th-century England: the use of the open-closed village model', *Journal of Peasant Studies*, 10 (1982–83), p. 259.

11 M. Home, *Winter Harvest: A Norfolk Boyhood*, 1969, pp. 42–4; A. Howkins, *Poor Labouring Men: Rural Radicalism in Norfolk 1872–1923*, 1985, pp. 51–2; N. Scotland, *Methodism and the Revolt of the Field*, Gloucester, 1981, p. 63.

12 T. Fontane, *Frau Jenny Treibel*, Frankfurt, 1984 edn, p. 20.

13 Marcelin, op.cit., p. 37.

14 On distinction, see Bourdieu, op. cit.

15 G. Crossick (ed.), *The Lower Middle Class in Britain 1870–1914*, 1976. See the classic humorous novel on such aspirations, G. and W. Grossmith, *The Diary of a Nobody*, 1892.

16 An example is J. Aubrey Rees, *The Grocery Trade: Its History and Romance*, 1910.

17 W.H. Sewell, Jr., *Work and Revolution in France: The Language of Labor from the Old Regime to 1848*, Cambridge,1980; I. Prothero, *Artisans and Politics in Early Nineteenth-century London*, 1979; C. Behagg, *Politics and Production in the Early Nineteenth Century*, 1990; F. Lenger, 'Beyond exceptionalism: notes on the artisanal phase of the labour movement in France, England, Germany and the US,' *International Review of Social History*, 36 (1991), pp. 1–23.

18 J. Rancière, however, offers a critique of that approach in 'The myth of the artisan. Critical reflections on a category of social history', *International Labor and Working Class History*, 24 (1983), pp. 1–16.

19 See the histories of artisanal trades and their traditions which appeared in France towards the end of the nineteenth century, such as A. Babeau, *Les artisans et les domestiques d'autrefois*, 1886, and F. Husson, *Artisans français. Les serruriers. Etude historique*, 1902.

20 On *Kunstgewerbe*, D. Blackbourn, 'The *Mittelstand* in German society and politics, 1871–1914', *Social History*, 4 (1977), p. 425.

21 B. Angleraud, 'Les boulangers lyonnais aux XIXe-XXe siècles (1836 à 1914). Une étude sur la petite bourgeoisie boutiquière', Thèse de doctorat, University of Lyon 2, 1993, vol. 2, pp. 516–17.

22 J. Ehmer, 'The artisan family in nineteenth-century Austria: embourgeoisement of the petite bourgeoisie?', in *Crossick and Haupt*, pp. 212–14; J. Boyer, *Political Radicalism in Late Imperial Vienna: Origins of the Christian Social Movement 1848–1897*, Chicago, 1981, pp. 40–121; H. Béraud, *La Gerbe d'Or*, 1928, pp. 48–55; T. Ericsson, 'Cults, myths and the Swedish petite bourgeoisie, 1870–1914', *European History Quarterly*, 23 (1993), pp. 245–6.

23 P. de Rousiers, *The Labour Question in Britain*, 1896, p. 5.

24 J. Schlumbohm, 'Traditional collectivity and modern individuality: some questions and suggestions for the historical study of socialisation. The examples of the German lower and upper bourgeoisies around 1800', *Social History*, 5 (1980), pp. 71–103.

25 O. Walcker, *Erinnerungen eines Orgelbauern*, Kassel, 1948, p. 5.

26 For the moral elements in German petit-bourgeois arguments, see D. Blackbourn, 'La petite bourgeoisie et l'Etat dans l'Allemagne impériale, 1871–1914', *le mouvement social*, 127 (1984), p. 13.

27 P. Dumont, *Etude de mentalité. La petite bourgeoisie vue à travers les contes quotidiens du Journal (1894–95)*, 1973, p. 18.

28 P. Nord, *Paris Shopkeepers and the Politics of Resentment*, Princeton, 1986, p. 262ff.

29 *Bexley Heath and Erith Observer*, 24 August 1894 and 28 September 1894.

30 Cited in M.J. Daunton, *Coal Metropolis: Cardiff 1870–1914*, Leicester, 1977, p. 156.

31 Y. Lequin in Duby, op. cit., p. 497.

32 W. Te Brake, *Regents and Rebels: The Revolutionary World of an Eighteenth-Century Dutch City*, Oxford, 1989; M. Walker, *German Home Towns: Community, State, and General Estate 1648- 1871*, Ithaca, 1971.

33 Ibid., p. 137.

34 E.J. Hobsbawm and T.W. Ranger (eds), *The Invention of Tradition*, Cambridge, 1983.

35 L. Abrams, *Workers' Culture in Imperial Germany: Leisure and Recreation in the Rhineland and Westphalia*, 1992, pp. 19, 50.

36 J.R. Eidson, 'German club life as a local cultural system', *Comparative Studies in Society and History*, 32 (1990), p. 367; C. Applegate, 'Localism and the German bourgeoisie: the *Heimat* movement in the Rhenish Palatinate before 1914', in D. Blackbourn and R.J. Evans (eds), *The German Bourgeoisie*, 1991, pp. 224–54; T.C. Bestor, *Neighbourhood Tokyo*, Stanford, 1989.

37 C. Tacke, 'Die 1900-Jahrfeier der Schlacht im Teutoburger Wald 1909', in M. Hettling and P. Nolte (eds), *Bürgerliche Feste*, Göttingen, 1993, pp. 197–9.

38 Behagg, op. cit.

39 For these values in the later twentieth century, F. Bechhofer and B. Elliott, 'A progress report on small shopkeepers and the class structure', SSRC Research Report, 1975.

40 R. Pernoud, *Histoire de la Bourgeoisie en France*, 1962, vol. 2, p. 583.

41 R. Mudie-Smith, *The Religious Life of London*, 1904, p. 200.

42 De Rousiers, op. cit., p. 34.

43 J.-P. Chaline, *Les bourgeois de Rouen. Une élite urbaine au XIXe siècle*, 1982, p. 137. On the property life cycle for larger bourgeois, see R.J. Morris, 'The middle class and the property cycle during the industrial revolution', in T.C. Smout (ed.), *The Search for Wealth and Stability*, 1979, pp. 91–113.

44 P. Léon, *Géographie de la fortune et structures sociales à Lyon au XIXe siècle (1815–1914)*, Lyon, 1974, p. 265.

45 A. Daumard, *La bourgeoisie parisienne de 1815 à 1848*, 1963, p. 488.

46 Daumard, op. cit., pp. 488, 504.

47 A. Daumard (ed.), *Les fortunes françaises au XIXe siècle. Enquêtes sur la répartition et la composition des capitaux privés à Paris, Lyon, Lille, Bordeaux et Toulouse d'apres l'enregistrement des déclarations de succession*, 1973, passim; Chaline, op. cit., pp. 143–5; Léon, op. cit., pp. 174–8; B. de Vries, 'Amsterdamse Vermogens en Vermogensbezitters, 1855–1875', in A.A.G. Bijdragen, 28, *Dertig Jaar Afdeling Agrarische Geschiedenis*, Wageningen, 1986, p. 204.

48 B. Elliott and D. McCrone, 'Landlords in Edinburgh: some preliminary findings', *Sociological Review*, 23 (1975), p. 559.

49 Léon, op. cit., pp. 208–9, 245; Daumard, *La bourgeoisie parisienne*, op. cit., pp. 484–5; B. Defaudon, 'Bourg-en-Bresse: aperçu d'une société urbaine au début du XIXe siècle 1815–1848', Mémoire de Maîtrise, Lyon 2, 1976, pp. 212–13, 224.

50 M. Boyer, 'Les métiers de la viande à Lyon de 1860 à 1914', Thèse de 3e cycle, Lyon 2, 1985, pp. 219–20.

51 Daunton, op. cit., pp. 121–4.

52 These highly personal advances prevailed amongst Lyon bakers before 1850, but yielded to secure government and local stocks: Angleraud, op. cit., pp. 431–2, 444.

53 R.J. Morris and S. Nenadic, 'The family and the small firm: Edinburgh 1861–1891', ESRC End of Award Report, 1992, pp. 16–17.

54 P. Ayçoberry, 'Histoire sociale de la ville de Cologne (1815–1875)', Thèse d'Etat, University of Paris 1, 1977, pp. 320–1; Boyer, op. cit., p. 233.

55 F.-P. Codaccioni, 'Les fortunes à Lille (1821–1908)', in Daumard, 'Les fortunes françaises', op. cit., pp. 390–1, 410–11.

56 See the comments in L. Aspe-Fleurimont, 'Une famille ouvrière à Paris', *La science sociale*, 2 (1886), p. 371.

57 S. Nenadic, 'The structure, values and influence of the Scottish urban middle class: Glasgow 1800 to 1870', PhD thesis, University of Glasgow, 1986, p. 142; A.N. Morgan, *David Morgan 1833–1919: The Life and Times of a Master Draper in South Wales*, Risca, 1977, p. 81.

58 Chaline, op. cit., pp. 158–60.

59 Quoted in H.-G. Haupt (ed.), *Die radikale Mitte. Lebensweise und Politik von Handwerkern und Kleinhändlern in Deutschland*, Munich, 1985, pp. 165–8.

60 For the power of collective reading and workshop proselytising in artisanal culture, see J. Hebrard, 'Les nouveaux lecteurs', in *Histoire de l'Edition française*, vol. 3, pp. 470–509.

61 E. Porter, *Victorian Cambridge: Josiah Chater's Diaries 1844–1884*, Chichester, 1975, pp. 71–6; E. Royle, 'Mechanics' Institutes and the working classes 1840–1860', *Historical Journal*, 14 (1971), pp. 305–21; C.E. Brent, 'The immediate impact of the Second Reform Act on a southern county town: voting patterns at Lewes Borough in 1865 and 1868', *Southern History*, 2 (1980), p. 173.

62 Lyons, op. cit., pp. 187–8. Lyon's petite bourgeoisie included a strong white-collar and professional element.

63 Essex Record Office D/ABWb167. We are grateful to Mrs J.E. Sellers for a copy of this inventory.

64 Daumard, *La Bourgeoisie* op. cit., p. 138; J.-C. Martin, 'Commerce et commerçants à Niort au XIXe siècle. Les faillites', *Bulletin de la Société Historique et Scientifique des Deux-Sèvres*, 13 (1980), pp. 413–14.

65 B. Schöne, *Kultur und Lebensweise Lausitzer Bandweber*, Berlin, 1977, pp. 92–3.

66 R. Qvarsell, *Kulturmiljö och idéspridning. Idédebatt, bokspridning och sällskapsliv kring 1800-talets mitt*, Stockholm, 1988, p. 127.

67 We are grateful to Bernadette Angleraud for supplying copies of these *inventaires* from the Archives Départementales du Rhône.

68 N. Fanjung, 'Serrurier–Forgeron du Quartier de Picpus, à Paris', Société d'économie sociale, *Les ouvriers des Deux-Mondes*, 2ème série, 42ème fascicule, 1897, p. 331.

69 F. Parent-Lardeur, *Les cabinets de lecture. La lecture publique à Paris sous la Restauration*, 1982. The limited data on the use of early public libraries in Britain suggests that the white-collar lower middle class (teachers, clerks, students) were especially numerous, together with a good percentage of shopkeepers from the more prosperous trades and artisans, though we cannot distinguish masters from

journeymen. See, for example, Return from each Library established under the Free Libraries Act, *PP*, 1877, lxviii, pp. 187ff.

70 Lyons, op. cit., pp. 190–1.

71 N. Hancock, *An Innocent Grows Up*, 1947, pp. 37–9; P. Searby, 'The schooling of Kipps: the education of lower middle class boys in England, 1860–1918', in P. Searby (ed.), *Educating the Victorian Middle Class*, 1982, pp. 113–31.

72 C. Ehrlich, *The Piano: A History*, 1990.

73 *La Conquête. Organe commercial, industriel, littéraire, artistique*, 1913–1914.

74 Walcker, op. cit., p. 6.

75 I. Weber-Kellermann, *Vom Handwerkersburschen zum Millionär. Eine Berliner Karriere des 19. Jahrhunderts*, Munich, 1990, p. 22.

76 E. Conrad, *Lebensführung von 22 Arbeiterfamilien Münchens*, Munich, 1909, p. 28 ff.

77 Angleraud, op. cit., pp. 208–22.

78 de Rousiers, op. cit., pp. 15–20.

79 That certainly emerges from the debates about luxury in Wilhelmine Germany. See W.G. Breckmann, 'Disciplining consumption: the debate about luxury in Wilhelmine Germany, 1890–1914', *Journal of Social History*, 25 (1991), pp. 485–505.

80 M. Albert, *Les théâtres des boulevards (1789–1848)*, 1902, p. 288; Crubellier and Agulhon, op. cit., pp. 395–6; Chaline, op. cit., p. 214.

81 C. Rearick, 'Song and society in turn-of-the-century France', *Journal of Social History*, 22, (1988), pp. 45–63.

82 On the last of these see L. Magnusson, 'Proto-industrialisation, culture et tavernes en Suède (1800–1850)', *Annales E.S.C.*, 1990, pp. 21–36.

83 A. Perdiguier, *Mémoires d'un compagnon*, 1964 edn, p. 80.

84 Quoted in M.J. Winstanley, *The Shopkeeper's World 1830–1914*, Manchester, 1983, p. 165.

85 Hancock, op. cit., pp. 73–5.

86 M. Agulhon, *Le cercle dans la France bourgeoise 1810–1848*, 1977.

87 C. Lipp, 'Verein als politisches Handlungsmuster. Das Beispiel des Württembergschen Vereinswesens von 1800 bis zur Revolution 1848–49', in F. Etienne (ed.), *Sociabilité et société bourgeoise en France, en Allemagne et en Suisse (1750–1850)*, 1987, pp. 274–97.

88 J. Quéniart, 'Les formes de sociabilité musicale en France et en Allemagne, 1750–1850', in ibid., p. 143.

89 On the role of voluntary societies in middle-class formation see R.J. Morris, *Class, Sect and Party: The Making of the British Middle Class. Leeds 1830–1850*, Manchester, 1990.

90 For examples of such associations: C. Hosgood, 'Shopkeepers and society: domestic and principal shopkeepers in Leicester, 1860–1914', PhD thesis, University of Manitoba, 1987, pp. 281- 93; C.O. Reid, 'Middle-class values and working-class culture in nineteenth-century Sheffield', PhD thesis, University of Sheffield, 1976, pp. 168–70; S. Nenadic, 'The structure, values and influence of the Scottish urban middle class: Glasgow 1800 to 1870', PhD thesis, University of Glasgow, 1986, p. 288.

91 C.H. Johnson, 'Patterns of proletarianization: Parisian tailors and Lodève woolens workers', in J. Merriman, (ed.), *Consciousness and Class Experience in Nineteenth-Century Europe*, New York, 1979, p. 80.

92 Morris, op. cit., pp. 306–11.

93 B. Lecoq, 'Les cercles parisiens au début de la Troisième République: de l'apogée au déclin', *Revue d'Histoire Moderne et Contemporaine*, xxxii (1985), p. 605.

94 D. Hervier, *Cafés et cabarets en Berry de 1851 à 1914*, 1980, pp. 63–6.

95 U. Krey, 'Petit-bourgeois association in Westphalia in the middle of the nineteenth century', unpublished paper to *5th Round Table*, Bad Homburg, 1987.
96 E. Knox, 'Between capital and labour: the petite bourgeoisie in Victorian Edinburgh', PhD thesis, University of Edinburgh, 1986, pp. 500–5.
97 P. Goujon, 'Associations et vie associative dans les campagnes au XIXe siècle: le cas du vignoble de Saône et Loire', *Cahiers d'Histoire*, 26 (1981), pp. 107–50; B. Lecoq, 'Les sociétés de gymnastique et de tir dans la France républicaine (1870–1914)', *Revue Historique*, 559 (1986), pp. 57–166.
98 Archives Départmentales du Rhône, 4M 584.
99 P. Goujon, 'La naissance des sociétés sportives en Saône et Loire avant 1914: la sociabilité sportive entre la tradition et la nouveauté', in P. Arnaud and J. Camy (eds), *La naissance du mouvement sportif en France*, Lyon, 1986, p. 211.
100 W. Hofmann, *Mit Grabstichel und Feder. Geschichte einer Jugend*, Stuttgart/ Tübingen, 1948, pp. 30–1.
101 D. Russell, *Popular Music in England 1840–1914*, 1987, p. 172.
102 Archives Départmentales du Rhône, 4M 622; W. Weber, *Music and the Middle Class: The Social Structure of Concert Life in London, Paris and Vienna*, 1975, pp. 90–108; Russell, op. cit., pp. 200–5.
103 Archives Départmentales du Rhône, 4M 525.
104 G. Duplat, *La classe moyenne. Son rôle social. Son action politique. Sa situation économique. Les réformes urgentes*, Brussels, 1914, pp. 303–4; Lecoq, 'Les cercles', op. cit., p. 595; Archives Départmentales du Rhône, 4M gr 12.
105 *Retailer and Associated Trader*, December, 1913; Hosgood, op. cit., pp. 297–8.
106 C. Booth, *Life and Labour of the People in London*, 1902 edn, 3rd series 'Religious Influences', vol. 1, p. 134.
107 Knox, op. cit., pp. 477–82. See also Reid, op. cit., pp. 108–32. For an example of a vigorously petit-bourgeois-led nonconformist community, see Finsbury Park Congregational Church in 1903, as described in Mudie-Smith, op. cit., p. 138.
108 D. Blackbourn, *Class, Religion and Local Politics in Wilhelmine Germany: The Centre Party in Württemberg before 1914*, New Haven, 1980; R. Gibson, *A Social History of French Catholicism 1789–1914*, 1989, p. 209.
109 *The Diaries of Thomas Carleton Skarratt (1818–1909): Draper of Kington Herefordshire*, Kington History Society, 1987, p. 25. See a similar picture in the reminiscences of a small-town bookseller and stationer: T. Owen, *Personal Reminiscences of Oswestry Fifty Years Ago*, Oswestry, 1904.

10 CONCLUSION: INTO THE TWENTIETH CENTURY

1 M. Weber, *Wirtschaft und Gesellschaft*, Tübingen, 1956, vol. 2, p. 538.
2 Key writings include V. Brants, *La petite industrie contemporaine*, 1902; F. Funck-Brentano, *Grandeur et décadences des classes moyennes*, 1903; G. Duplat, *La classe moyenne. Son rôle social. Son action politique. Sa situation économique. Les réformes urgentes*, Brussels, 1914; L. Rivière, 'La notion des classes moyennes', in *Les Classes Moyennes dans le Commerce et l'Industrie. XXIXe Congrès de la Société internationale d'économie sociale*, 1910, pp. 2–10. For this discourse, G. Crossick, 'Metaphors of the middle: the discovery of the petite bourgeoisie 1880–1914', *Transactions of the Royal Historical Society*, 6th series, 4 (1994), pp. 251–79.
3 M. Gribaudi, *Mondo operaio e mito operaio*, Turin, 1987; K.U. Mayer, 'Lebenslaufforschung', in W. Voges (ed.), *Methoden der Biographie- und Lebenslaufforschung*, Opladen, 1987, pp. 51–74; J.C. Passeron, 'Biographies flux, itinéraires, trajectoires', *Revue française de sociologie*, 31 (1989), pp. 3–22.

4 J. Kocka, *Arbeitsverhältnisse und Arbeitsexistenzen. Grundlagen der Klassen-bildung im 19. Jahrhundert*, Bonn, 1990, pp. 508–15.
5 J.-P. Chaline, *Les bourgeois de Rouen. Une élite urbaine au XIXe siècle*, 1982. See especially Chapter 5, pp. 94–123.
6 R.J. Morris, *Class, Sect and Party: The Making of the British Middle Class: Leeds, 1820–1850*, Manchester, 1990.
7 The formulation is that of F. Gresle, *L'univers de la boutique. Les petits patrons du Nord (1920–1975)*, Lille, 1981, pp. 156–7.
8 We are grateful to Yves Lequin for this information.
9 On the innovative nature of the last of these, see J.K. Walton, *Fish and Chips and the British Working Class 1870–1914*, Leicester, 1992.
10 P. Marcelin, 'Souvenirs d'un passé artisanal', *Les cahiers rationalistes*, 253 (1968), pp. 42–4.
11 A good example is P. du Maroussem, *La question ouvrière. vol. 3: le jouet parisien. Grands Magasins. 'Sweating-system'*, 1894, pp. 37, 241–62.
12 F. Funck-Brentano, *Compte Rendu Sténographique du Congrès International de la Petite Bourgeoisie, tenu à Anvers le 17 et 18 septembre 1899*, Brussels, 1900, p. 89.
13 G. Simmel, *Sociologie et Epistémologie*, 1981 edn, pp. 200–1.
14 P. Bourdieu, *Distinction: A Social Critique of the Judgement of Taste*, 1984.
15 On the *classe objet* applied to the peasantry, see P. Bourdieu, 'Une classe objet', *Actes de la recherche en sciences sociales*, 17/18 (1977), pp. 2–5.
16 Compare the argument that the artisanal vision in late-Weimar Germany did indeed constitute an attempt to create a new and different economic and social system, in F. Domurad, 'The politics of corporatism: Hamburg handicraft in the late Weimar Republic, 1927–1933', in R. Bessel and E.J. Feuchtwanger (eds), *Social Change and Political Development in Weimar Germany*, 1981, pp. 198–9.
17 R. Koshar (ed.), *Splintered Classes: Politics and the Lower Middle Classes in Interwar Europe*, New York, 1990. This valuable collection contains a particularly useful essay by the editor surveying the broad problematic of interwar politics.
18 Important works on the period include P.J. Lyth, *Inflation and the Merchant Economy: The Hamburg Mittelstand 1914–1924*, Oxford, 1990; Gresle, op. cit.; S.M. Zdatny, *The Politics of Survival: Artisans in Twentieth-Century France*, Oxford, 1990; B. Zarca, 'Survivance ou transformation de l'artisanat dans la France d'aujourd'hui', Doctoral Thesis, Institut d'études politiques de Paris, 1983.
19 Cited in R.F. Hamilton, *Who Voted for Hitler?*, Princeton, 1982, p. 463.
20 T. Geiger, 'Panik im Mittelstand', *Die Arbeit*, 7 (1930), pp. 637–59.
21 E. Bloch, *Erbschaft dieser Zeit*, Frankfurt, 1935, pp. 104–10.
22 S.M. Lipset, *Political Man: The Social Bases of Politics*, 1959, pp. 131–76.
23 See the penetrating discussion in P. Baldwin, 'Social interpretations of Nazism: renewing a tradition', *Journal of Contemporary History*, 25 (1990), pp. 5–37.
24 R. Koshar, 'On the politics of the splintered classes: an introductory essay', in Koshar, op. cit., p. 6.
25 I. Kershaw, *Popular Opinion and Political Dissent in the Third Reich: Bavaria 1933–1945*, Oxford, 1983, p. 119.
26 P.H. Merkl, 'Comparing fascist movements' in S.U. Larsen, B. Hagtuet and J.P. Myklebust (eds), *Who were the Fascists? Social Roots of European Fascism*, Bergen, 1980, p. 765; D. Mühlberger, 'Germany', in D. Mühlberger, *The Social Bases of European Fascist Movements*, 1987, pp. 40–139.
27 J.W. Falter *et al.*, *Wahlen und Abstimmungen in der Weimarer Republik. Materialen zum Wahlverhalten*, Munich, 1986; C.D. Krohn and D. Stegmann, 'Kleingewerbe und Nazionalsozialismus in einer agrarisch-mittelständischen Region. Das Beispiel Lüneburg', *Archiv für Sozialgeschichte*, 17 (1977), pp. 41–98;

J.W. Falter and M.H. Kater, 'Wähler und Mitglieder der NSDAP. Neue Forschungsergebnisse zur Soziographie des Nationalismus 1925 bis 1933', *Geschichte und Gesellschaft*, 19 (1993), pp. 155–77.

28 Hamilton, op. cit. Botz has similar reservations about the Austrian evidence: G. Botz, 'The changing patterns of popular support for Austrian National Socialism (1918–45)', in Larsen, op. cit., pp. 202–25.

29 M. Revelli, 'Italy', in Mühlberger, op. cit., pp. 1–39; M. Berezin, 'Created constituencies: the Italian middle classes and fascism', in Koshar, op. cit., pp. 142–63; R. de Felice, 'Italian fascism and the middle classes', in Larsen *et al.*, op. cit., pp. 312–7; D. Roberts, 'Petty bourgeois fascism in Italy: form and content', in ibid., pp. 337–47.

30 E. Witte and J. Craeybeckx, *La Belgique politique de 1830 à nos jours*, Brussels, 1987, pp. 225–43; C. Strikwerda, 'Corporatism and the lower middle classes: interwar Belgium', in Koshar, op. cit., pp. 210–39.

31 Ibid., p. 221.

32 H.A. Winkler, *Mittelstand, Demokratie und Nationalsozialismus. Die politische Entwicklung von Handwerk und Kleinhandel in der Weimarer Republik*, Cologne/ Berlin, 1972.

33 *Bremer Nationalsozialistische Zeitung*, 24 September 1933; *Bremer Adressbuch*, Bremen, 1932. See H.-G. Haupt and C. Niermann, 'Between solidarity and splintering: Bremen shopkeepers in the Weimar Republic', in Koshar, op. cit., pp. 55–69.

34 P. Wulf, *Die politische Haltung des schleswig-holsteinischen Handwerks, 1928–32*, Vienna, 1969; R. Koshar, *Social Life, Local Politics and Nazism: Marburg 1880–1935*, 1986; W. Schieder, 'Die NSDAP vor 1933. Profil einer faschistischen Partie', in *Geschichte und Gesellschaft*, 19 (1993), pp. 141–54.

35 T. Childers, 'The middle classes and National Socialism', in D. Blackbourn and R.J. Evans (eds), *The German Bourgeoisie: Essays on the Social History of the German Middle Class from the Late Eighteenth to the Early Twentieth Century*, 1991, p. 319.

36 Mühlberger, op. cit., p. 124.

37 T. Childers, *The Nazi Voter: The Social Foundations of Fascism in Germany, 1919–1933*, Chapel Hill, 1983.

38 Kershaw, op. cit., pp. 120–39. See also A. v. Saldern, *Mittelstand im Dritten Reich. Handwerker Einzelhandel, Bauern*, Frankfurt, 1979.

39 Strikwerda, op. cit. On the new measures see J. Boddewyn, *Belgian Public Policy towards Retailing since 1789: The Socio-Politics of Distribution*, East Lansing, 1971, pp. 35–58.

40 Zdatny, op. cit., p. 184. See the whole of Zdatny's book for artisanal politics in interwar France, on which this discussion draws. S. Berstein, *Histoire du parti radical*, vol. 2, 1980; P. Machever, 'Le Parti Social Français et la petite entreprise', *Bulletin du Centre d'Histoire de la France Contemporaine*, 8 (1987), pp. 35–46; K. Müller, 'Protest-Modernisierung-Integration. Bemerkungen zum Problem faschistischer Phänomene in Frankreich 1924–1934', *Francia*, 8 (1980), pp. 465–524.

41 Baldwin, op. cit., p. 11.

42 Koshar's introductory essay cited above provides interesting points of continuity with the period with which we have been concerned in this book. For *Heimat*, see C. Applegate, *A Nation of Provincials: The German Idea of Heimat*, Berkeley, 1990.

43 T. Jeffery, 'A place in the nation: the lower middle class in England', in Koshar, op. cit., pp. 70–96 shows how political parties tussled over the new white-collar lower middle class in rival attempts to define and redefine the nation.

44 For a long-term historical analysis of these concepts in France, see K.-P. Sick, 'Le concept de classes moyennes. Notion sociologique ou slogan politique?', *Vingtième Siècle*, no. 37 (1993), pp. 13–33. L. Boltanski, *Les cadres. La formation d'un groupe social*, 1982, is an interesting analysis of the way a new social group is constructed in contemporary discussion.

45 For sociological discussion, R. Aron *et al.*, *Inventaires III. Classes moyennes*, 1939, especially M. Halbwachs, 'Les caractéristiques des classes moyennes', pp. 28–52, and H. Mougin, 'Un projet d'enquête dur les classes moyennes', pp. 287–325. L. Moulin and L. Aerts, 'Les classes moyennes. Essai de bibliographie critique d'une définition', *Revue d'histoire économique et sociale*, 32 (1954), pp. 268–86, 293–309 is an assessment rooted in the interwar debates. A wide-ranging Social Catholic discussion is O. Melun, *L'ordre social et les classes moyennes*, Liège and Ghent, 1933.

46 S. Hoffmann *et al.*, *Le Mouvement Poujade*, 1956; D. Borne, *Petits bourgeois en révolte? Le mouvement Poujade*, 1977.

47 The elder statesman of the international movement for the petite bourgeoisie observed this fragmentation with regret at his retirement celebration in 1931: H. Lambrechts, *Trente années au service des classes moyennes*, Dison, n.d. (1931), p. 330.

48 For a fuller consideration of some of these issues, see Geoffrey Crossick, 'L'histoire comparée et la petite bourgeoisie', *Bulletin du Centre Pierre Léon d'histoire économique et sociale*, June (1992), pp. 13–25; Geoffrey Crossick, 'E che cosa si può sapere dell'Inghilterra? La storia comparata in Gran Bretagna', *Passato e Presente*, 28 (1993), pp. 30–41, and the articles as a whole in that special issue.

FURTHER READING

This bibliography is no more than a selected reading list of some of the major works through which the themes of the book may be pursued further. It is not a full list of the primary sources and secondary works that appear in the references to each chapter, and those interested in pursuing aspects in more detail are directed to these. As in the notes, place of publication, unless otherwise indicated, is London for English-language titles and Paris for titles in French.

AUTOBIOGRAPHIES AND NOVELS

Béraud, H. (1928) *La Gerbe d'Or*.

Bullen, F.T. (1908) *Confessions of a Tradesman*.

Hancock, N. (1947) *An Innocent Grows Up*.

Hofmann, W. (1948) *Mit Grabstichel und Feder. Geschichte einer Jugend*, Stuttgart/ Tübingen.

Marcelin, P. (1968) 'Souvenirs d'un passé artisanal', *Les cahiers rationalistes*, 253, pp. 33–72.

Roberts, R. (1973) *The Classic Slum: Salford Life in the First Quarter of the Century*, Harmondsworth.

Roche, D. (ed.) (1982) *Journal de ma vie. Jacques-Louis Ménétra. Compagnon vitrier au 18ème siècle*. (English edition as J.-L. Ménétra, *Journal of My Life*, New York, 1986.)

Zola, E. (1883) *Au bonheur des dames*. (English translation as *The Ladies Paradise*, Berkeley, 1992.)

SECONDARY BOOKS AND ARTICLES

Alexander, D. (1970) *Retailing in England during the Industrial Revolution*.

Allen, G.C. (1929) *The Industrial Development of Birmingham and the Black Country 1860–1927*, 1966 edn.

Aron, R. *et al.*, (1939) *Inventaires III. Classes moyennes*.

Bechhofer, F. and Elliott, B. (1976) 'Persistence and change: the petite bourgeoisie in industrial society', *European Journal of Sociology*, 17, pp. 74–99.

Bechhofer, F. and Elliott, B. (eds) (1981) *The Petite Bourgeoisie: Comparative Studies of the Uneasy Stratum*.

Behagg, C. (1990) *Politics and Production in the Early Nineteenth Century*.

Benson, J. and Shaw, G. (eds) (1992) *The Evolution of Retail Systems, c.1800–1914*, Leicester.

Bergmann, J. (1973) *Das Berliner Handwerk in den Frühphasen der Industrialisierung*, Berlin.

Bergmann, J. (1986) *Wirtschaftskreise und Revolution. Handwerker und Arbeiter im 1848*, Stuttgart.

Berstein, S. (1988) 'L'enracinement de la République au sein des classes moyennes au début du XXe siècle', in P. Isoart and C. Bidegaray (eds) *Des Républiques françaises*, pp. 261–83.

Blackbourn, D. (1977) 'The *Mittelstand* in German society and politics, 1871–1914', *Social History*, 4, pp. 409–33.

Blackbourn, D. (1980) *Class, Religion and Local Politics in Wilhelmine Germany: The Centre Party in Württemberg before 1914*, New Haven.

Blackbourn, D. (1984) 'La petite bourgeoisie et l'Etat dans l'Allemagne impériale, 1871–1914', *le mouvement social*, 127, pp. 3–28.

Bossenga, G. (1991) *The Politics of Privilege: Old Regime and Revolution in Lille*, Cambridge.

Bourillon, F. (1987) 'La rénovation de Paris sous le Second Empire: étude d'un quartier', *Revue historique*, 278, pp. 135–60.

Boyer, J.W. (1981) *Political Radicalism in Late Imperial Vienna: Origins of the Christian Social Movement 1848–1897*, Chicago.

Burdy, J.-P. (1989) *Le Soleil noir. Un quartier de Saint-Etienne 1840–1940*, Lyon.

Caglioti, D.L. (1989) 'I fallimenti del Tribunale di Commercio di Napoli: una fonte per lo studio del piccolo e medio commercio cittadino', *Società e Storia*, 12, pp. 443–53.

Chaline, J.-P. (1982) *Les bourgeois de Rouen. Une élite urbaine au XIXe siècle*.

Commission Internationale d'Histoire des Mouvements Sociaux et des Structures Sociales, (1981) *Petite entreprise et croissance industrielle dans le monde au XIXe et XXe siècle*, 2 vols.

Corbin, A. (1975) *Archaïsme et modernité en Limousin au XIXe siècle (1845–1880)*.

Crossick, G. (ed.) (1977) *The Lower Middle Class in Britain 1870–1914*.

Crossick, G. (1978) *An Artisan Elite in Victorian Society: Kentish London 1840–1880*.

Crossick, G. (1984) 'Al di la della Metafora: Studi recenti sui ceti medi inferiori in Europa prima del 1914' in *Quaderni Storici*, 56, pp. 573–612.

Crossick, G. (1986) 'The petite bourgeoisie in nineteenth-century Europe: problems and research' in *Historische Zeitschrift* Sonderheft 15, 'Arbeiter und Arbeiterbewegung im Vergleich', Munich, pp. 227–77.

Crossick, G. (1992) 'L'histoire comparée et la petite bourgeoisie', *Bulletin du Centre Pierre Léon d'histoire économique et sociale*, June, pp. 13–25.

Crossick, G. (1995) 'Metaphors of the middle: the discovery of the petite bourgeoisie 1880–1914', *Transactions of the Royal Historical Society 1994*, 6th series, 4, pp. 251–79.

Crossick, G. and Haupt, H.-G. (eds) (1984) *Shopkeepers and Master Artisans in Nineteenth-Century Europe*.

Daumard, A. (1963) *La bourgeoisie parisienne de 1815 à 1848*.

Dupeux, G. (1962) *Aspects de l'histoire sociale et politique du Loir-et-Cher 1848–1914*.

Edgren, L. (1986) 'Crafts in transformation?: Masters, journeymen, and apprentices in a Swedish town, 1800–1850', *Continuity and Change*, 1, pp. 363–83.

Engelhardt, U. (ed.) (1984) *Handwerker in der Industrialisierung*, Stuttgart.

Ericsson, T. (1984) 'The *Mittelstand* in Swedish class society', *Scandinavian Journal of History*, 9, pp. 313–28.

Ericsson, T. (1993) 'Cults, myths and the Swedish petite bourgeoisie, 1870–1914', *European History Quarterly*, 23, pp. 233–51.

Fischer, W. (ed.) (1957) *Quellen zur Geschichte des deutschen Handwerks*, Göttingen.

Gaillard, J. (1976) *Paris, la Ville (1852–1870)*, Lille.

FURTHER READING

Garrioch, D. (1986) *Neighbourhood and Community in Paris 1740–1790*, Cambridge.
Gellately, R. (1974) *The Politics of Economic Despair: Shopkeepers and German Politics 1890–1914*.
Georges, D. (1991) 'Zwischen Reaktion und Liberalismus. Die Organisation hand-werklicher Interessen zwischen 1849 und 1869', in H.J. Puhle (ed.) *Bürger in der Gesellschaft der Neuzeit*, Göttingen, pp. 223–37.
Gresle, F. (1981) *L'univers de la boutique. Les petits patrons du Nord (1920–1975)*, Lille.
Haupt, H.-G. (ed.) (1978) *'Bourgeois und Volk zugleich'? Zur Geschichte des Kleinbürgertums im 19. und 20. Jahrhundert*, Frankfurt/New York 1978.
Haupt, H.-G. (1982) 'Kleinhändler und Arbeiter in Bremen zwischen 1890 und 1914', *Archiv für Sozialgeschichte*, 22, pp. 95–134.
Haupt, H.-G. (ed.) (1982) *Der Bremer Kleinhandel um 1900*, Bremen.
Haupt, H.-G. (ed.) (1985) *Die radikale Mitte. Lebensweise und Politik von Hand-werkern und Kleinhändelern in Deutschland seit 1848*, Munich.
Haupt, H.-G. (1987) 'Les petits commerçants et la politique sociale: l'exemple de la loi sur le repos hebdomadaire', *Bulletin du Centre d'Histoire de la France contemporaine*, 8, pp. 7–34.
Haupt, H.-G. (1987) 'Les employés lyonnais devant le Conseil de prud'hommes du commerce (1910–1914)', *le mouvement social*, no. 141, pp. 81–99.
Haupt, H.-G. (1993) 'La petite bourgeoisie en France et en Allemagne dans l'entre-deux-guerres', in H. Möller *et al.* (eds) *Gefährdete Mitte? Mittelschichten und politische Kultur zwischen den Weltkriegen: Italien, Frankreich und Deutschland*, Sigmaringen, pp. 35–55.
Haupt H.-G. and Vigier, P. (eds) (1979) 'L'atelier et la boutique', special issue of *le mouvement social*, 108.
Haupt H.-G. and Vigier, P. (eds) (1981) 'Petite entreprise et politique', special issue of *le mouvement social*, 114.
Holderness, B.A. (1972) 'Rural tradesmen, 1660–1850. A regional study in Lindsey', *Lincolnshire History and Archaeology*, 7, pp. 77–83.
Hosgood, C. (1989) 'The "Pigmies of Commerce" and the working-class community: small shopkeepers in England, 1870–1914', *Journal of Social History*, 33, pp. 439–60.
Hosgood, C. (1992) 'A "Brave and Daring Folk"? Shopkeepers and trade associational life in Victorian and Edwardian England', *Journal of Social History*, 36, pp. 285–308.
Jacquemet, G. (1984) *Belleville au XIXe. Du faubourg à la ville*.
Jefferys, J.B. (1954) *Retail Trading in Britain 1850–1950*, Cambridge.
Kaplan, S.L. and Koepp, C.J. (eds) (1986) *Work in France: Representations, Meaning, Organization, and Practices*, Ithaca.
Kellett, J.R. (1957–8) 'The breakdown of gild and corporation control over the handicraft and retail trade in London', *Economic History Review*, New Series, 10, pp. 381–94.
Koshar, R. (ed.) (1990) *Splintered Classes: Politics and the Lower Middle Classes in Interwar Europe*, New York.
Krohn, C.D. and Stegmann, D. (1977) 'Kleingewerbe und Nazionalsozialismus in einer agrarisch-mittelständischen Region. Das Beispiel Lüneburg', *Archiv für Sozialgeschichte*, 17, pp. 41–98.
Kurgan-van Hentenryk, G. (1983) 'A la recherche de la petite bourgeoisie: l'Enquête orale de 1902–1904', *Revue belge d'histoire contemporaine*, 14, pp. 294–8.
Kurgan-van Hentenryk, G. and Jaumain, S. (eds), (1992) *Aux Frontières des Classes Moyennes. La petite bourgeoisie belge avant 1914*, Brussels.
Kurgan-van Hentenryk, G. and Viré, G. (1981) 'Les registres des patentables, source de l'histoire de Bruxelles à la fin du XIXe siècle', *Acta Historica Bruxellensia*, 4.

286

Lenger, F. (1986) *Zwischen Kleinbürgertum und Proletariat. Studien zur Sozialgeschichte der Düsseldorfer Handwerker 1816–1878*, Göttingen.

Lenger, F. (1988) *Sozialgeschichte der deutschen Handwerker seit 1800*, Frankfurt.

Lequin, Y. (ed.) (1982) 'Ouvriers dans la ville', special issue of *le mouvement social*, 118.

Levau, G. Grunberg, G. and Mayer, N. (eds) (1983) *L'Univers politique des classes moyennes.*

Le Yaouanq, J. (1993) 'Trajectoires sociales à Paris au XIXe siècle: le monde de la boutique', *Bulletin du Centre Pierre Léon*, pp. 25–40.

Lorçin, J. (1968) 'Un essai de stratigraphie sociale: chefs d'atelier et compagnons dans la grève des passementiers de Saint-Etienne en 1900', *Cahiers d'Histoire*, 13, pp. 179–92.

Lyth, P.J. (1990) *Inflation and the Merchant Economy: The Hamburg Mittelstand 1914–1924*, Oxford.

Martin, J.-C. (1980) 'Commerce et commerçants à Niort au XIXe siècle. Les faillites', *Bulletin de la Société Historique et Scientifique des Deux-Sèvres*, 13, pp. 337–501.

Martin, J.-C. (1980) 'Le commerçant, la faillite et l'historien', *Annales E.S.C.*, 35, pp. 1251–68.

Martin, J.M. (1984) 'Village traders and the emergence of a proletariat in south Warwickshire, 1750–1851', *Agricultural History Review*, 32, pp. 179–88.

Mayer, A.J. (1975) 'The lower middle class as a historical problem', *Journal of Modern History*, 47, pp. 409–36.

Miles, A. (1993) 'Lower middle class mobility in England, 1839–1914', *Bulletin du Centre Pierre Léon*, pp. 41–59.

Miller, M.B. (1981) *The Bon Marché: Bourgeois Culture and the Department Store, 1869–1920*, Princeton.

Morris, J. (1993) *The Political Economy of Shopkeeping in Milan 1886–1922*, Cambridge.

Morris, R.J. (1990) *Class, Sect and Party: The Making of the British Middle Class. Leeds 1820–1850*, Manchester.

Moulin, L. and Aerts, L. (1954) 'Les classes moyennes. Essai de bibliographie critique d'une définition', *Revue d'histoire économique et sociale*, 32, pp. 268–86, 293–309.

Noll, A. (1975) *Sozio-ökonomischer Strukturwandel des Handwerks in der zweiten Phase der Industrialisierung unter besonderer Berücksichtigung der Regierungsbezirke Arnsberg und Münster*, Göttingen.

Nord, P. (1986) *Paris Shopkeepers and the Politics of Resentment*, Princeton.

Nord, P. (1986) 'Les mouvements de petits propriétaires et la politique (des années 1880 à la première guerre mondiale)', *Revue historique*, 558, pp. 407–33.

Pinol, J.-L. (1991) *Les mobilités de la grande ville. Lyon fin XIXe – début XXe.*

Raison-Jourde, F. (1976) *La colonie auvergnate de Paris au XIXe siècle.*

Rebérioux, M. (1981) 'Les socialistes français et le petit commerce au tournant du siècle', *le mouvement social*, 114, pp. 57–70.

Reith, R. (1988) *Arbeits- und Lebensweise im städtischen Handwerk. Zur Sozialgeschichte Augsburger Handwerksgesellen im 18. Jahrhundert (1700–1806)*, Göttingen.

Renzsch, W. (1980) *Handwerker und Lohnarbeiter in der frühen Arbeiterbewegung. Zur sozialen Basis von Gewerkschaftsbewegung und Sozialdemokratie im Reichsgründungsjahrzehnt*, Göttingen.

Sabel, C. and Zeitlin, J. (1985) 'Historical alternatives to mass production: politics, markets and technology in nineteenth-century industrialization', *Past and Present*, 108, pp. 133–76.

Schötz, S. (1991) 'On the recruitment of the Leipzig middle strata from the working class, 1830–1870', in G. Iggers (ed.) *Marxist Historiography in Transformation: East German Social History in the 1980s*, New York/Oxford, pp. 95–113.

Schraut, S. (1989) *Sozialer Wandel in Industrialisierungsprozeß. Esslingen 1800–1870*, Sigmaringen.

Sedatis, H. (1979) *Liberalismus und Handwerk in Südwestdeutschland. Wirtschafts- und Gesellschaftskonzeption des Liberalismus und die Krise des Handwerks im 19. Jahrhundert*, Stuttgart.

Sick, K.-P. (1993) 'Le concept de classes moyennes. Notion sociologique ou slogan politique?', *Vingtième Siècle*, 37, pp. 13–33.

Sinner, E. (1981) 'La politique de la social-démocratie allemande vis-à-vis de l'artisanat à la fin du XIXe siècle', *le mouvement social*, 114, pp. 105–23.

Te Brake, W. (1989) *Regents and Rebels: The Revolutionary World of an Eighteenth-Century Dutch City*, Oxford.

van Lente, D. (1991) 'The crafts in industrial society: ideals and policy in the Netherlands, 1890–1930', *Economic and Social History in the Netherlands*, 2, pp. 99–119.

Volkov, S. (1978) *The Rise of Popular Antimodernism in Germany: The Urban Master Artisans, 1873–1896*, Princeton.

Walker, M. (1971) *German Home Towns: Community, State, and General Estate 1648–1871*, Ithaca.

Wengenroth, U. (ed.) (1981) *Prekäre Selbständigkeit. Zur Standortbestimmung von Handwerk, Hausindustrie und Kleingewerbe im Industrialisierungsprozess*, Stuttgart.

Winkler, H.A. (1972) *Mittelstand, Demokratie und Nationalsozialismus. Die politische Entwicklung von Handwerk und Kleinhandel in der Weimarer Republik*, Cologne/Berlin.

Winstanley, M. (1983) *The Shopkeeper's World 1830–1914*, Manchester.

Zdatny, S.M. (1990) *The Politics of Survival: Artisans in Twentieth-Century France*, Oxford.

UNPUBLISHED THESES

Angleraud, B. (1993) 'Les boulangers lyonnais aux XIXe-XXe siècles (1836 à 1914). Une étude sur la petite bourgeoisie boutiquière', Thèse de doctorat, University of Lyon 2.

Ayçoberry, P. (1977) 'Histoire sociale de la ville de Cologne (1815–1875)', Thèse d'Etat, University of Paris 1.

Boyer, M. (1985) 'Les métiers de la viande à Lyon de 1860 à 1914', Thèse de 3e Cycle, University of Lyon 2.

Cagliotti, D. (1992) 'Il guadagno difficile. Commercianti e artigiani napoletani nella seconda metà dell'800', PhD thesis, EUI Florence.

Hosgood, C. (1987) 'Shopkeepers and society: domestic and principal shopkeepers in Leicester, 1860–1914', PhD thesis, University of Manitoba.

Jaumain, S. (1991) 'Les petits commerçants belges face à la modernité (1880–1914)', Thèse de doctorat, Université Libre de Bruxelles.

Knox, E. (1986) 'Between capital and labour: the petite bourgeoisie in Victorian Edinburgh', PhD thesis, University of Edinburgh.

INDEX